FIRE PUNCH

8

STORY AND ART BY
TATSUKI FUJIMOTO

CHARACTERS

AGNI

A Blessed with the power of regeneration, his little sister is killed by Doma, who engulfs Agni in flames that will never extinguish.

JUDAH

A Blessed with the power of regeneration, she has lost her memory and is suffering from infantile regression.

SUN

A Blessed with the power of electricity. Agni saves his life.

NENETO

A girl taken to Behemdorg with Sun.

ICE WITCH

An unidentified person who has appeared out of nowhere claiming to be the Ice Witch.

TOGATA

A mysterious girl who is trying to film a movie starring Agni.

Humans who possess unique powers are called Blessed, and two such Blessed, Agni and Luna, live in a world frozen over by the Ice Witch. One day, Agni and Luna's village is attacked by a Behemdorg soldier named Doma, who's a Blessed whose flames won't extinguish until they've completely consumed their fuel. Luna loses her life, but Agni survives to suffer a living hell for eight years until he masters the art of controlling his flames and becomes Fire Punch. He then begins a journey to exact revenge on Doma, which he finally does. But after Doma's comrade Judah loses her memory, Agni takes her under his wing as his sister Luna. When his flames finally extinguish, he takes up peaceful residence with a band of girls who all love Doma and once followed his teachings. All of Agni's lies and crimes weigh on his psyche, slowly eating away at his sanity, until one day, Neneto and several followers of Agniism show up to take Judah from him. When Agni's past is exposed to his housemates, he reverts back to Fire Punch and immediately sets off to rescue Judah. Meanwhile, Sun, who is now grown and a central figure of Agniism, kills the Ice Witch!

STORY

FIRE PUNCH

STORY AND ART BY
TATSUKI FUJIMOTO

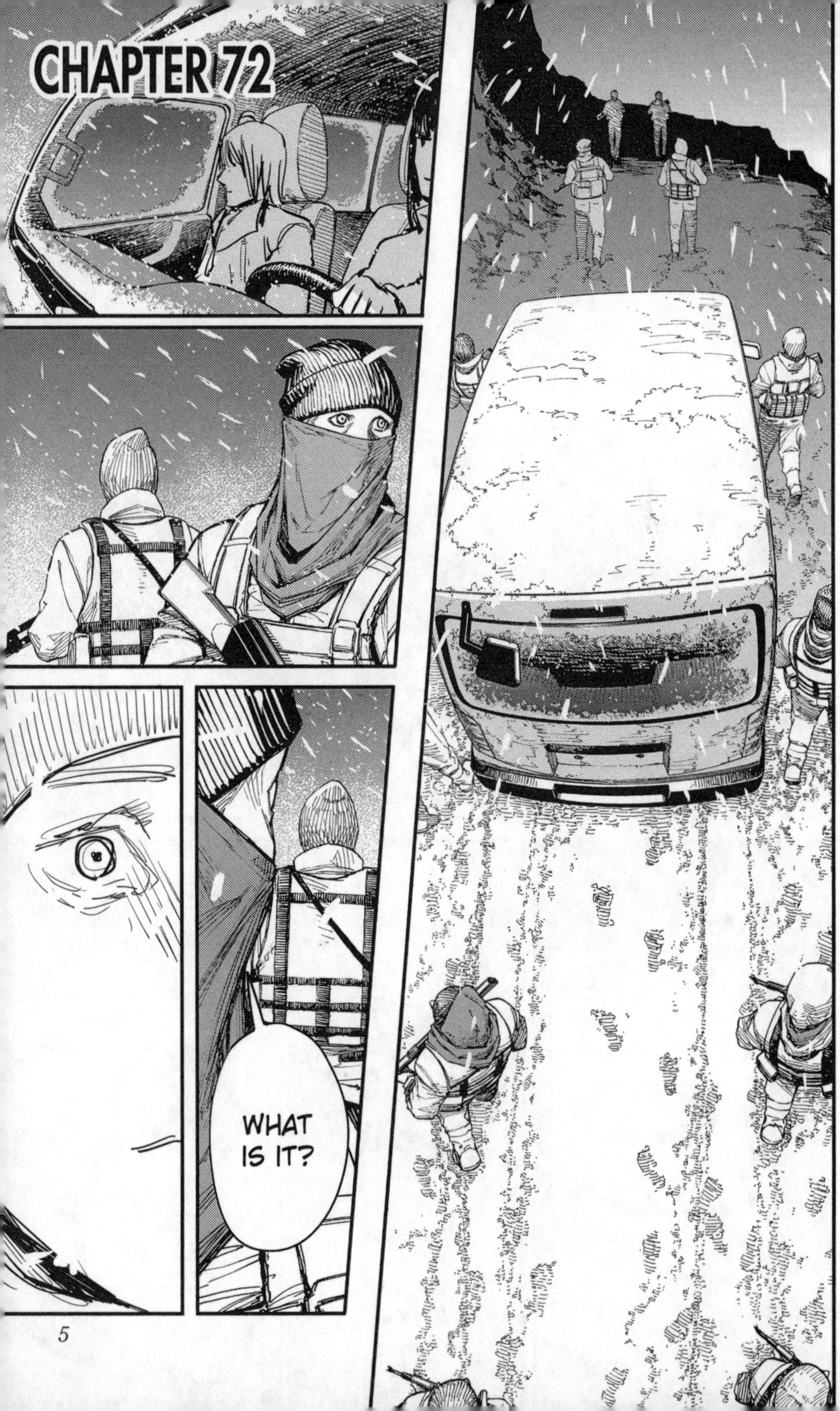
CHAPTER 72
WHAT IS IT?

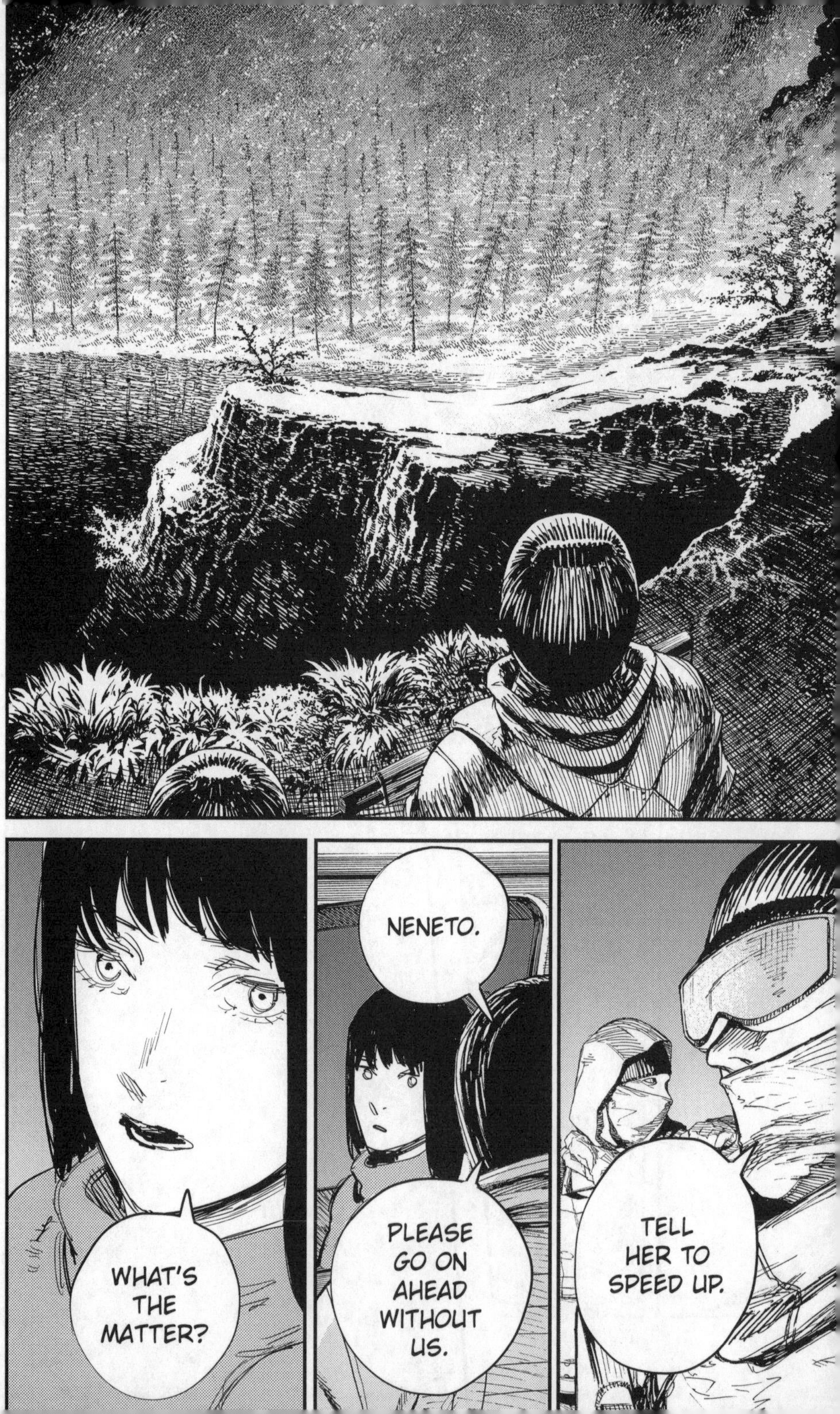
TELL HER TO SPEED UP.
NENETO.
PLEASE GO ON AHEAD WITHOUT US.
WHAT'S THE MATTER?

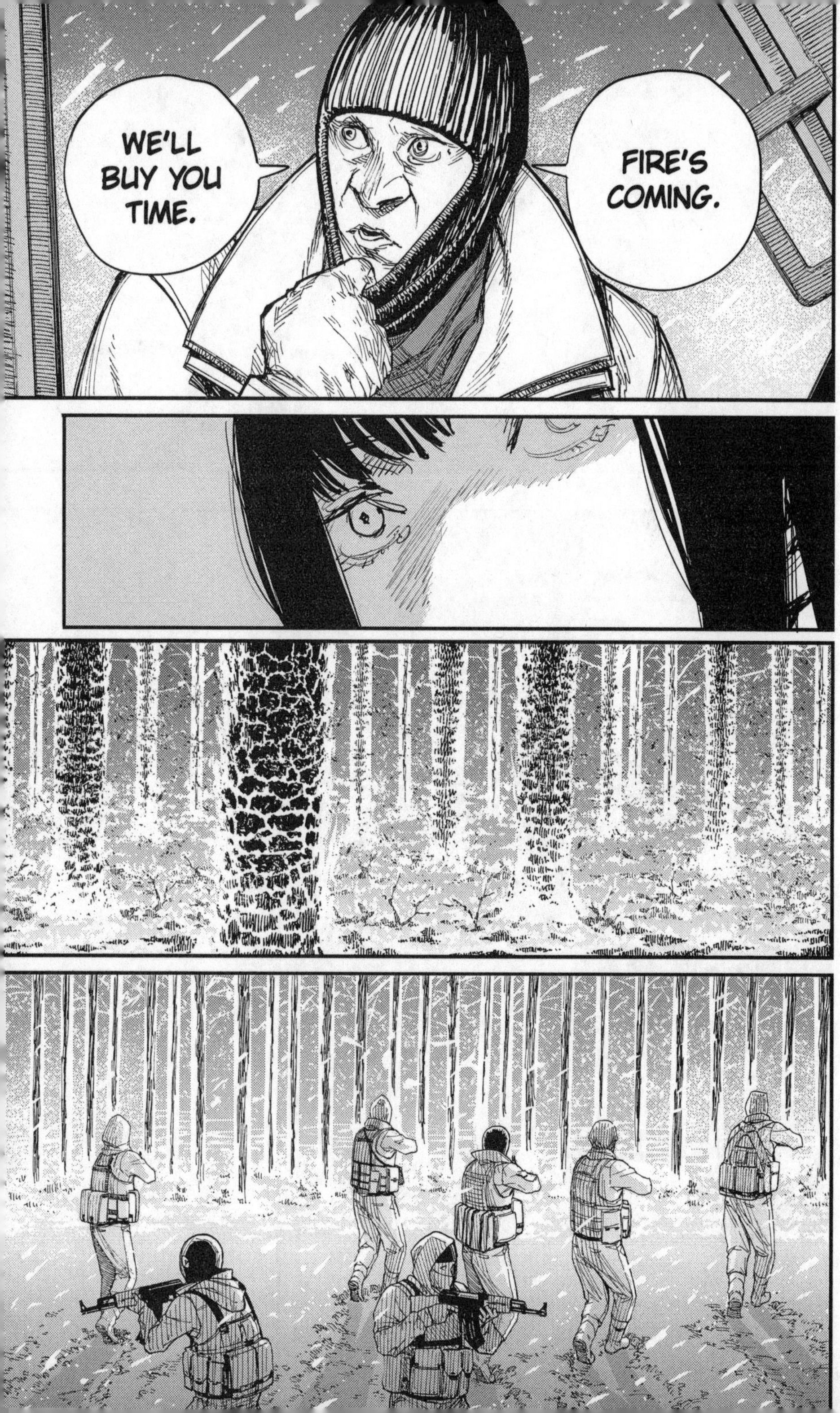
FIRE'S COMING.
WE'LL BUY YOU TIME.

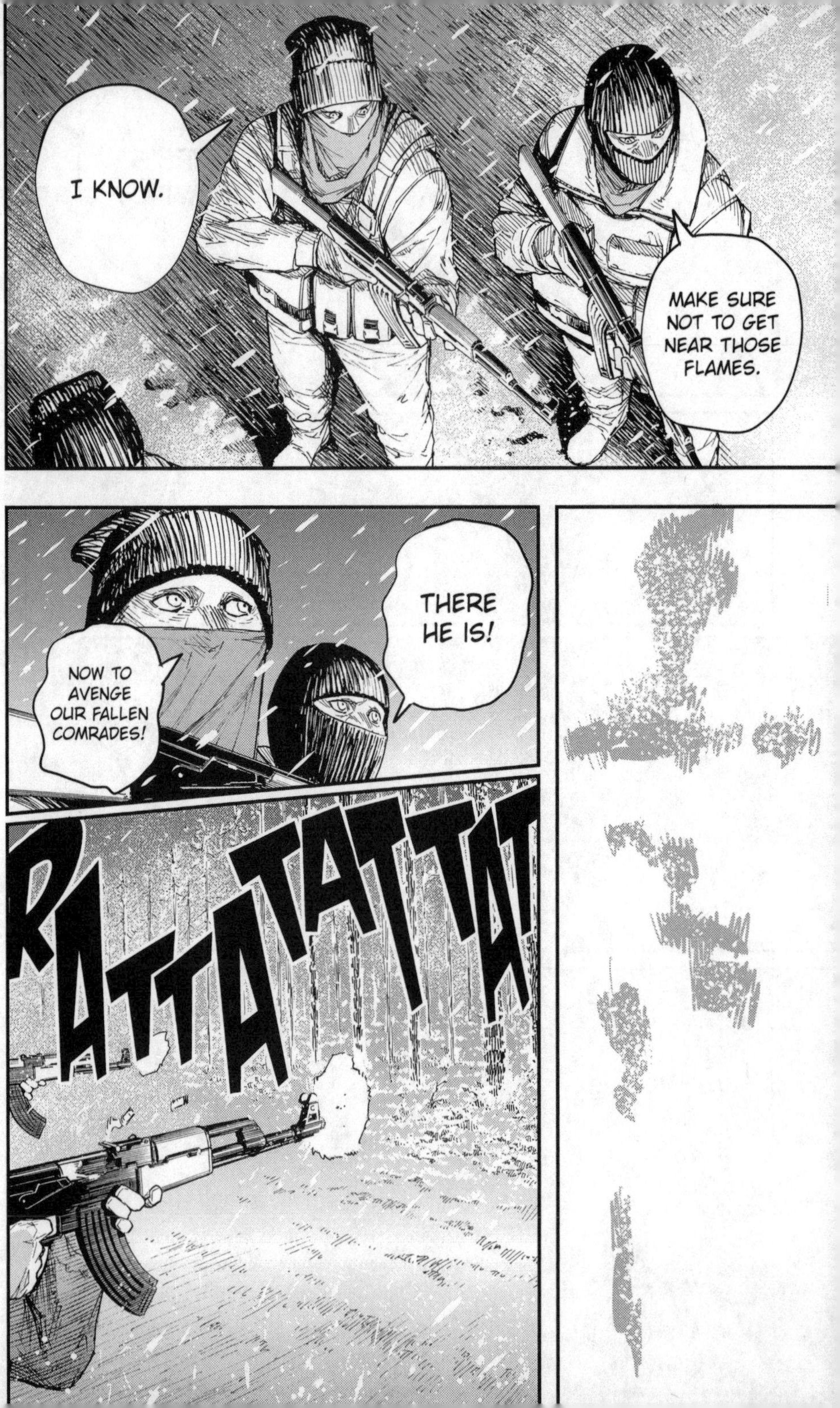
MAKE SURE NOT TO GET NEAR THOSE FLAMES.
I KNOW.
THERE HE IS!
NOW TO AVENGE OUR FALLEN COMRADES!
RATTATATTA

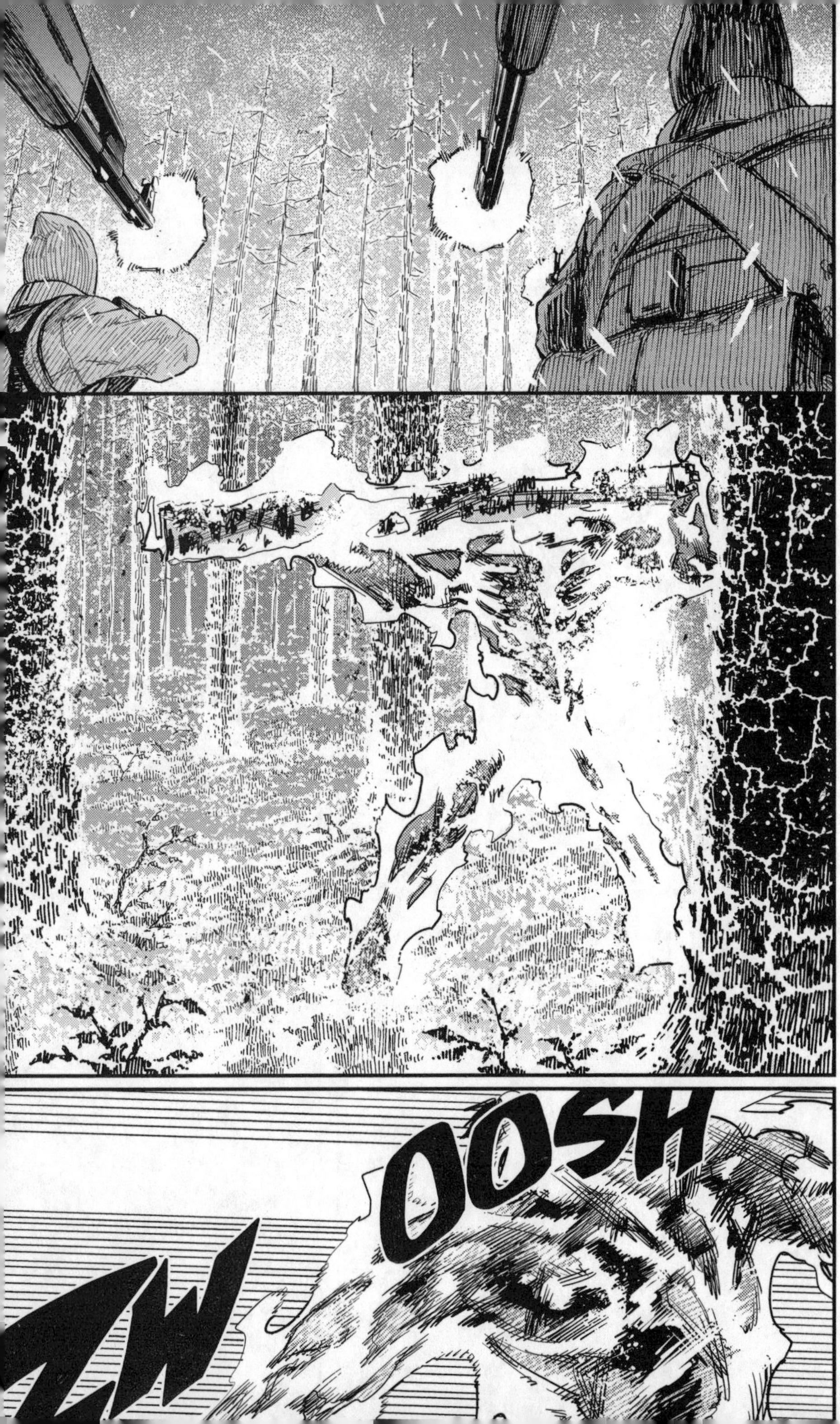
ZWOOSH

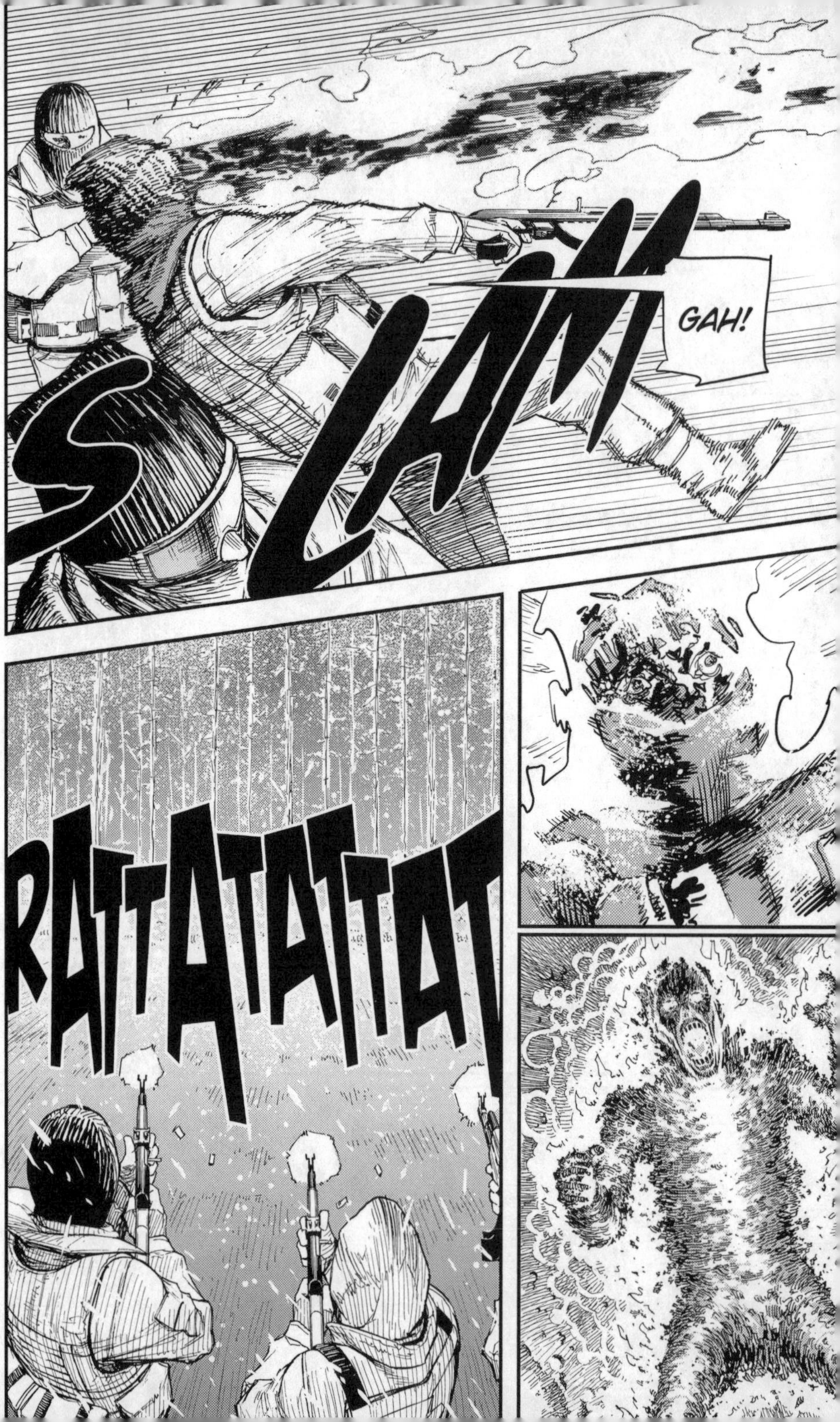
SLAM
GAH!
RATTATATTAT

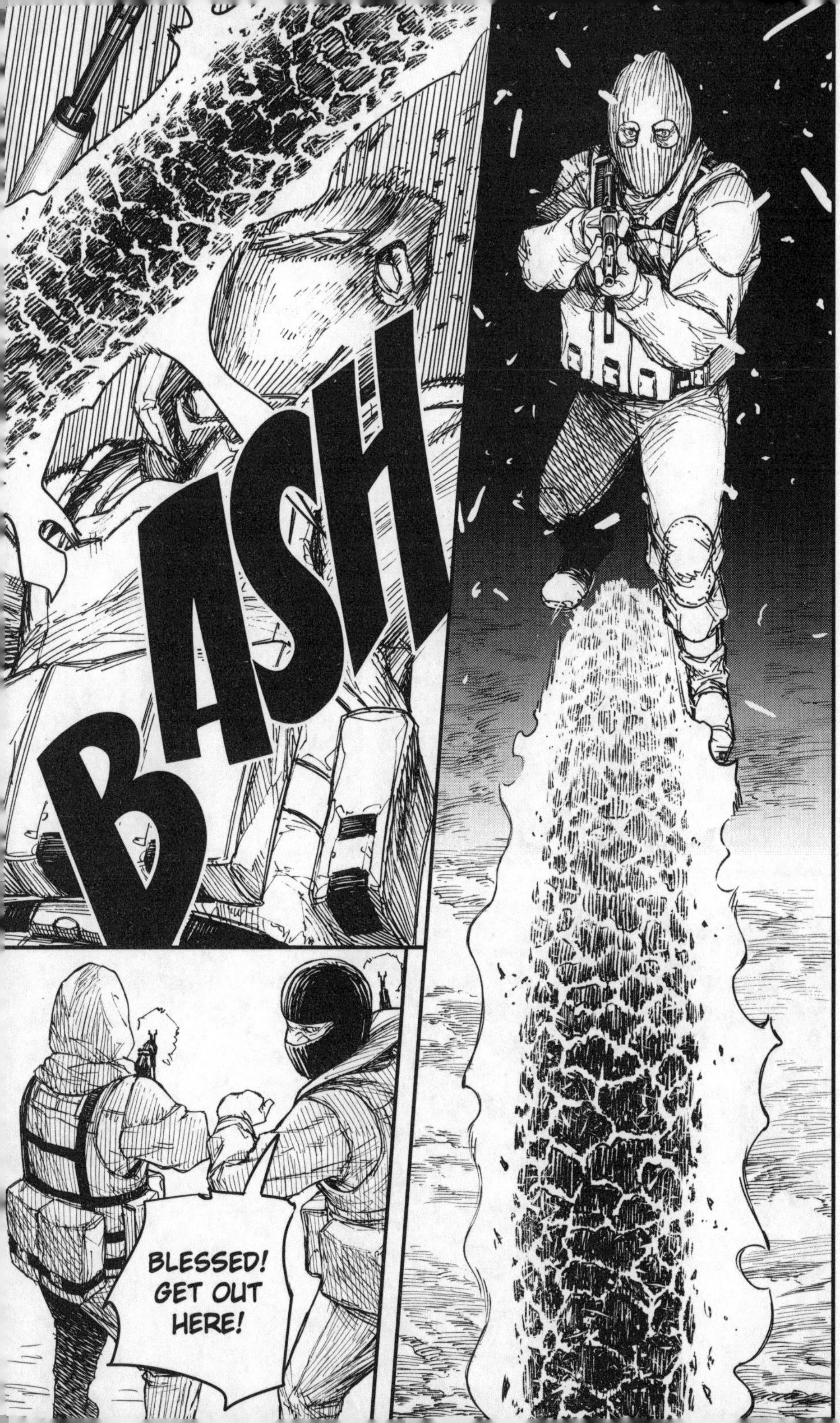
BASH
BLESSED! GET OUT HERE!

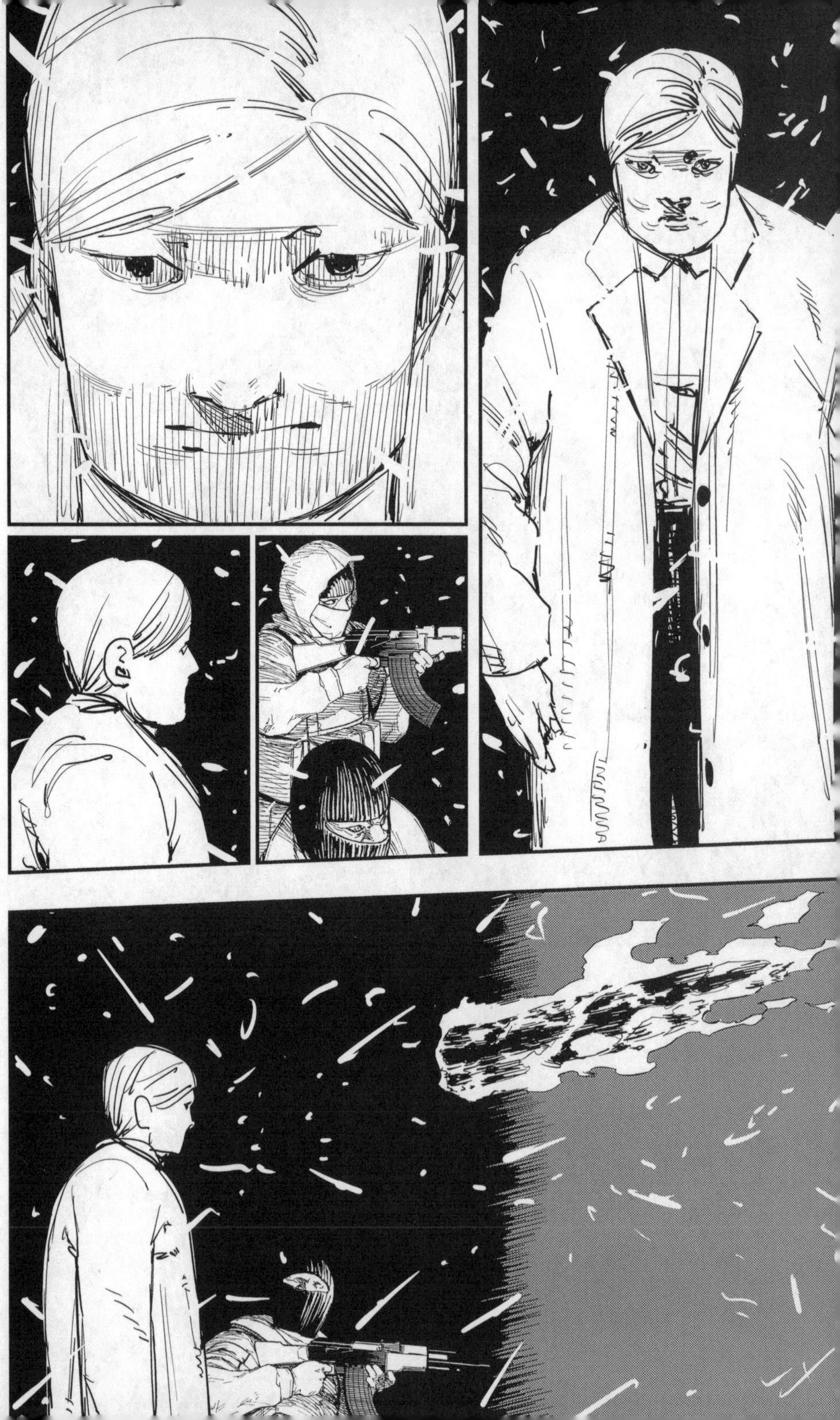

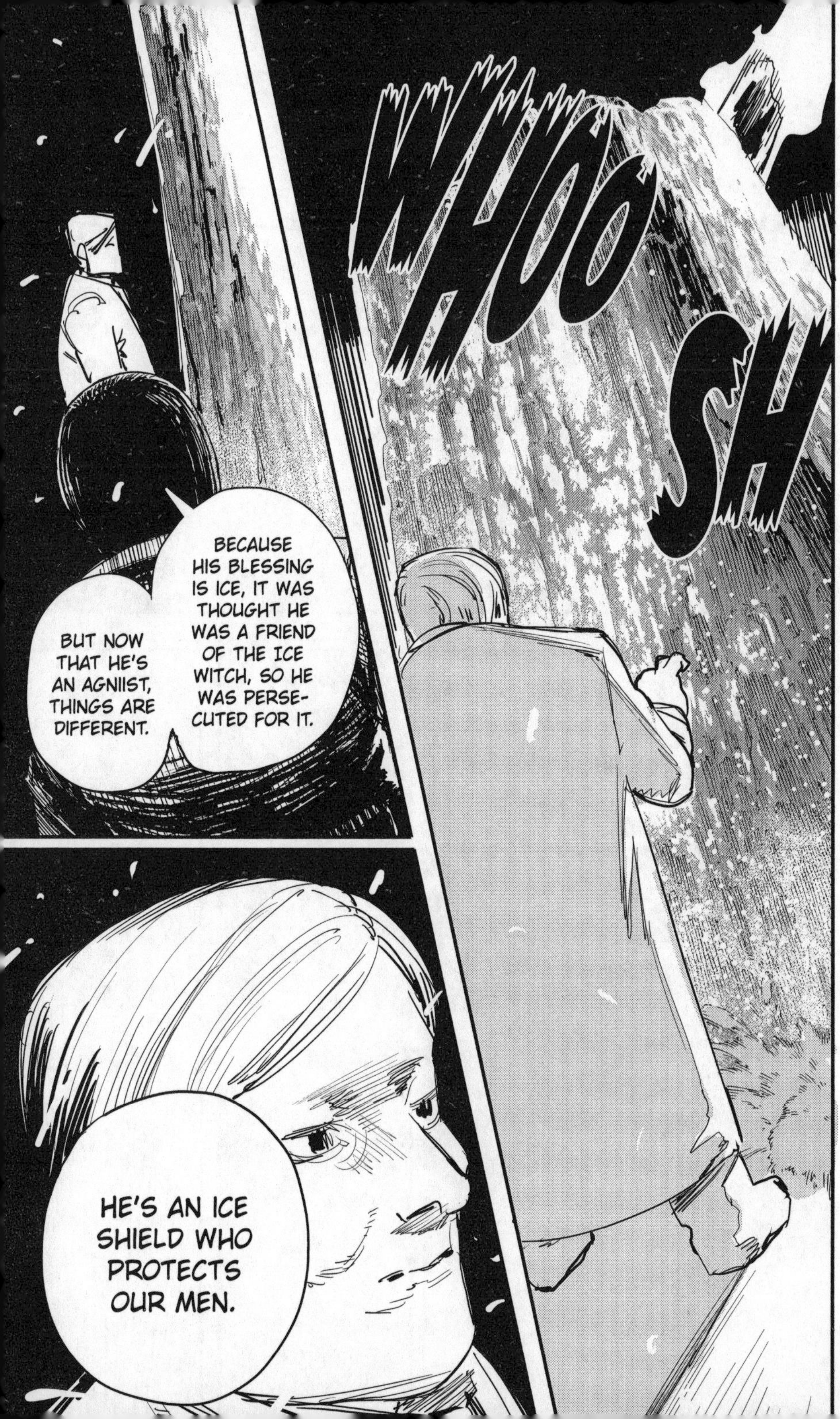
WHOOSH
BECAUSE HIS BLESSING IS ICE, IT WAS THOUGHT HE WAS A FRIEND OF THE ICE WITCH, SO HE WAS PERSECUTED FOR IT.
BUT NOW THAT HE'S AN AGNIIST, THINGS ARE DIFFERENT.
HE'S AN ICE SHIELD WHO PROTECTS OUR MEN.

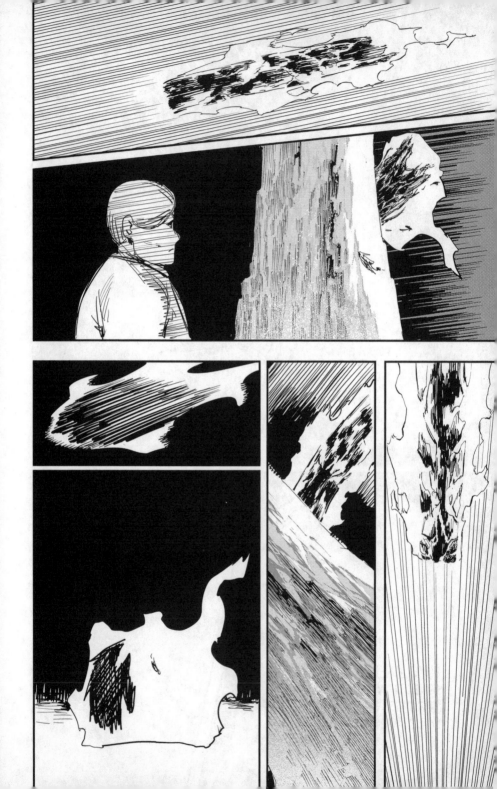

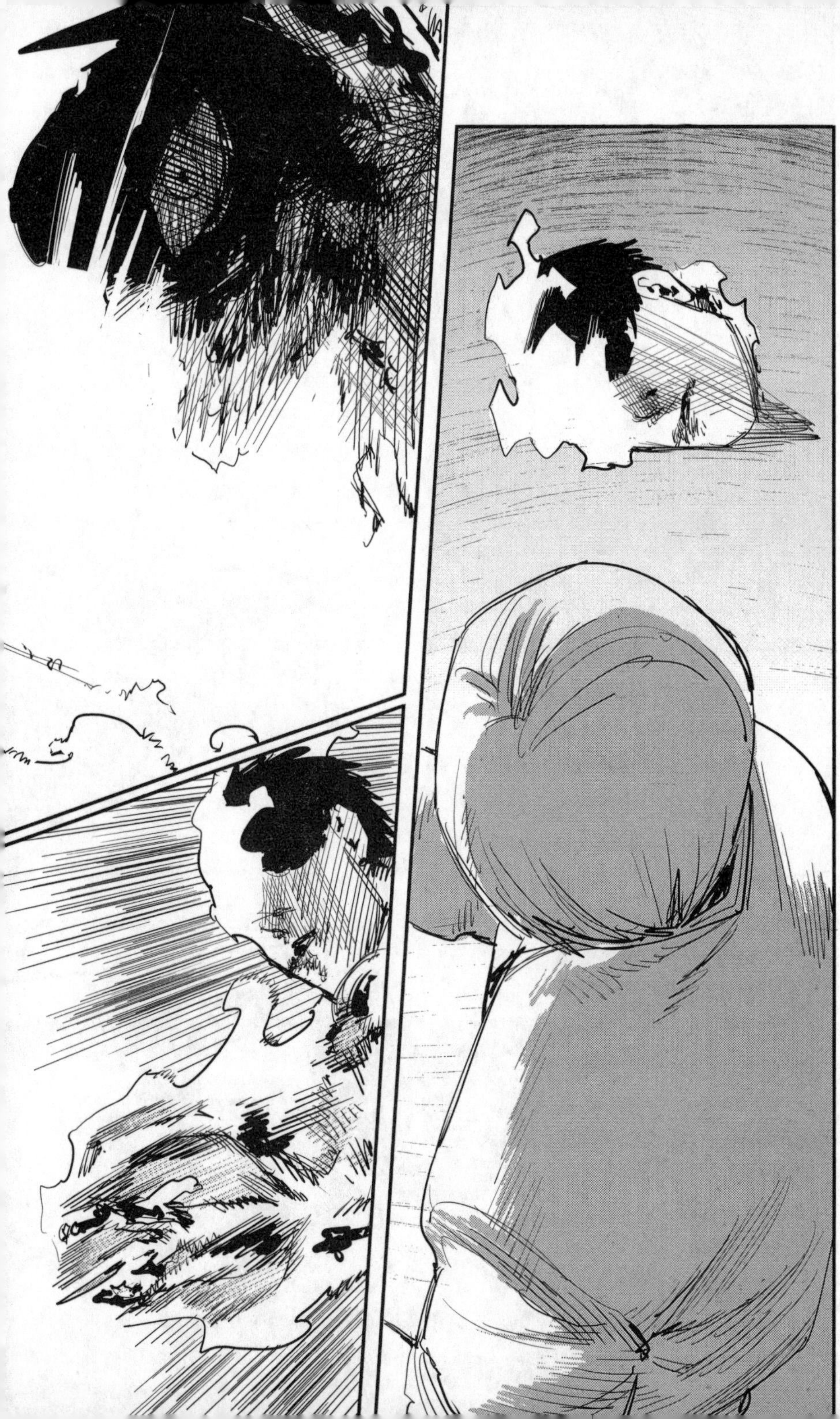

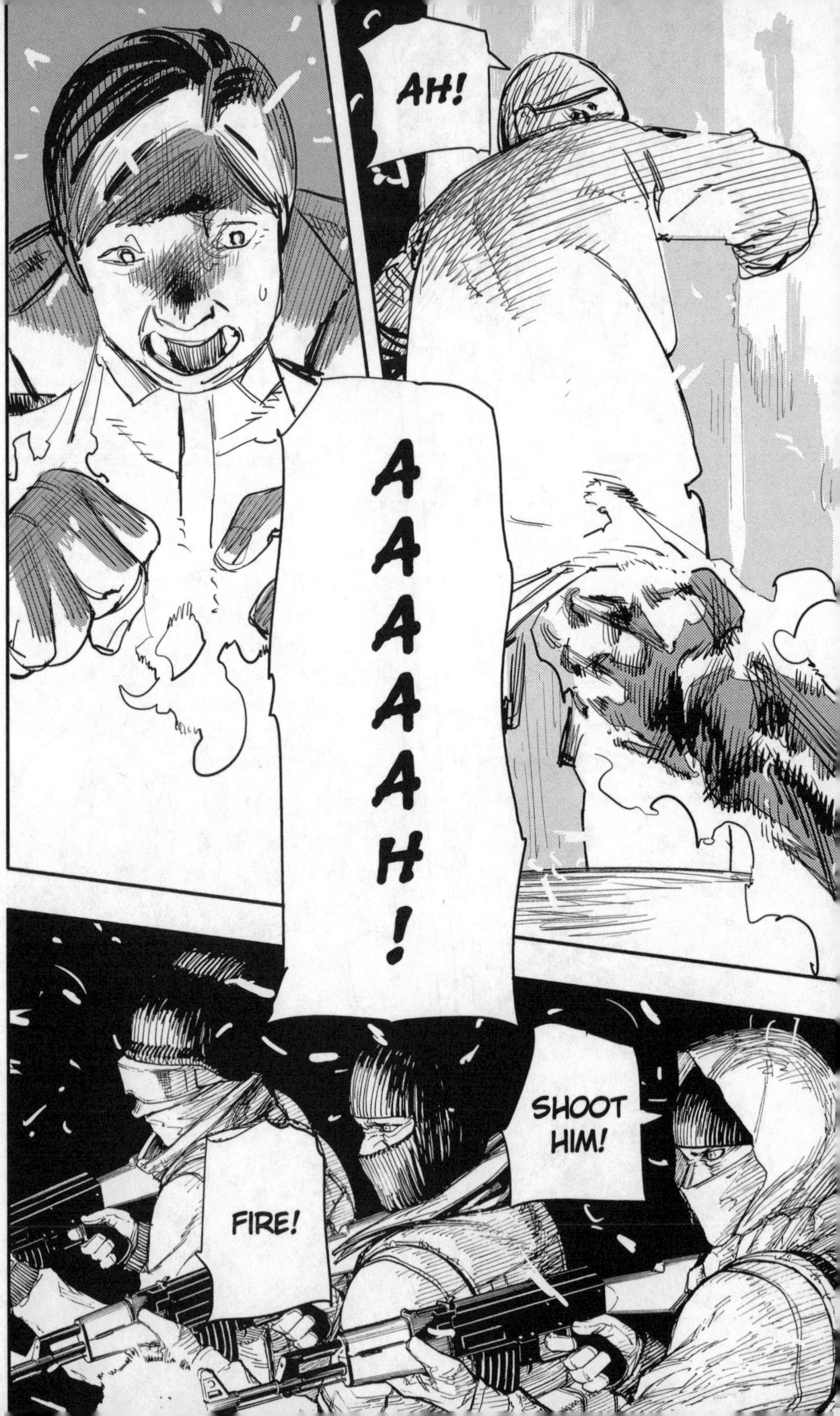
AH!
AAAAAH!
SHOOT HIM!
FIRE!

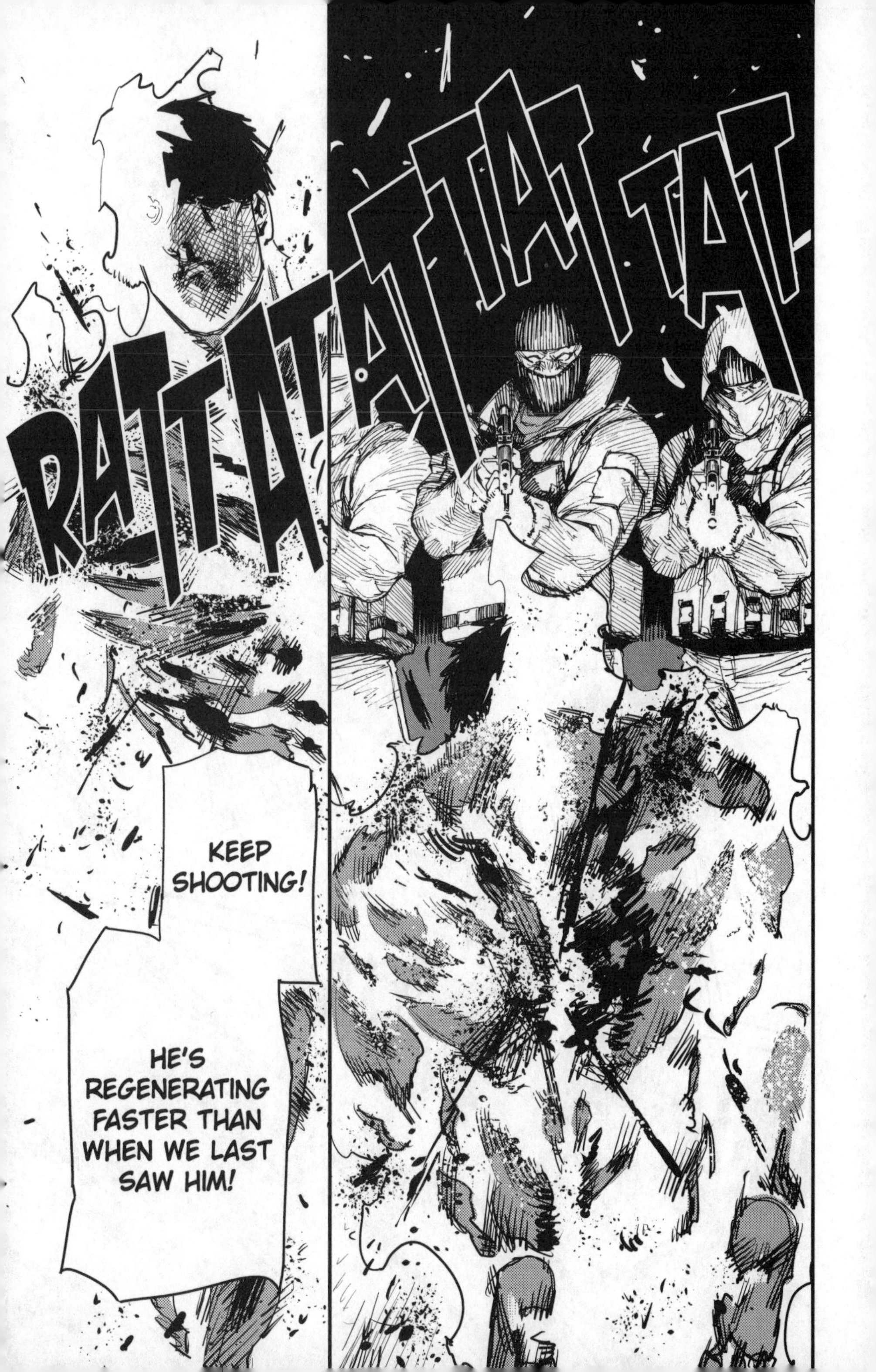
RATTATATTATTAT
KEEP SHOOTING!
HE'S REGENERATING FASTER THAN WHEN WE LAST SAW HIM!

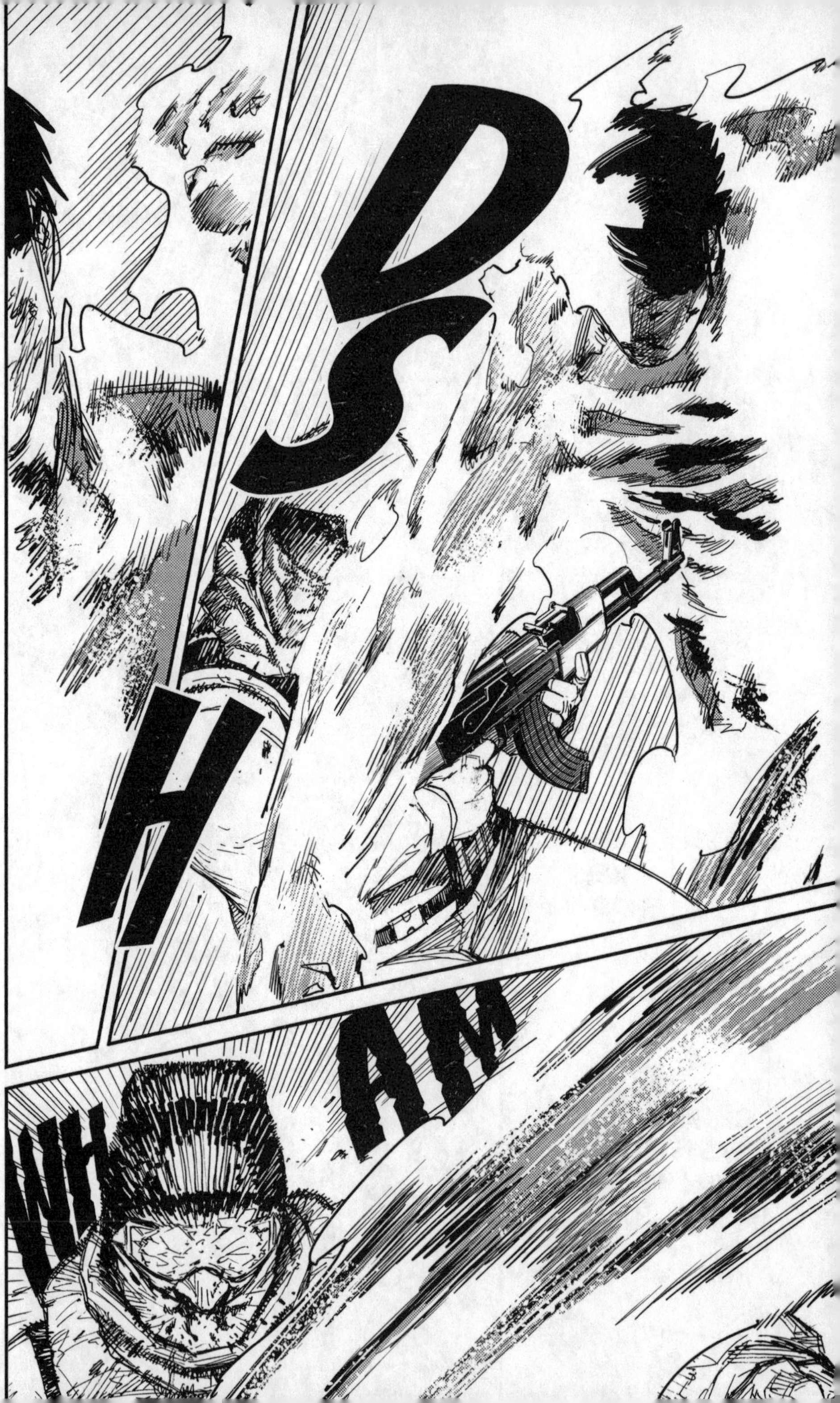
DSH
WHAM

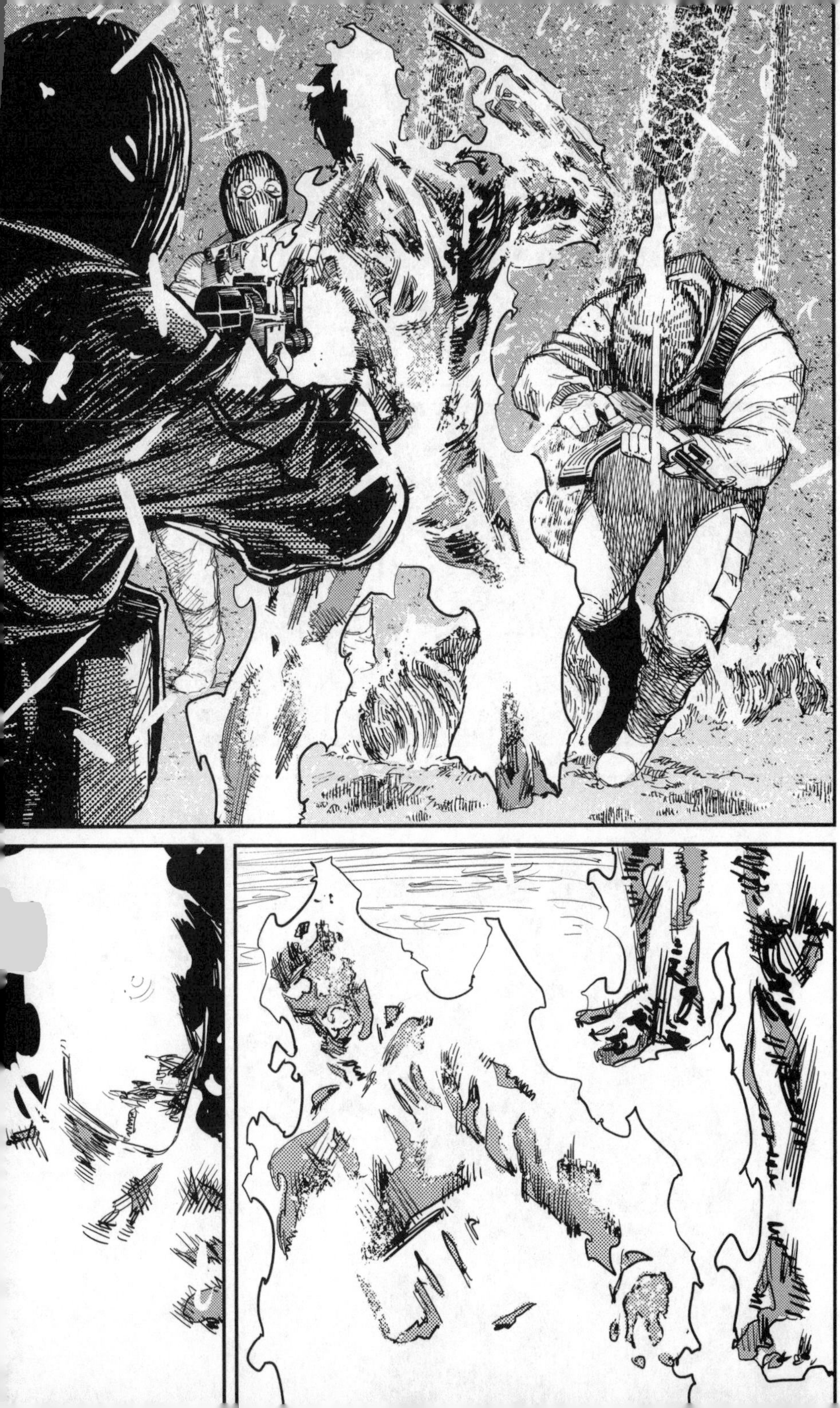

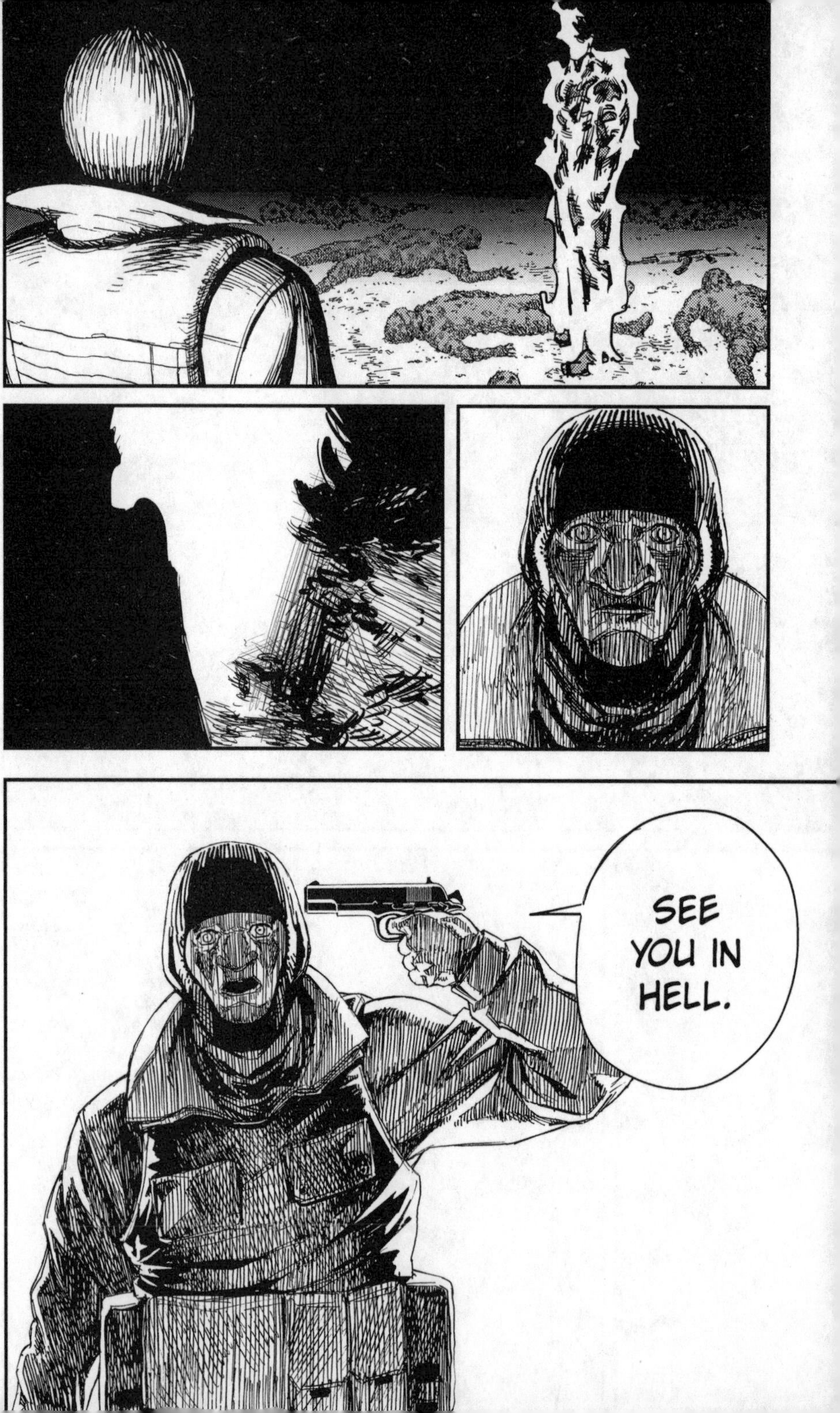
SEE YOU IN HELL.

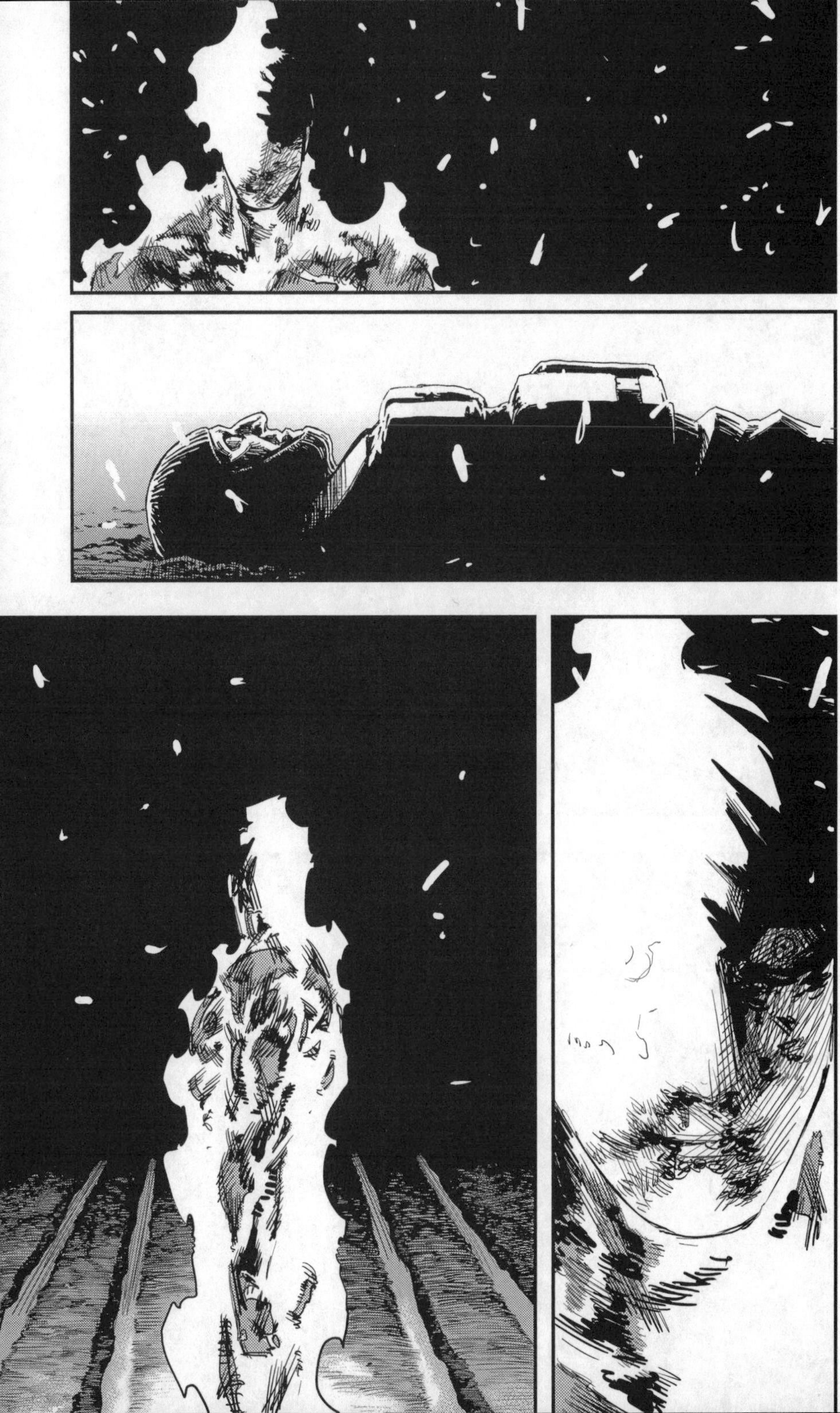

CHAPTER 73

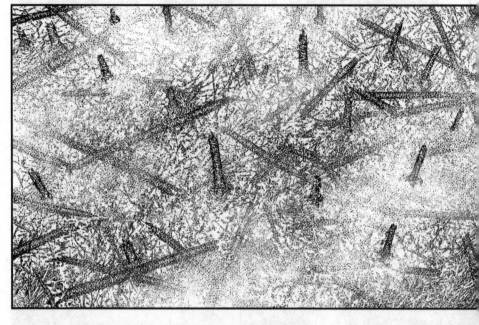

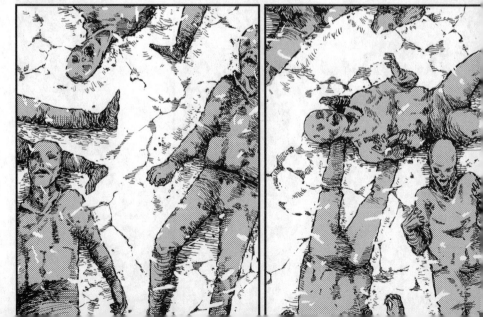

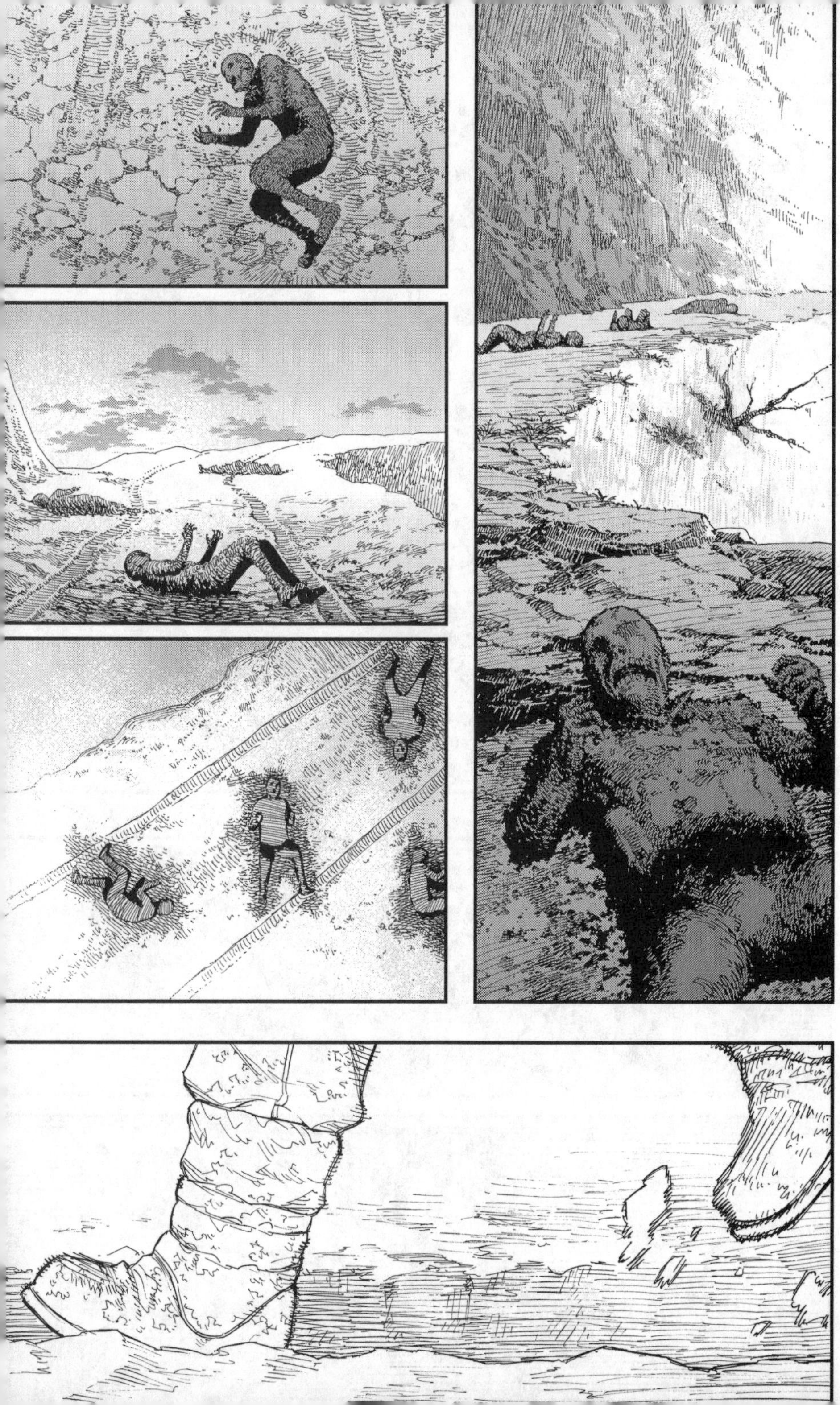

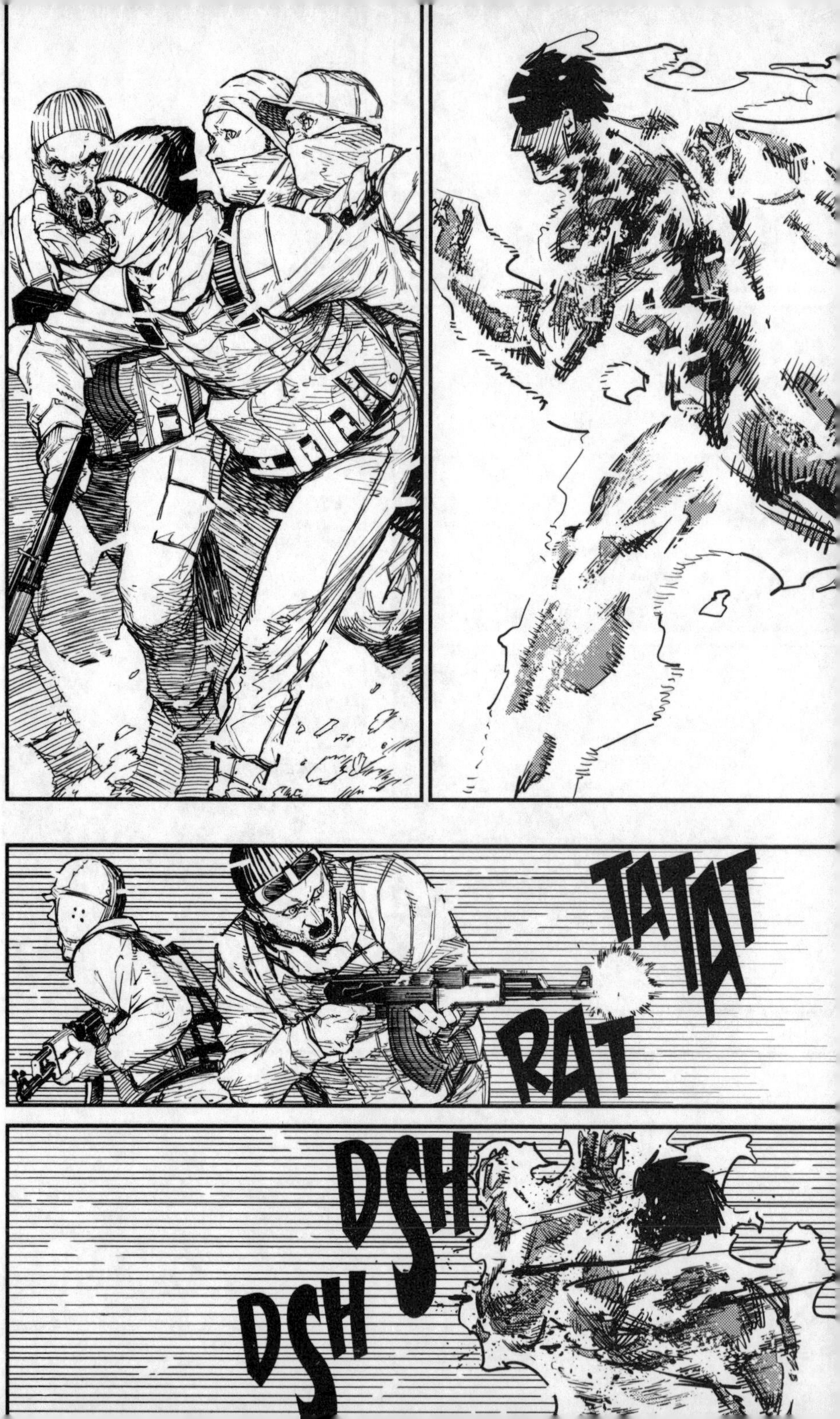
TATAT
RAT
DSH
DSH

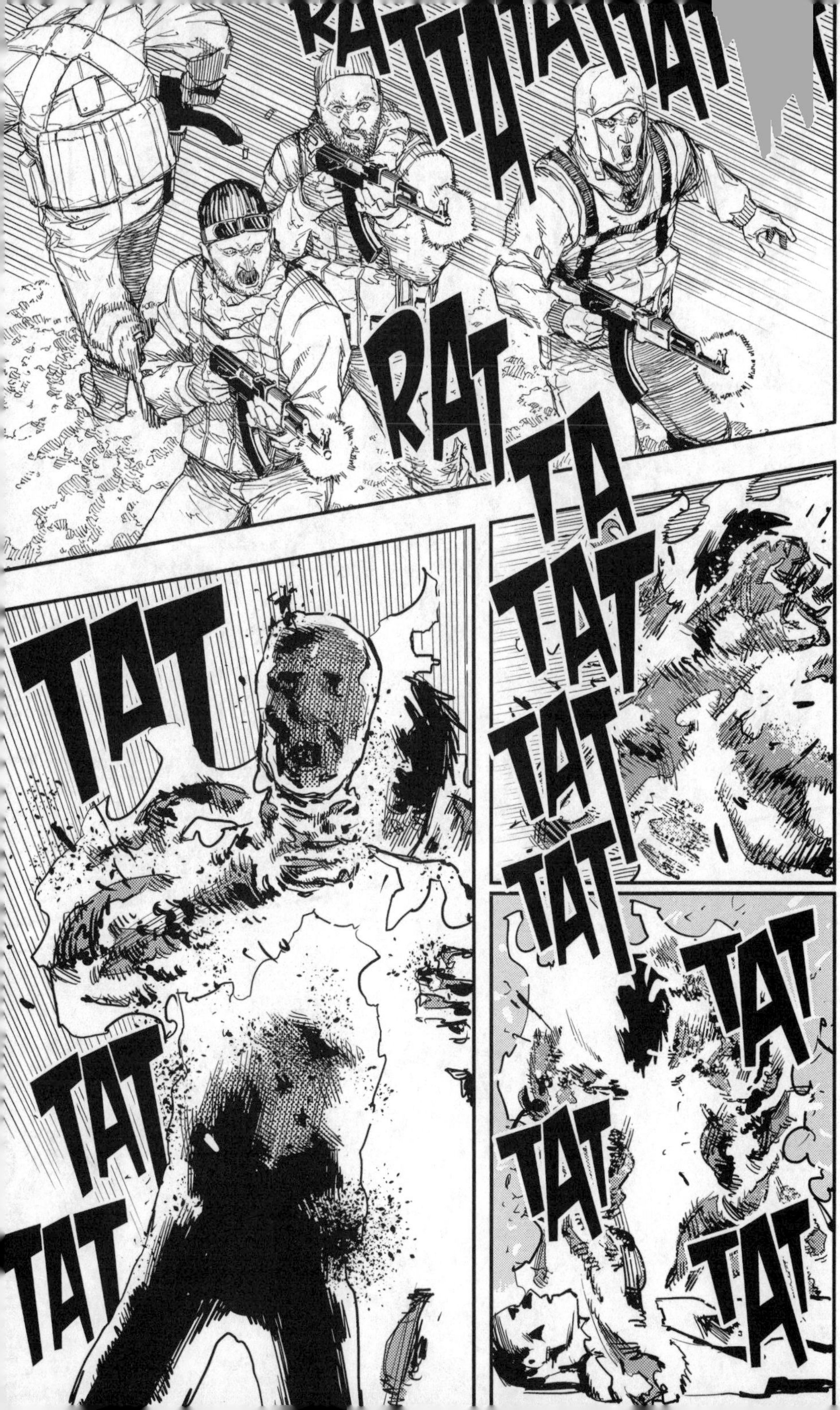
RATTATATAT
RAT
TA
TAT
TAT
TAT
TAT
TAT
TAT
TAT
TAT
TAT

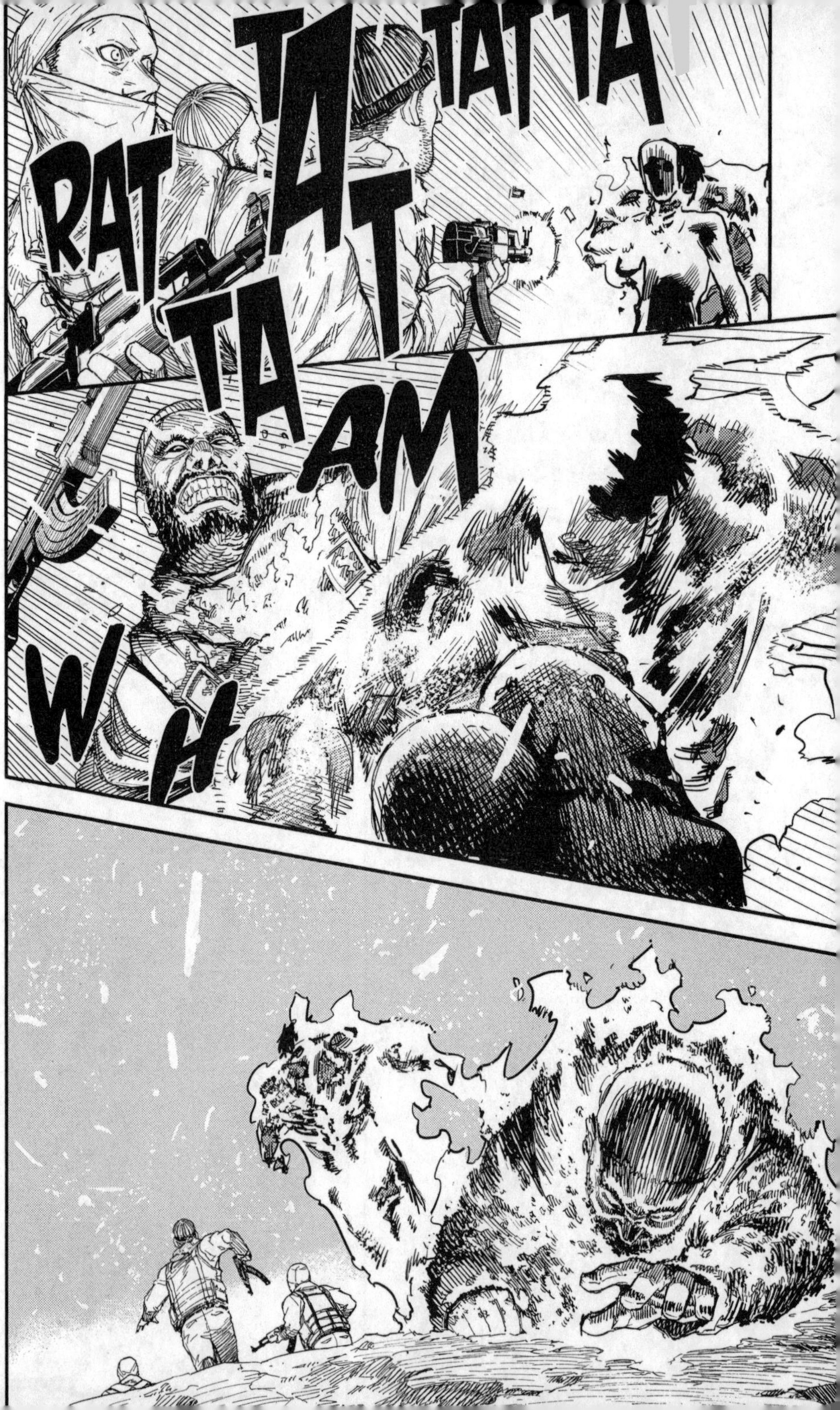
TATTA
TAT
RAT
TA
WHAM

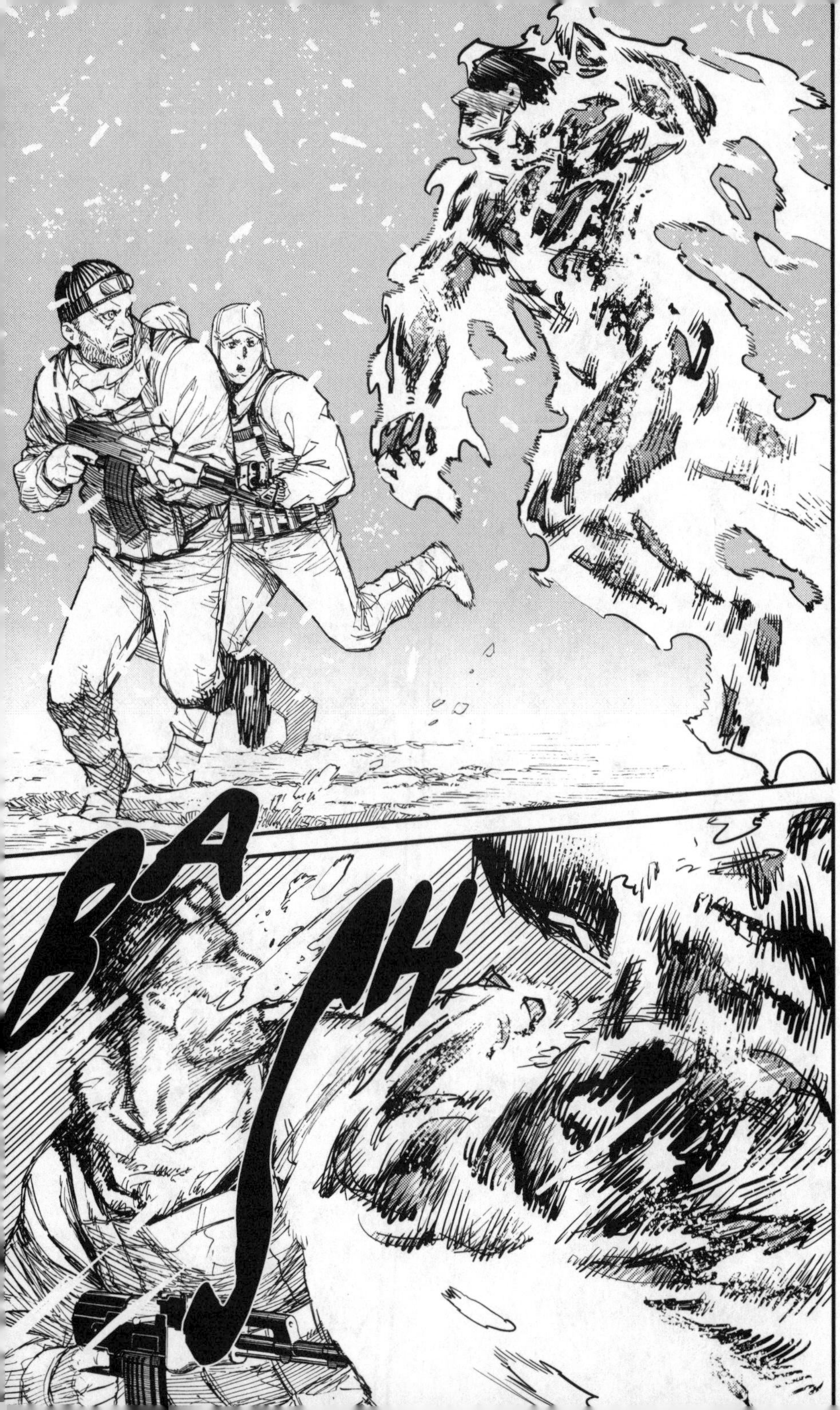
BASH

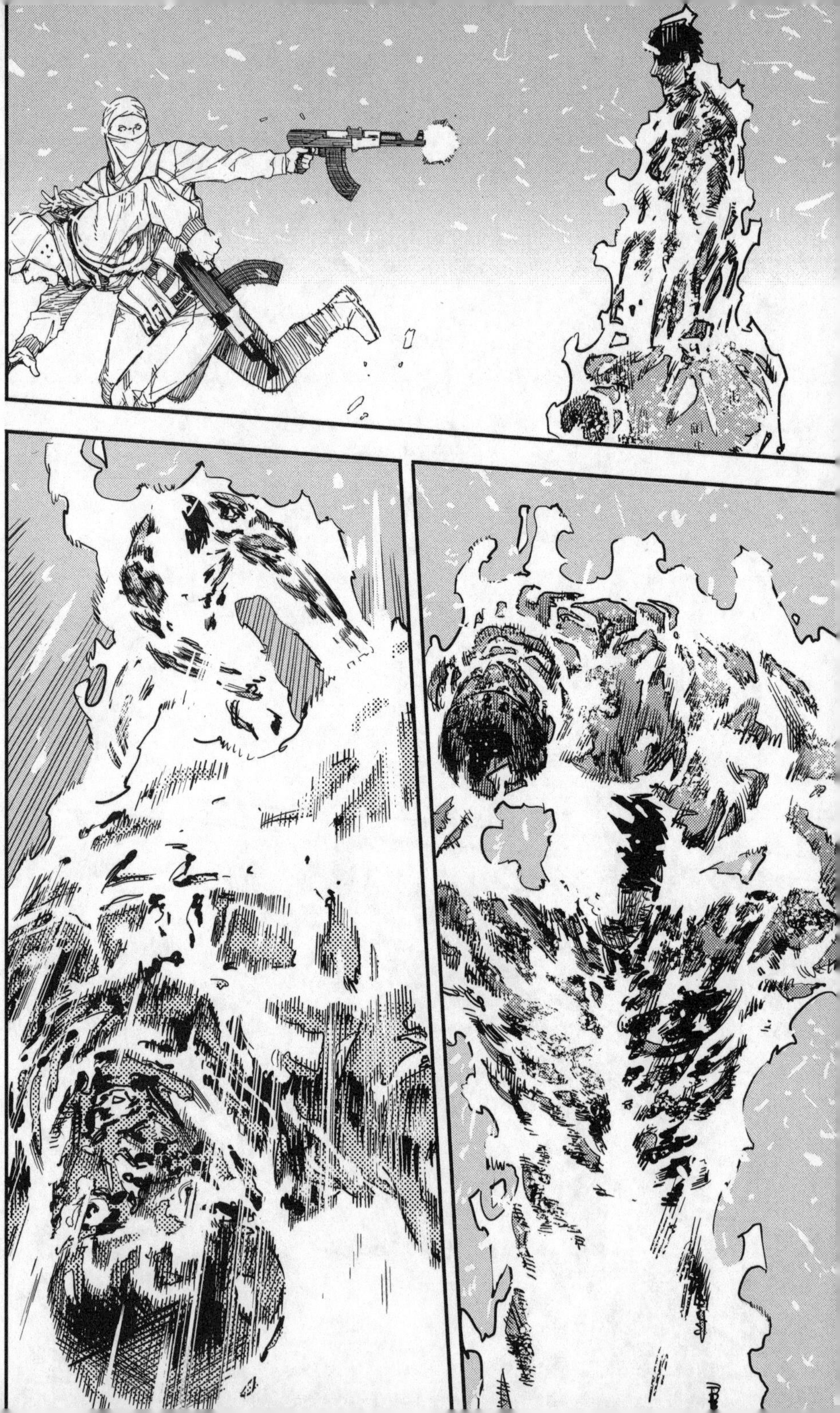

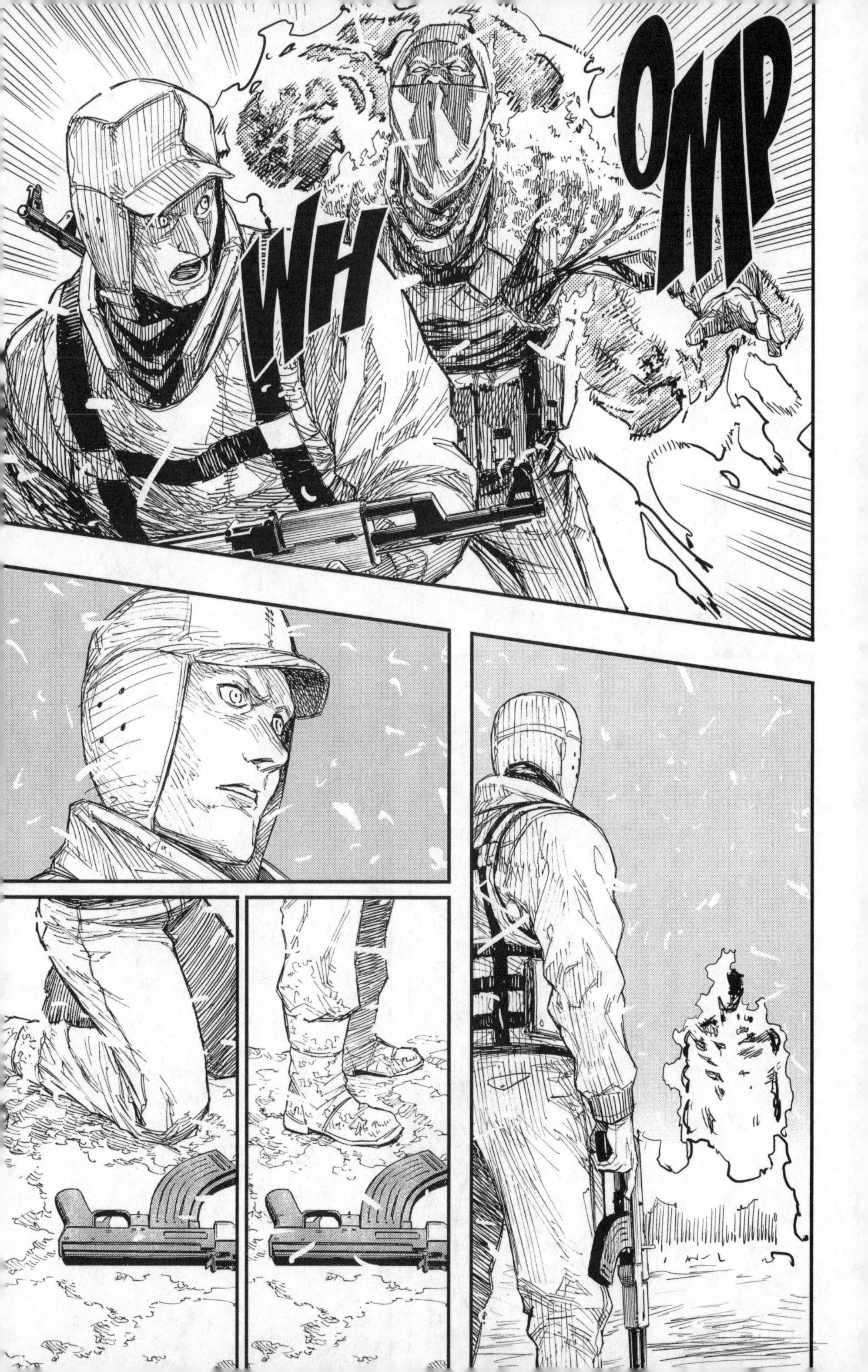
WH
OMP

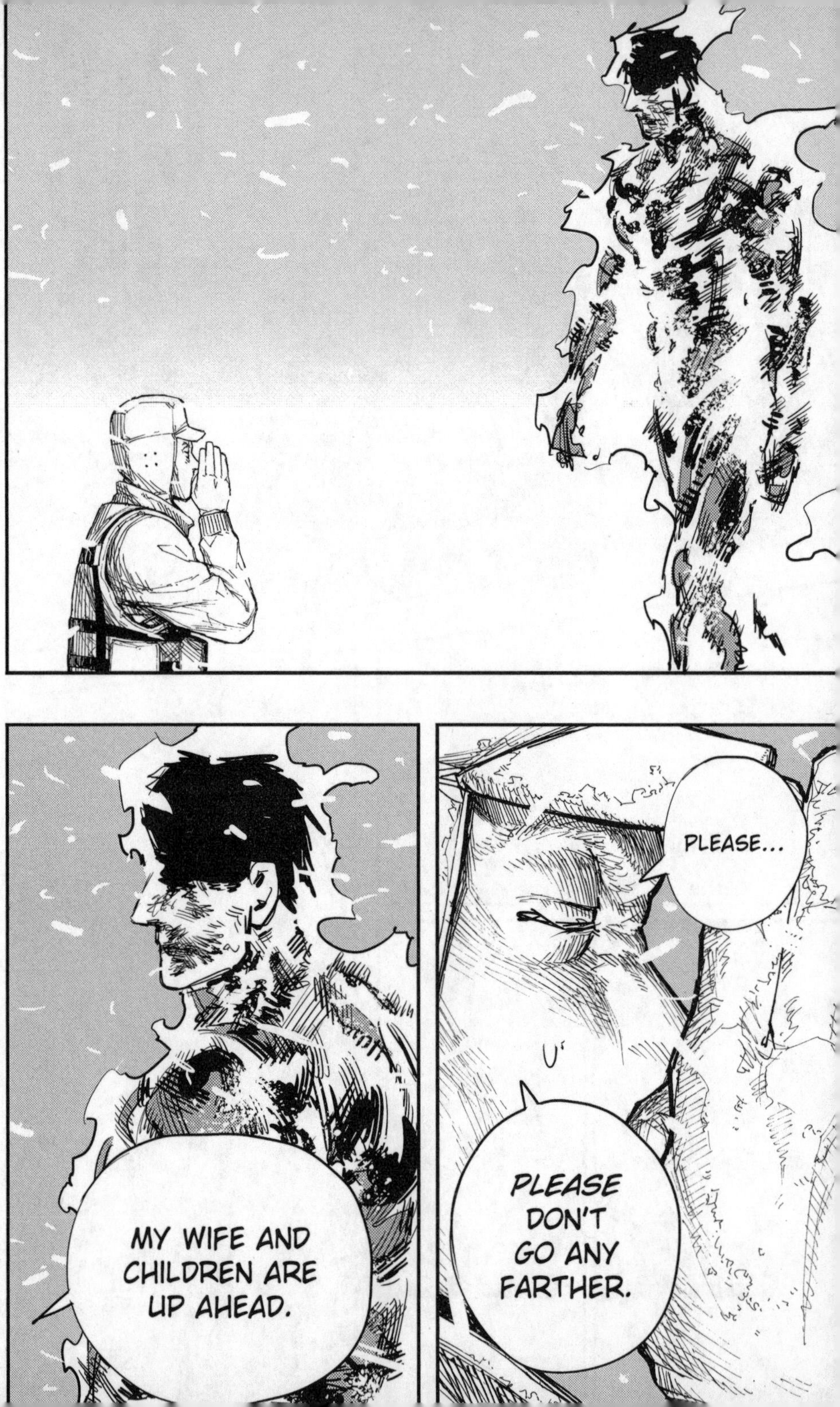
PLEASE...
PLEASE DON'T GO ANY FARTHER.
MY WIFE AND CHILDREN ARE UP AHEAD.

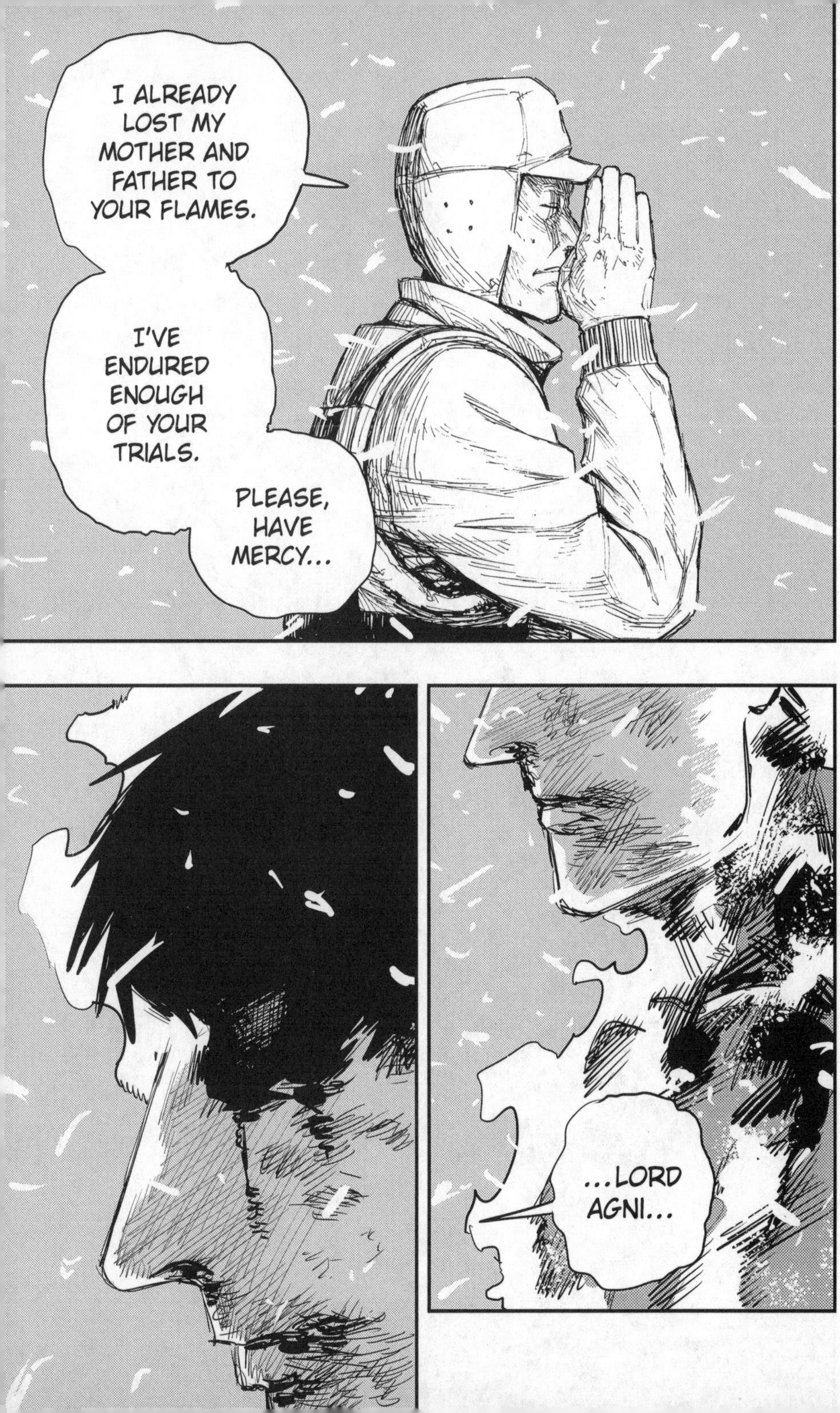
I ALREADY LOST MY MOTHER AND FATHER TO YOUR FLAMES.
I'VE ENDURED ENOUGH OF YOUR TRIALS.
PLEASE, HAVE MERCY...
...LORD AGNI...

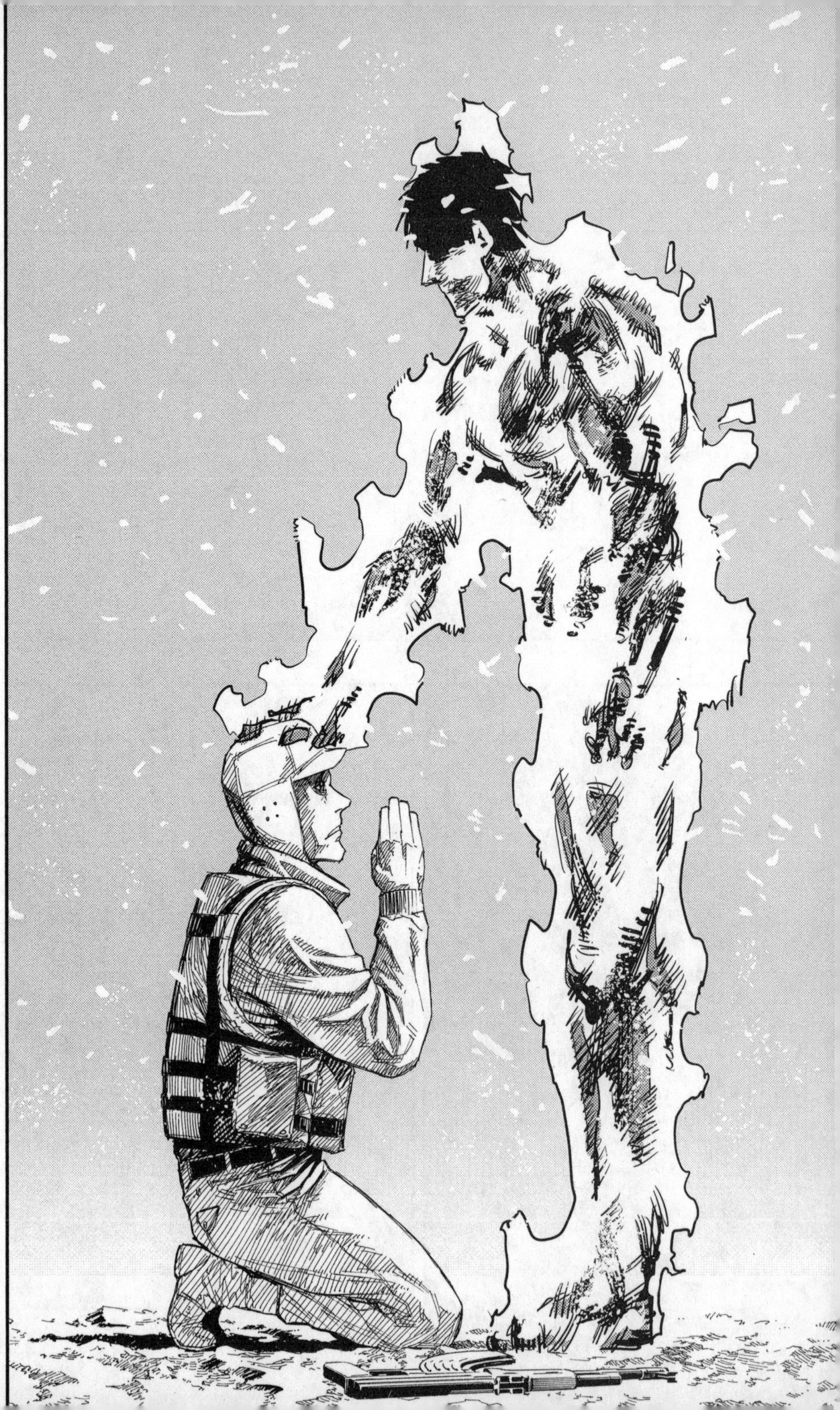

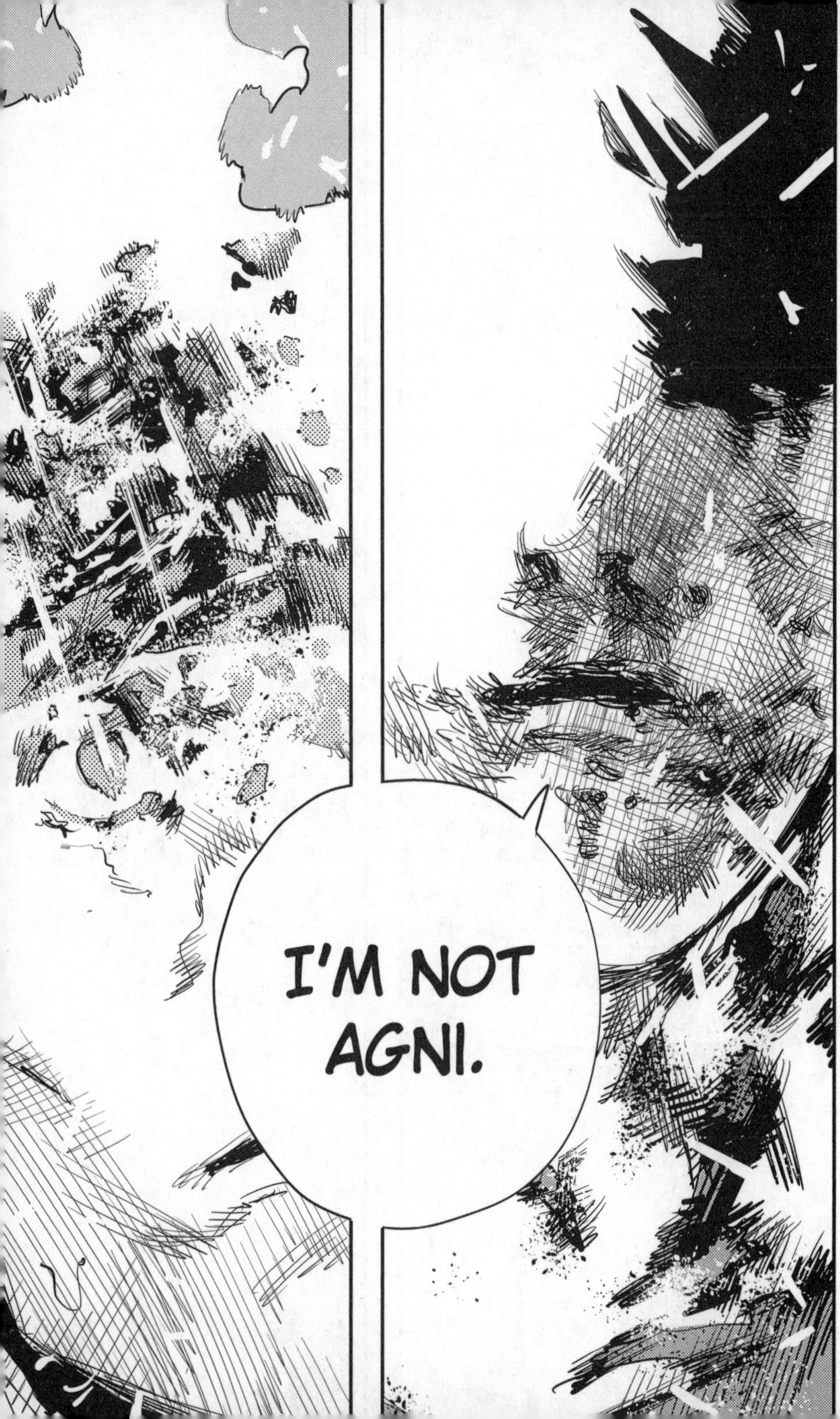
I'M NOT AGNI.

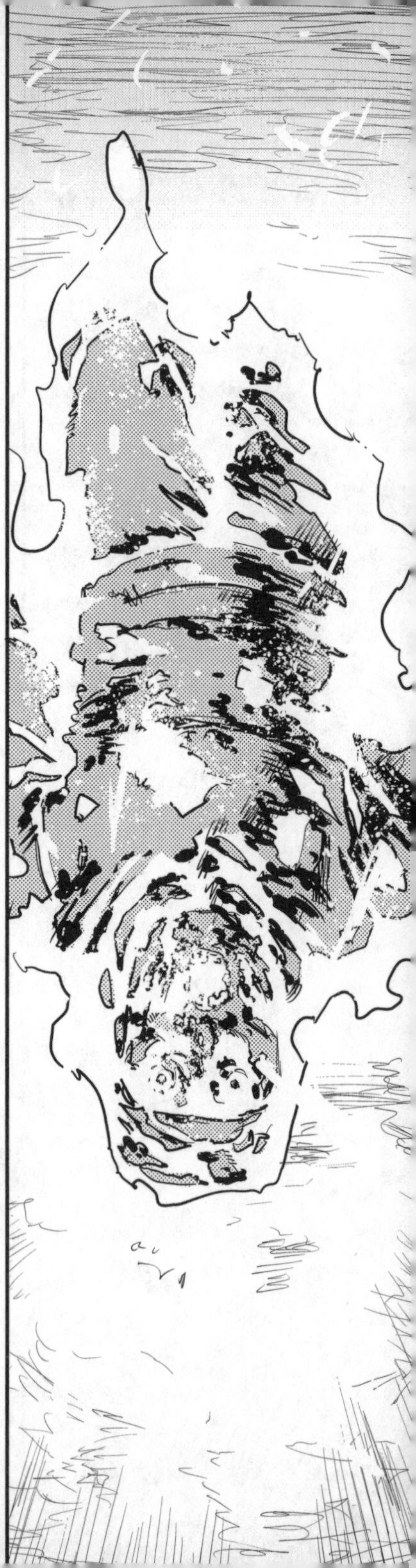
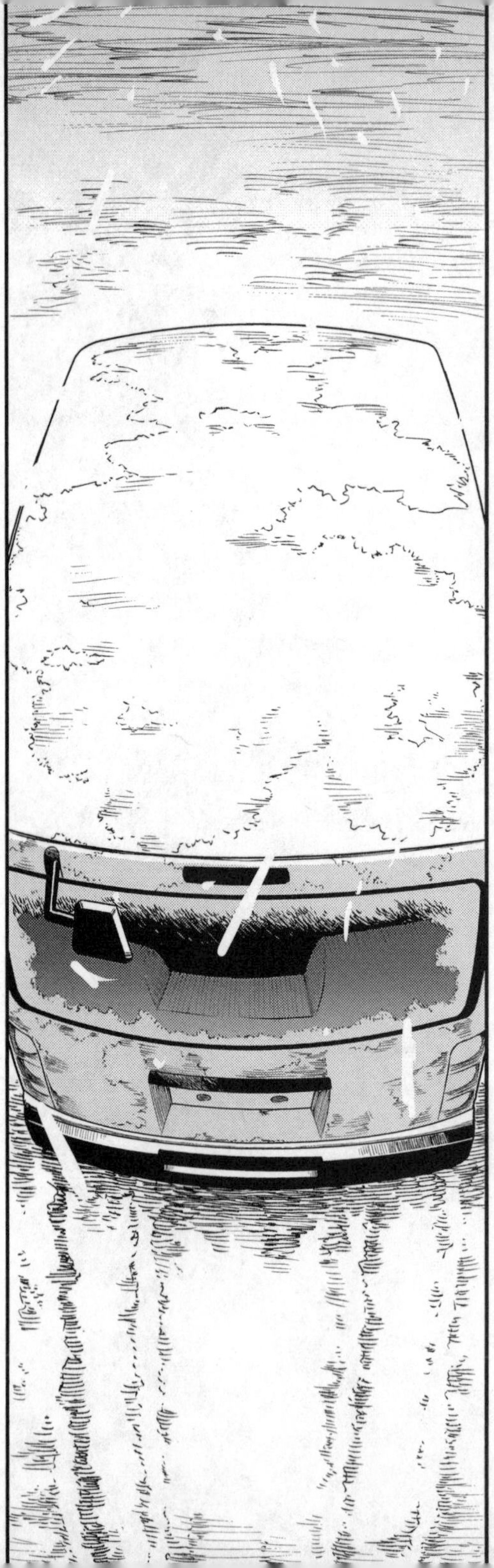

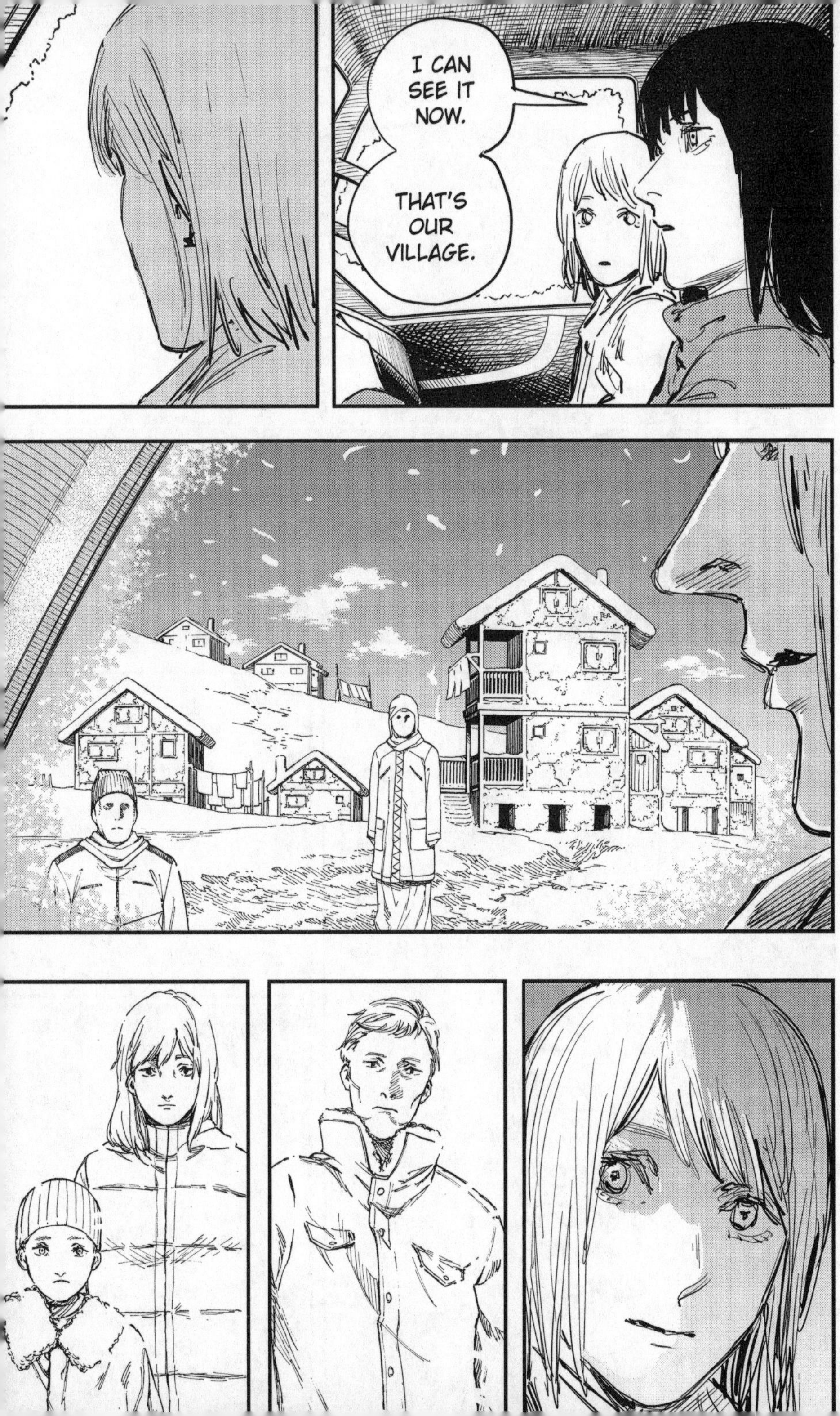
I CAN SEE IT NOW.
THAT'S OUR VILLAGE.

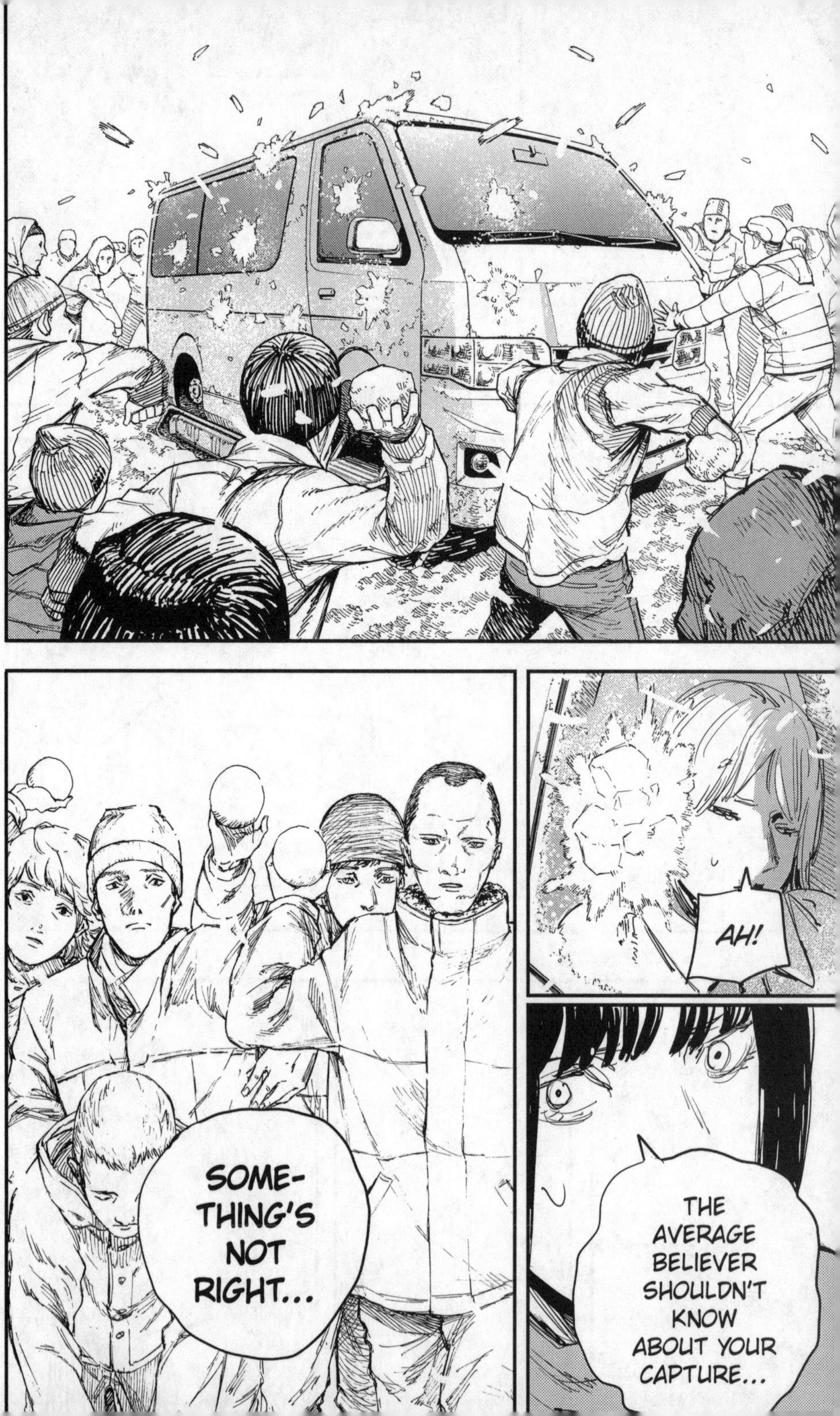
AH!
THE AVERAGE BELIEVER SHOULDN'T KNOW ABOUT YOUR CAPTURE...
SOME-THING'S NOT RIGHT...

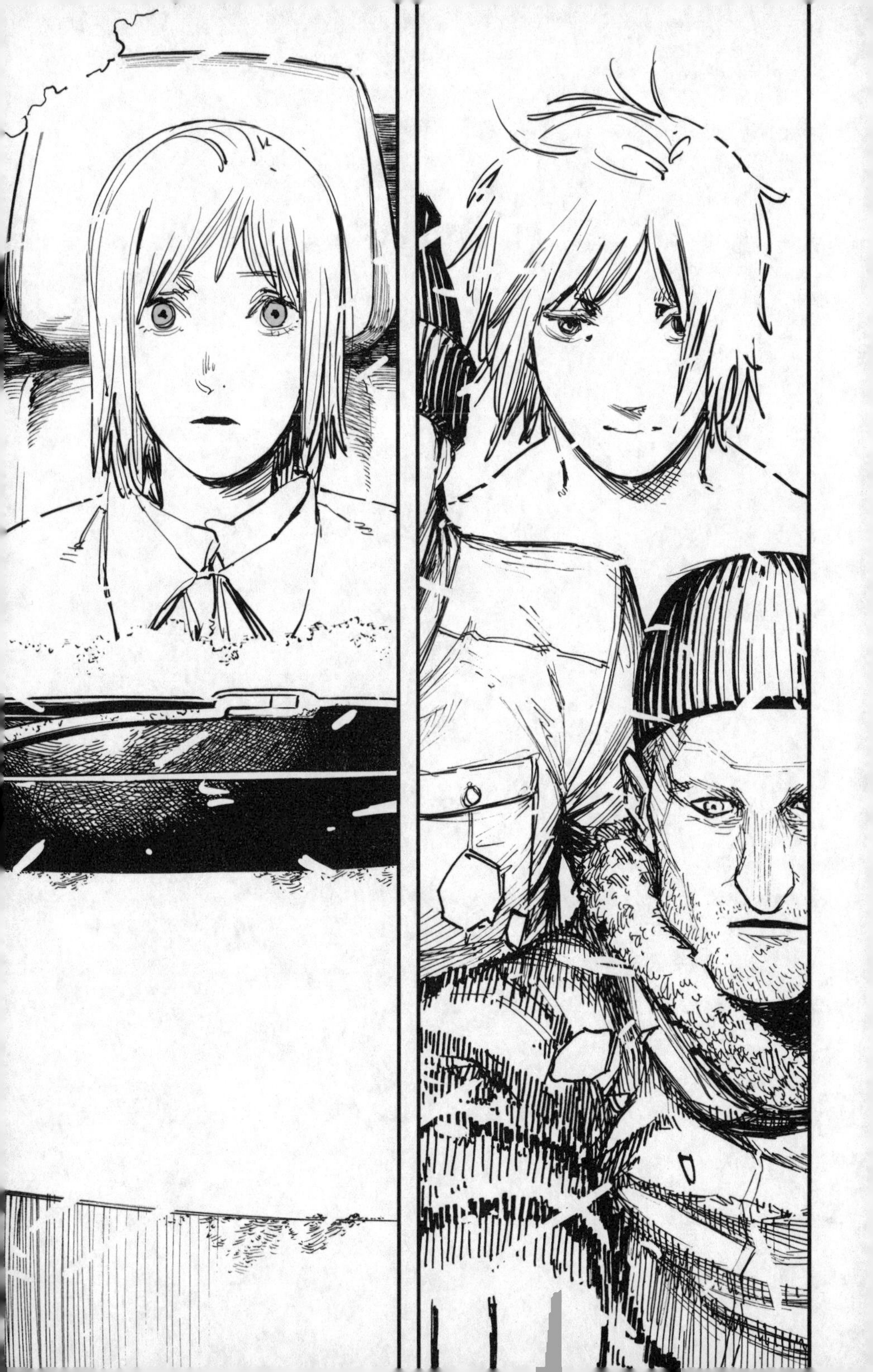

FIRE PUNCH

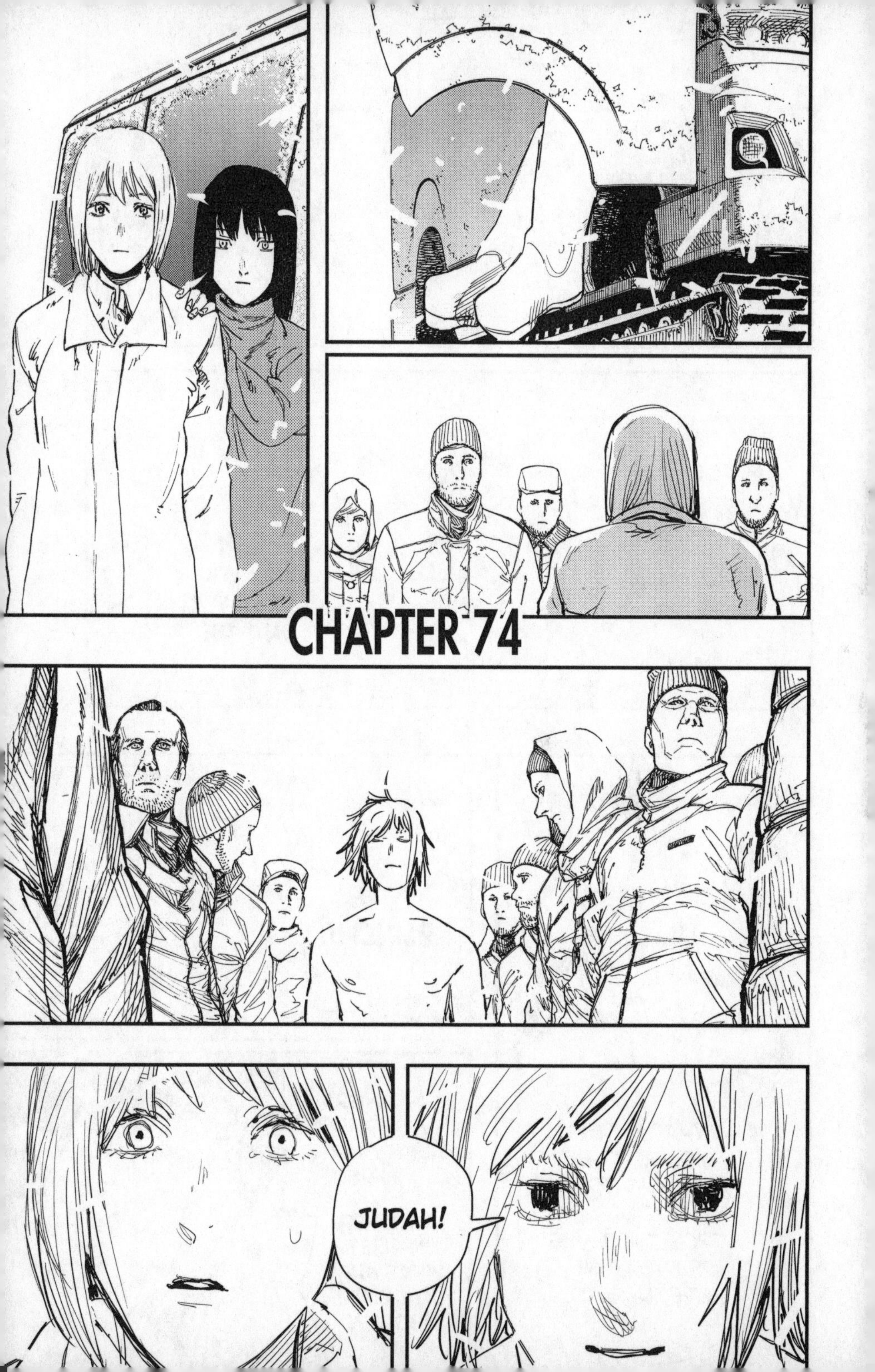
CHAPTER 74
JUDAH!

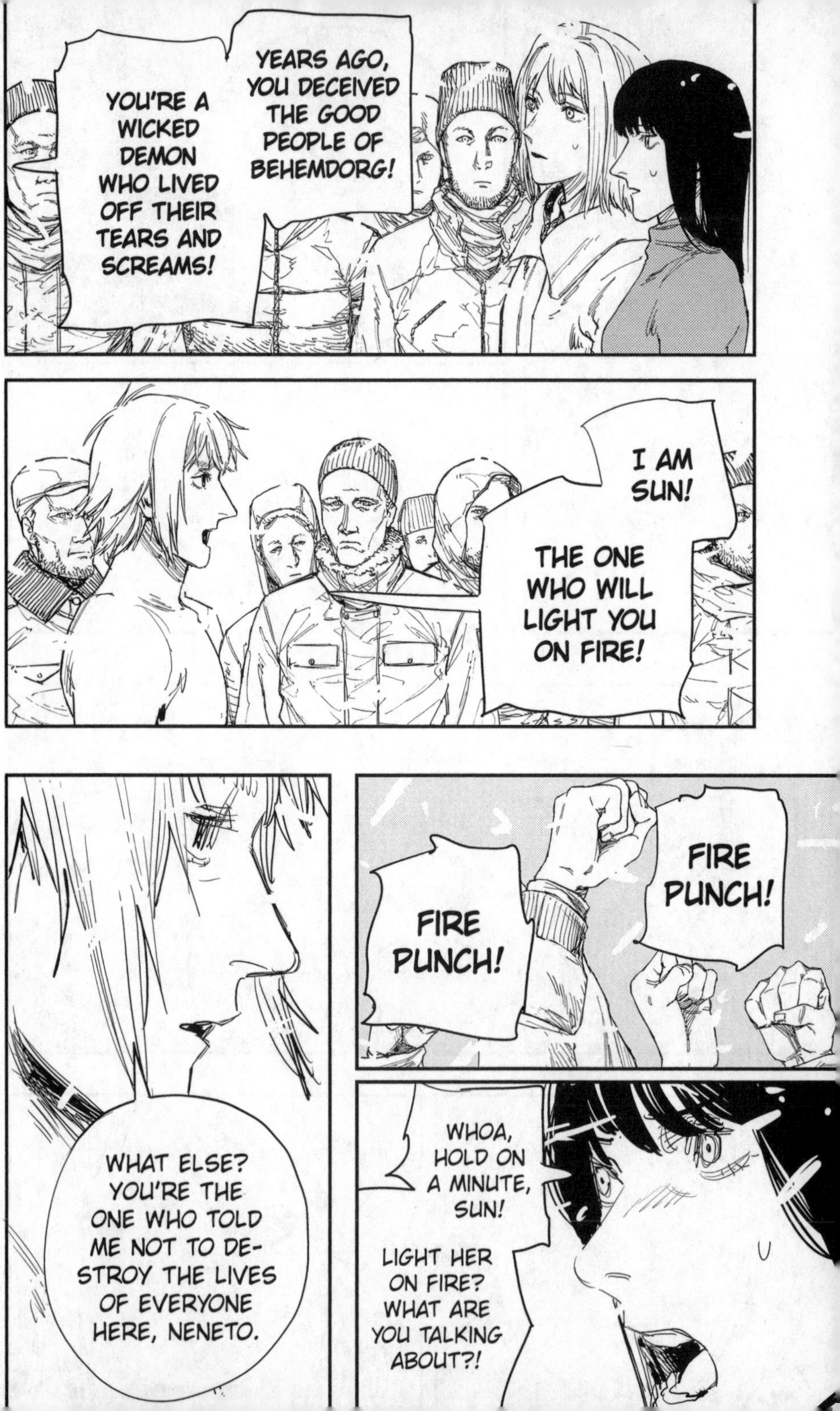
YEARS AGO, YOU DECEIVED THE GOOD PEOPLE OF BEHEMDORG!
YOU'RE A WICKED DEMON WHO LIVED OFF THEIR TEARS AND SCREAMS!
I AM SUN!
THE ONE WHO WILL LIGHT YOU ON FIRE!
FIRE PUNCH!
FIRE PUNCH!
WHOA, HOLD ON A MINUTE, SUN!
LIGHT HER ON FIRE? WHAT ARE YOU TALKING ABOUT?!
WHAT ELSE? YOU'RE THE ONE WHO TOLD ME NOT TO DESTROY THE LIVES OF EVERYONE HERE, NENETO.

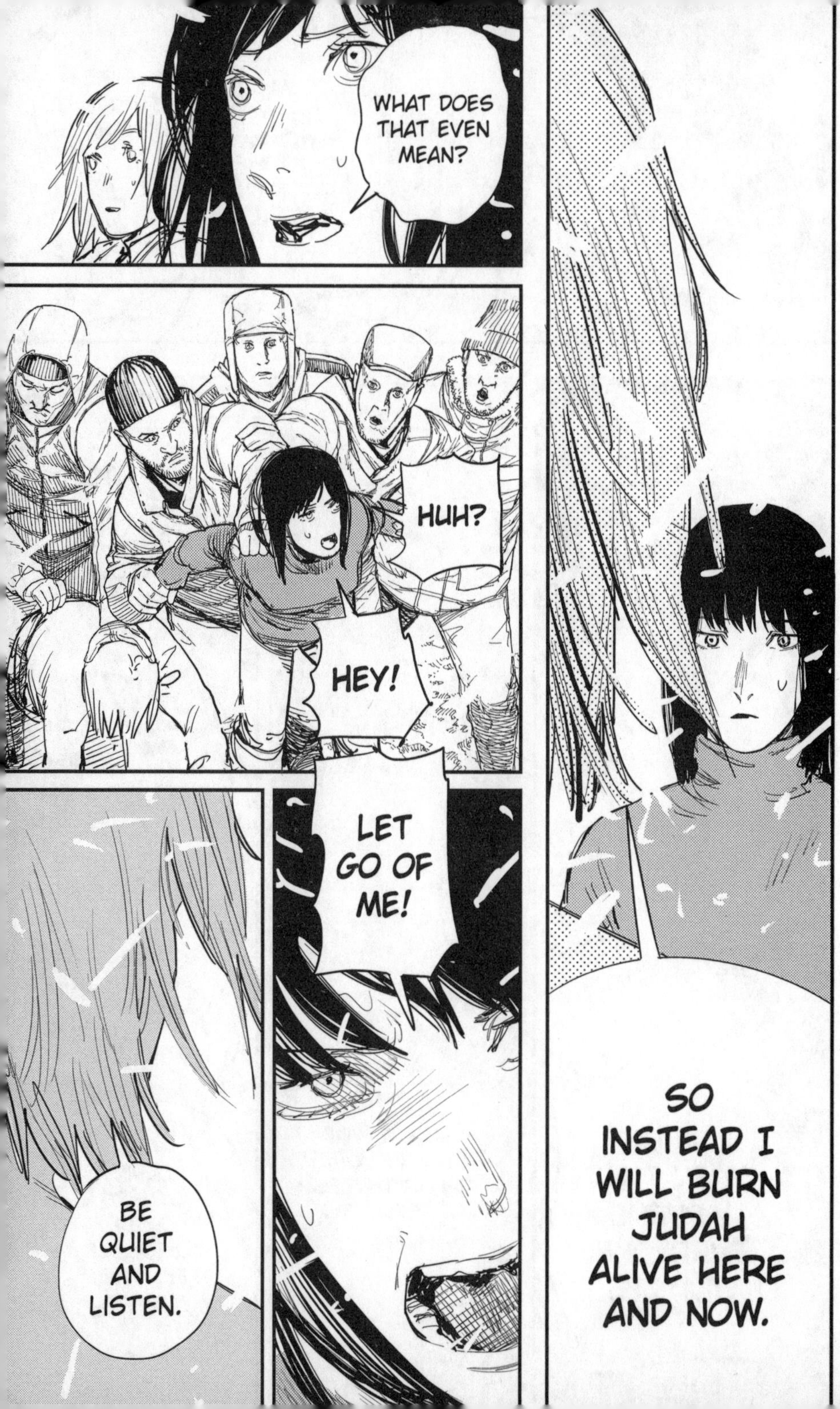
WHAT DOES THAT EVEN MEAN?
HUH?
HEY!
LET GO OF ME!
BE QUIET AND LISTEN.
SO INSTEAD I WILL BURN JUDAH ALIVE HERE AND NOW.

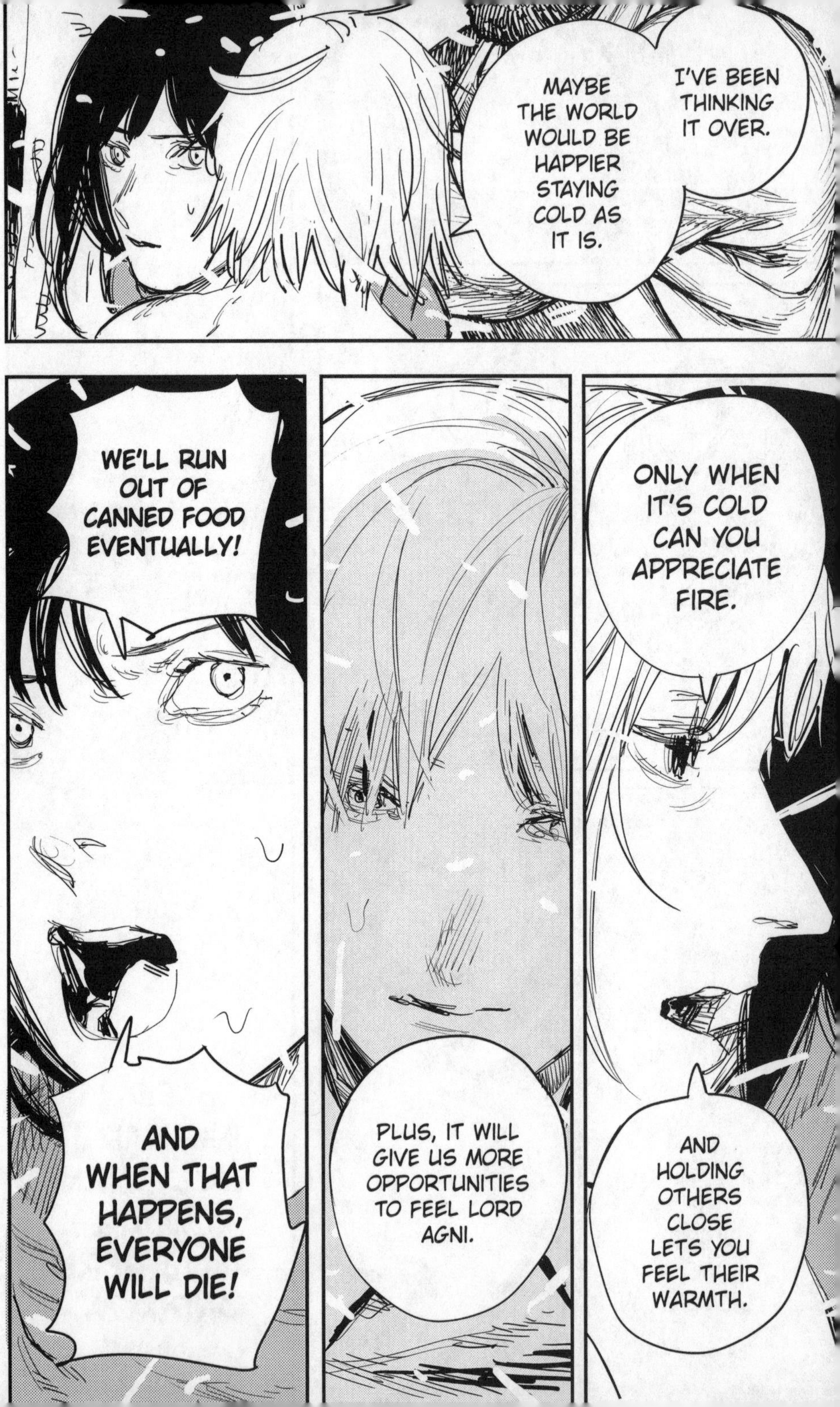
I'VE BEEN THINKING IT OVER.
MAYBE THE WORLD WOULD BE HAPPIER STAYING COLD AS IT IS.
ONLY WHEN IT'S COLD CAN YOU APPRECIATE FIRE.
AND HOLDING OTHERS CLOSE LETS YOU FEEL THEIR WARMTH.
PLUS, IT WILL GIVE US MORE OPPORTUNITIES TO FEEL LORD AGNI.
WE'LL RUN OUT OF CANNED FOOD EVENTUALLY!
AND WHEN THAT HAPPENS, EVERYONE WILL DIE!

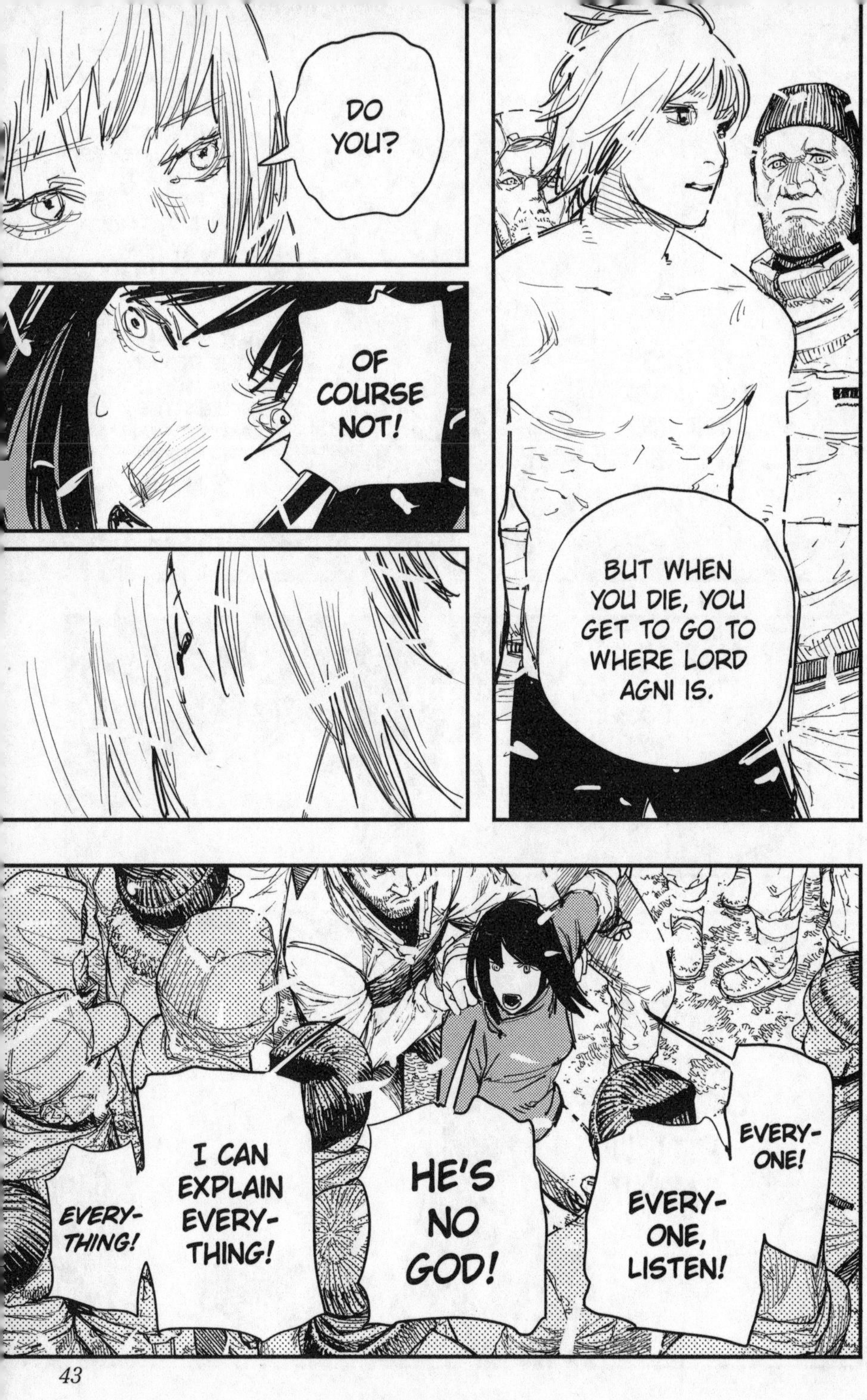
BUT WHEN YOU DIE, YOU GET TO GO TO WHERE LORD AGNI IS.
DO YOU?
OF COURSE NOT!
EVERY-ONE!
EVERY-ONE, LISTEN!
HE'S NO GOD!
I CAN EXPLAIN EVERY-THING!
EVERY-THING!

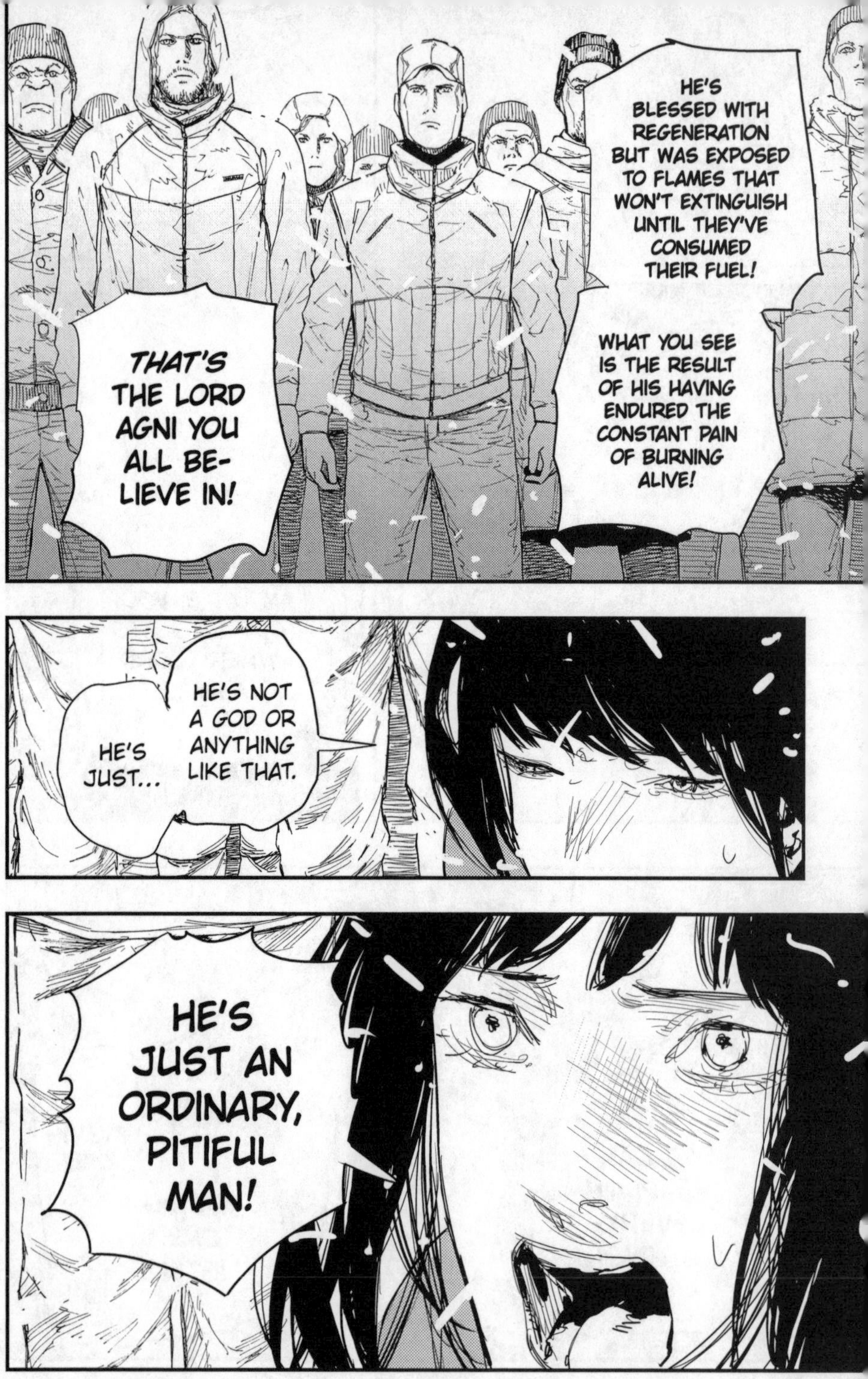
HE'S BLESSED WITH REGENERATION BUT WAS EXPOSED TO FLAMES THAT WON'T EXTINGUISH UNTIL THEY'VE CONSUMED THEIR FUEL!
WHAT YOU SEE IS THE RESULT OF HIS HAVING ENDURED THE CONSTANT PAIN OF BURNING ALIVE!
THAT'S THE LORD AGNI YOU ALL BE-LIEVE IN!
HE'S NOT A GOD OR ANYTHING LIKE THAT.
HE'S JUST...
HE'S JUST AN ORDINARY, PITIFUL MAN!

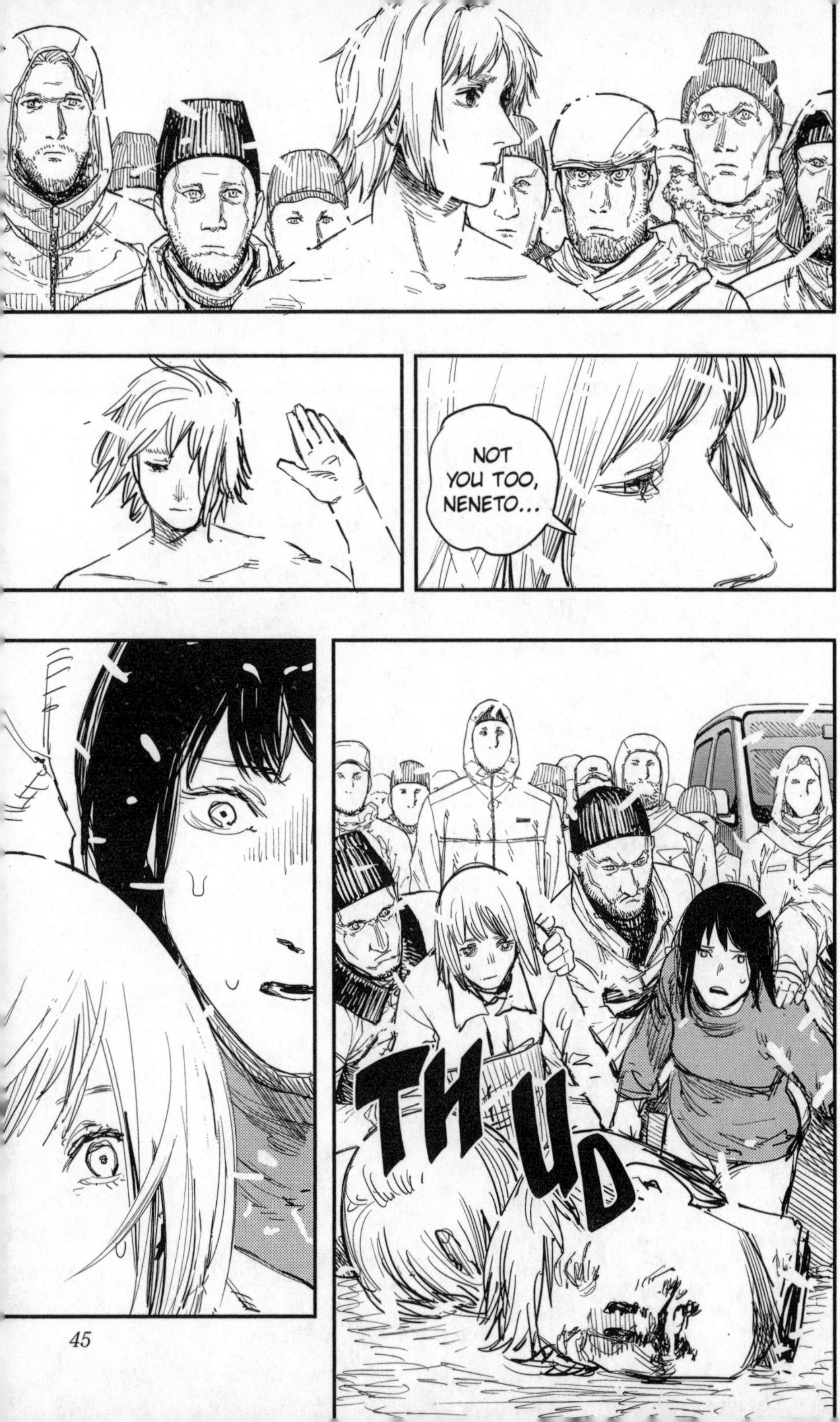
NOT YOU TOO, NENETO...
THUD

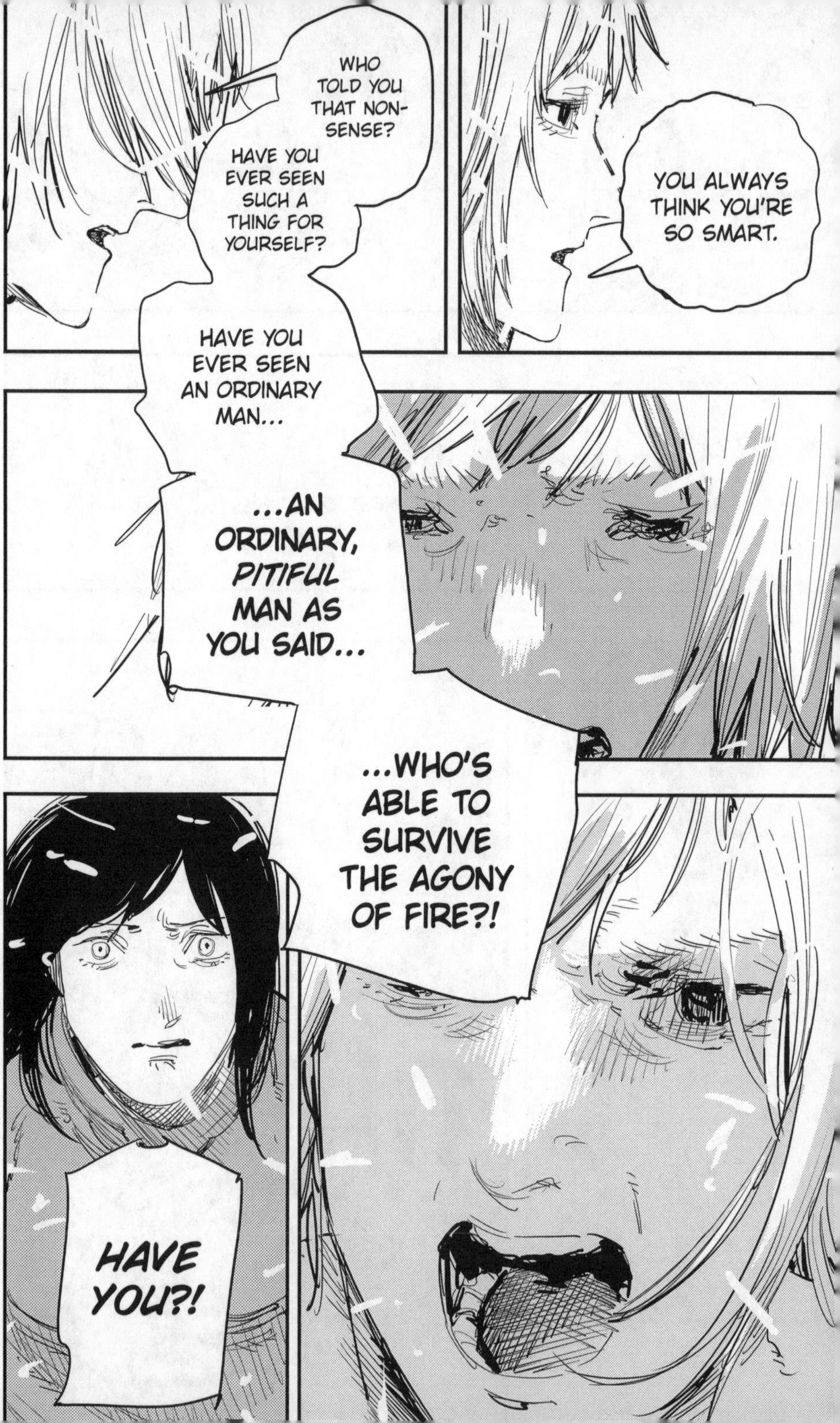
YOU ALWAYS THINK YOU'RE SO SMART.
WHO TOLD YOU THAT NON-SENSE?
HAVE YOU EVER SEEN SUCH A THING FOR YOURSELF?
HAVE YOU EVER SEEN AN ORDINARY MAN...
...AN ORDINARY, PITIFUL MAN AS YOU SAID...
...WHO'S ABLE TO SURVIVE THE AGONY OF FIRE?!
HAVE YOU?!

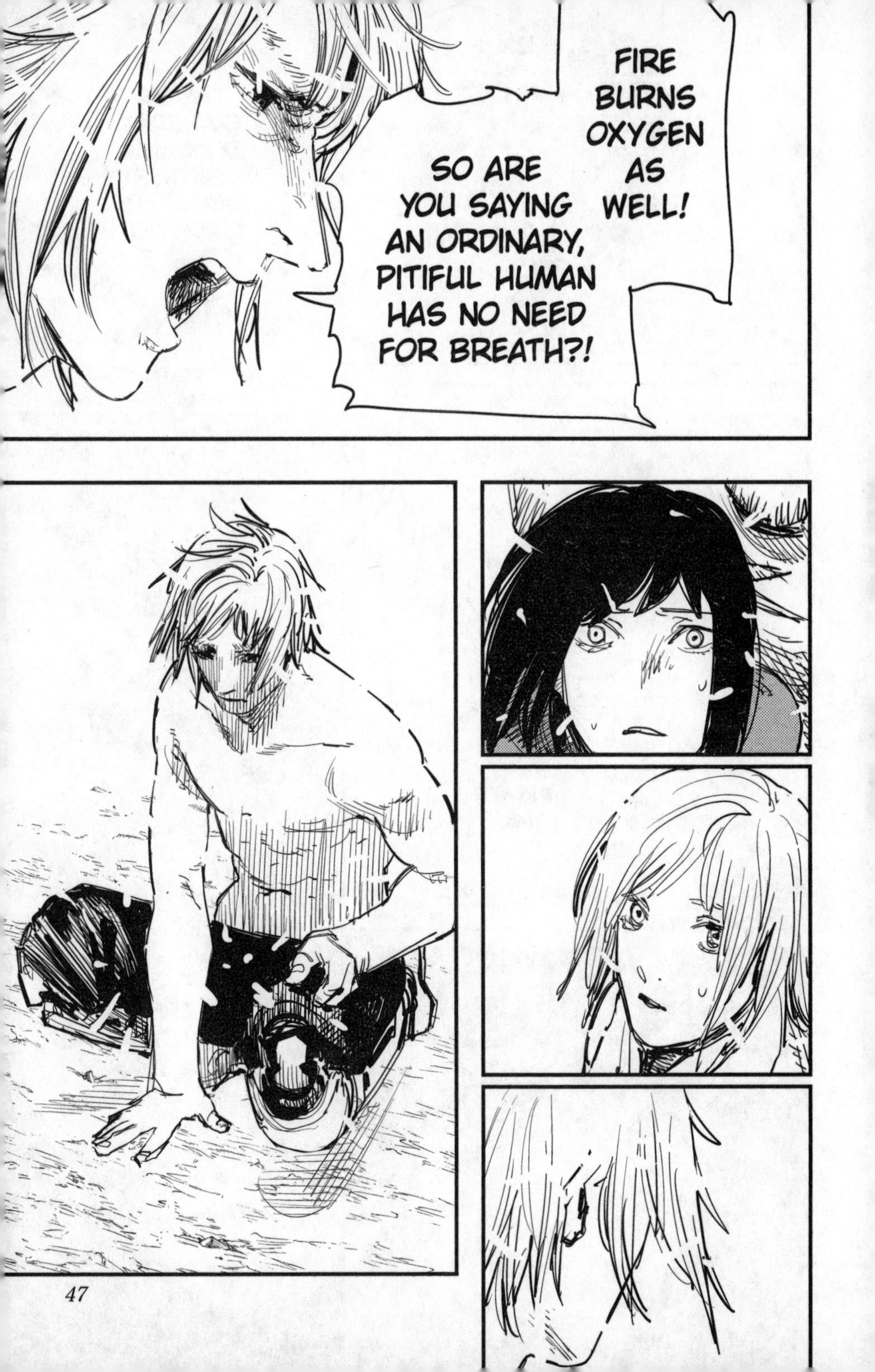
SO ARE YOU SAYING AN ORDINARY, PITIFUL HUMAN HAS NO NEED FOR BREATH?!
FIRE BURNS OXYGEN AS WELL!

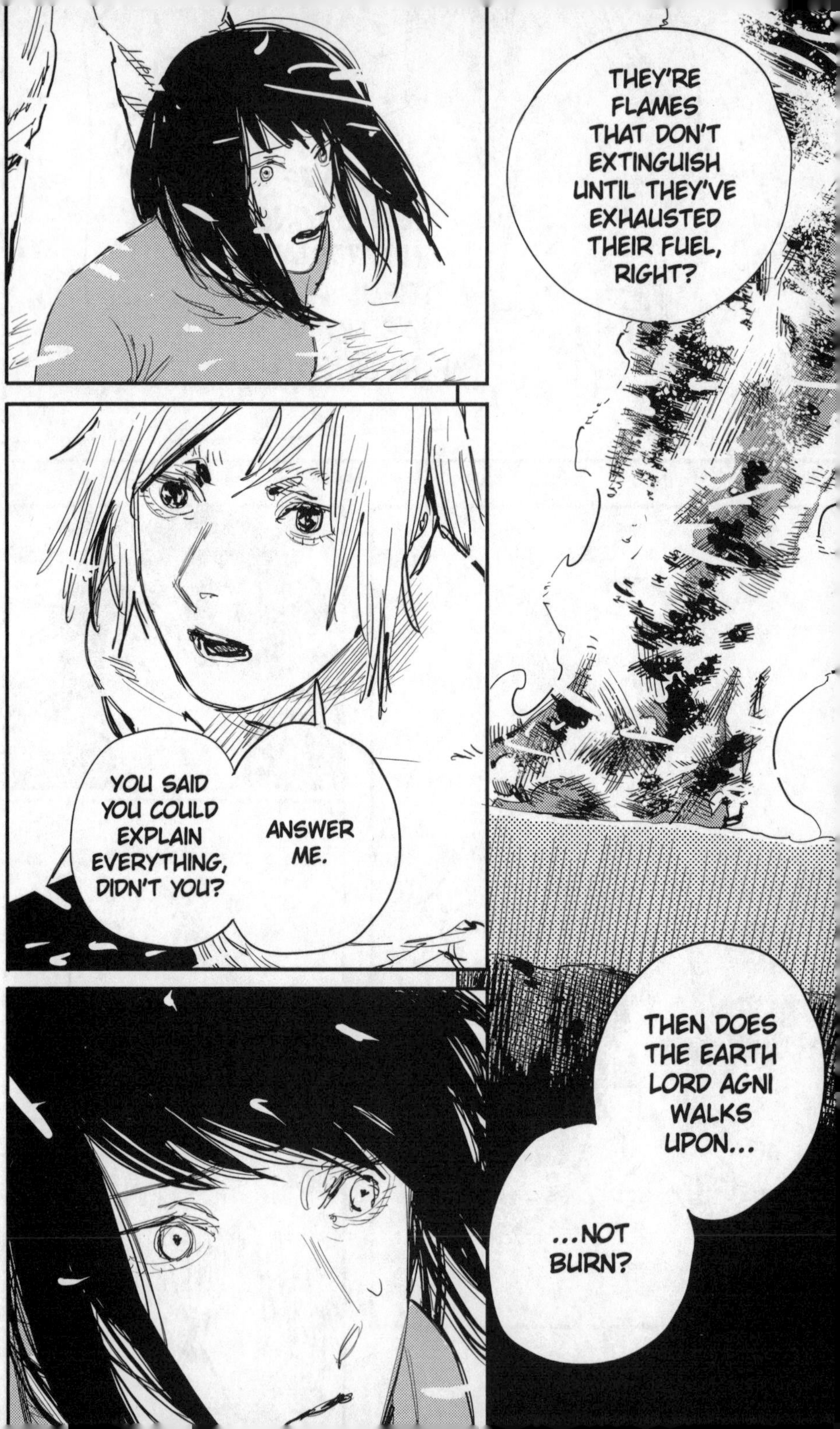
THEY'RE FLAMES THAT DON'T EXTINGUISH UNTIL THEY'VE EXHAUSTED THEIR FUEL, RIGHT?
ANSWER ME.
YOU SAID YOU COULD EXPLAIN EVERYTHING, DIDN'T YOU?
THEN DOES THE EARTH LORD AGNI WALKS UPON...
...NOT BURN?

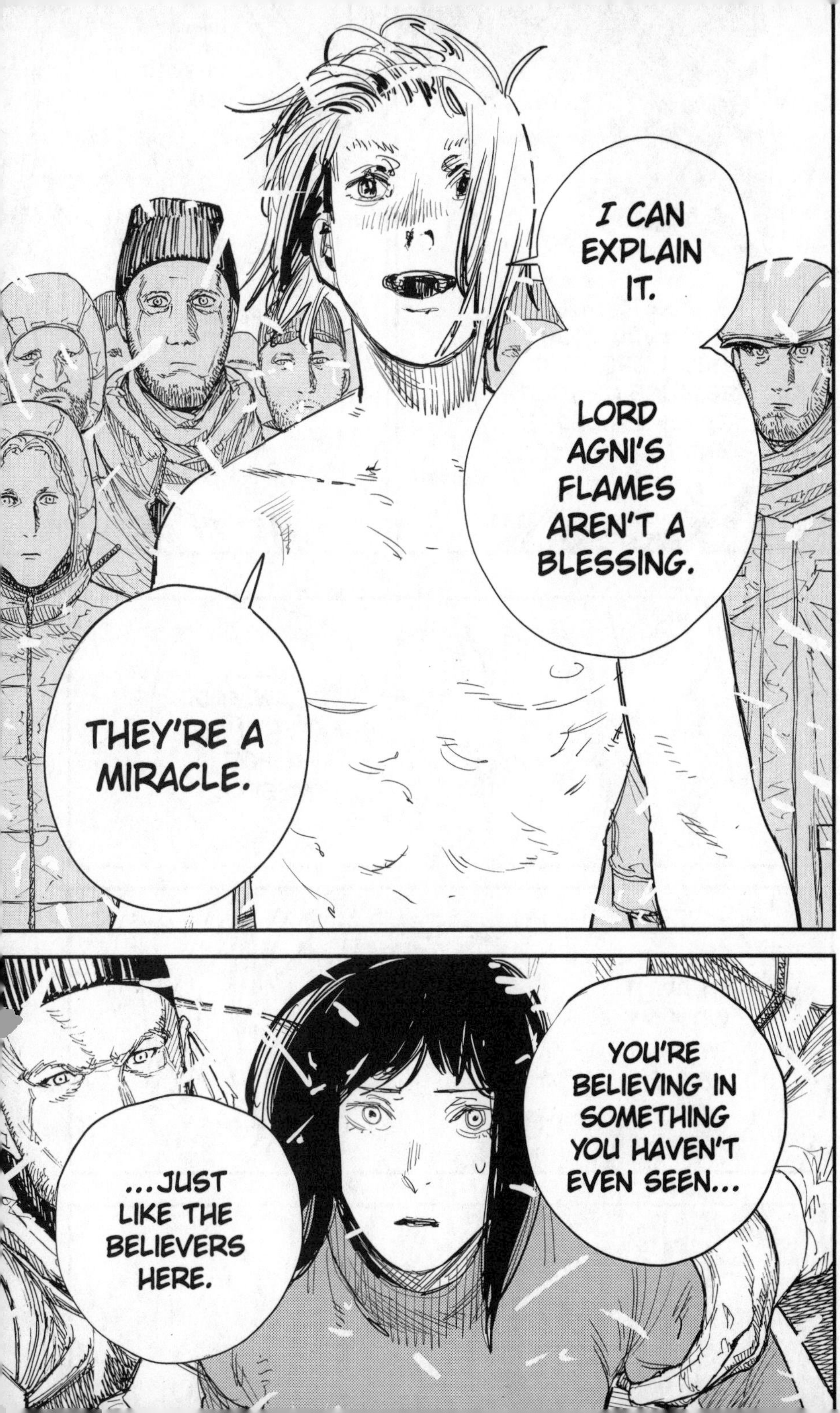
I CAN EXPLAIN IT.
LORD AGNI'S FLAMES AREN'T A BLESSING.
THEY'RE A MIRACLE.
YOU'RE BELIEVING IN SOMETHING YOU HAVEN'T EVEN SEEN...
...JUST LIKE THE BELIEVERS HERE.

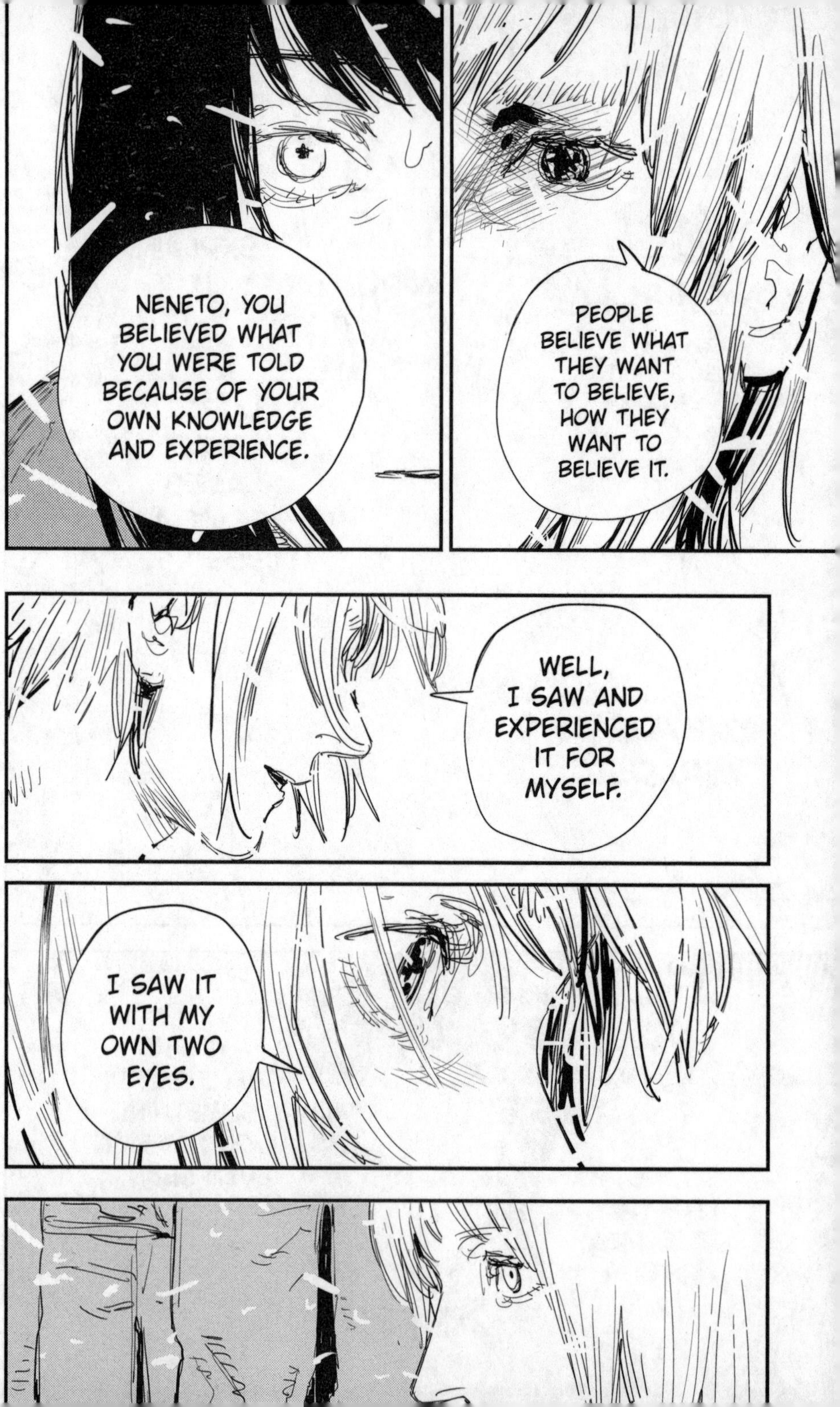
PEOPLE BELIEVE WHAT THEY WANT TO BELIEVE, HOW THEY WANT TO BELIEVE IT.
NENETO, YOU BELIEVED WHAT YOU WERE TOLD BECAUSE OF YOUR OWN KNOWLEDGE AND EXPERIENCE.
WELL, I SAW AND EXPERIENCED IT FOR MYSELF.
I SAW IT WITH MY OWN TWO EYES.

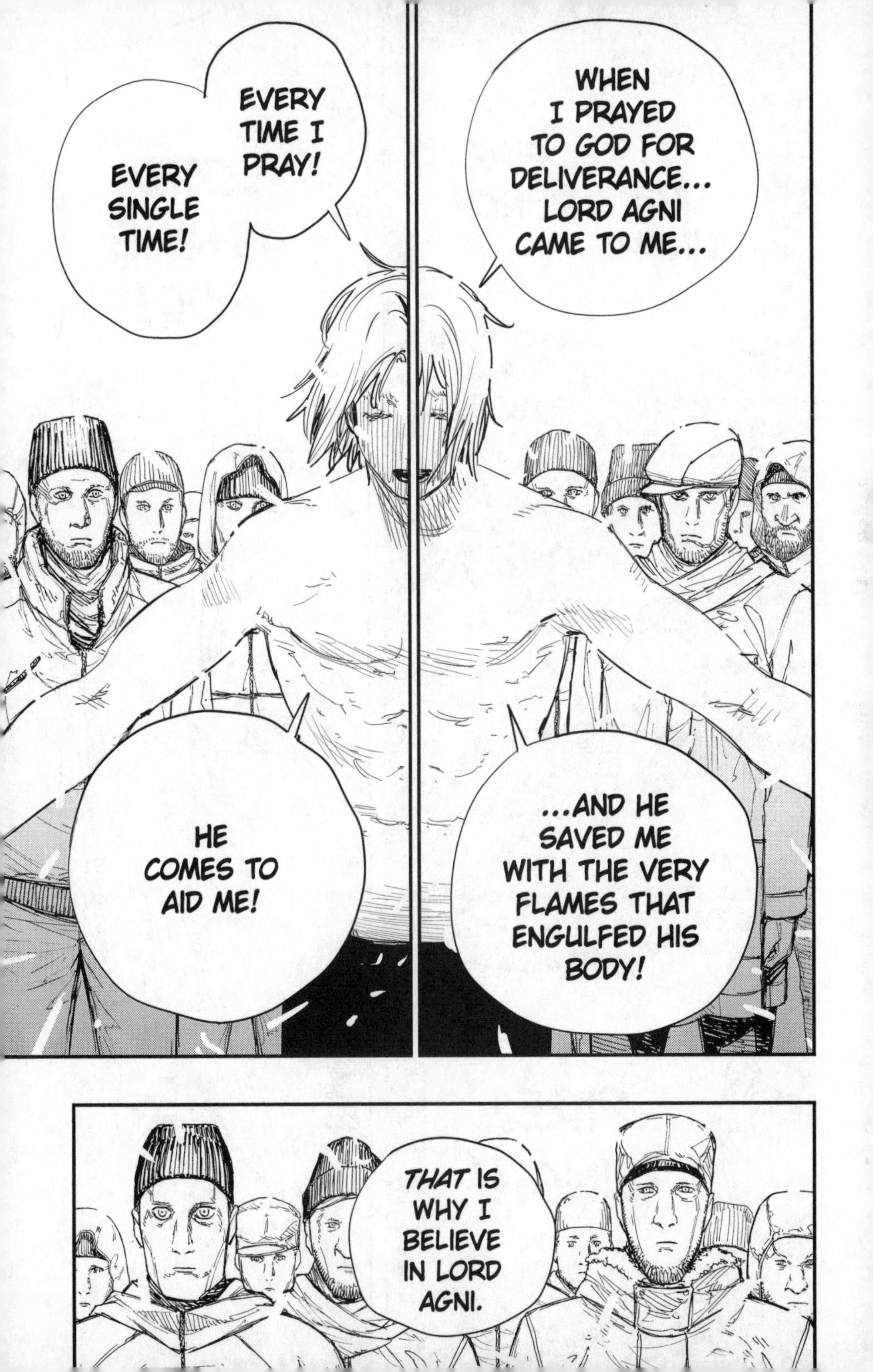
WHEN I PRAYED TO GOD FOR DELIVERANCE... LORD AGNI CAME TO ME...
...AND HE SAVED ME WITH THE VERY FLAMES THAT ENGULFED HIS BODY!
EVERY TIME I PRAY!
EVERY SINGLE TIME!
HE COMES TO AID ME!
THAT IS WHY I BELIEVE IN LORD AGNI.

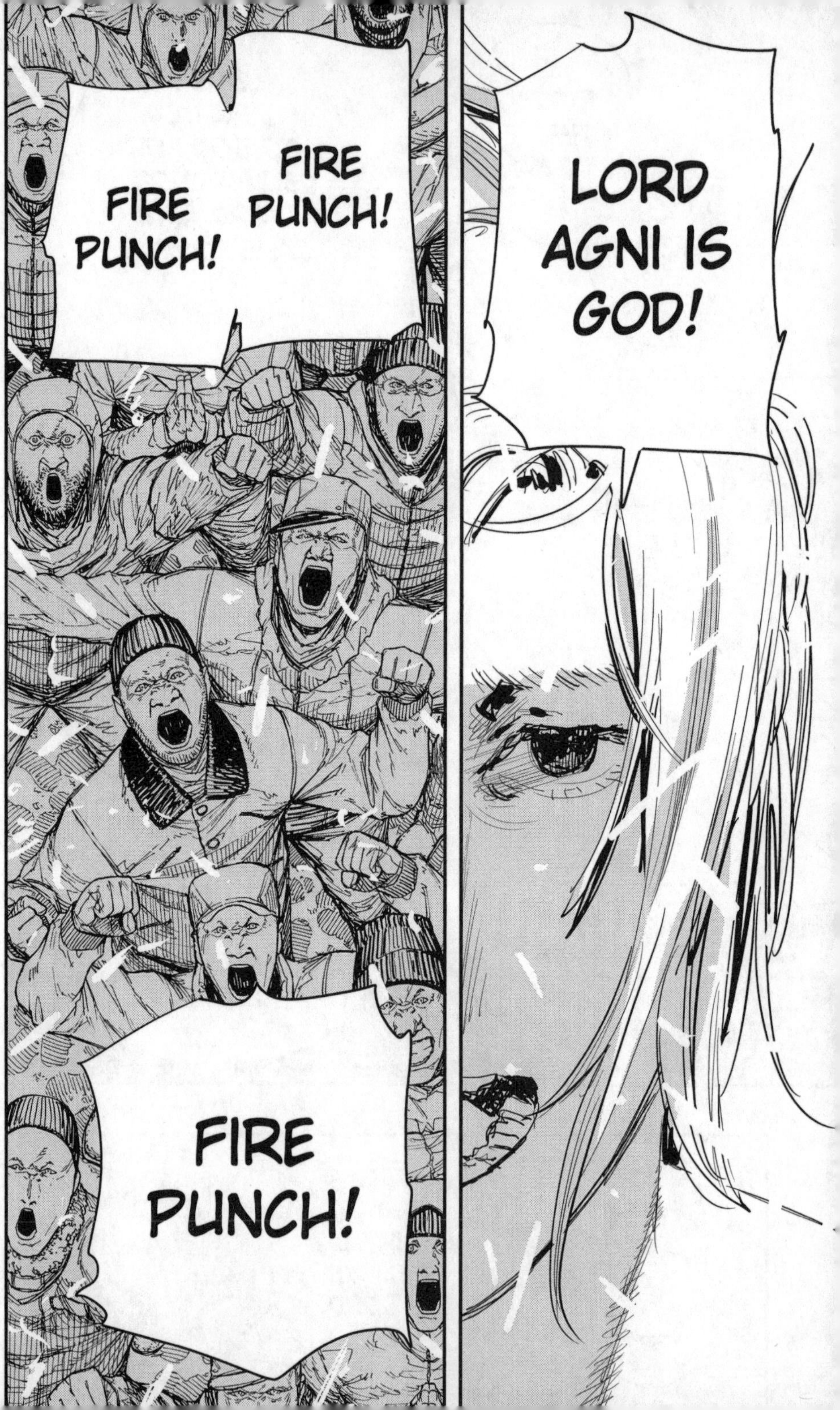
LORD AGNI IS GOD!
FIRE PUNCH!
FIRE PUNCH!
FIRE PUNCH!

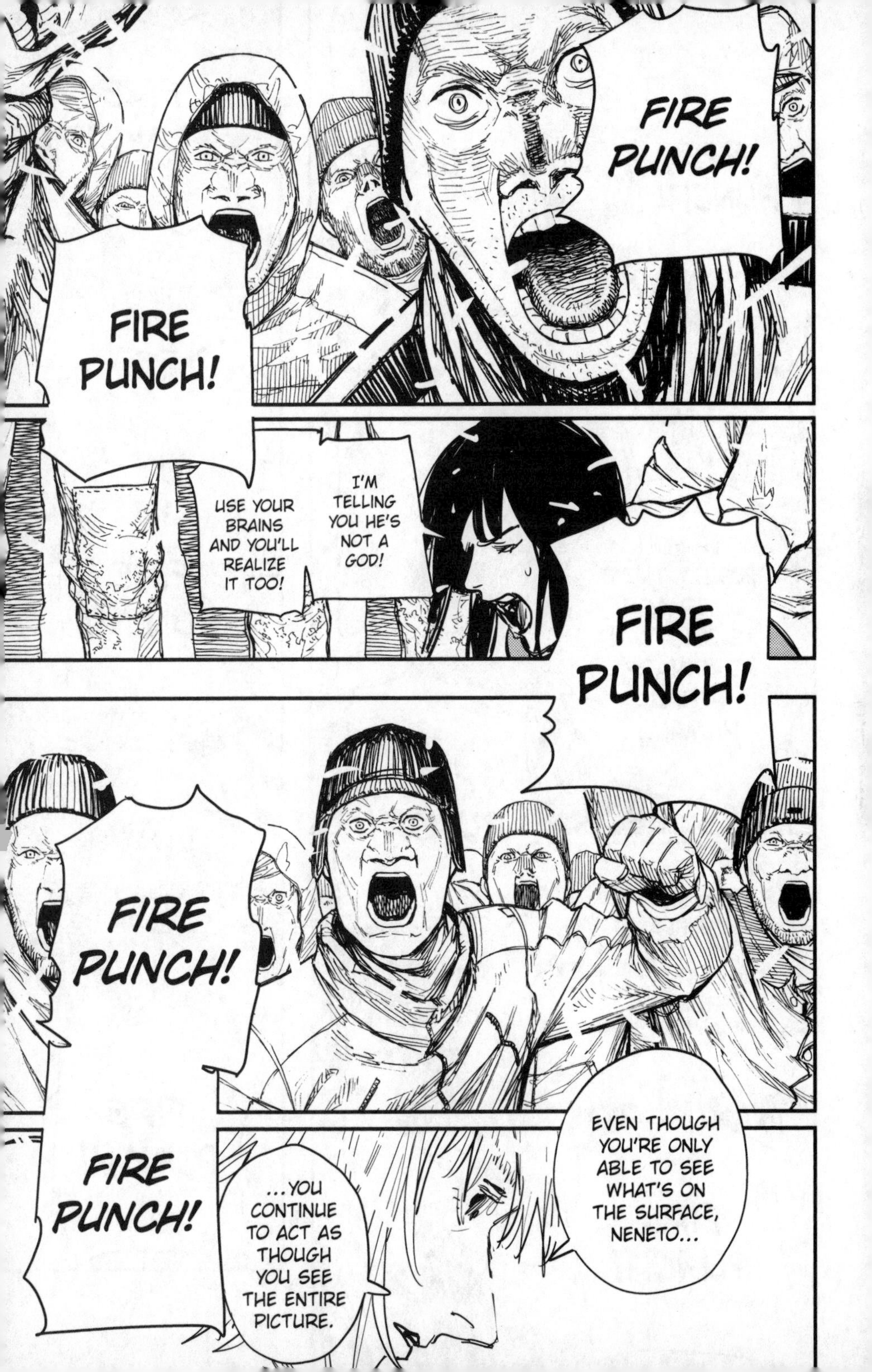
FIRE PUNCH!
FIRE PUNCH!
FIRE PUNCH!
I'M TELLING YOU HE'S NOT A GOD!
USE YOUR BRAINS AND YOU'LL REALIZE IT TOO!
FIRE PUNCH!
EVEN THOUGH YOU'RE ONLY ABLE TO SEE WHAT'S ON THE SURFACE, NENETO...
...YOU CONTINUE TO ACT AS THOUGH YOU SEE THE ENTIRE PICTURE.
FIRE PUNCH!

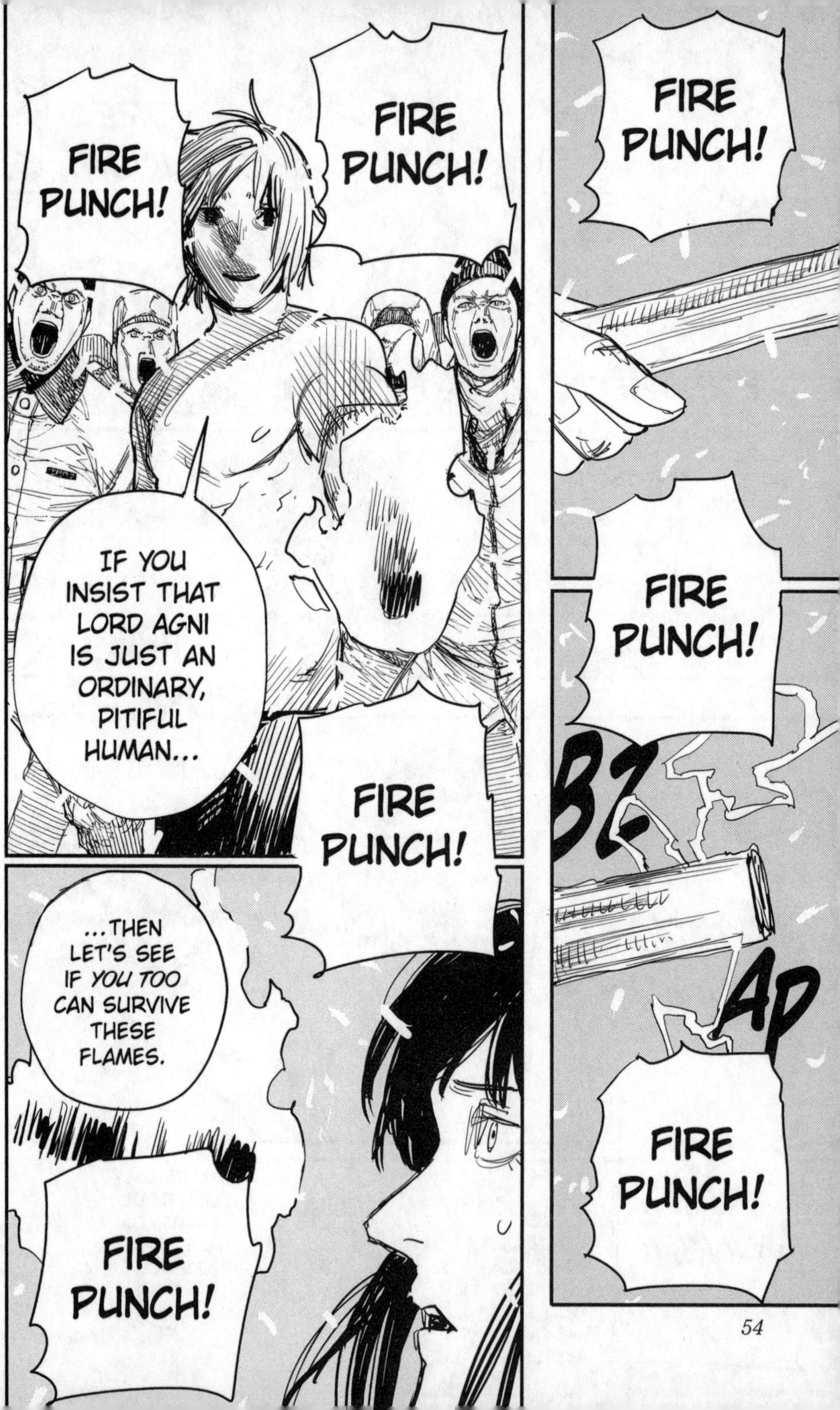
FIRE PUNCH!
FIRE PUNCH!
FIRE PUNCH!
BZ
AP
FIRE PUNCH!
FIRE PUNCH!
FIRE PUNCH!
IF YOU INSIST THAT LORD AGNI IS JUST AN ORDINARY, PITIFUL HUMAN...
FIRE PUNCH!
...THEN LET'S SEE IF *YOU TOO* CAN SURVIVE THESE FLAMES.
FIRE PUNCH!

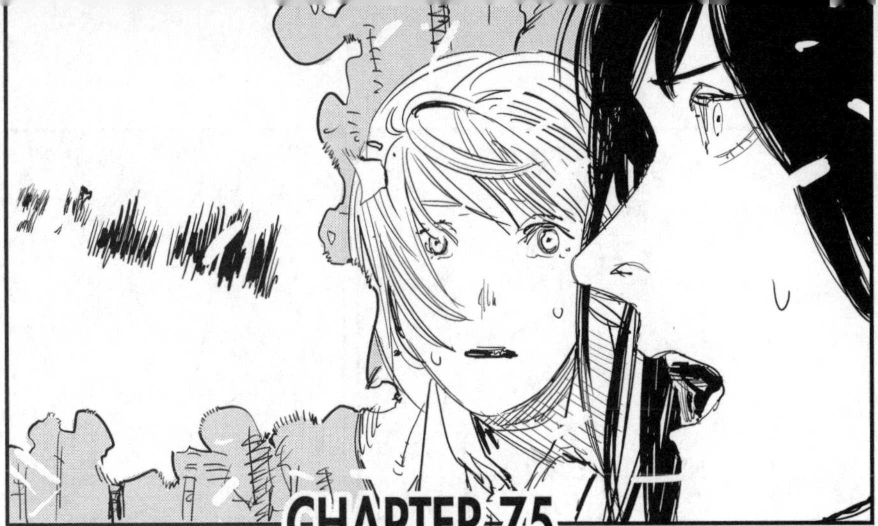

CHAPTER 75

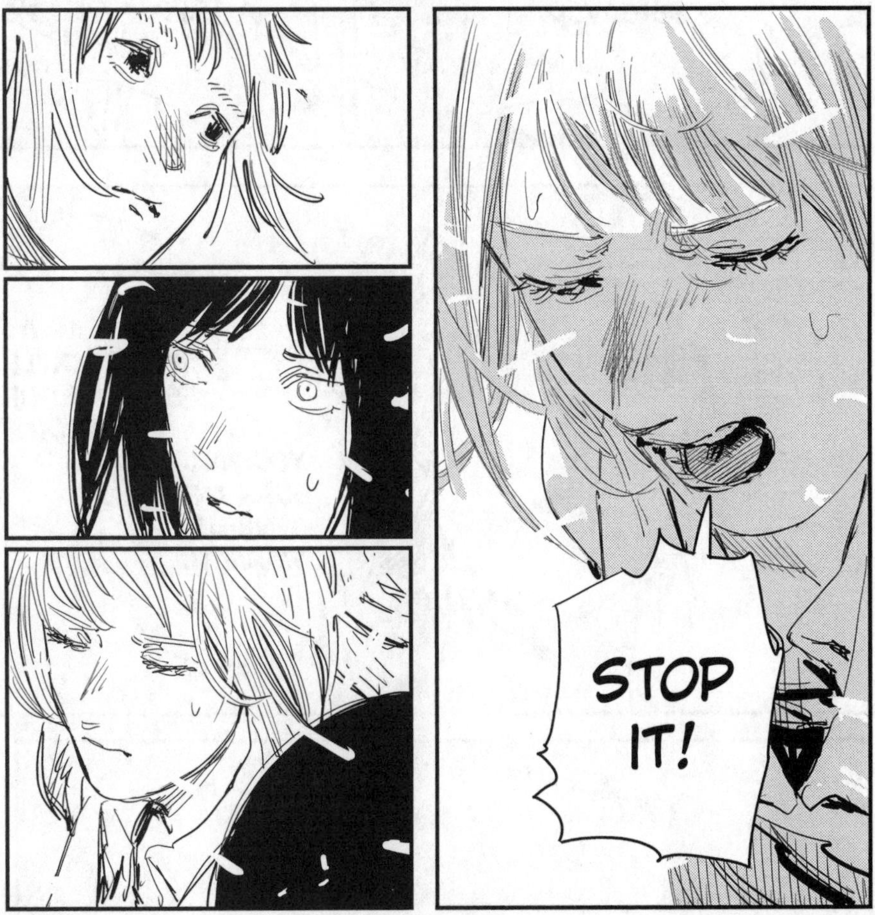
STOP IT!

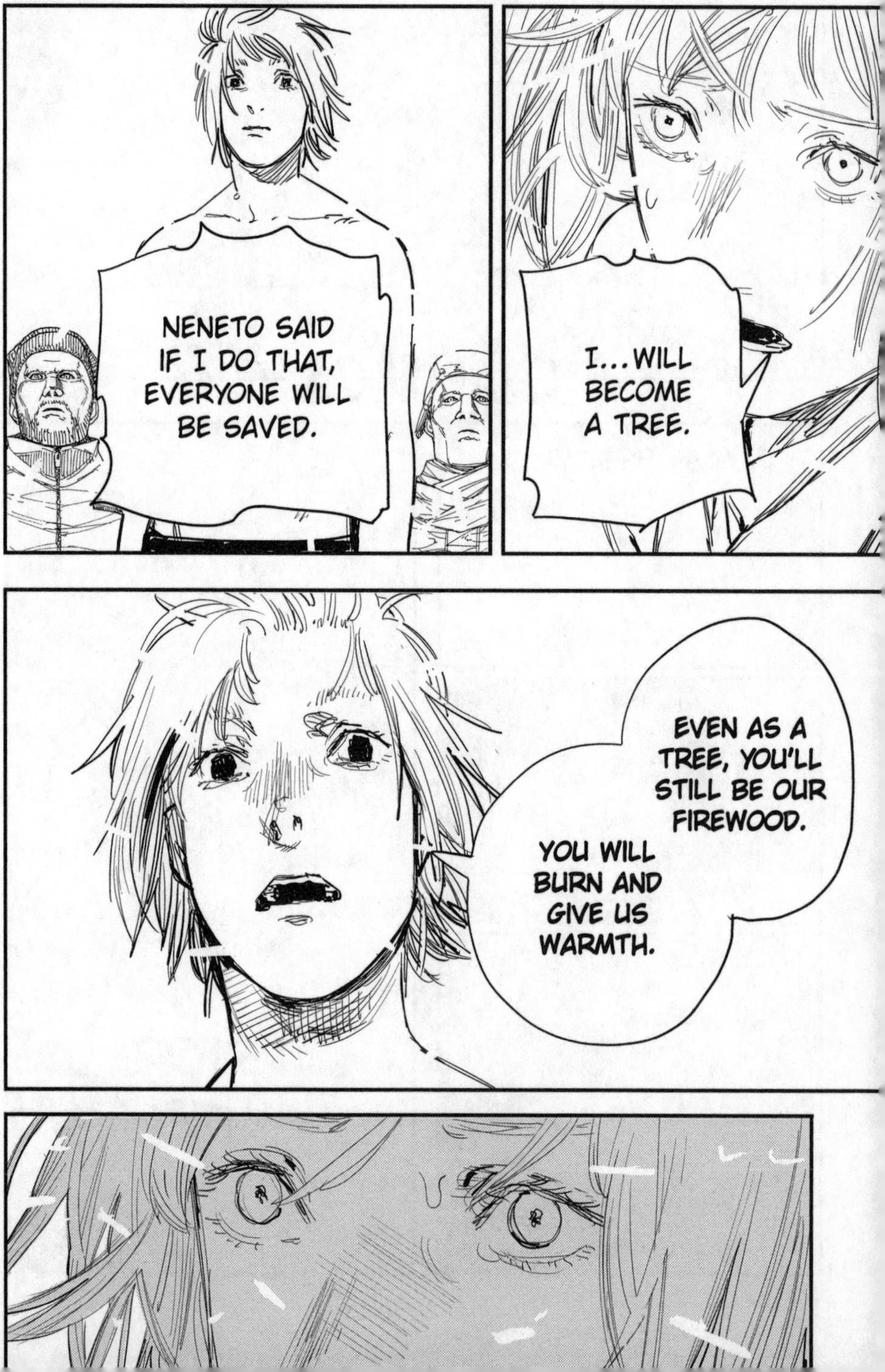
I...WILL BECOME A TREE.
NENETO SAID IF I DO THAT, EVERYONE WILL BE SAVED.
EVEN AS A TREE, YOU'LL STILL BE OUR FIREWOOD.
YOU WILL BURN AND GIVE US WARMTH.

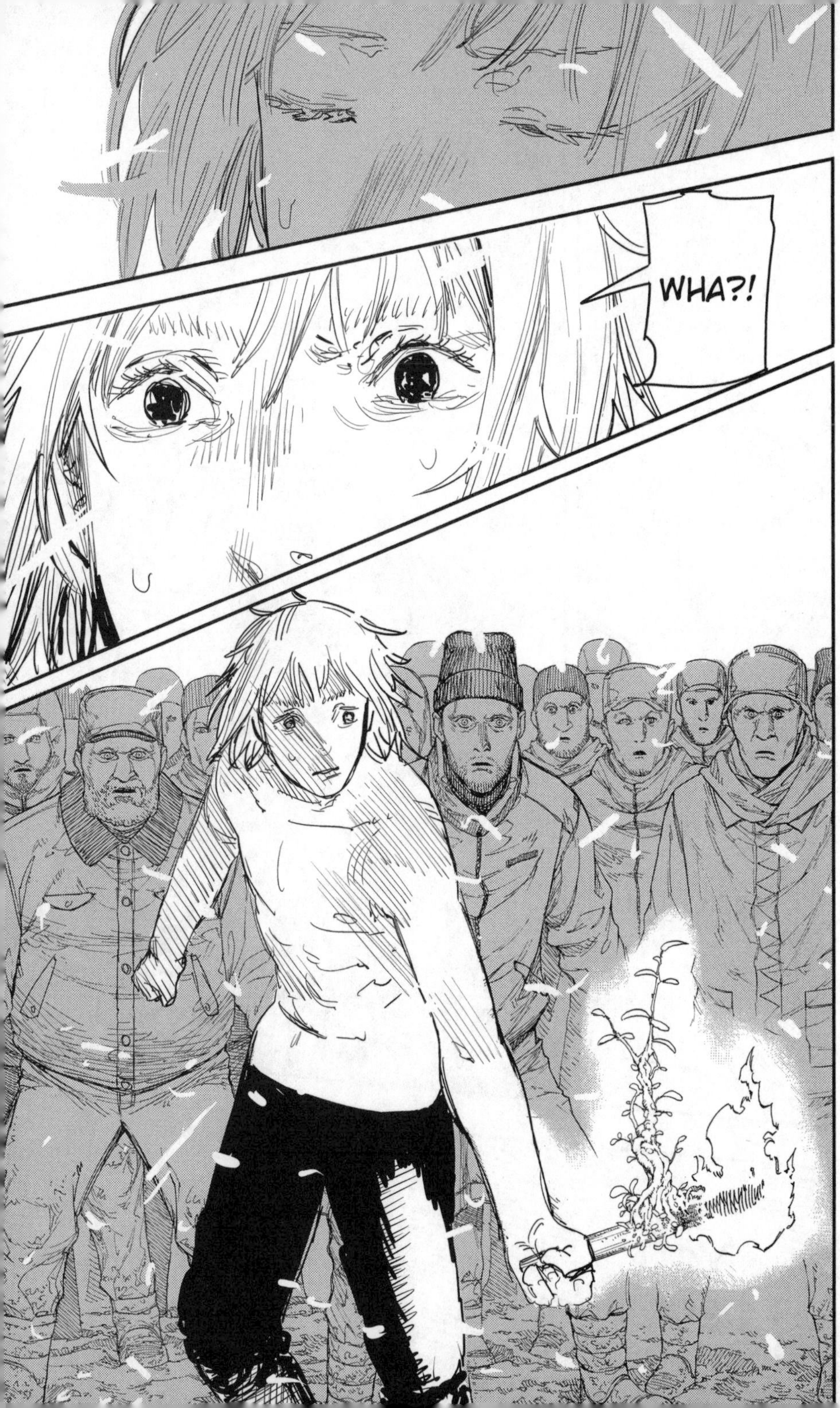
WHA?!

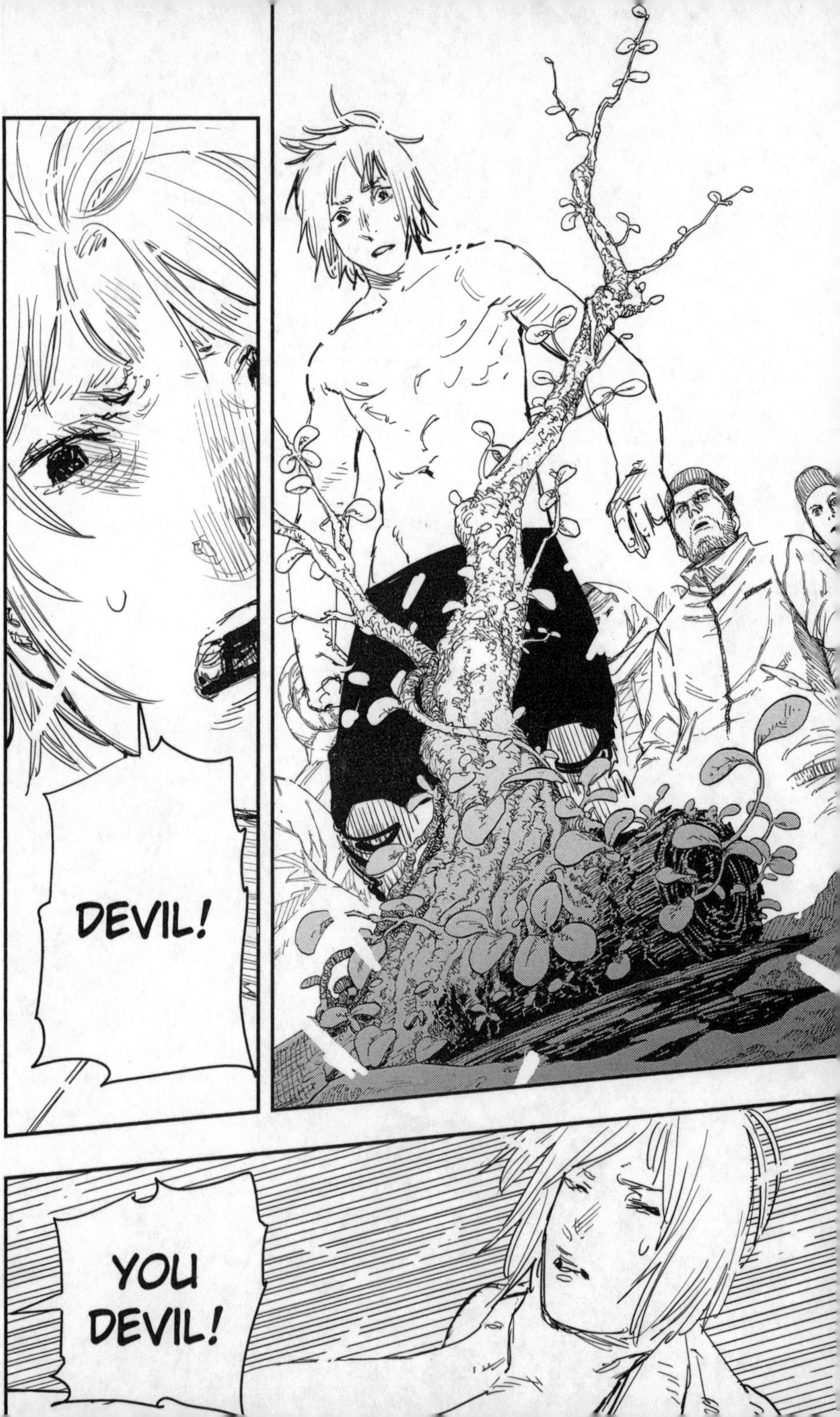
DEVIL!
YOU DEVIL!

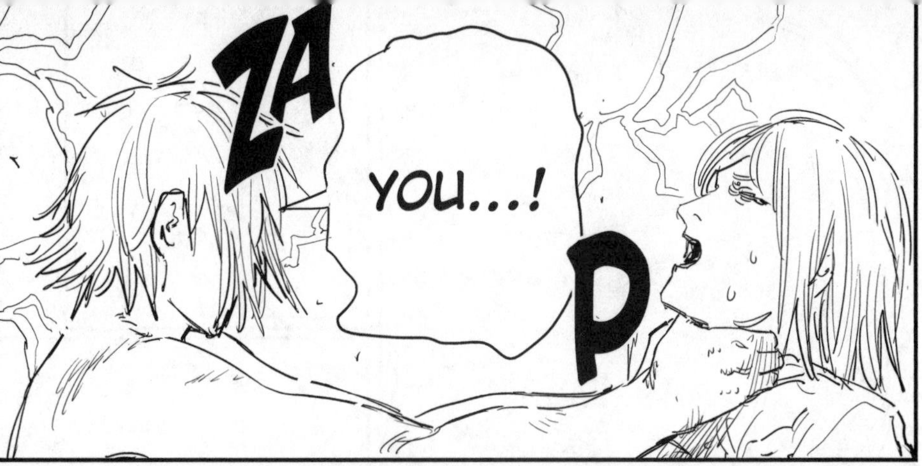
ZAP
YOU...!
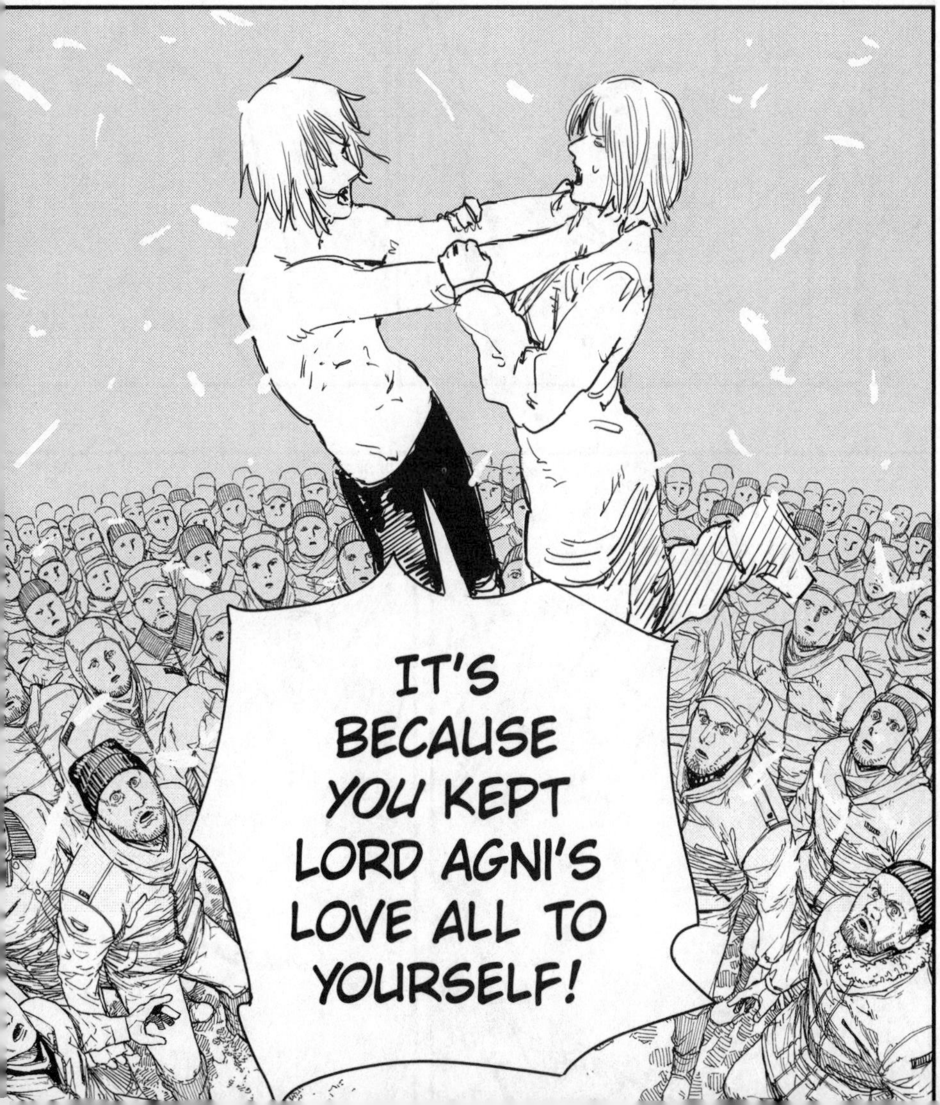
IT'S BECAUSE YOU KEPT LORD AGNI'S LOVE ALL TO YOURSELF!

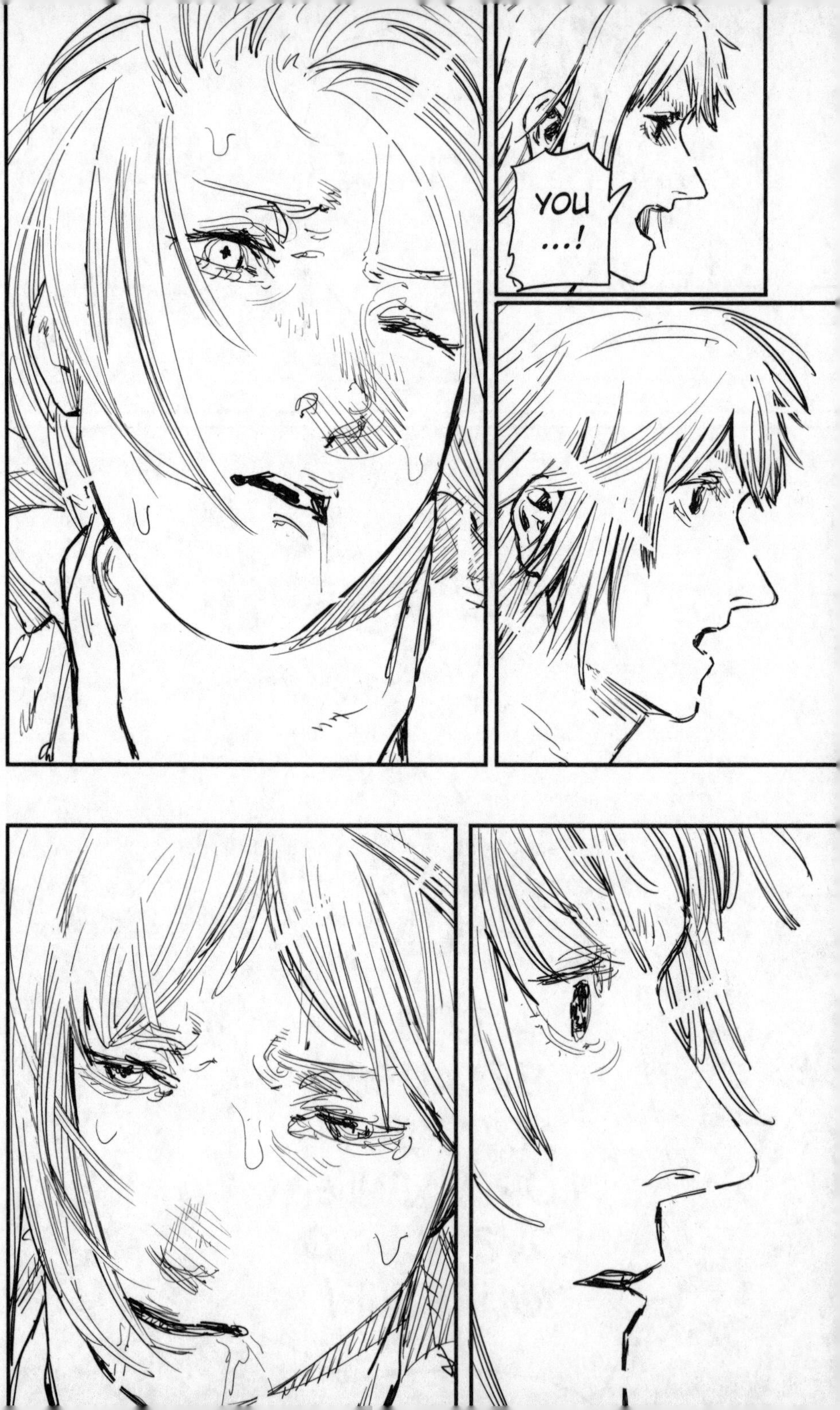
YOU ...!

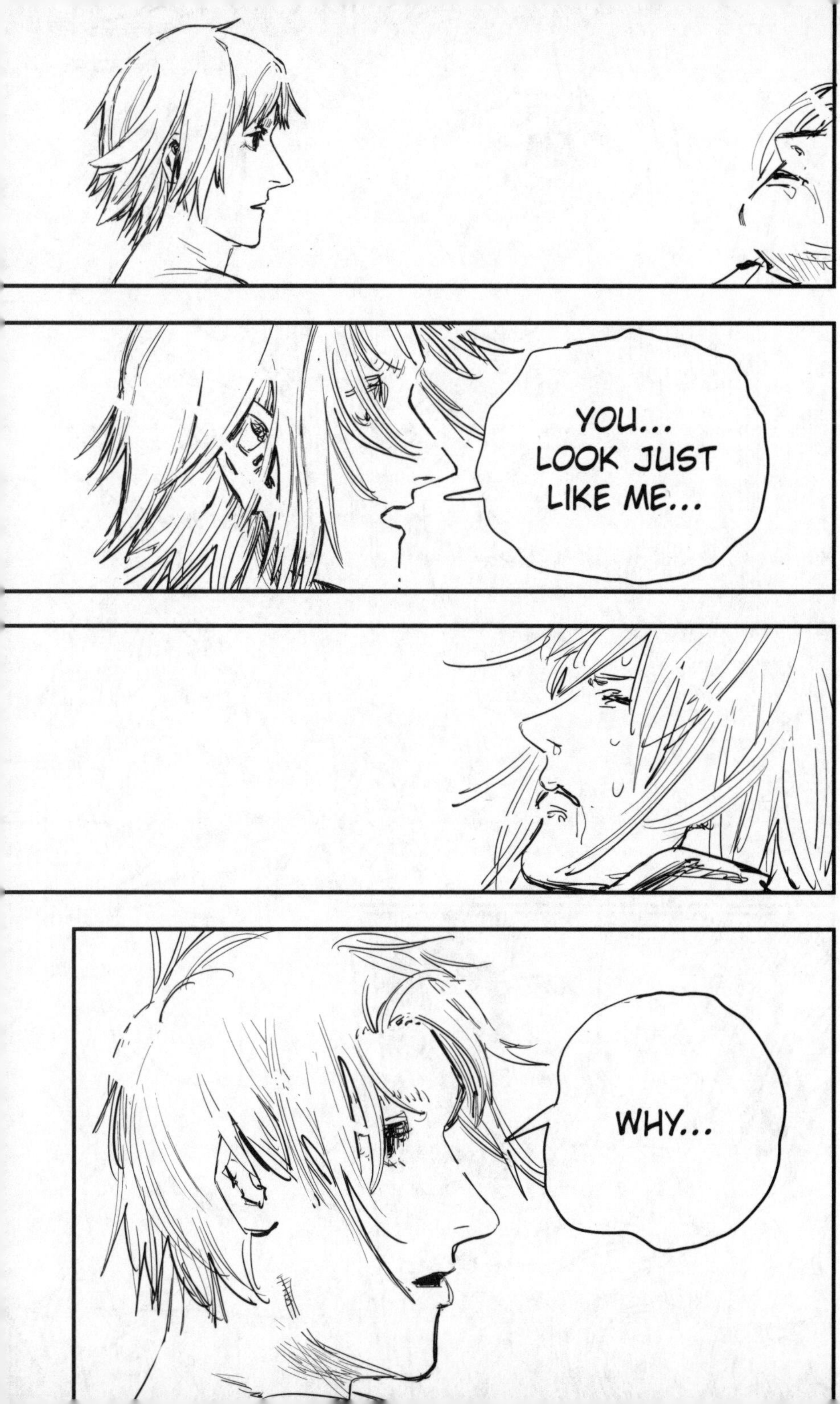
YOU... LOOK JUST LIKE ME...
WHY...

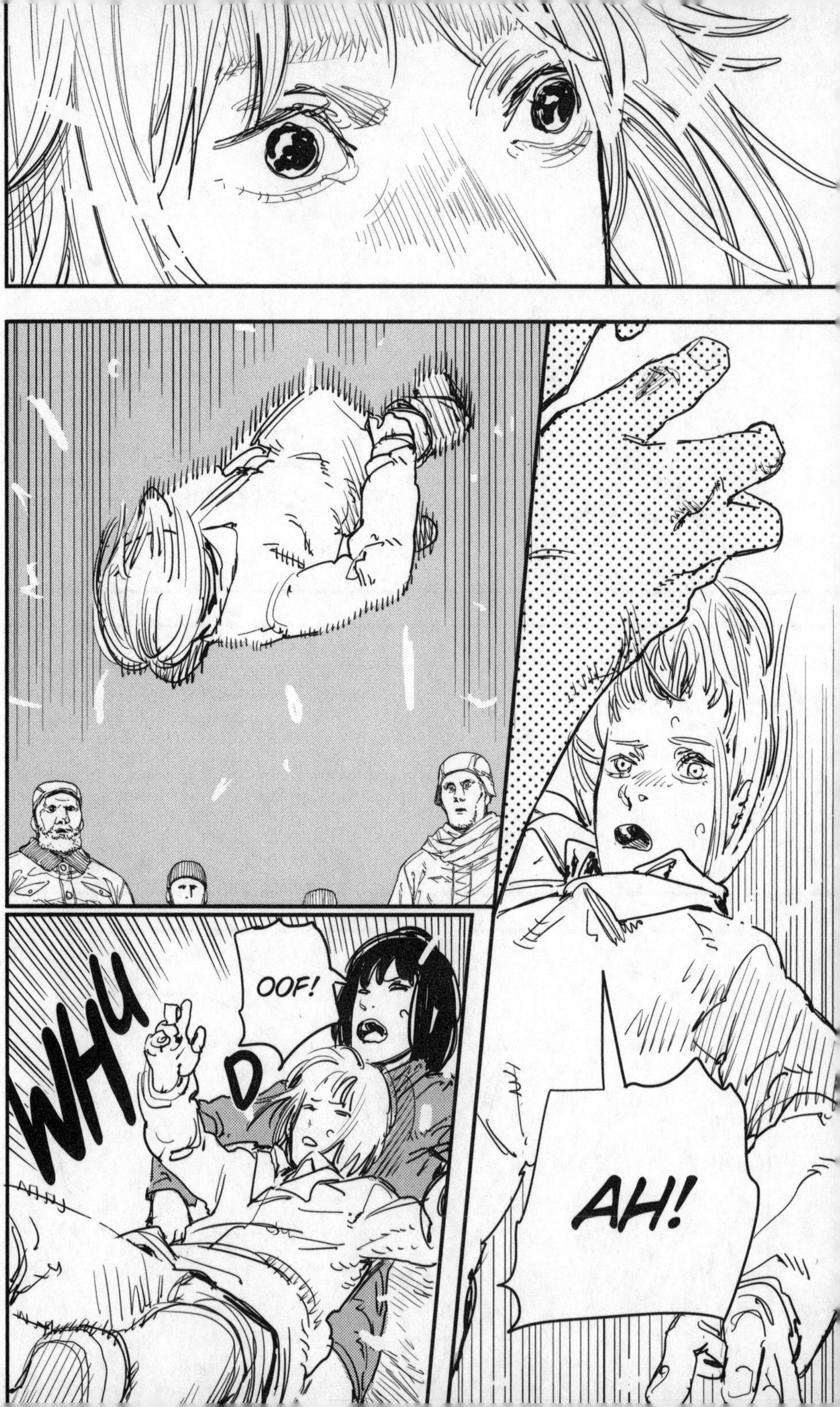
AH!
OOF!
WHUD

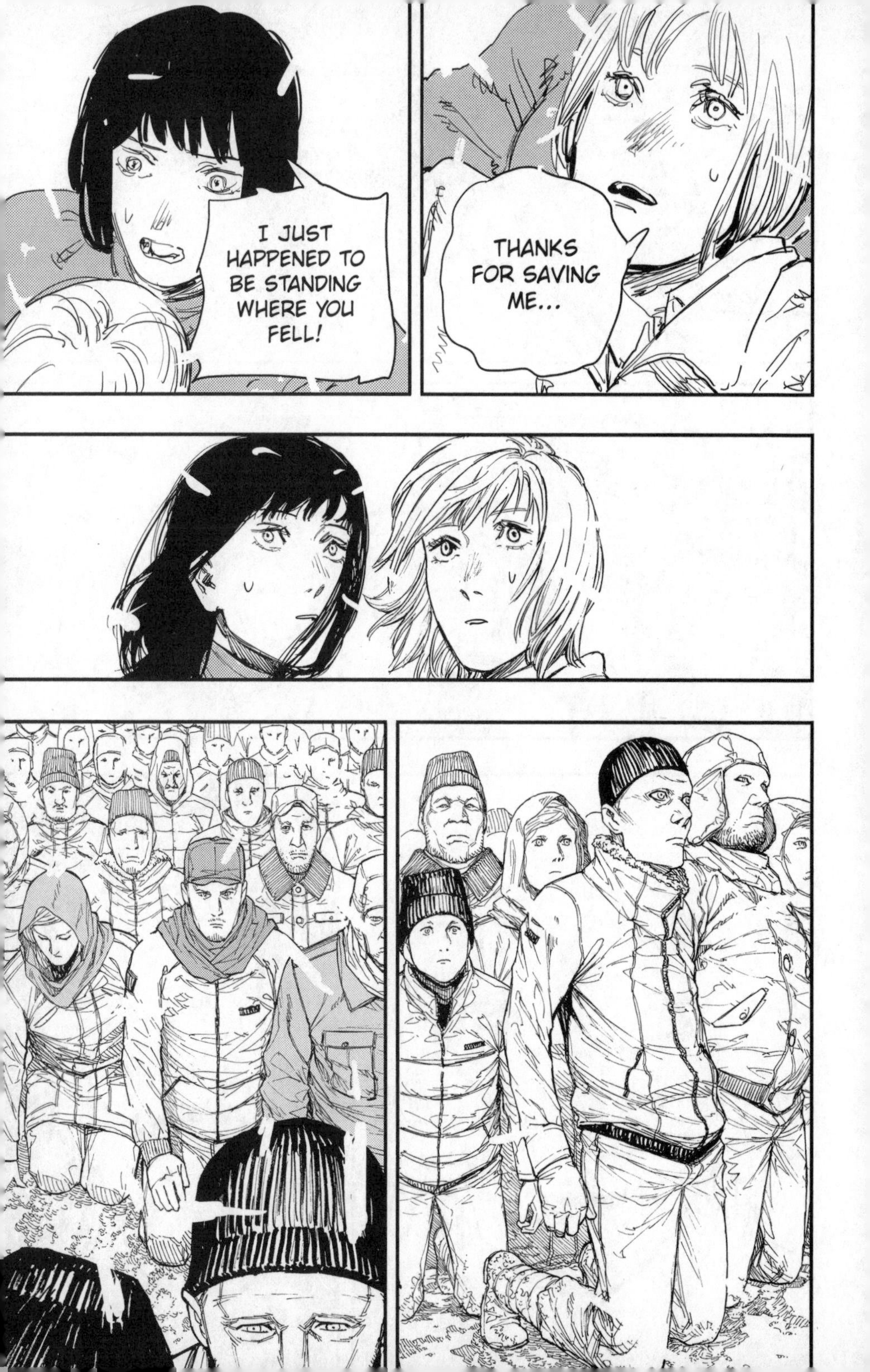
THANKS FOR SAVING ME...
I JUST HAPPENED TO BE STANDING WHERE YOU FELL!

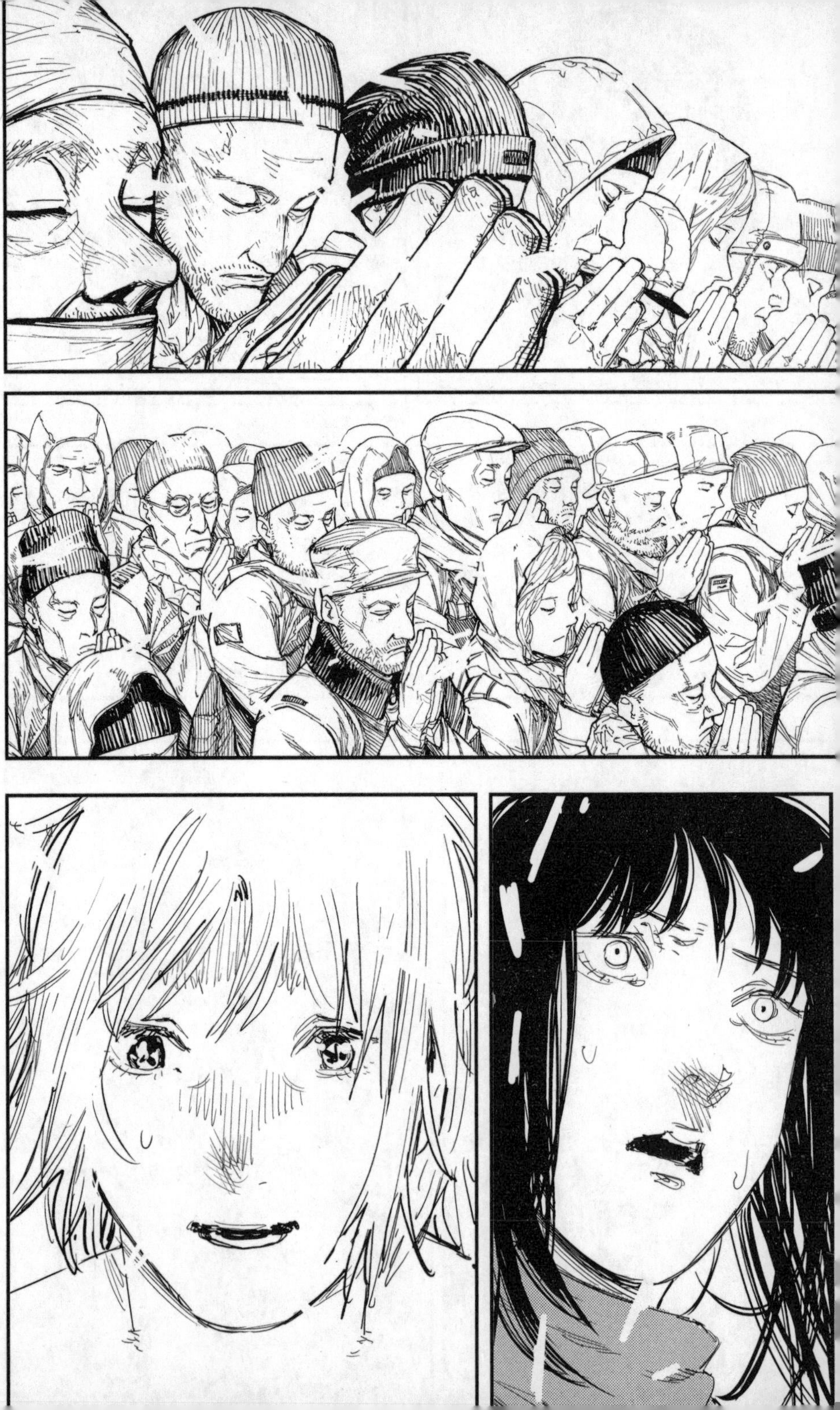

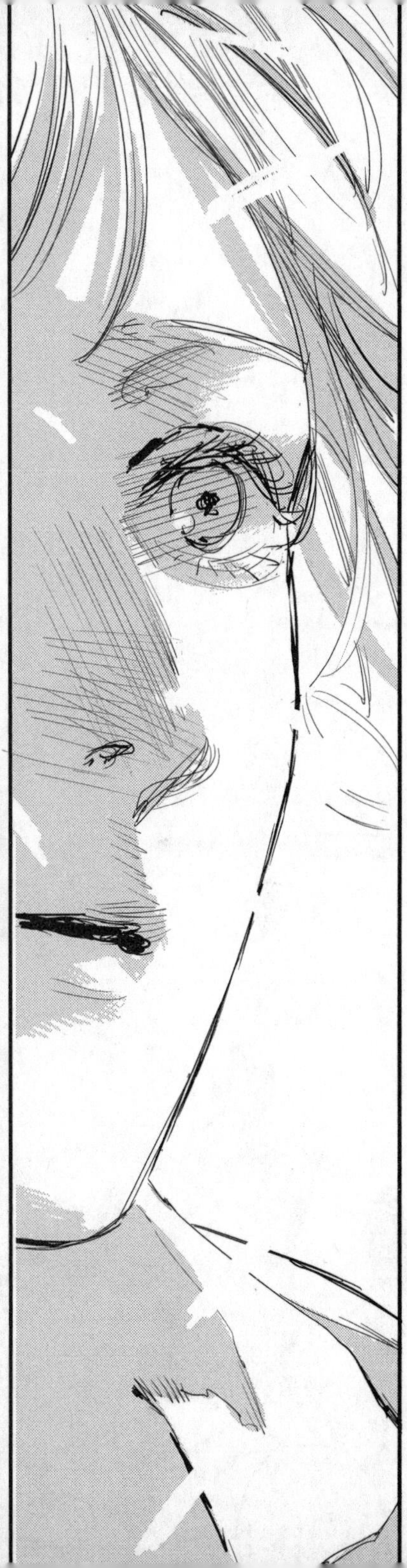
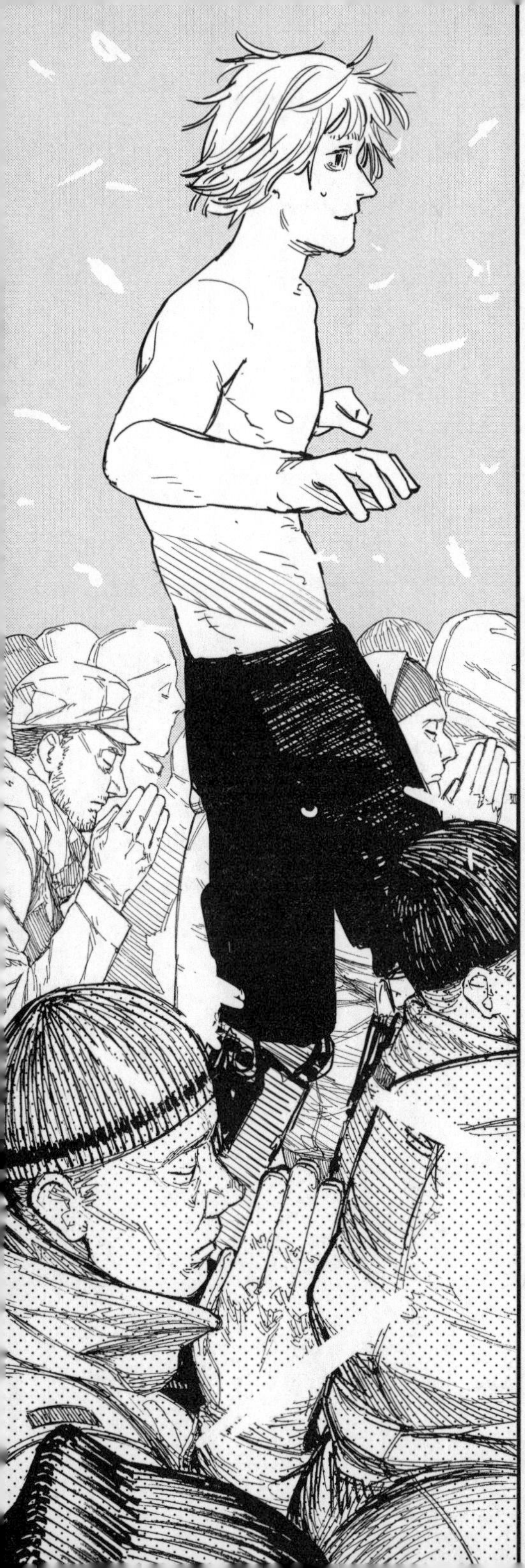

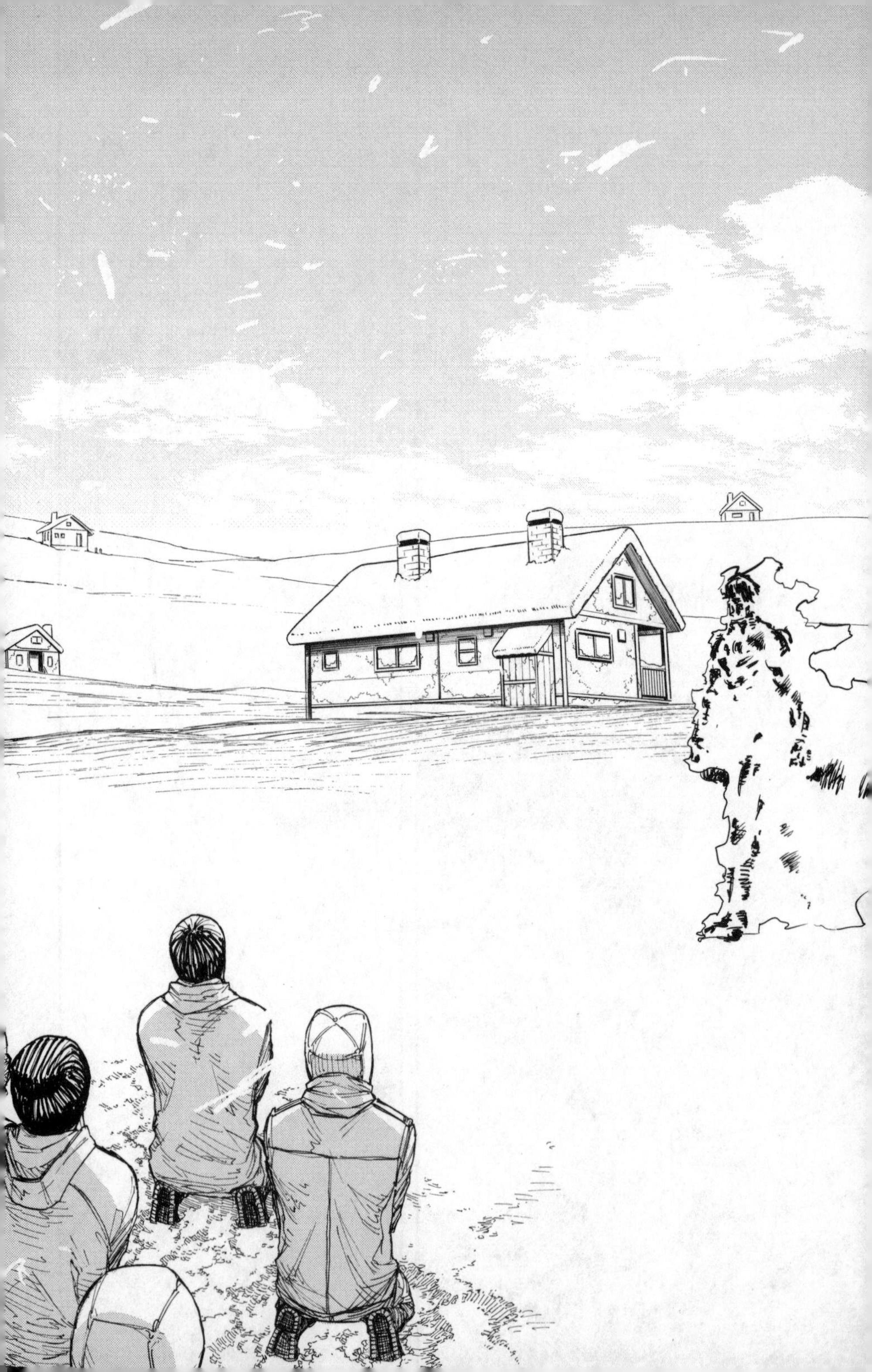

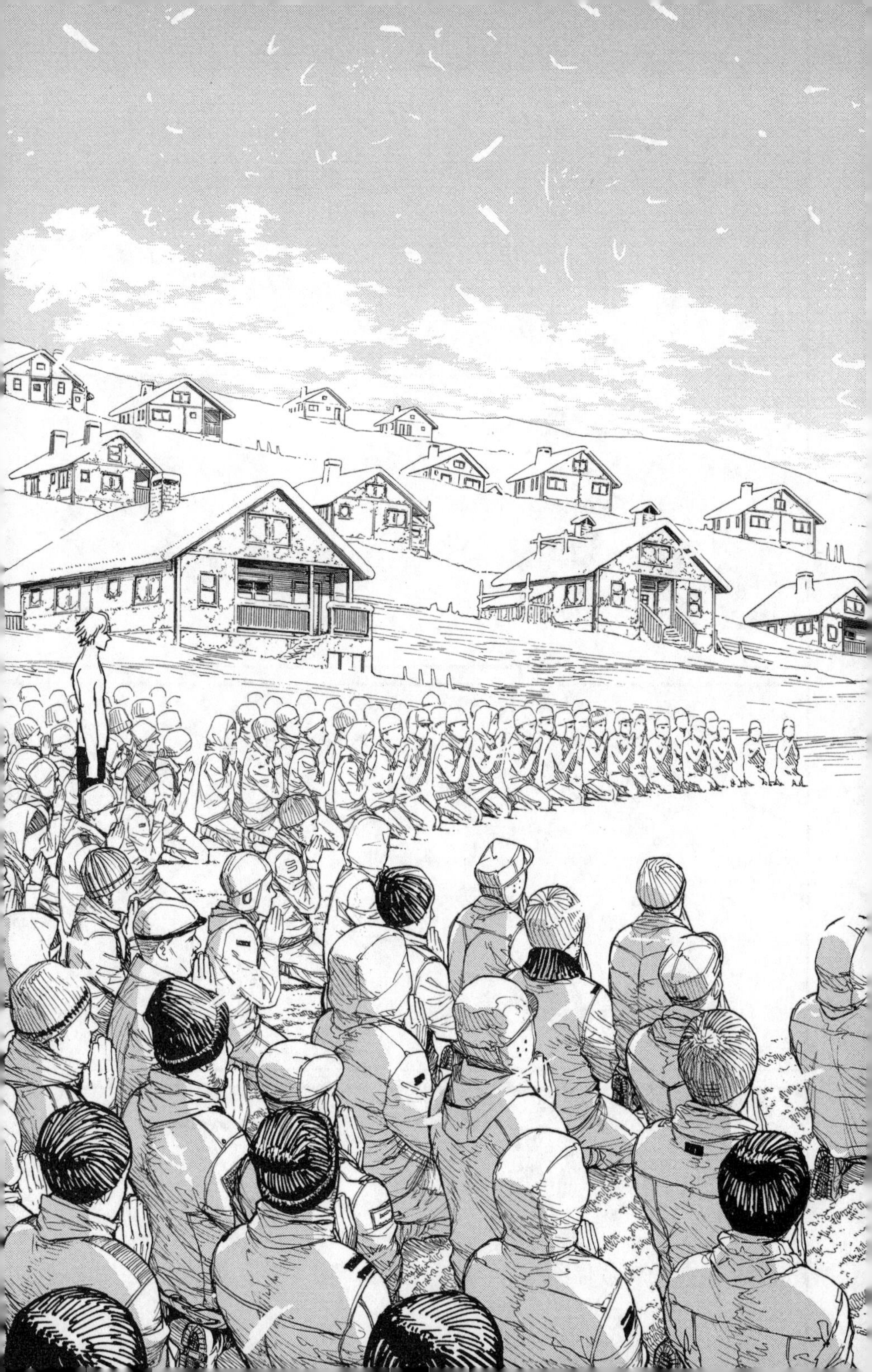

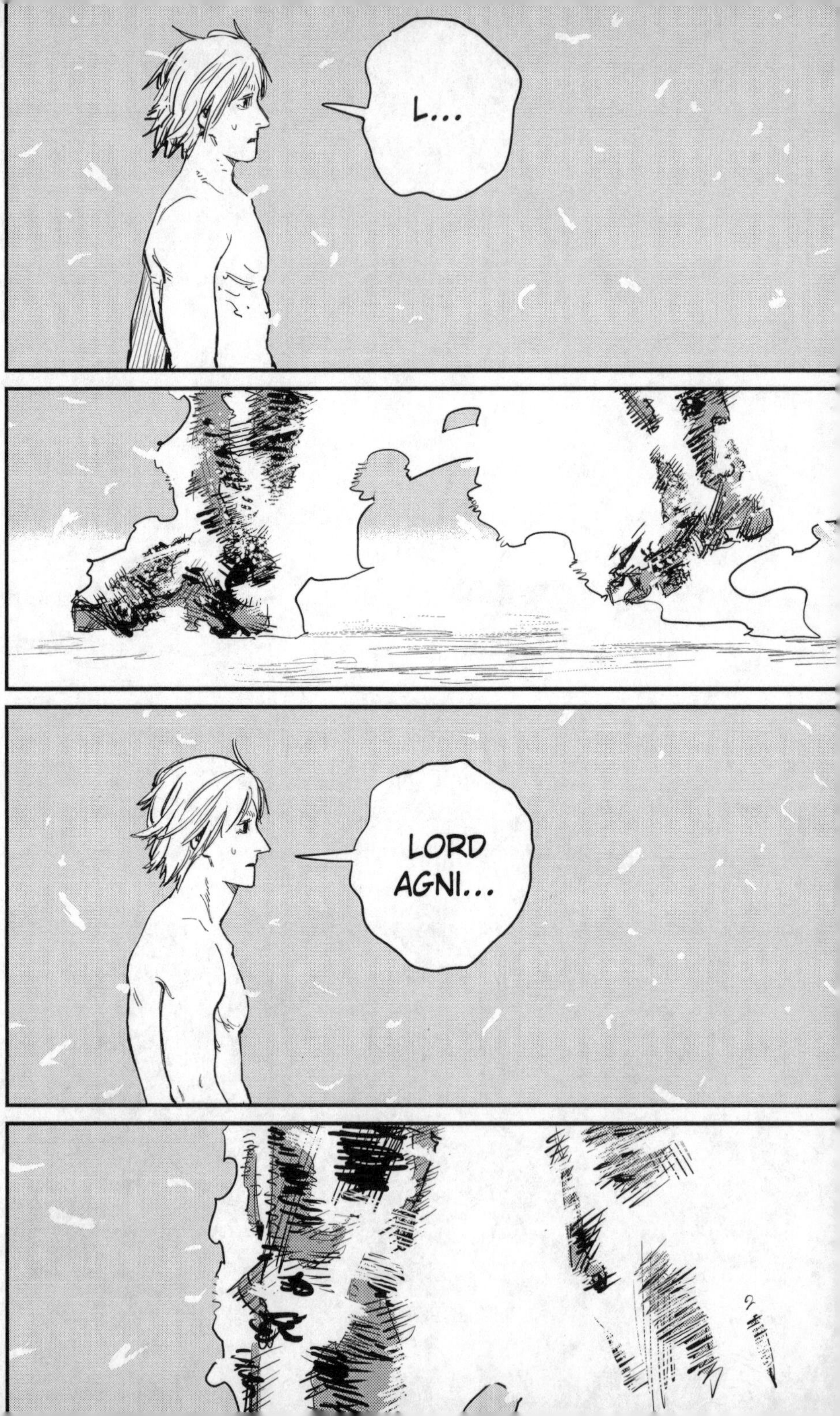
L...
LORD AGNI...

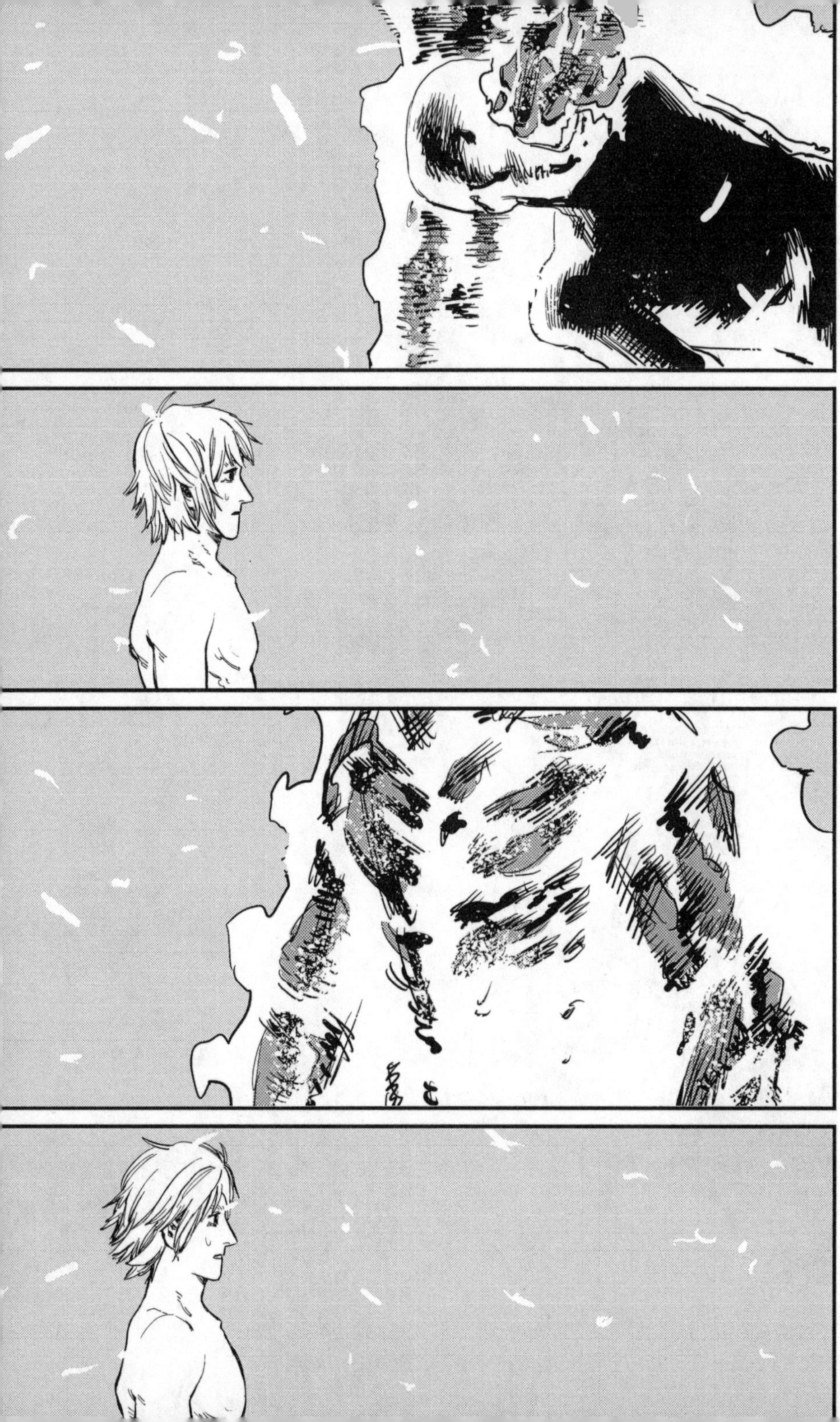

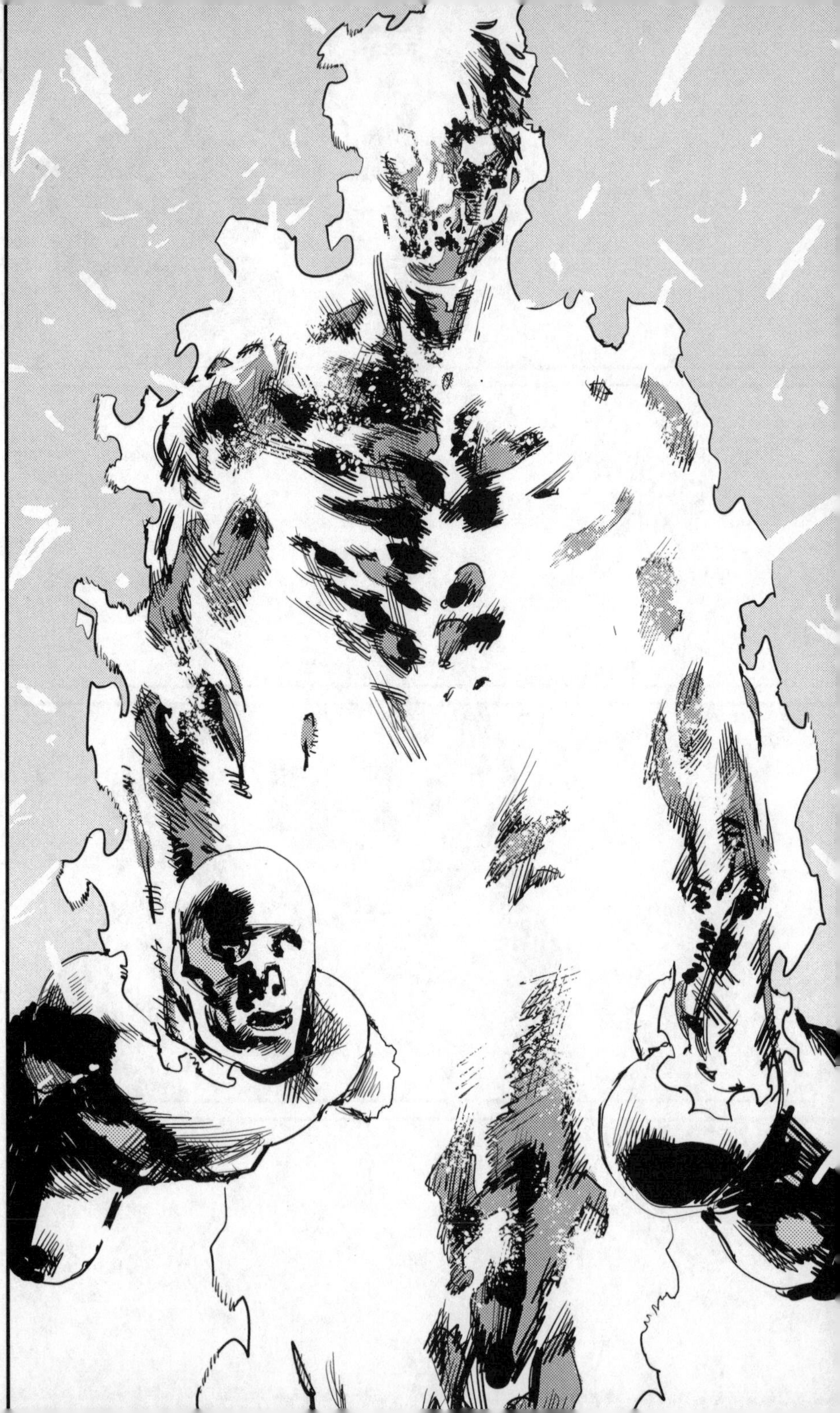

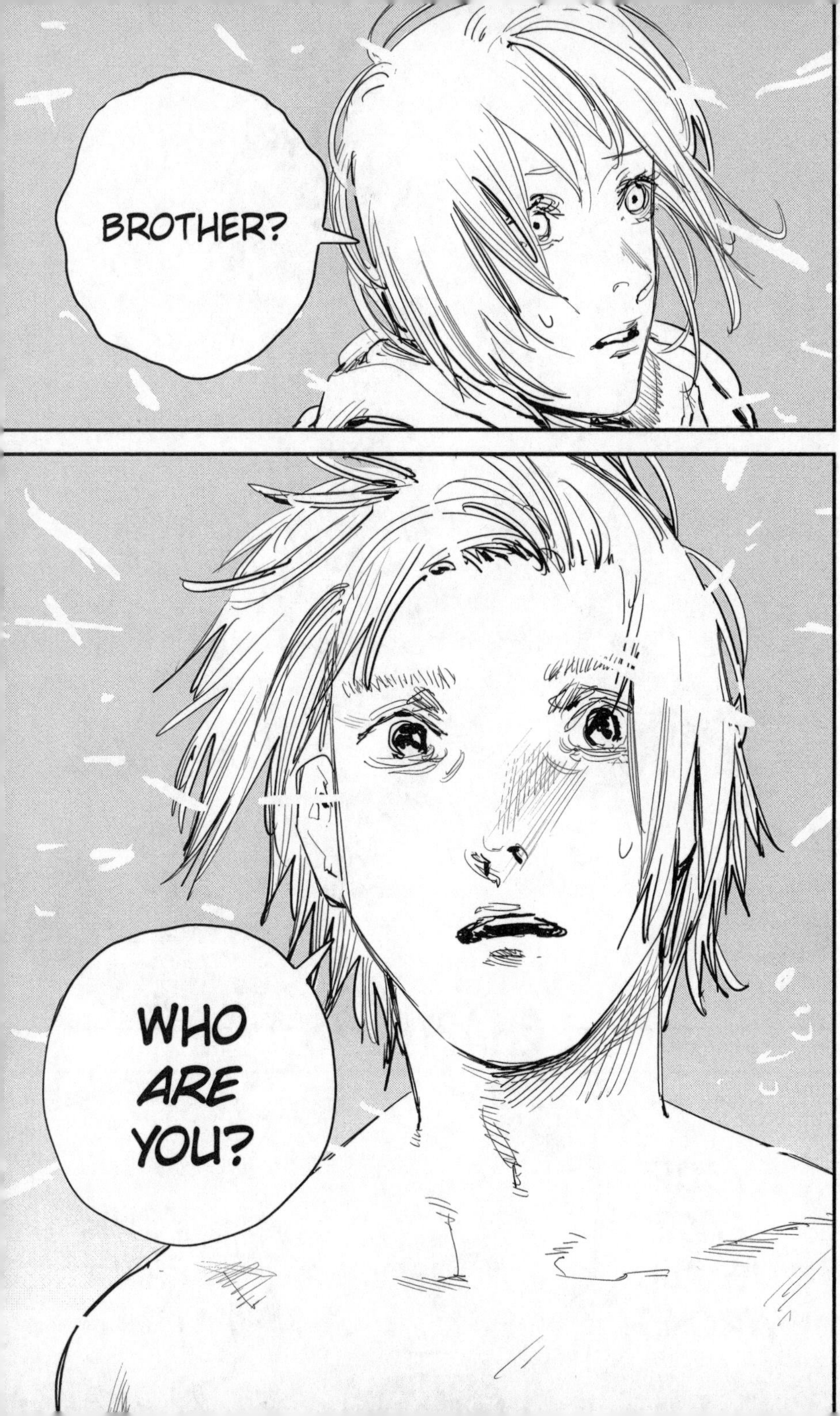
BROTHER?
WHO ARE YOU?

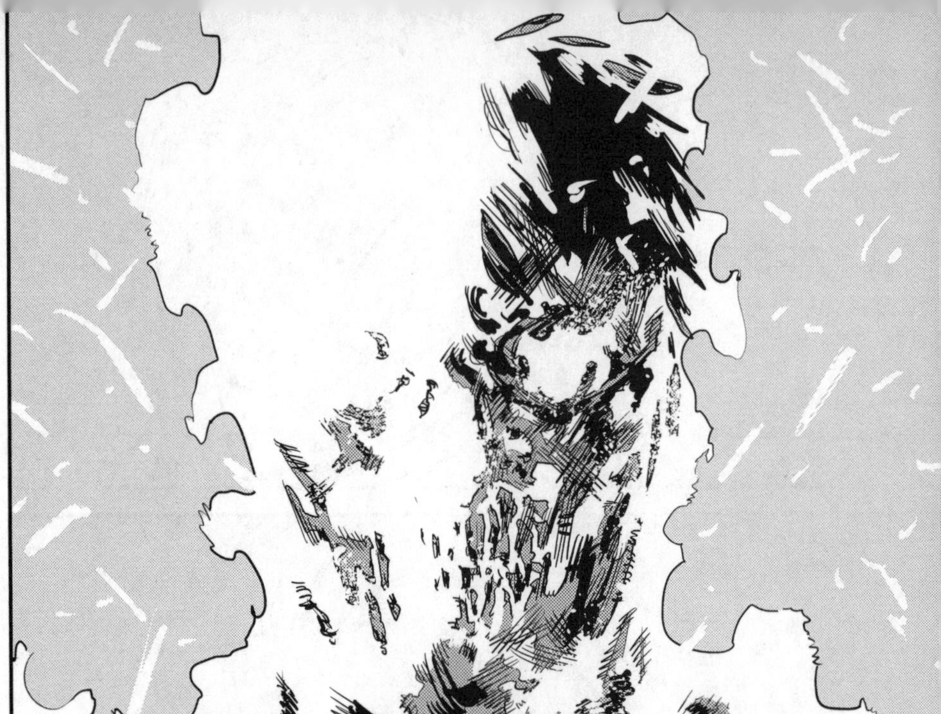

CHAPTER 76

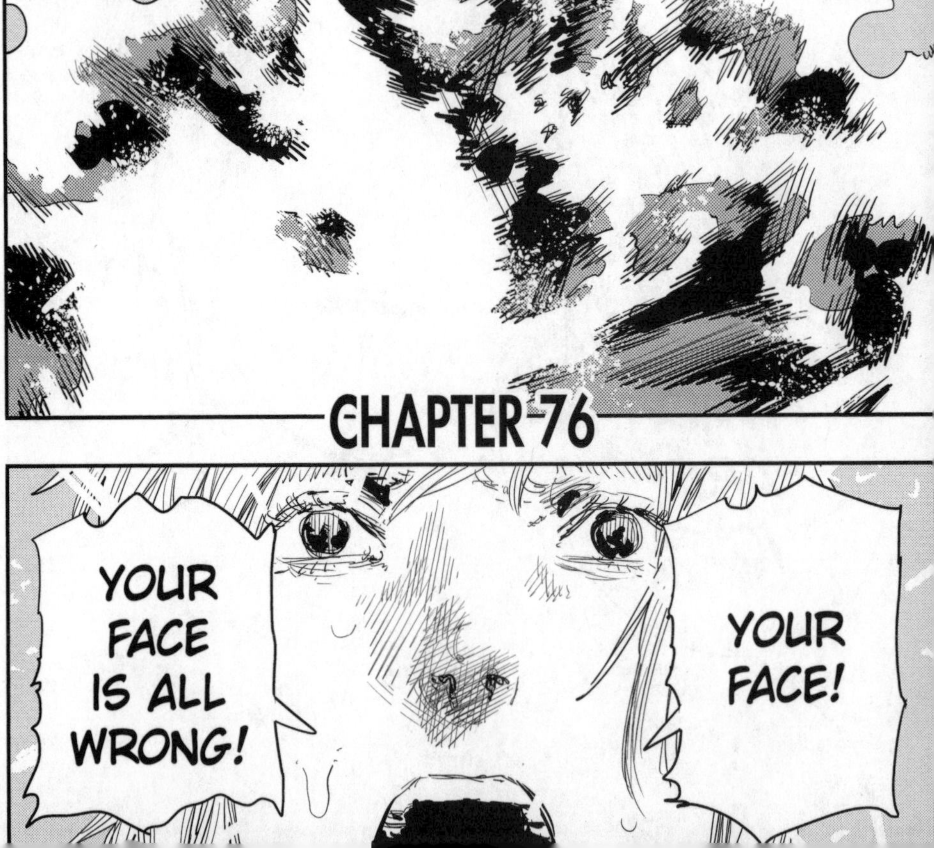
YOUR FACE!
YOUR FACE IS ALL WRONG!

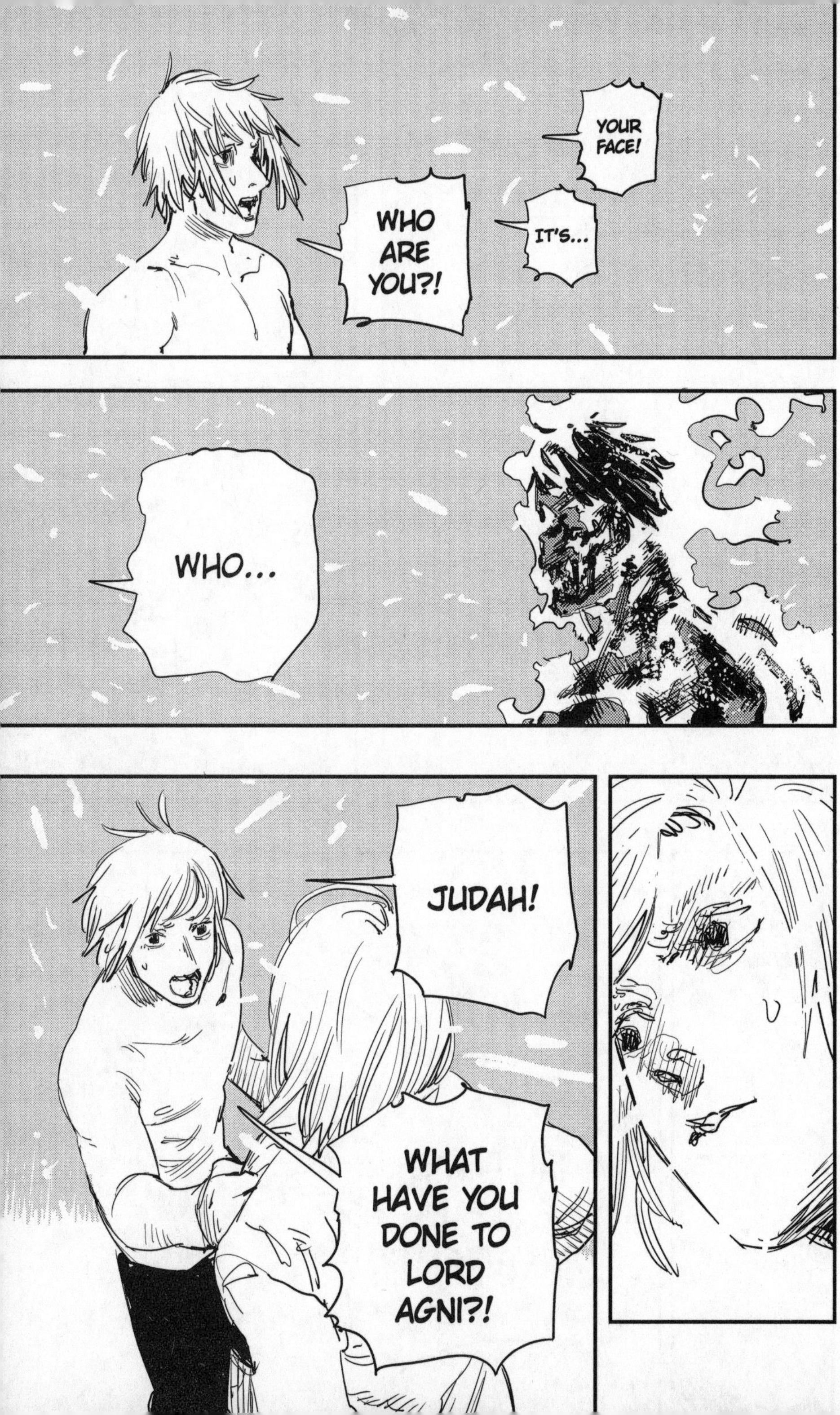
YOUR FACE!
IT'S...
WHO ARE YOU?!
WHO...
JUDAH!
WHAT HAVE YOU DONE TO LORD AGNI?!

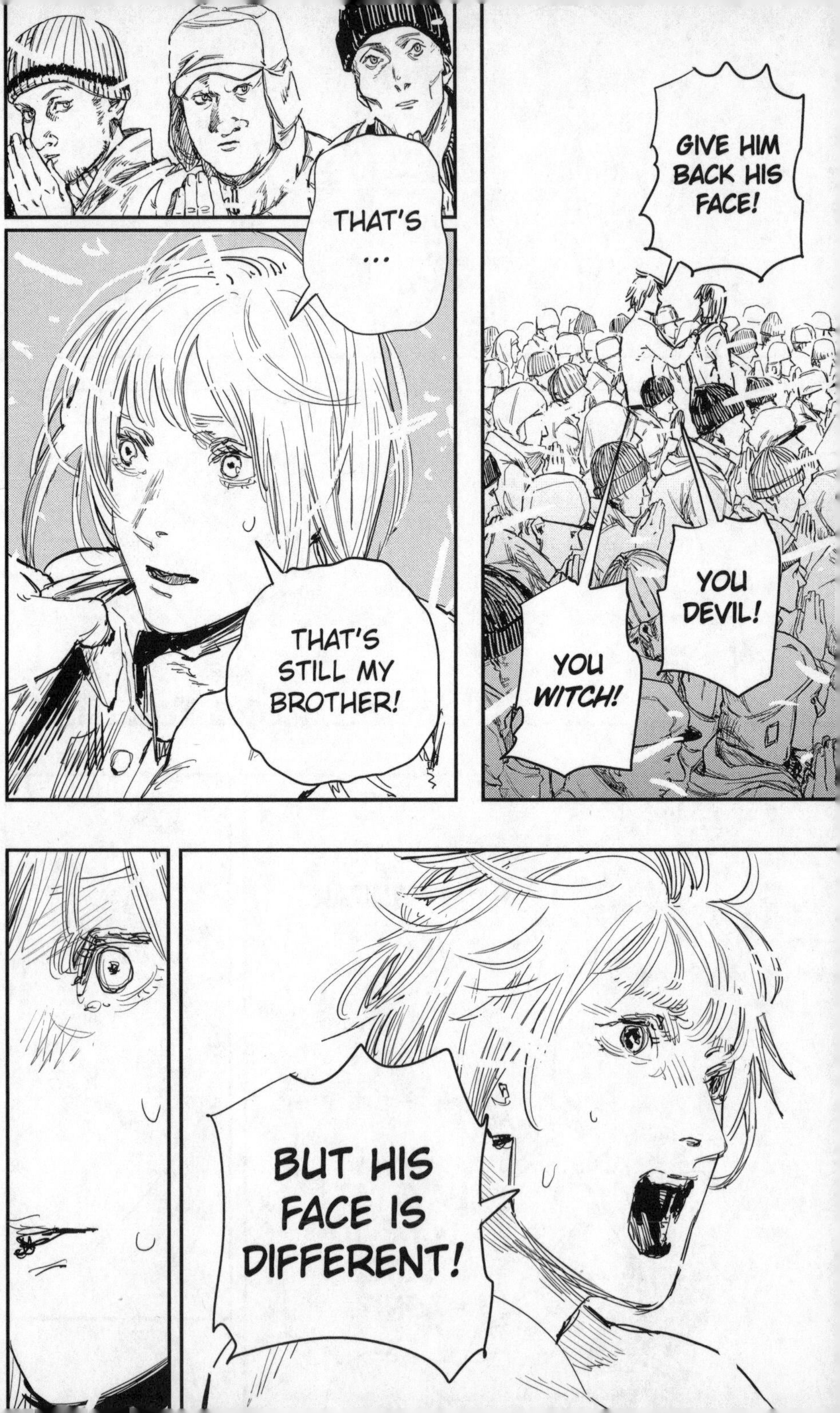
GIVE HIM BACK HIS FACE!
YOU DEVIL!
YOU WITCH!
THAT'S ...
THAT'S STILL MY BROTHER!
BUT HIS FACE IS DIFFERENT!

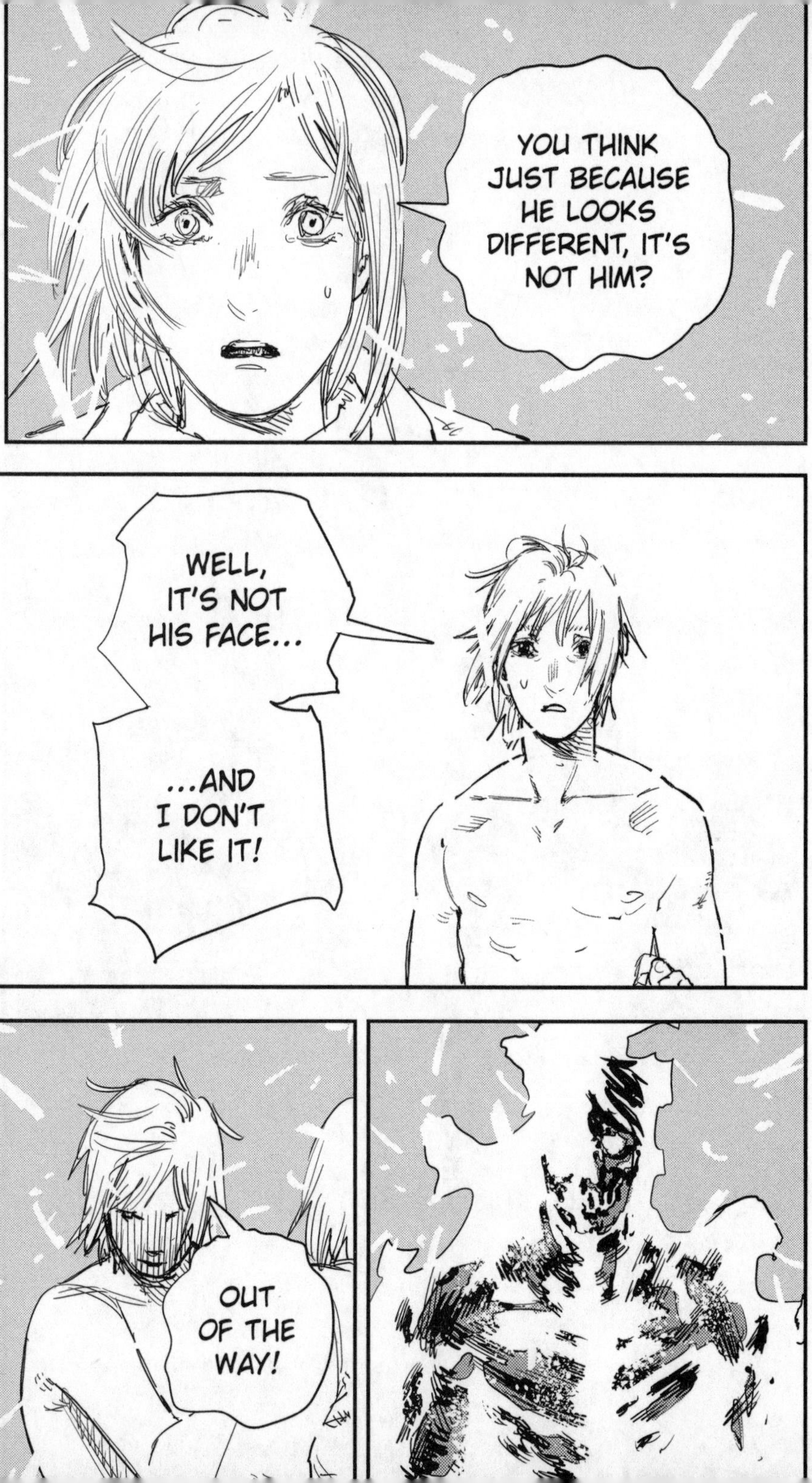
YOU THINK JUST BECAUSE HE LOOKS DIFFERENT, IT'S NOT HIM?
WELL, IT'S NOT HIS FACE...
...AND I DON'T LIKE IT!
OUT OF THE WAY!

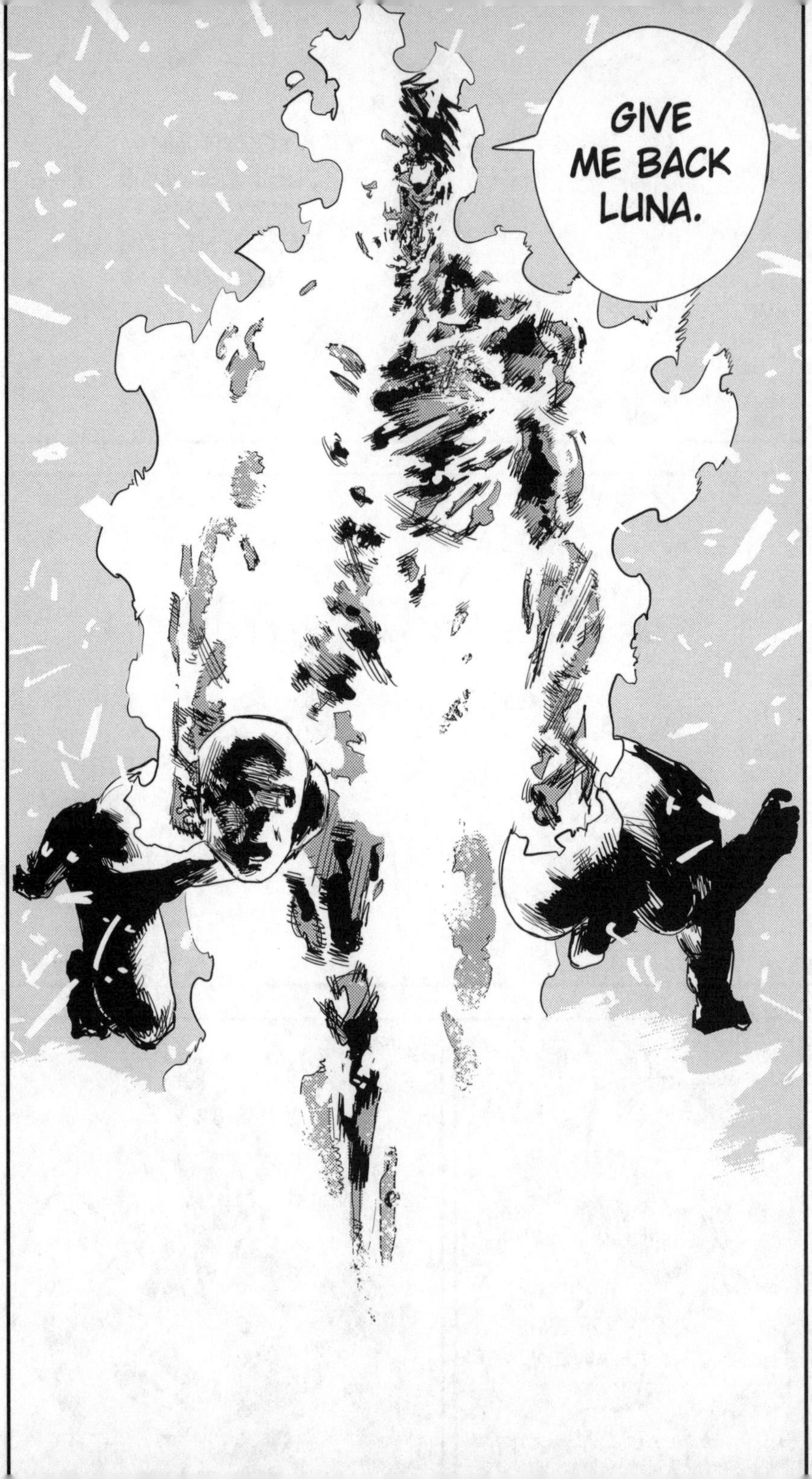
GIVE ME BACK LUNA.

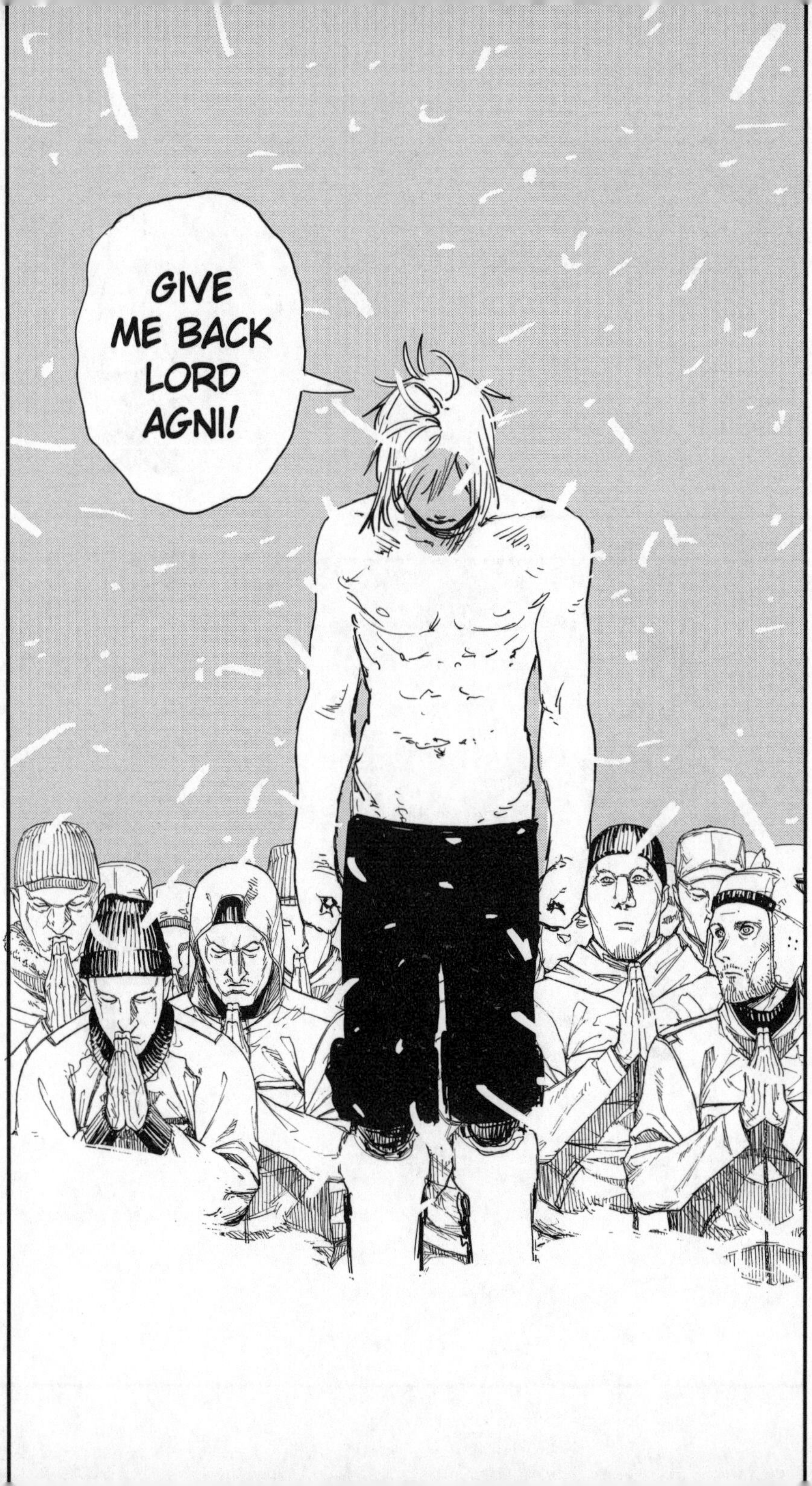
GIVE ME BACK LORD AGNI!

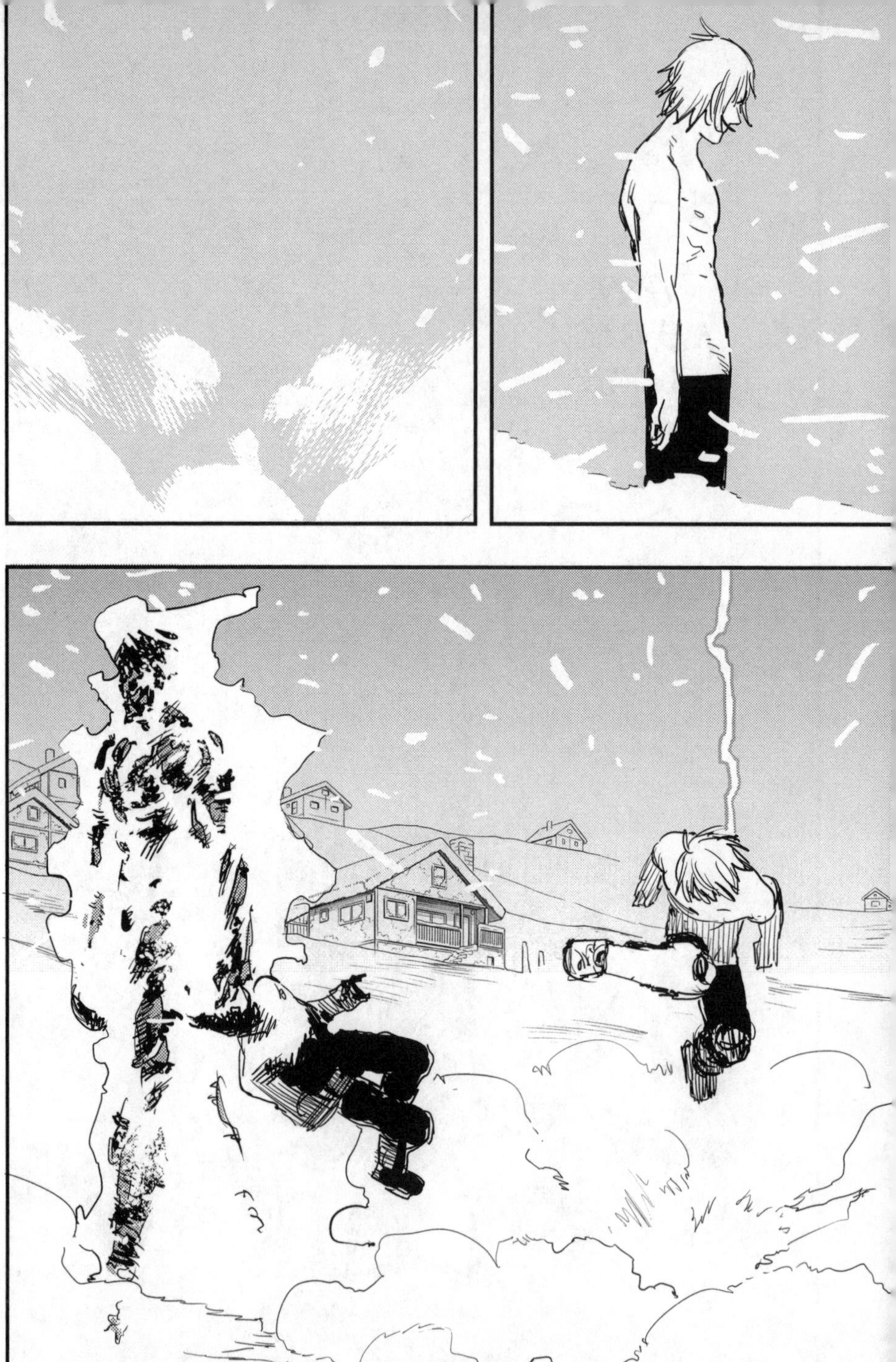

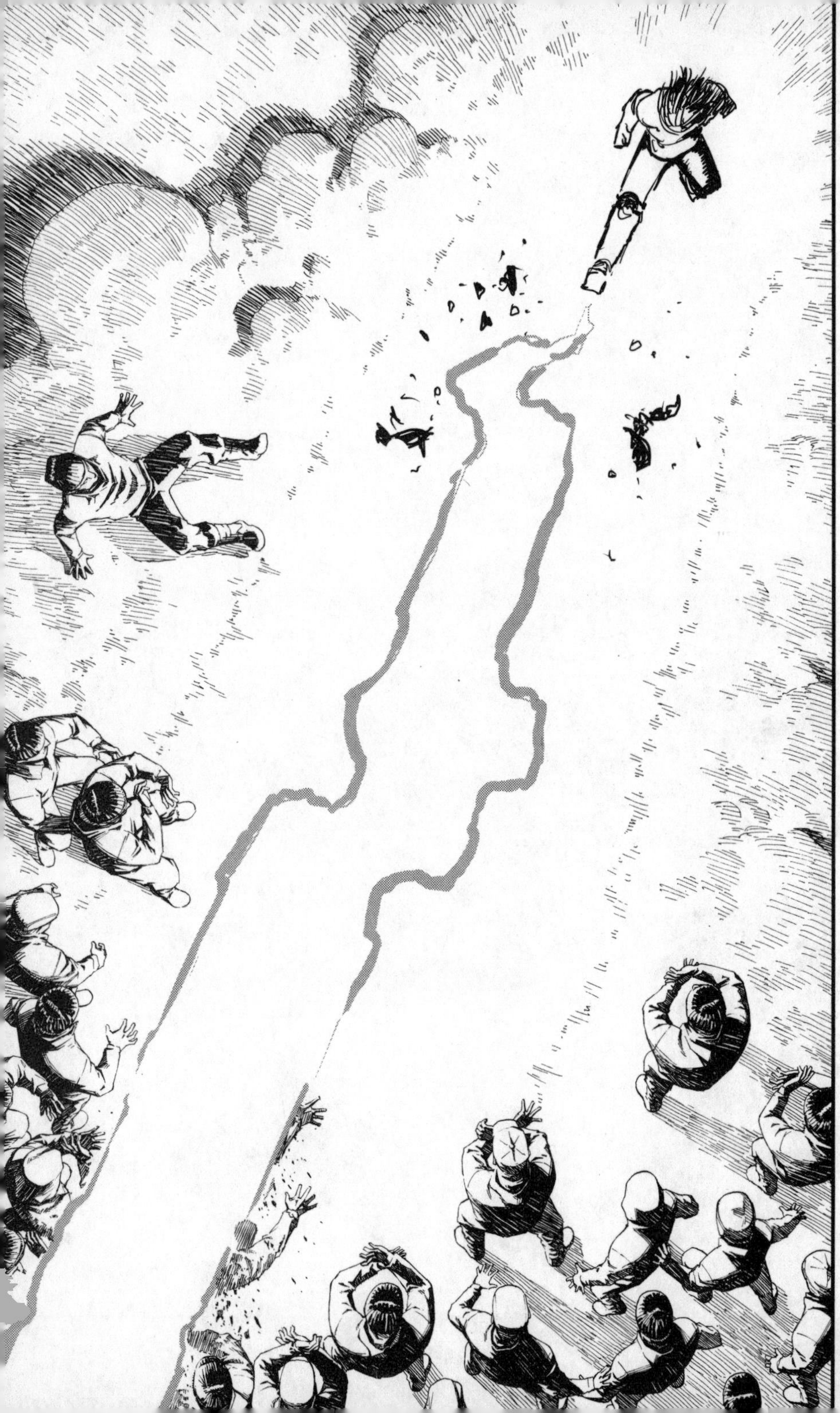

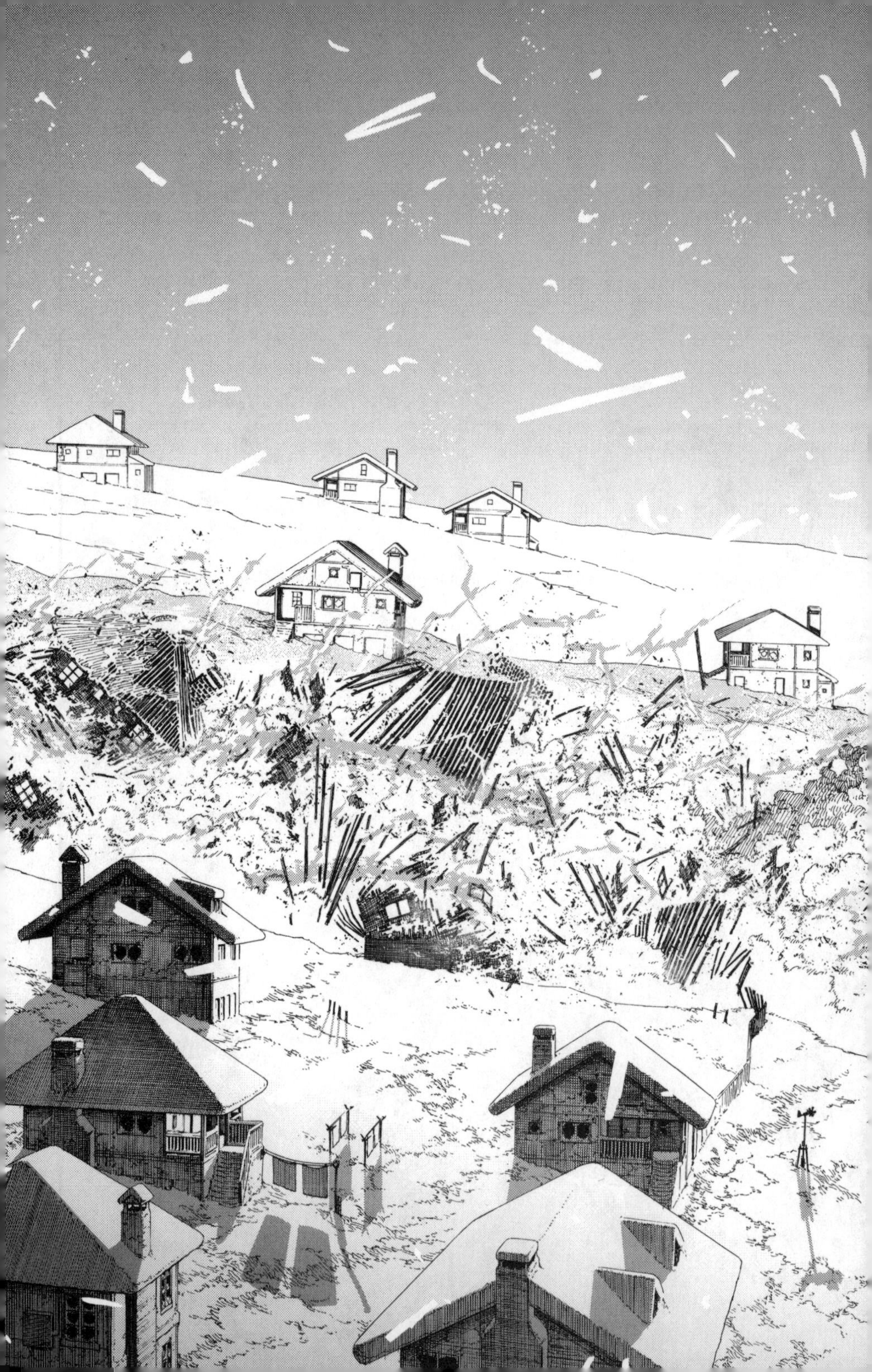

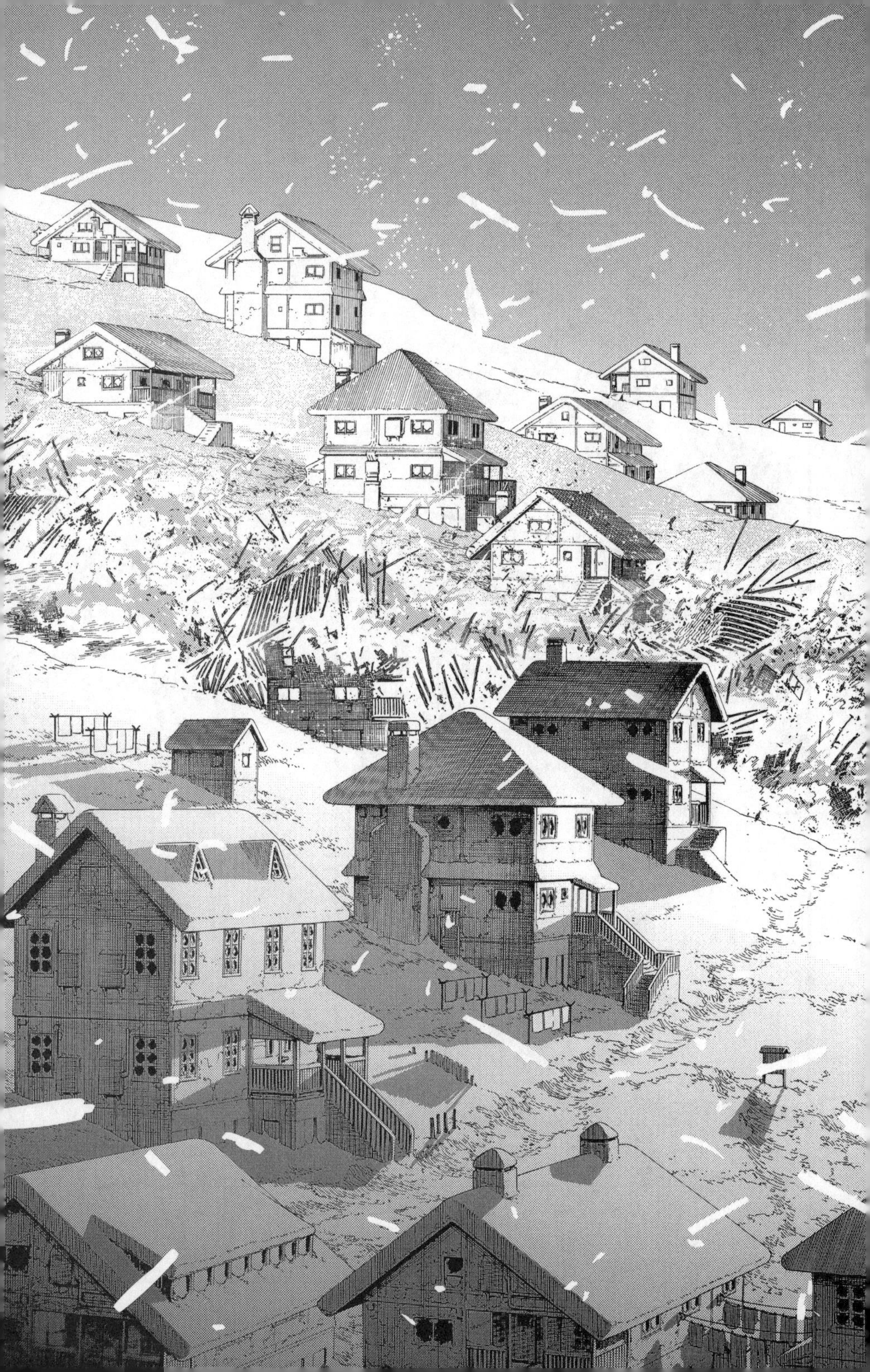

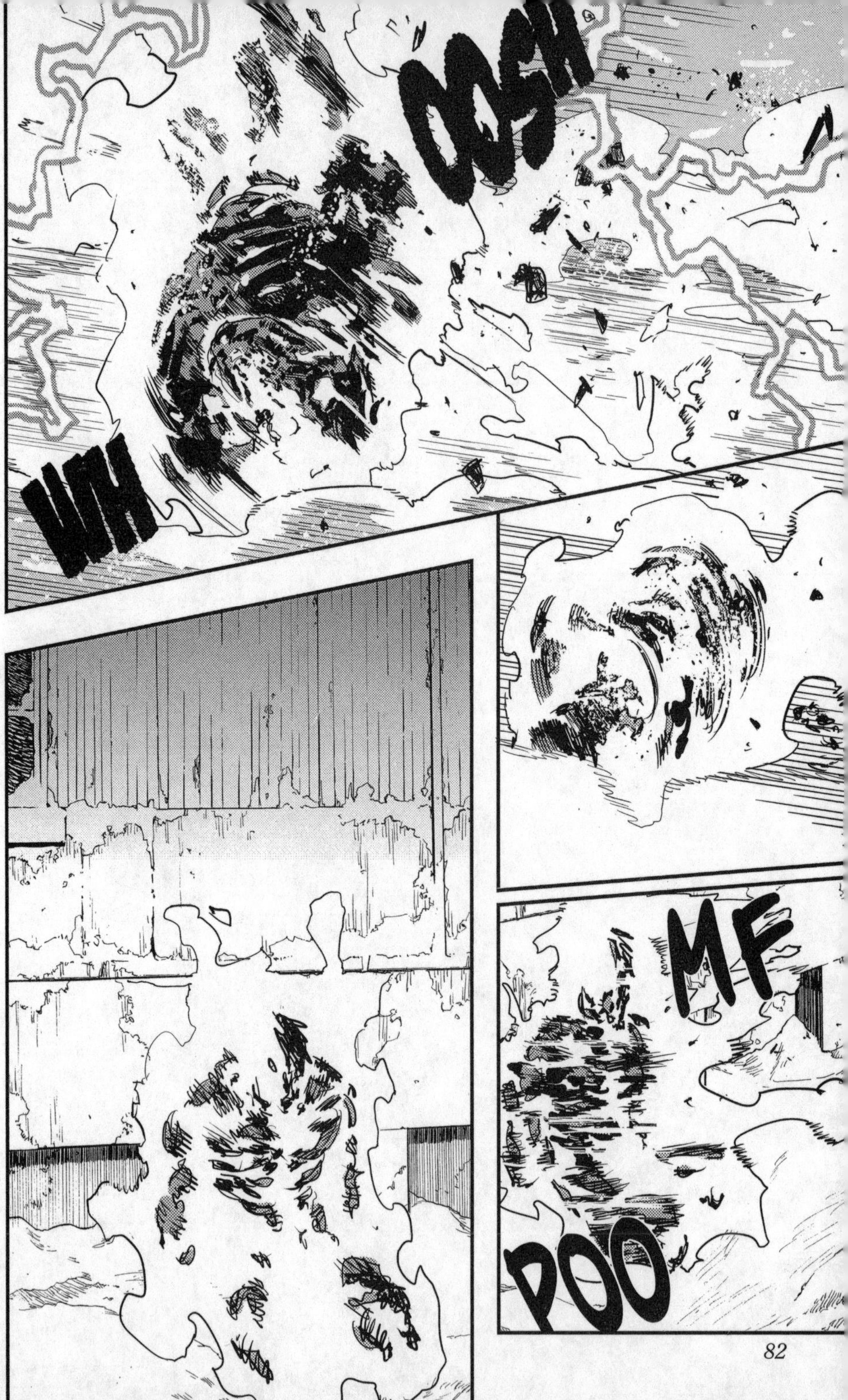
WH
OOSH
POO
MF

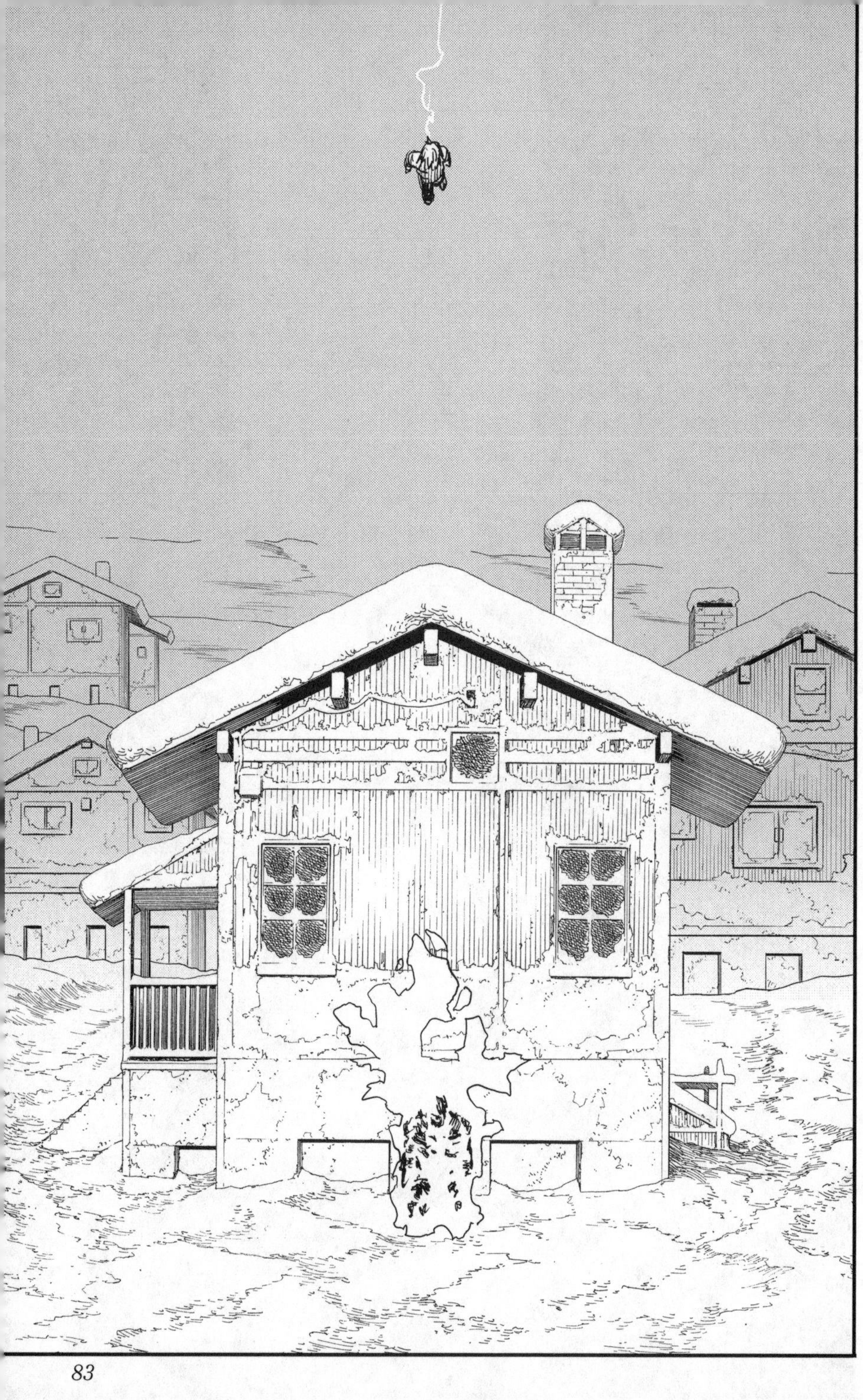

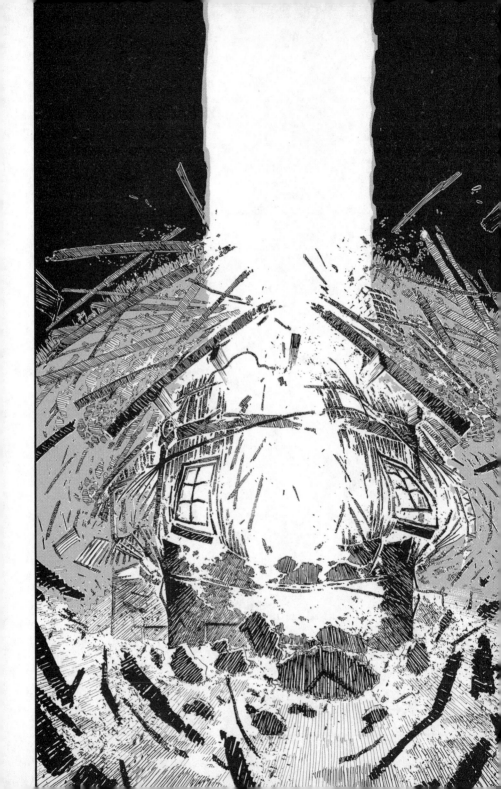

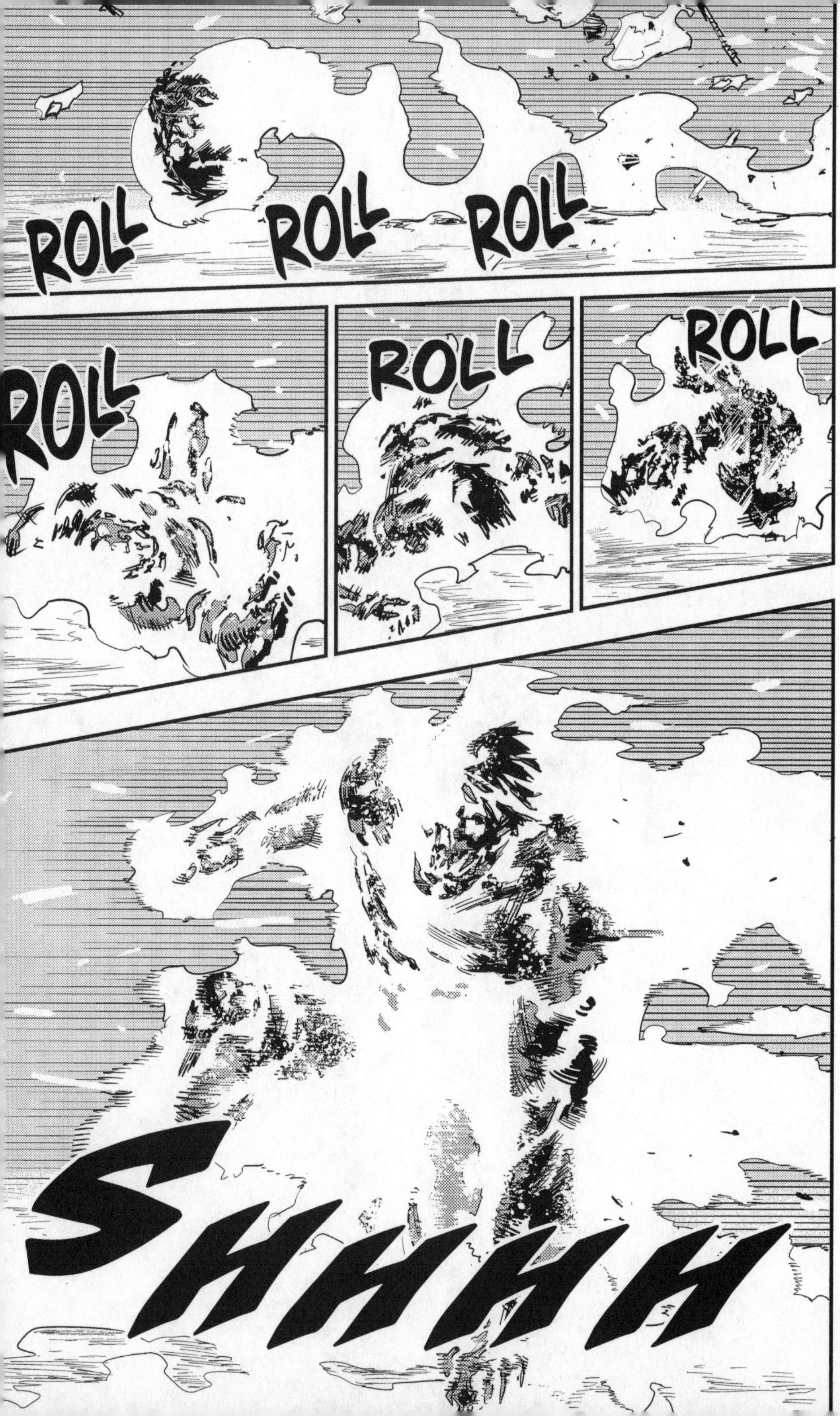
ROLL
ROLL
ROLL
ROLL
ROLL
ROLL
SHHHH

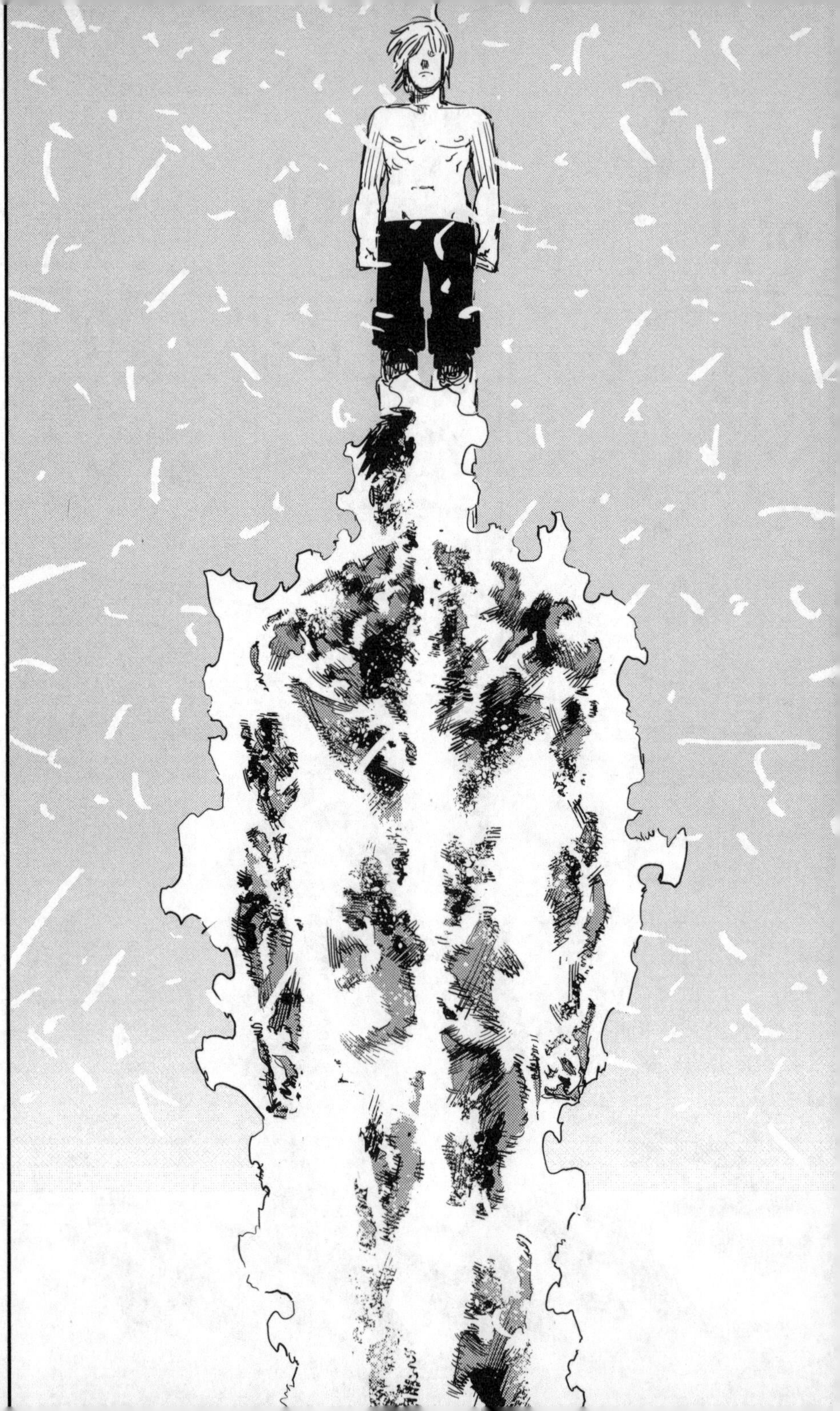

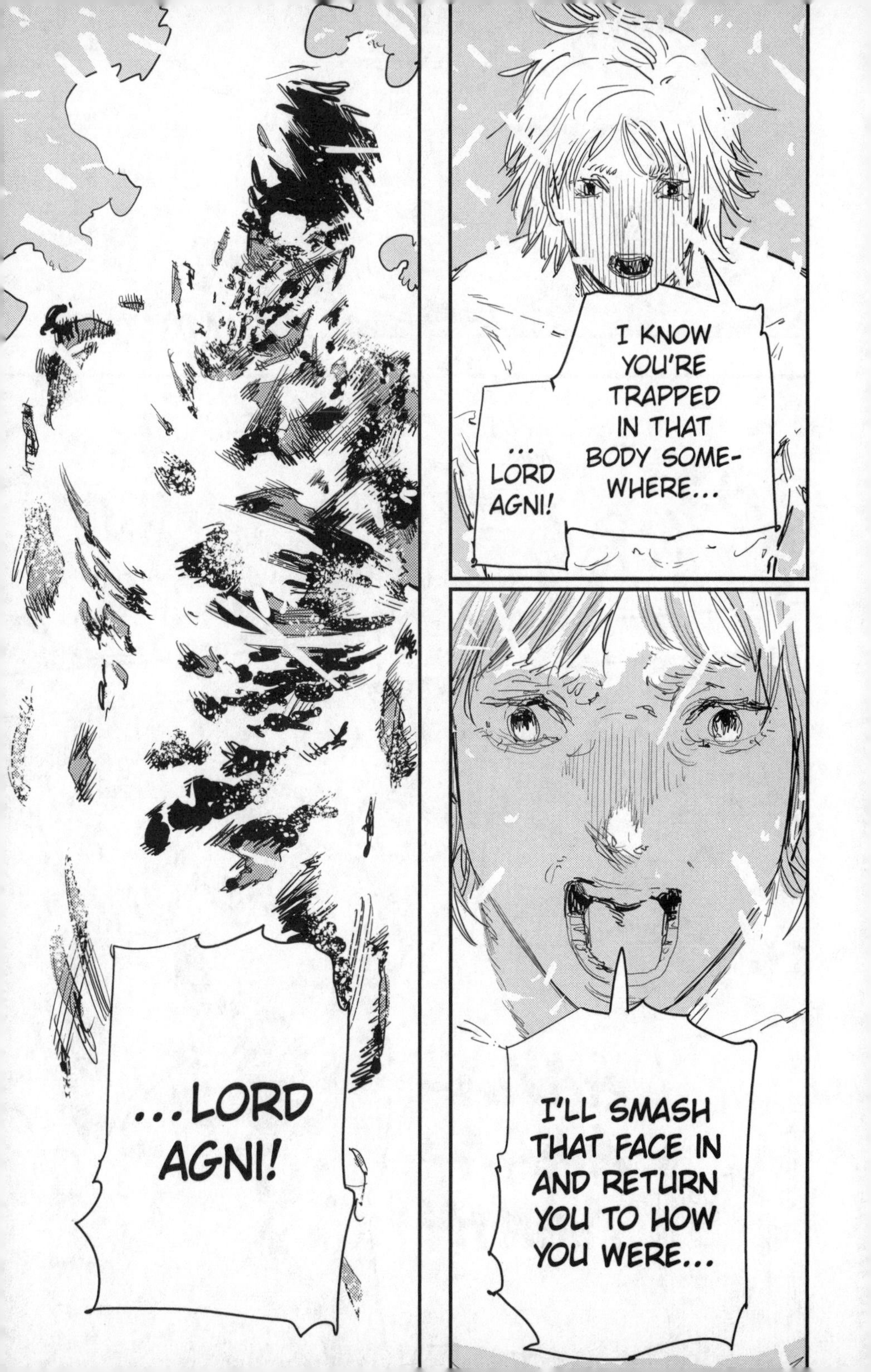
I KNOW YOU'RE TRAPPED IN THAT BODY SOMEWHERE...
... LORD AGNI!
I'LL SMASH THAT FACE IN AND RETURN YOU TO HOW YOU WERE...
...LORD AGNI!

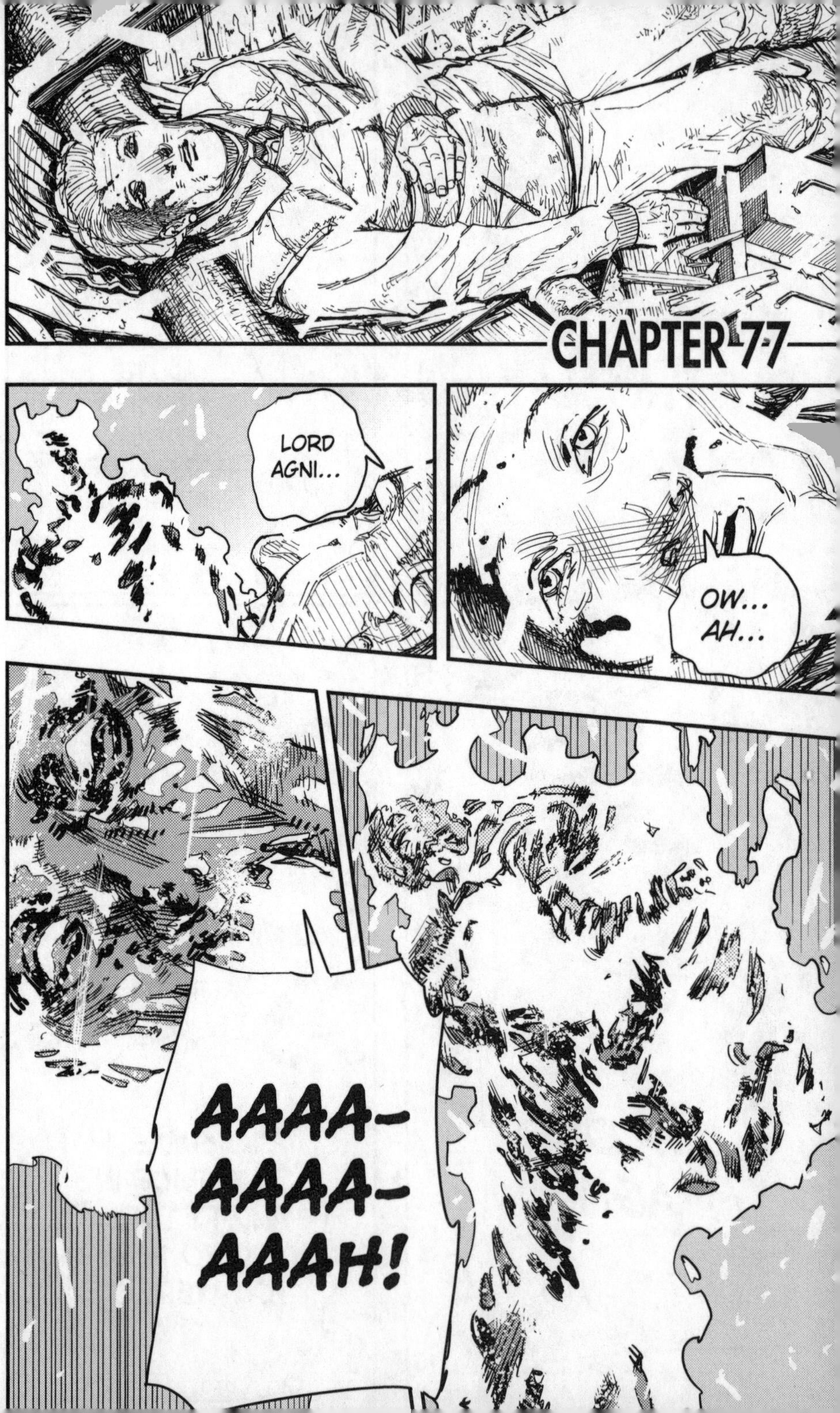
CHAPTER 77
OW... AH...
LORD AGNI...
AAAA-AAAA-AAAH!

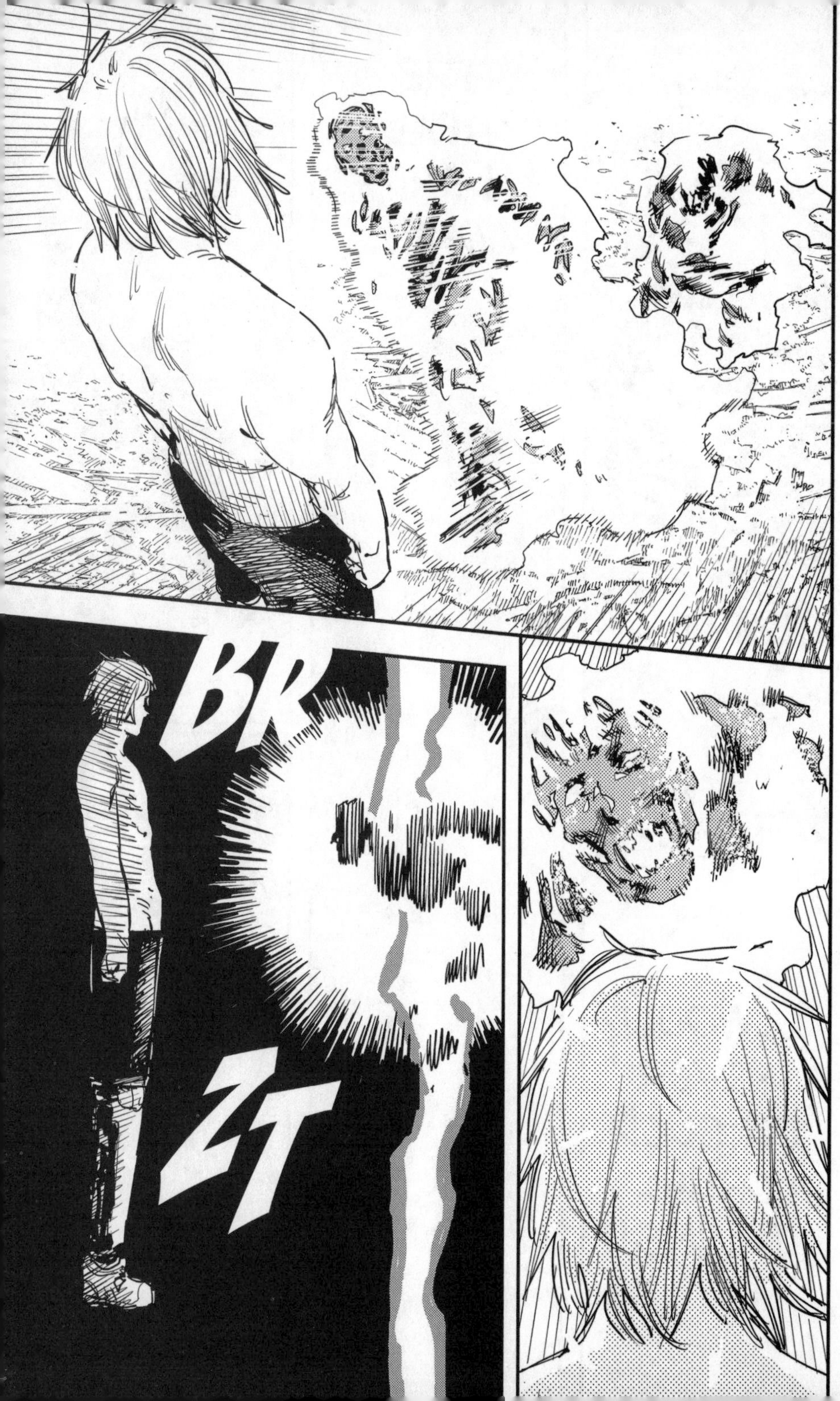
BR
ZZT

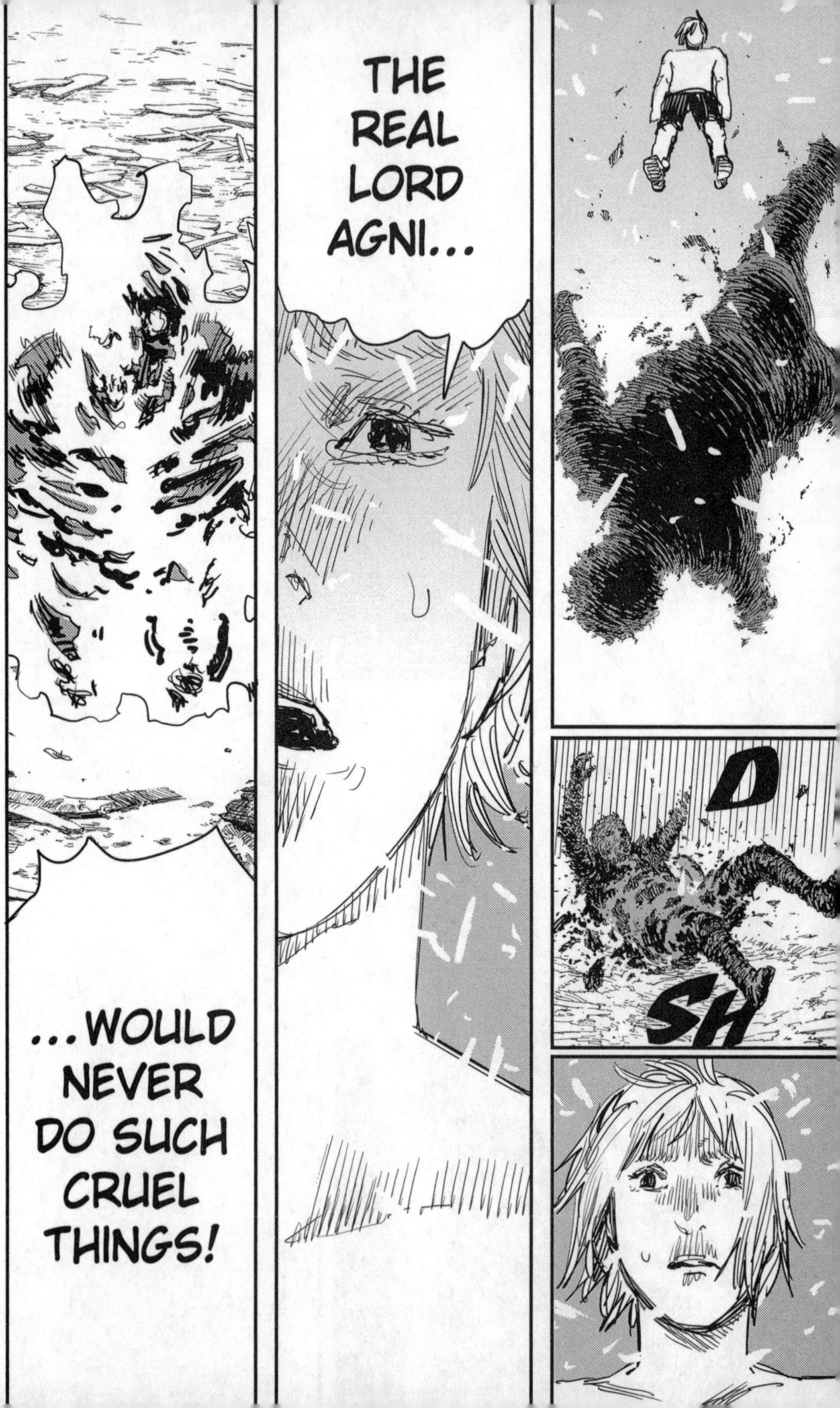
D
SH
THE REAL LORD AGNI...
...WOULD NEVER DO SUCH CRUEL THINGS!

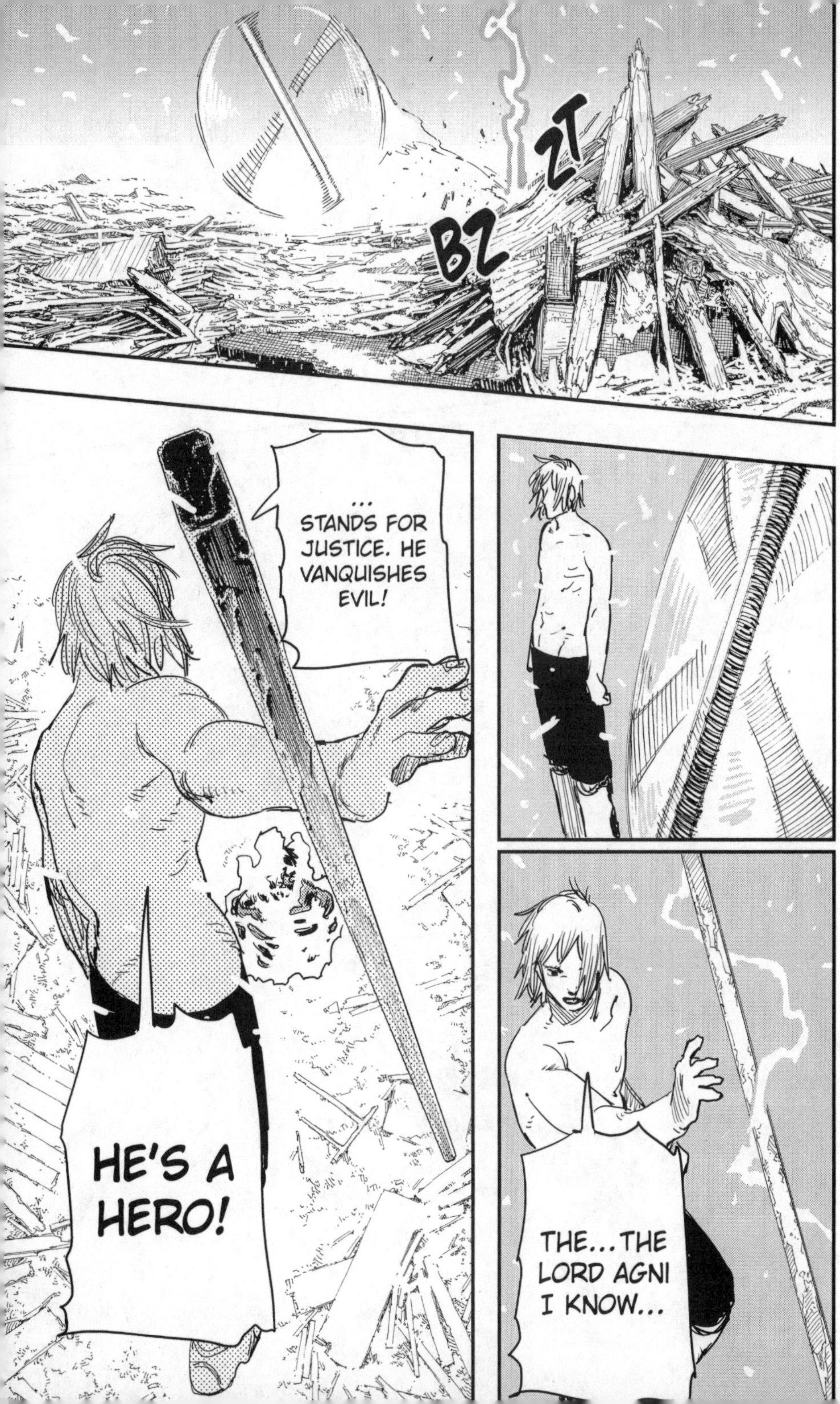
BZZT
THE...THE LORD AGNI I KNOW...
... STANDS FOR JUSTICE. HE VANQUISHES EVIL!
HE'S A HERO!

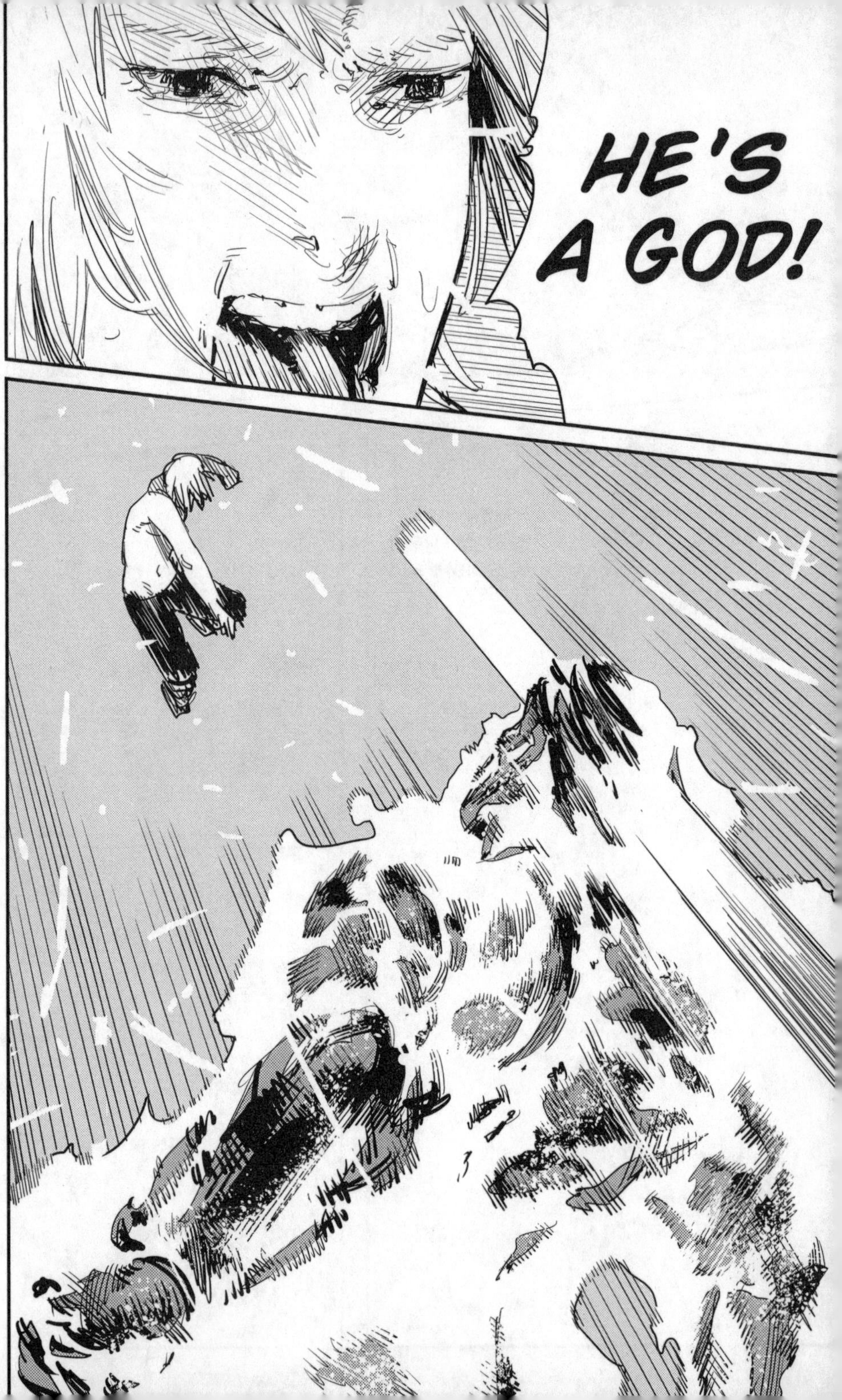
HE'S A GOD!

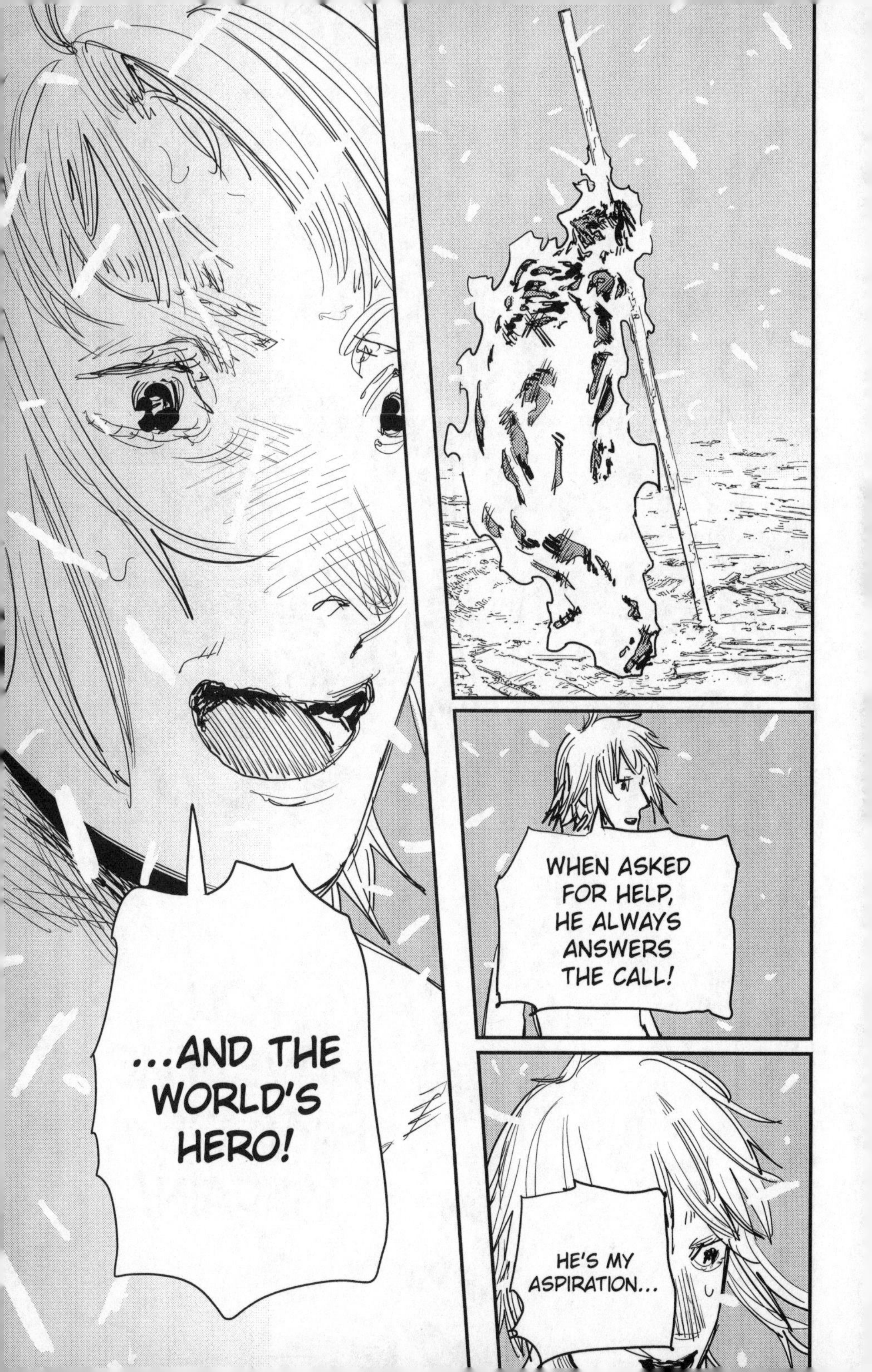
WHEN ASKED FOR HELP, HE ALWAYS ANSWERS THE CALL!
HE'S MY ASPIRATION...
...AND THE WORLD'S HERO!

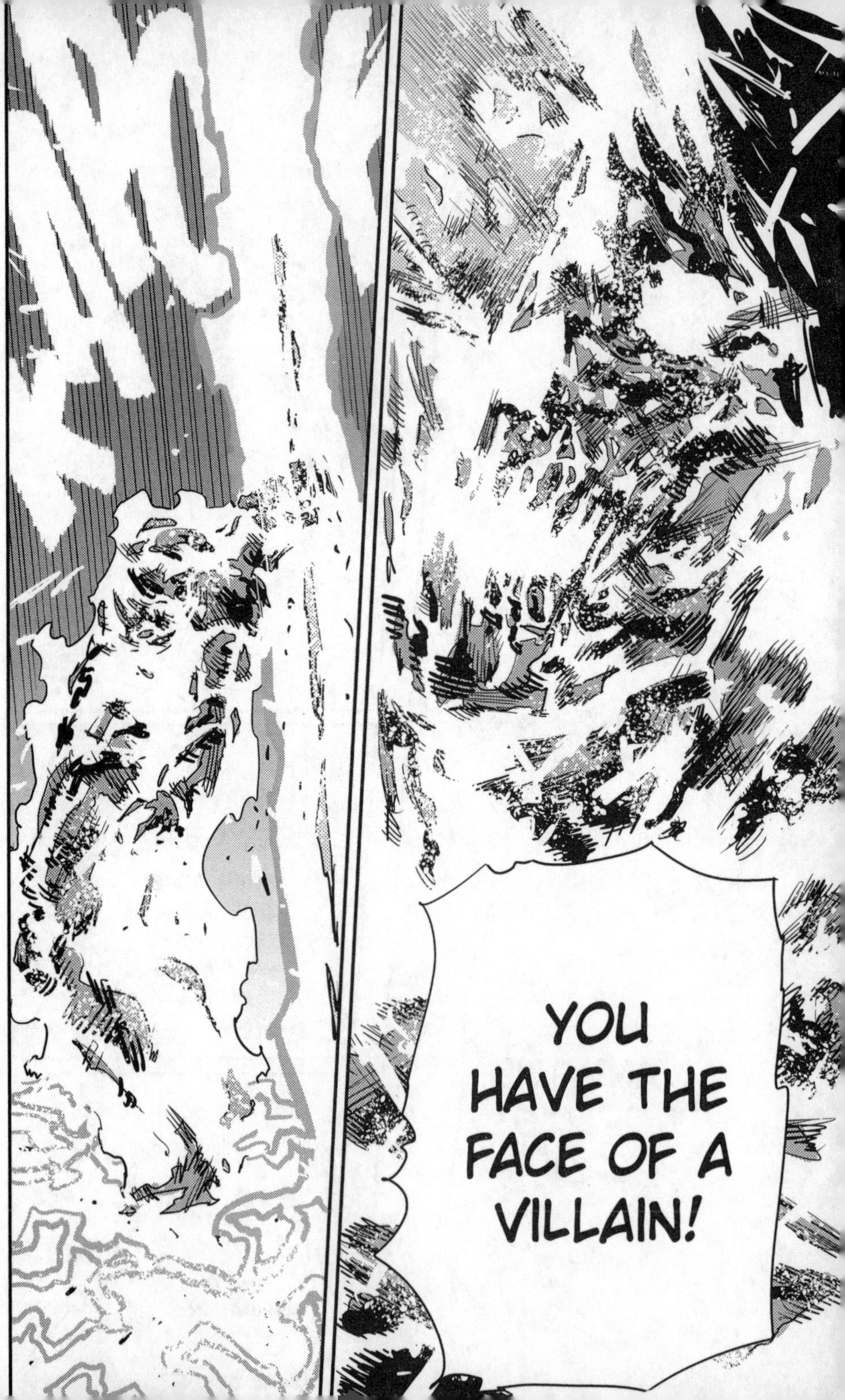
YOU HAVE THE FACE OF A VILLAIN!

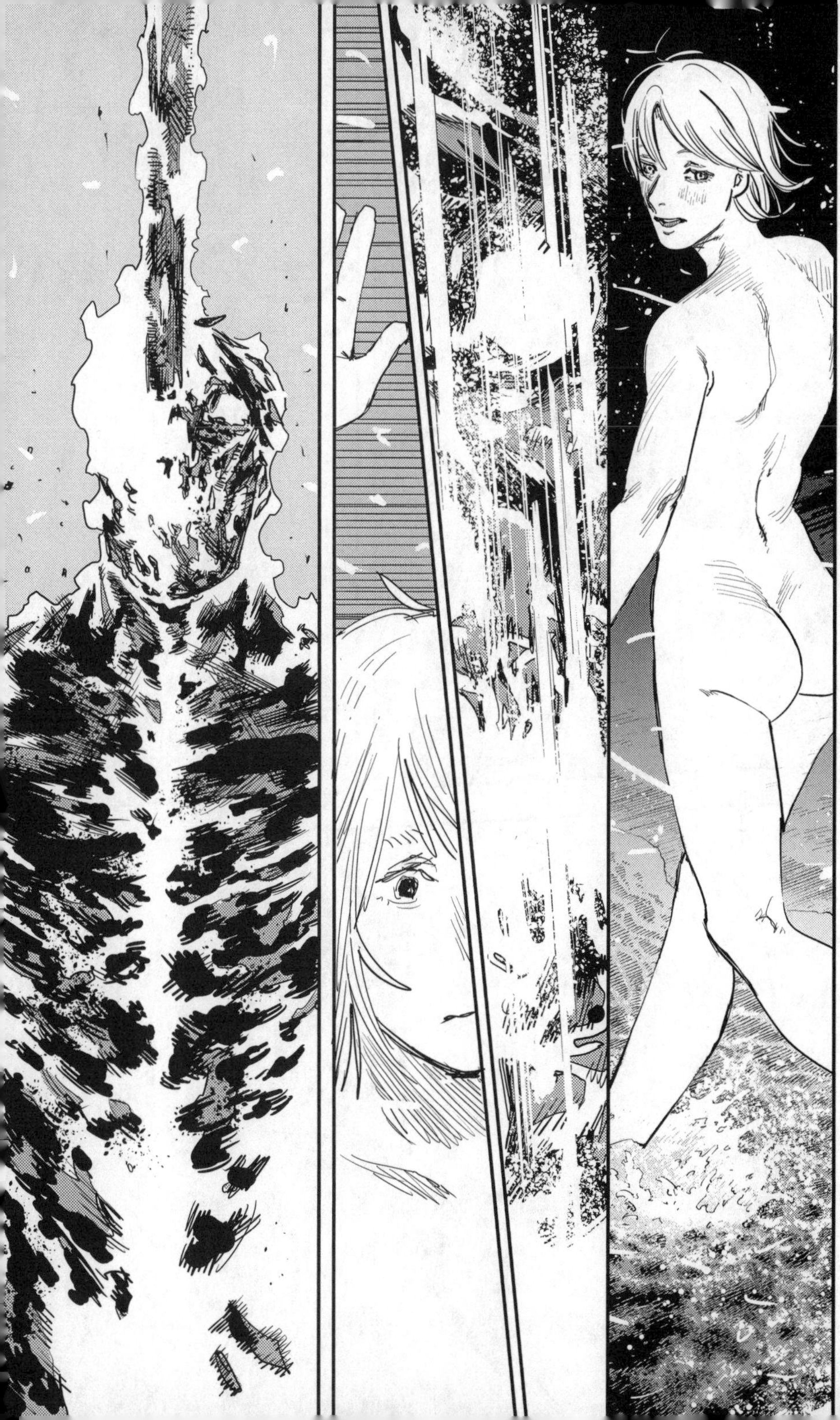

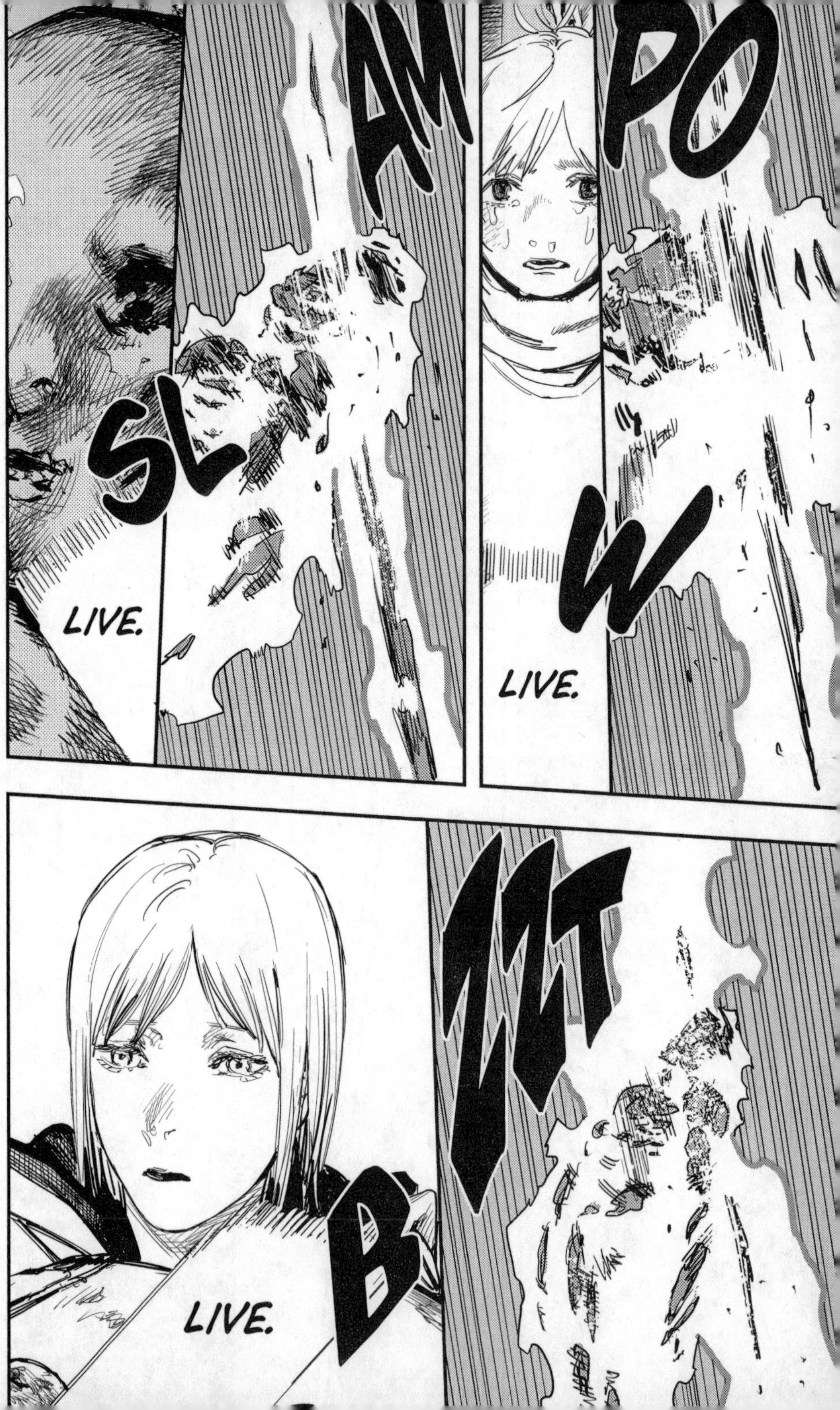
PO
W
LIVE.
AM
SL
LIVE.
ZZT
B
LIVE.

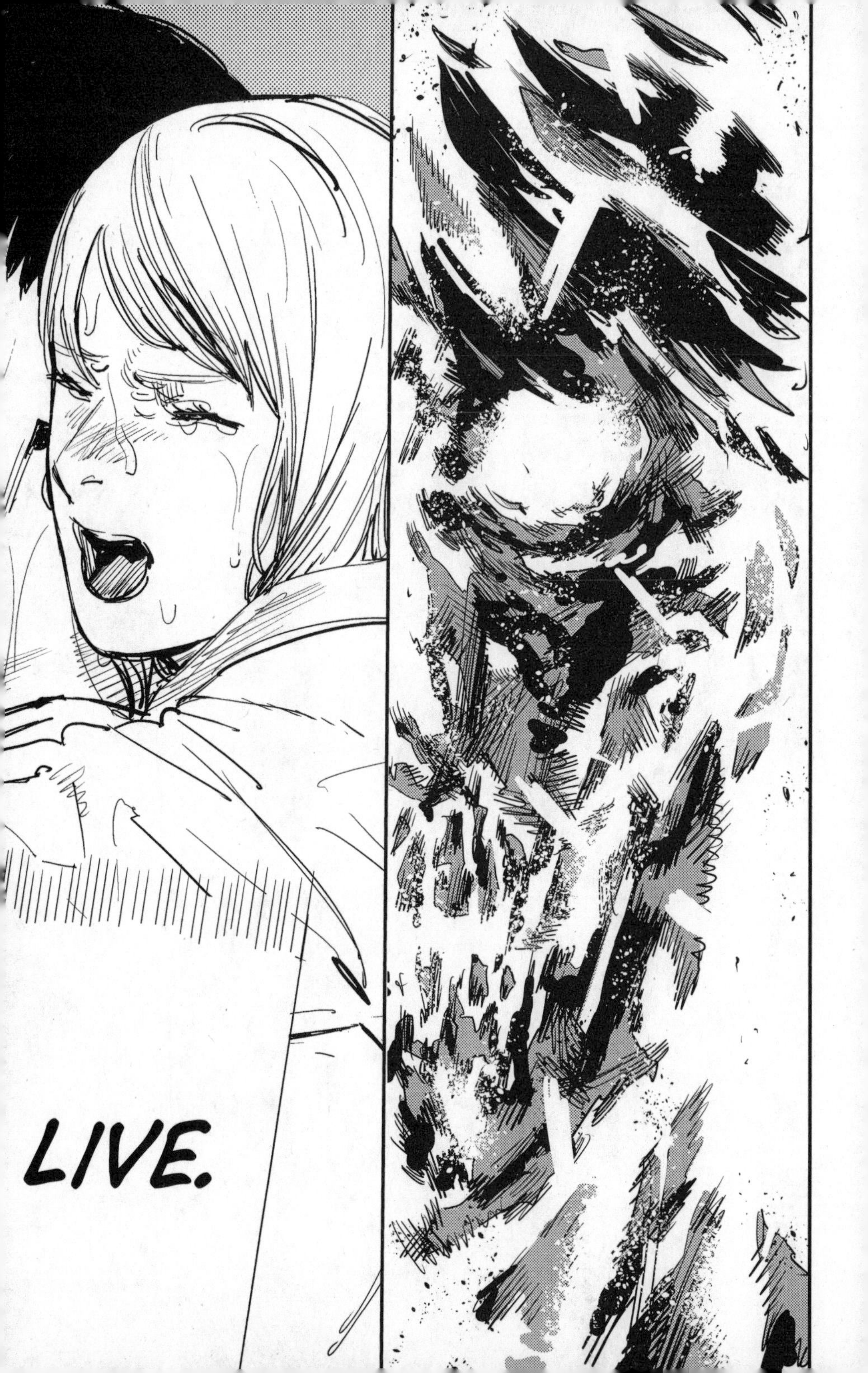
LIVE.

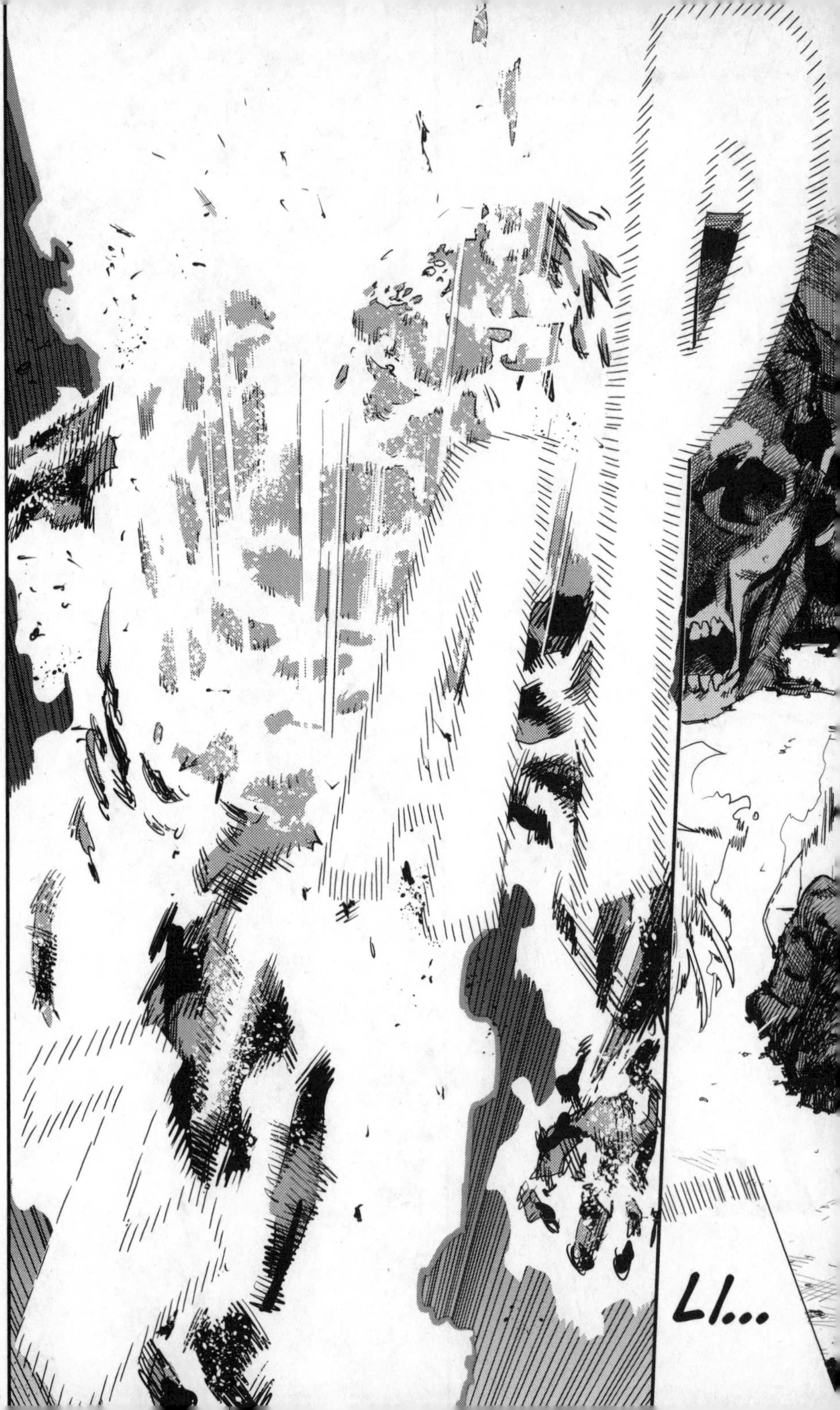

LI...

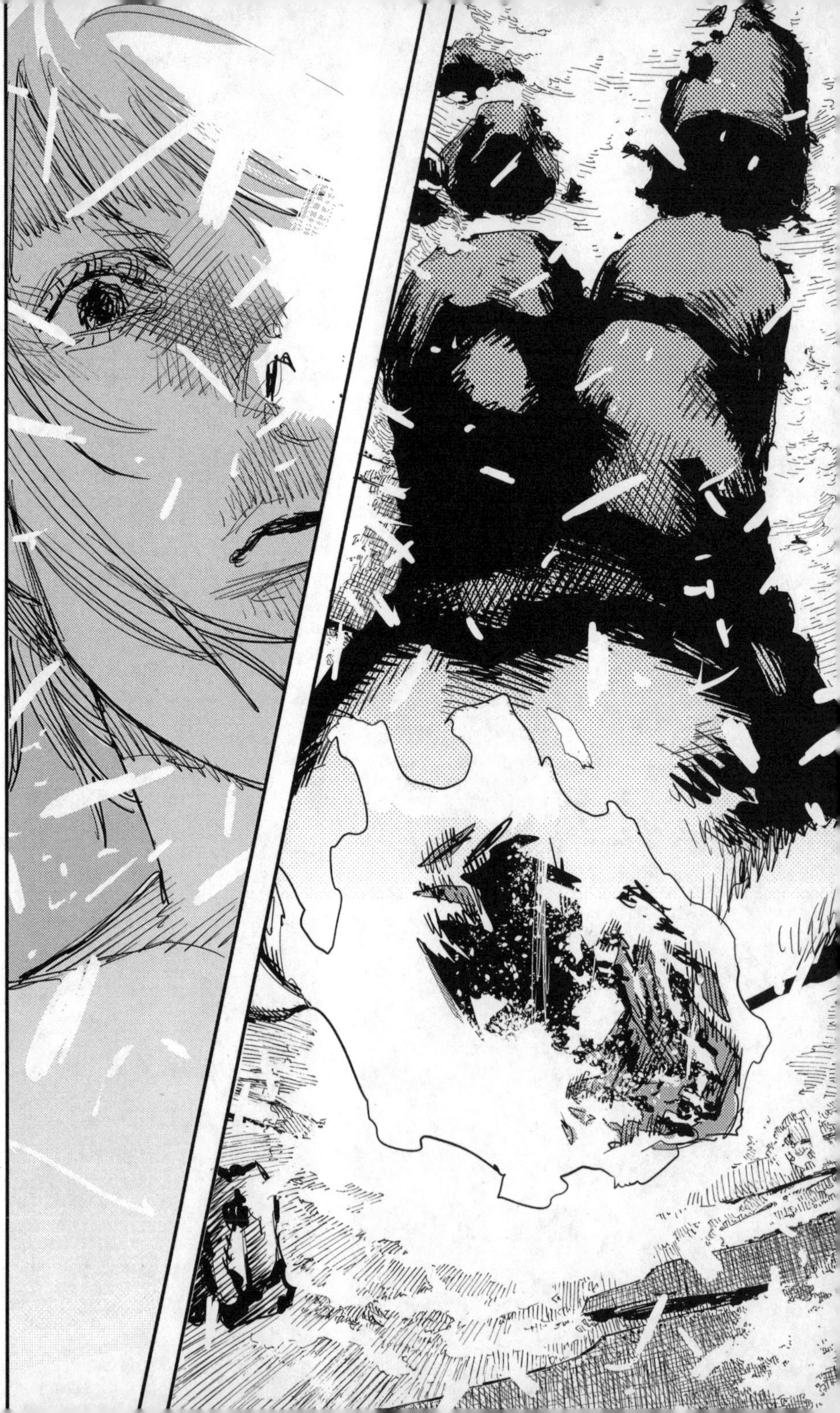

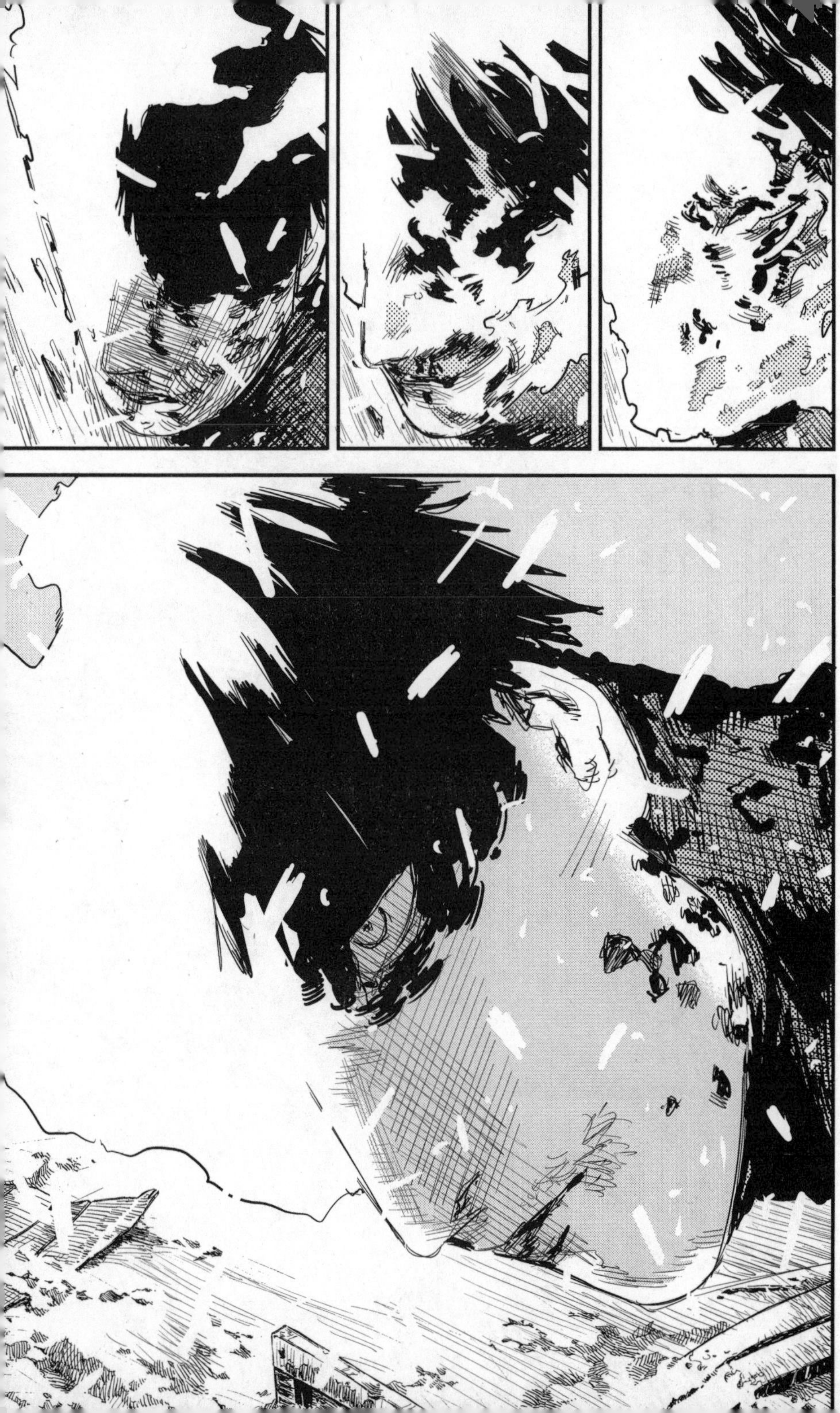

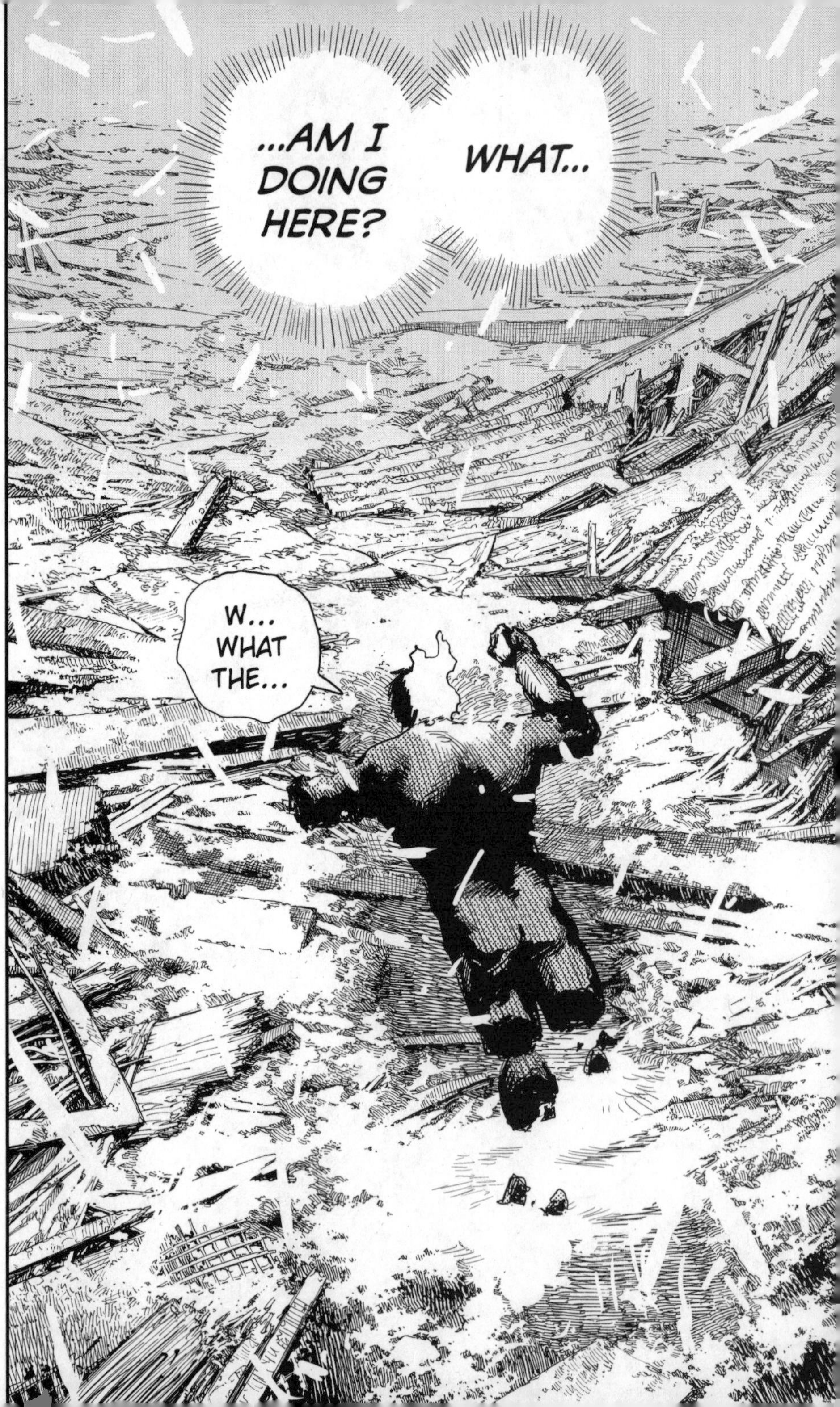
WHAT...
...AM I DOING HERE?
W... WHAT THE...

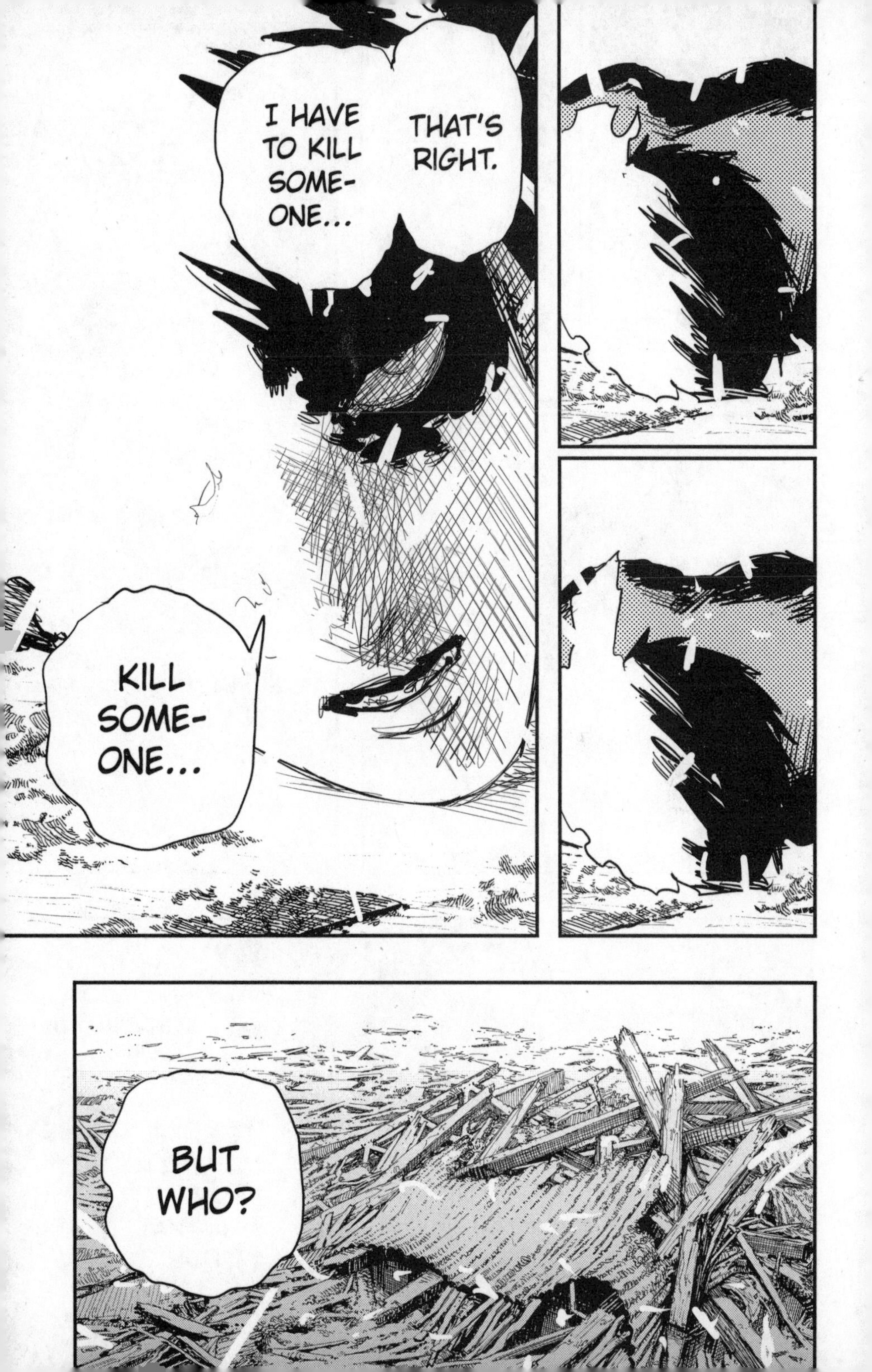
THAT'S RIGHT.
I HAVE TO KILL SOME-ONE...
KILL SOME-ONE...
BUT WHO?

DOMA?

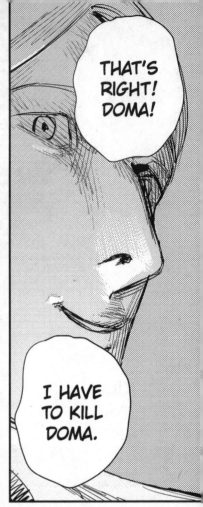

THAT'S RIGHT! DOMA!

I HAVE TO KILL DOMA.

NO... WHAT AM I TALKING ABOUT?

IT'S THE ICE WITCH I HAVE TO KILL. THAT WITCH.

THE ICE...

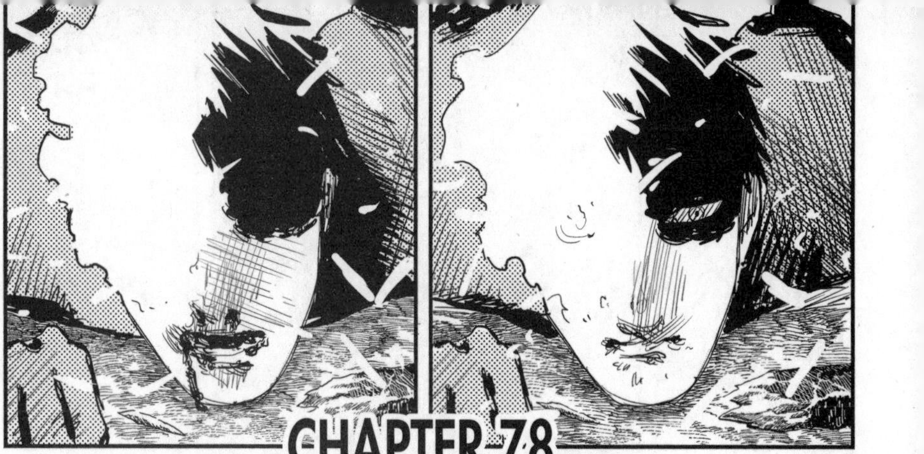

CHAPTER 78

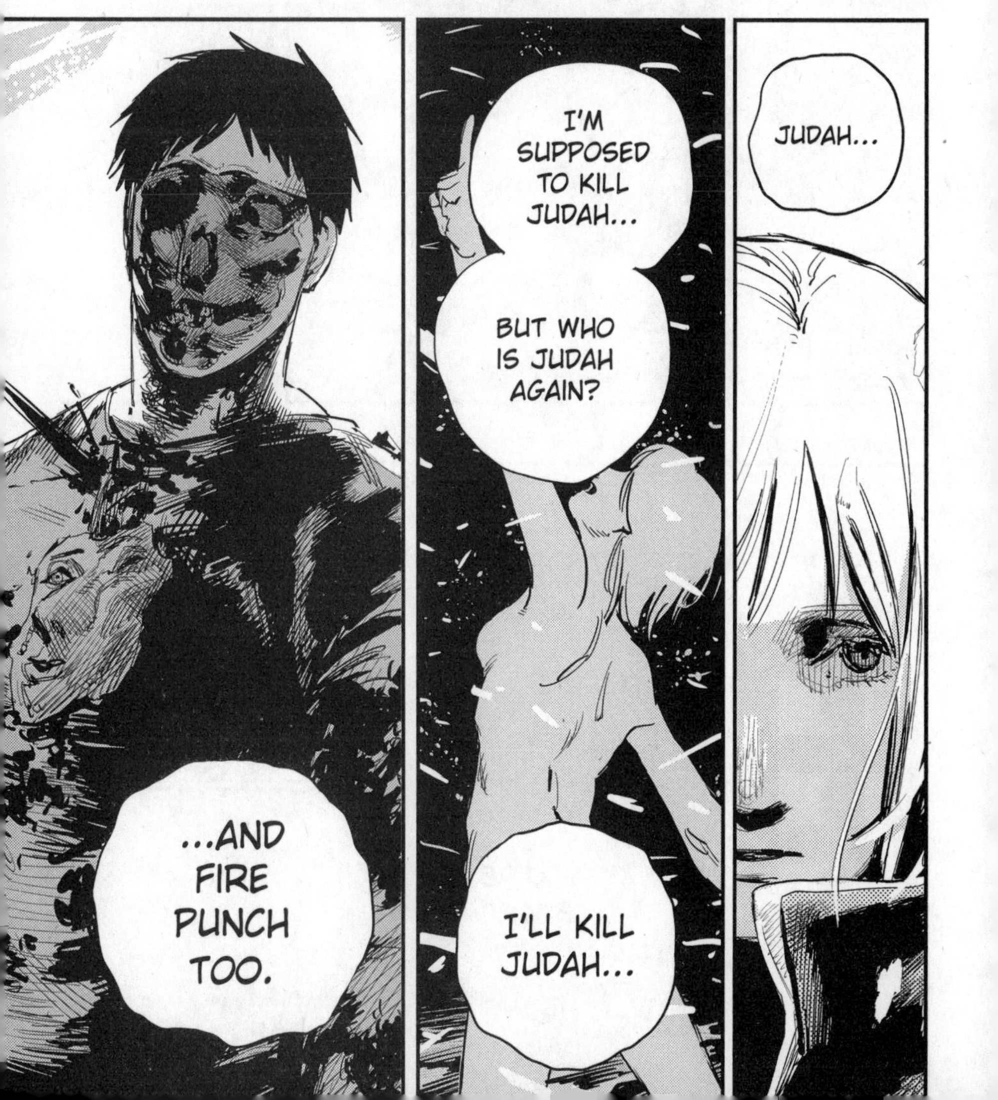
JUDAH...
I'M SUPPOSED TO KILL JUDAH...
BUT WHO IS JUDAH AGAIN?
I'LL KILL JUDAH...
...AND FIRE PUNCH TOO.

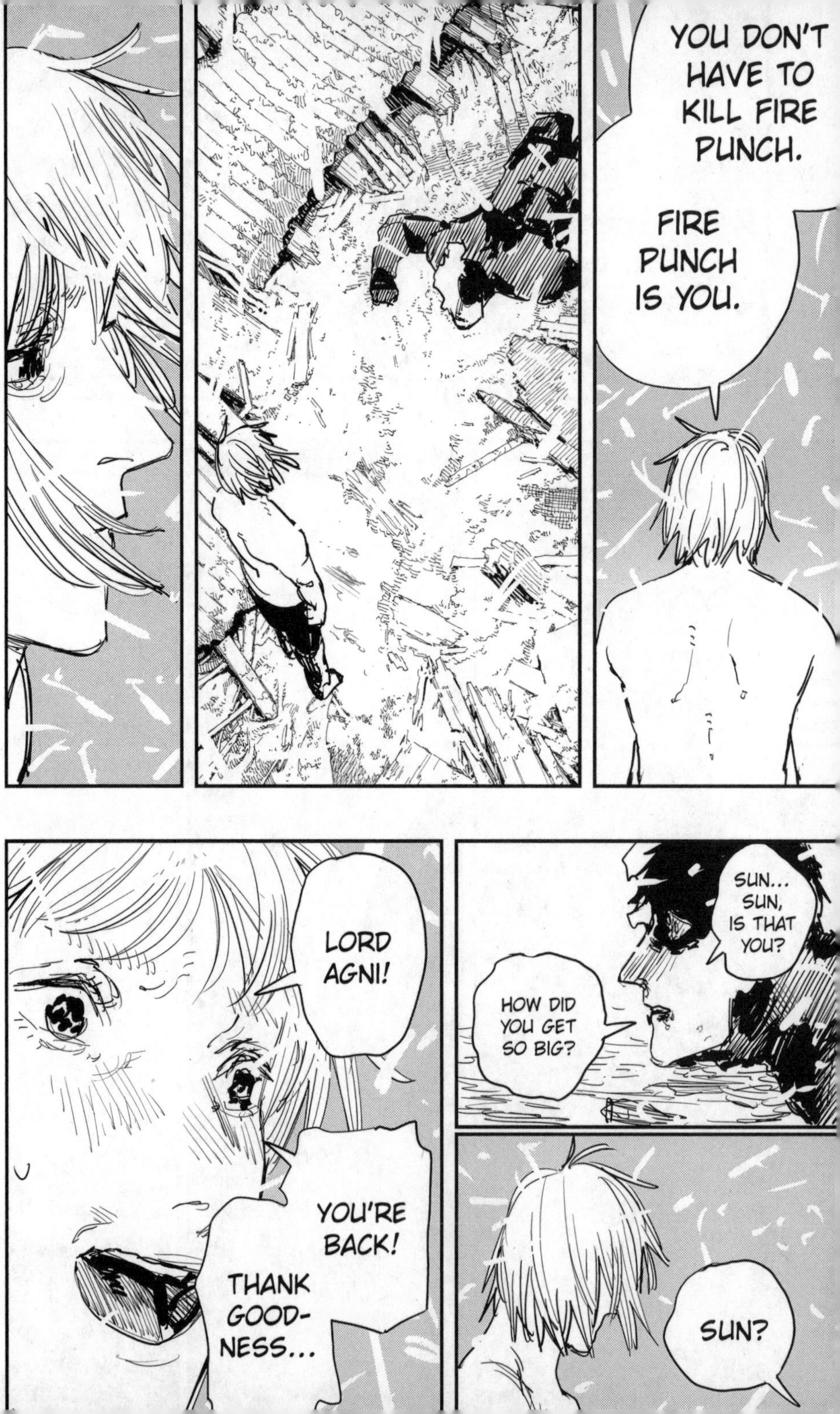
YOU DON'T HAVE TO KILL FIRE PUNCH.
FIRE PUNCH IS YOU.
SUN... SUN, IS THAT YOU?
HOW DID YOU GET SO BIG?
SUN?
LORD AGNI!
YOU'RE BACK!
THANK GOODNESS...

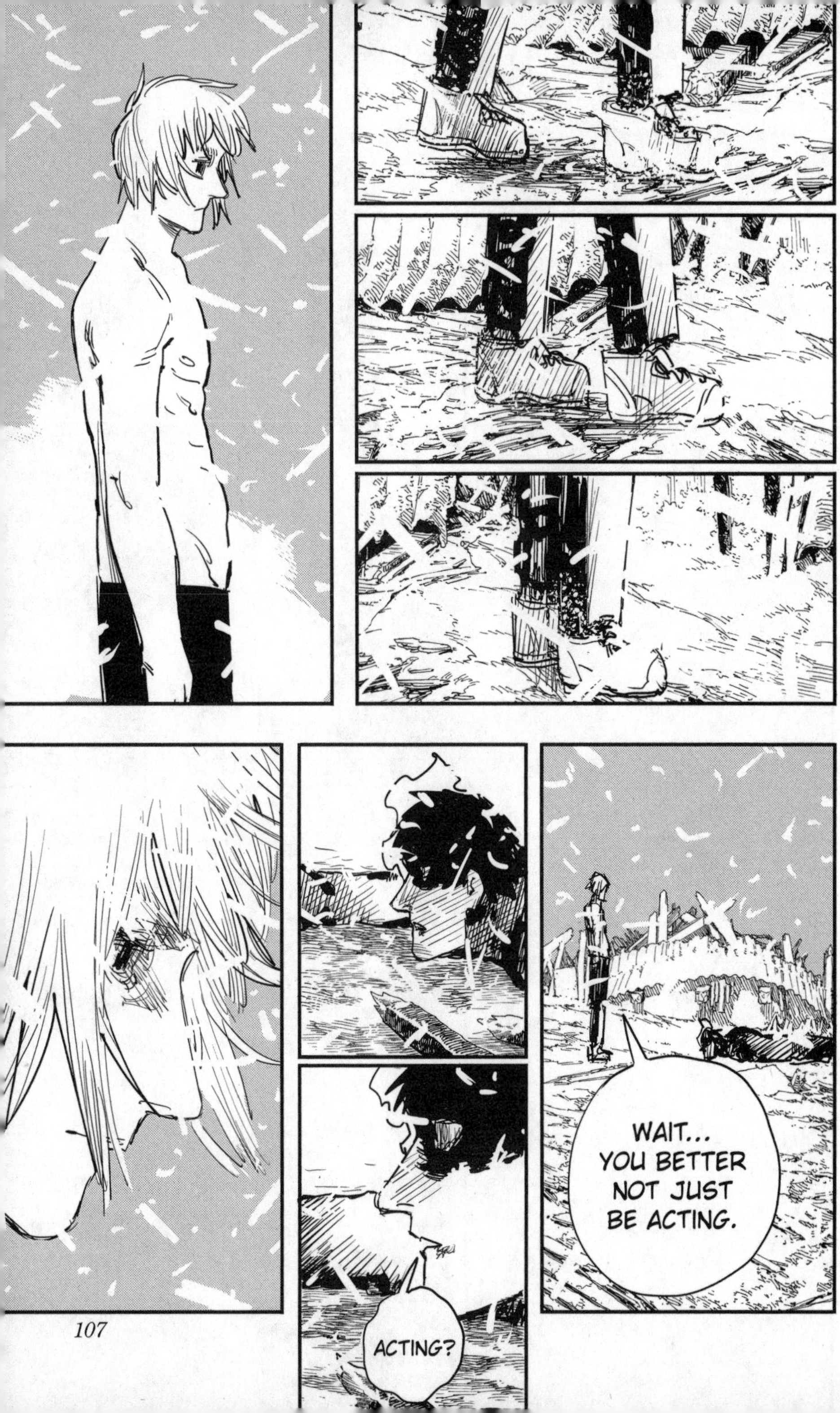
WAIT... YOU BETTER NOT JUST BE ACTING.
ACTING?

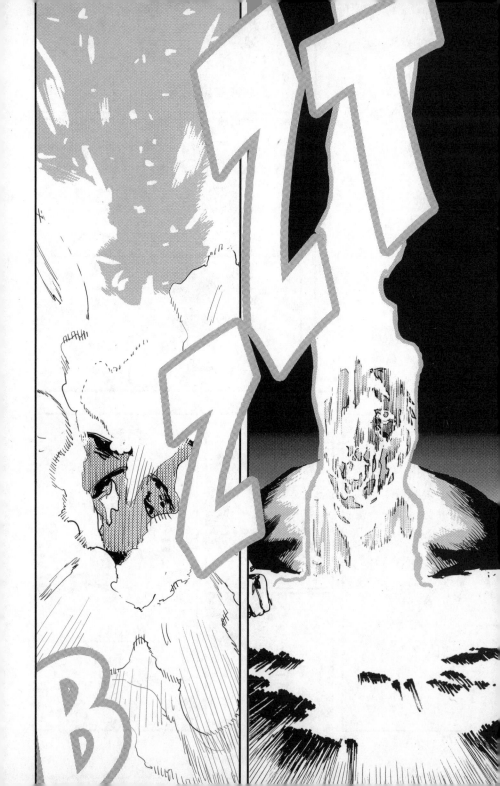

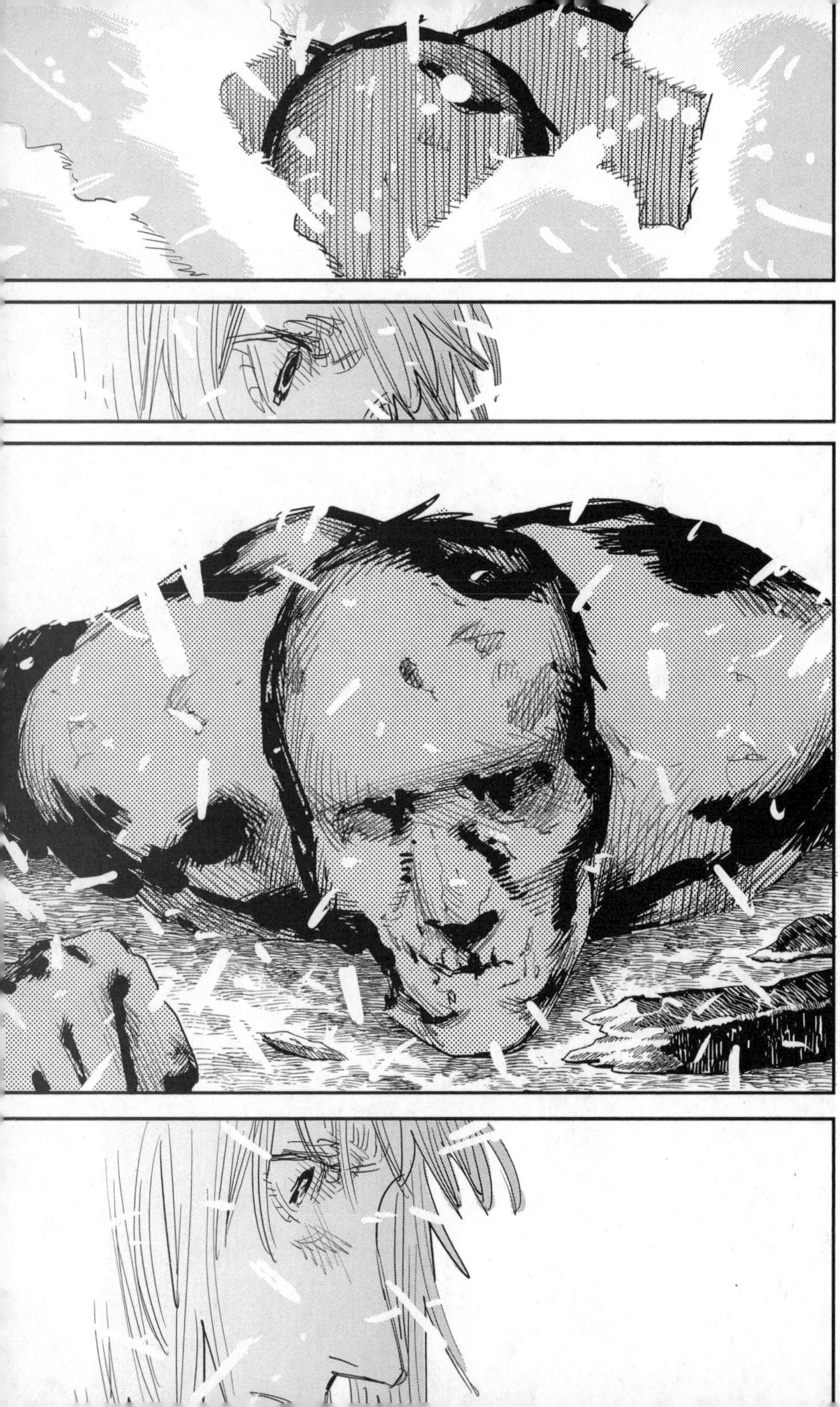

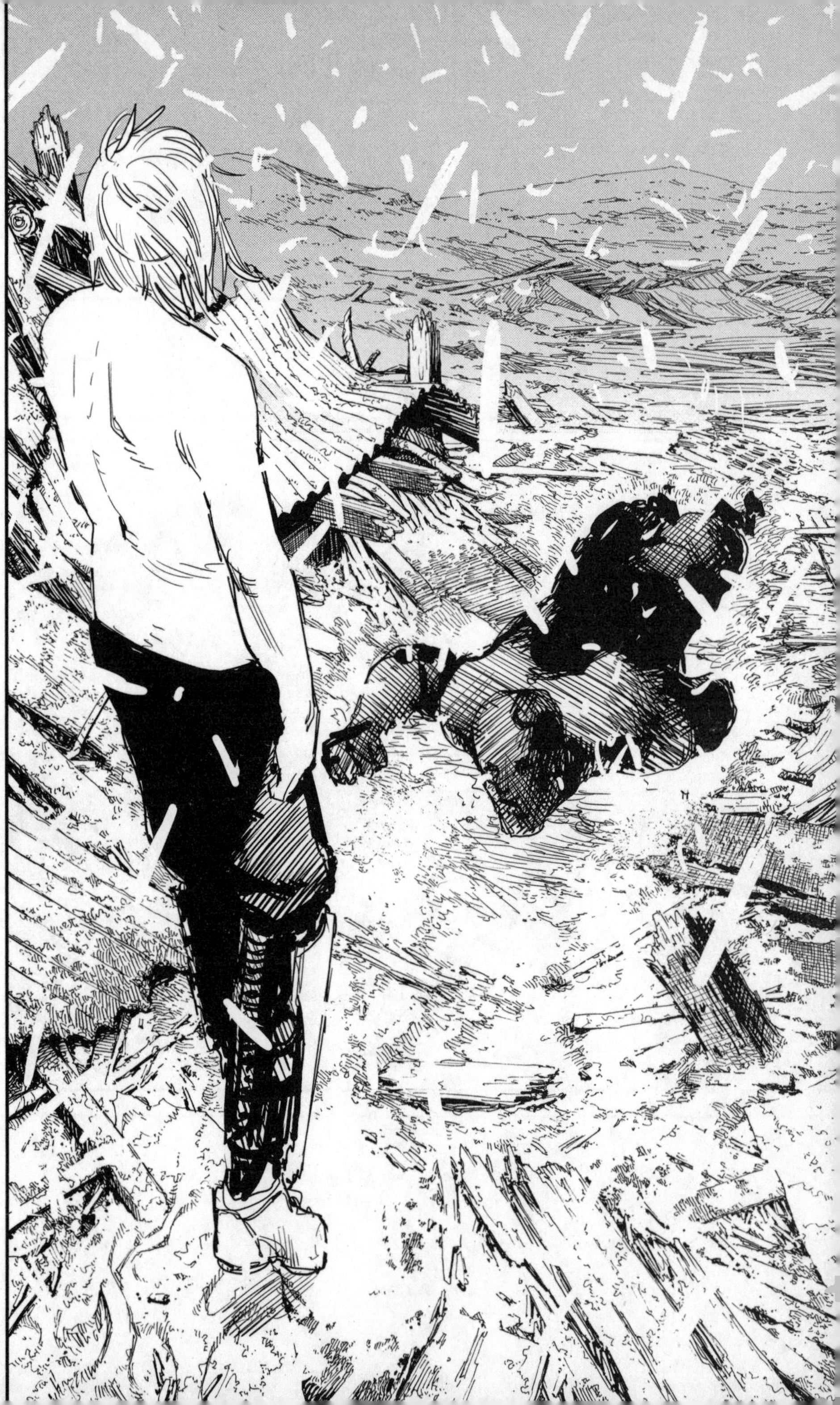

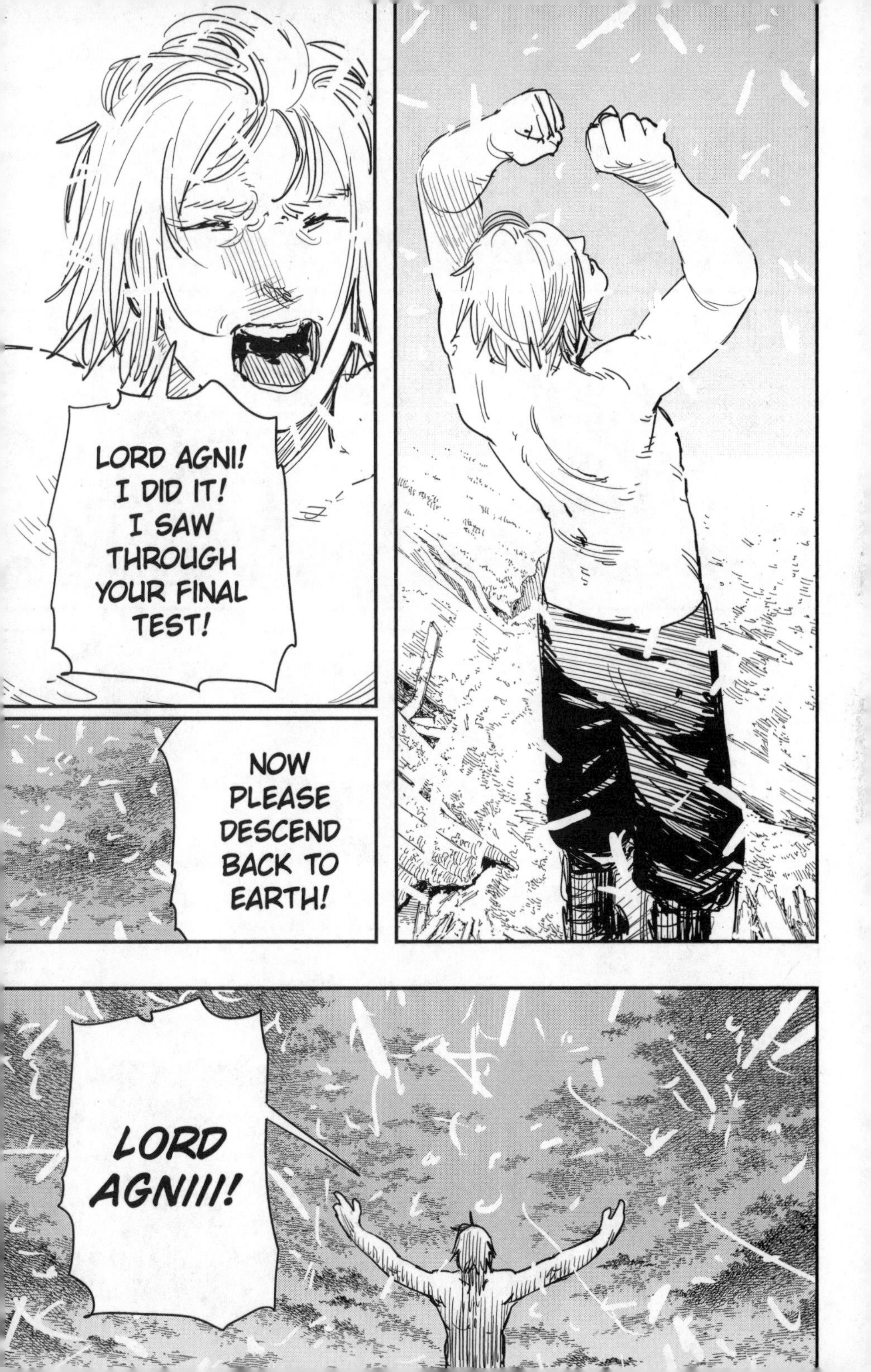
LORD AGNI! I DID IT! I SAW THROUGH YOUR FINAL TEST!
NOW PLEASE DESCEND BACK TO EARTH!
LORD AGNIII!

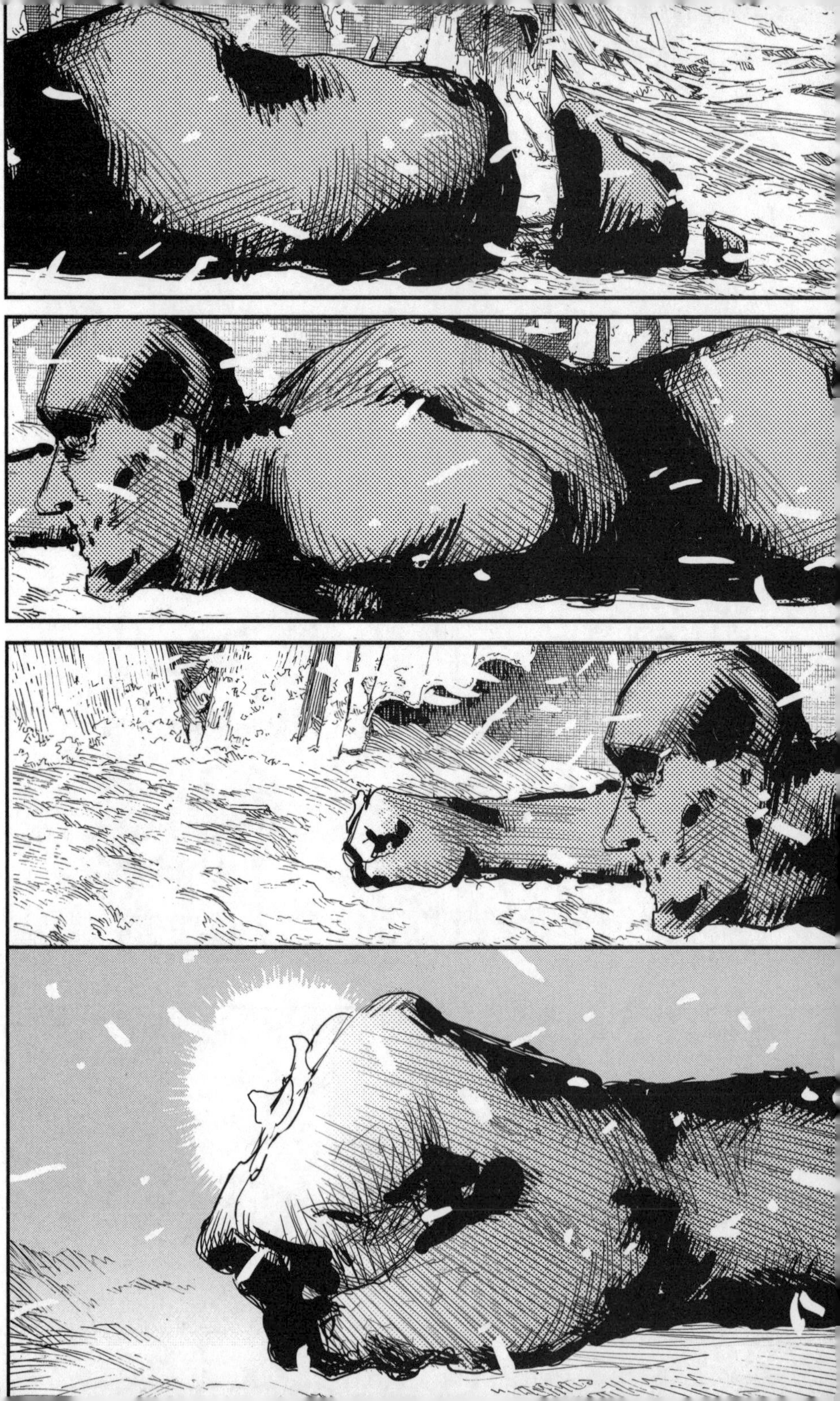

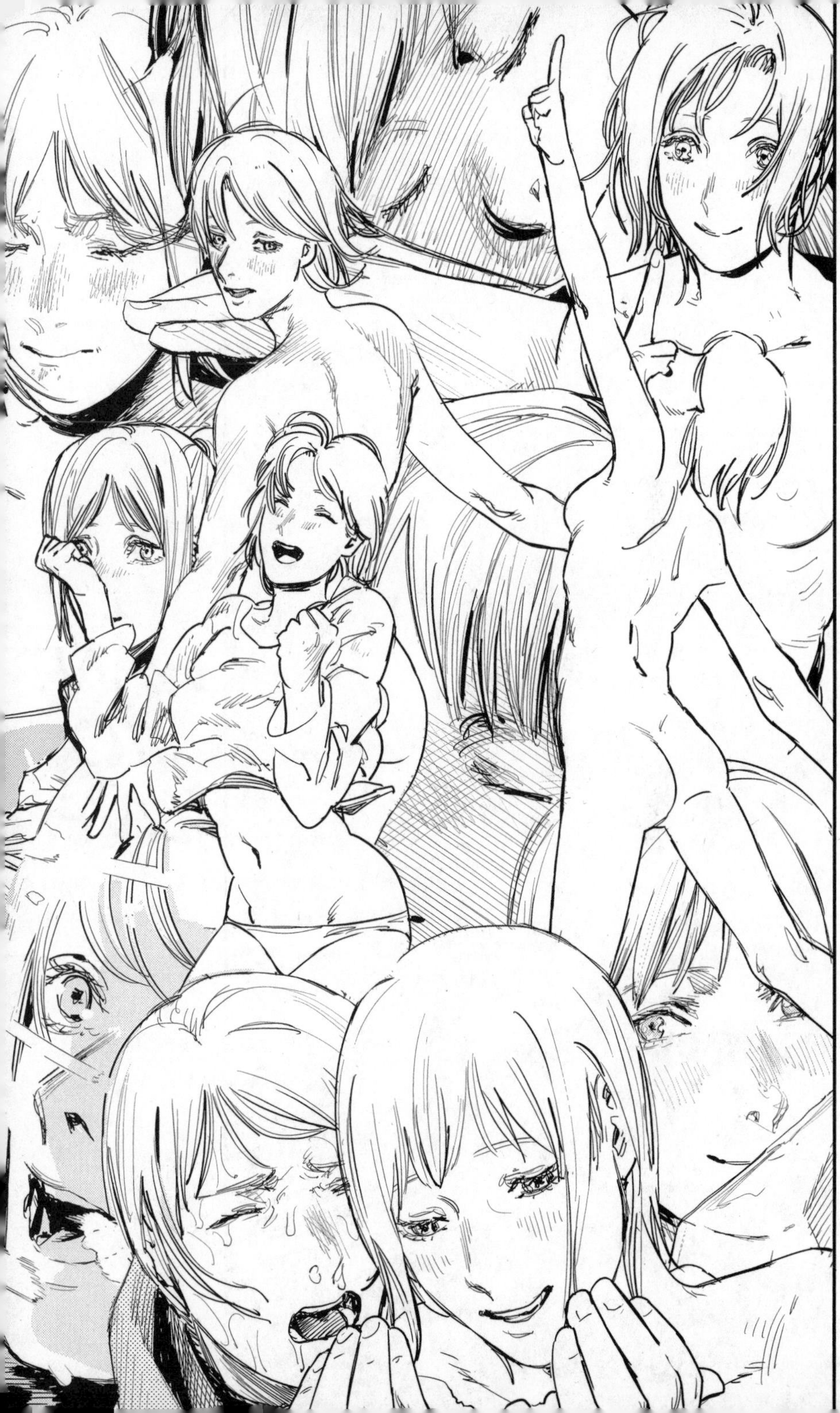

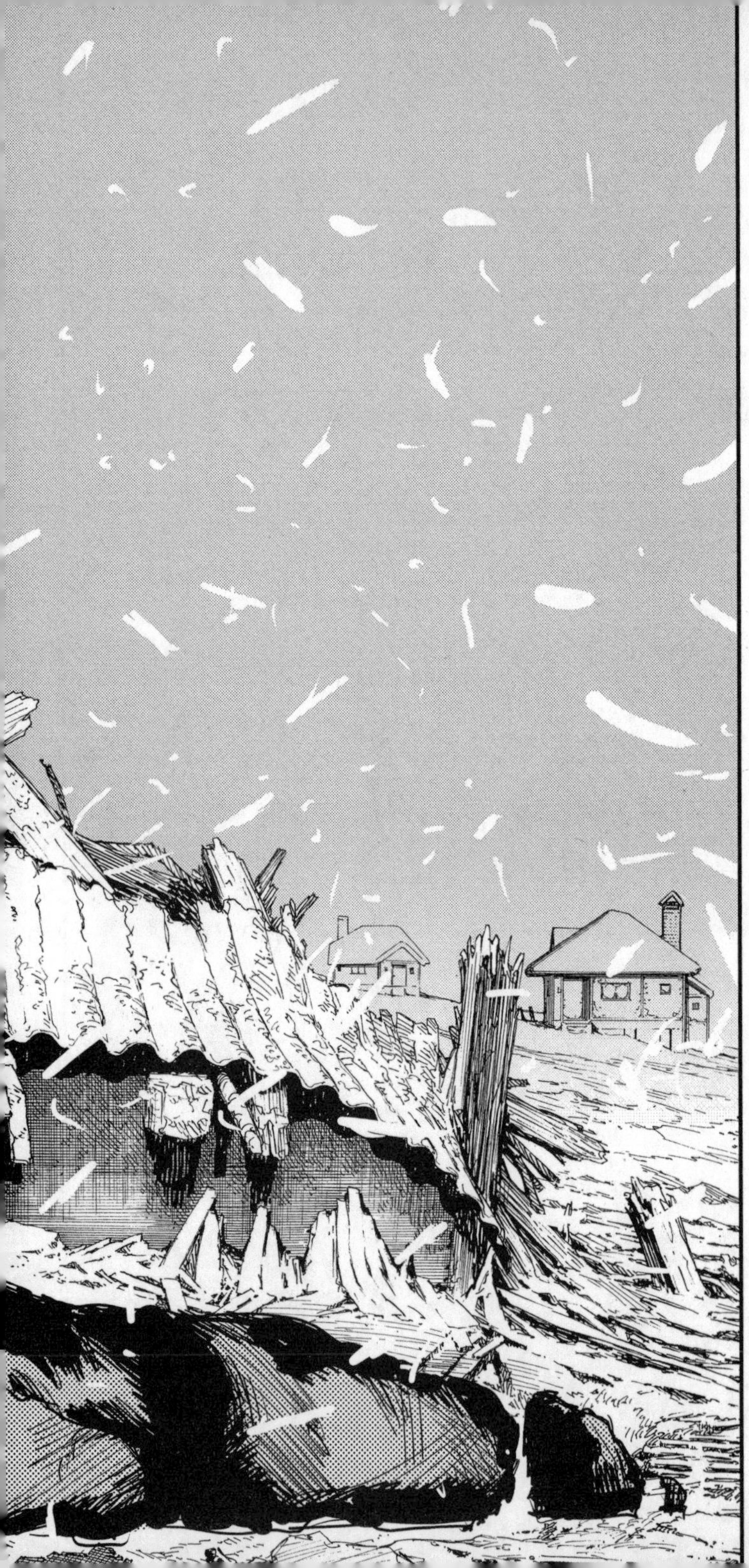

I WANT TO LIVE.

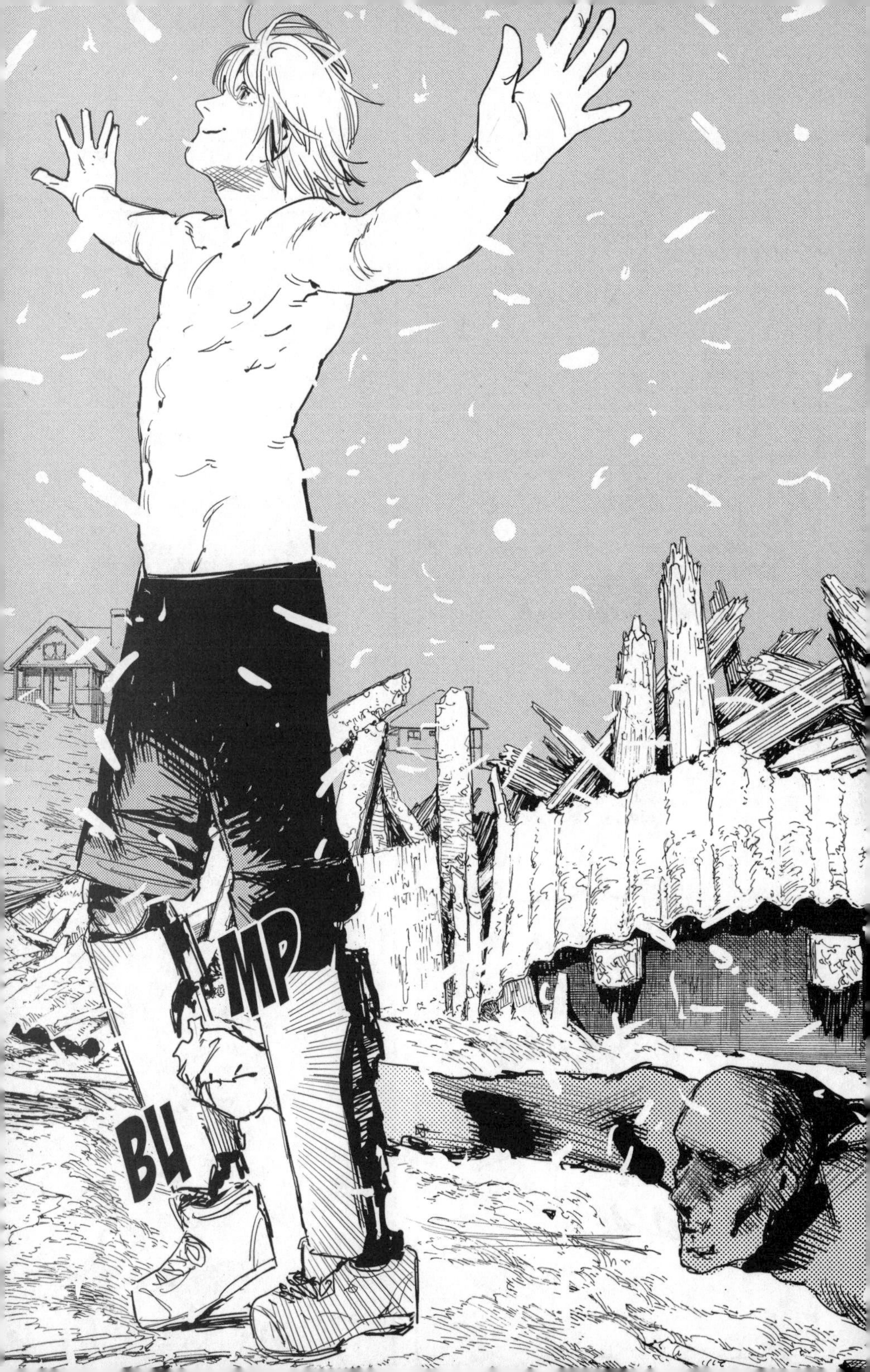
BUMP

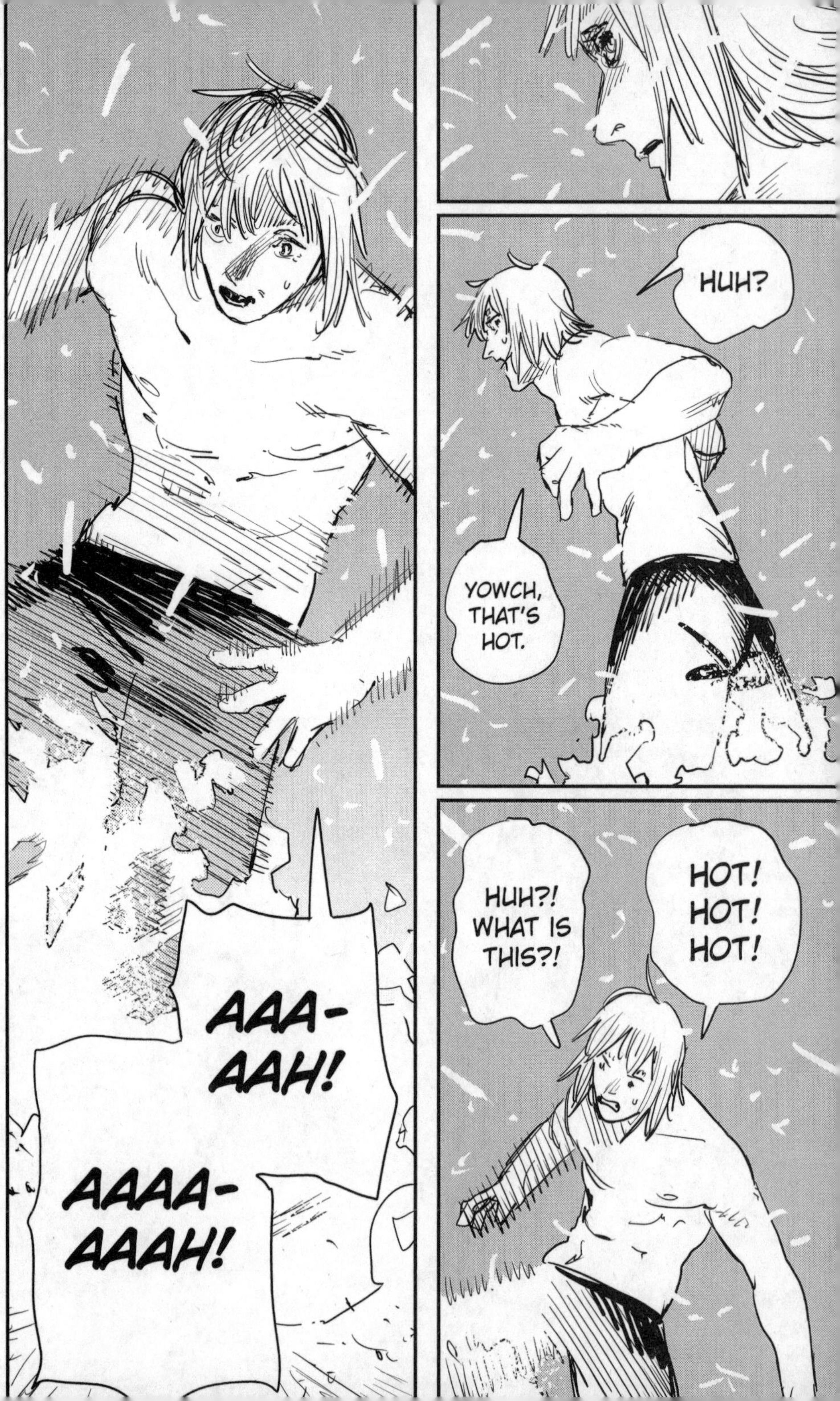
HUH?
YOWCH, THAT'S HOT.
HOT! HOT! HOT!
HUH?! WHAT IS THIS?!
AAA-AAH!
AAAA-AAAH!

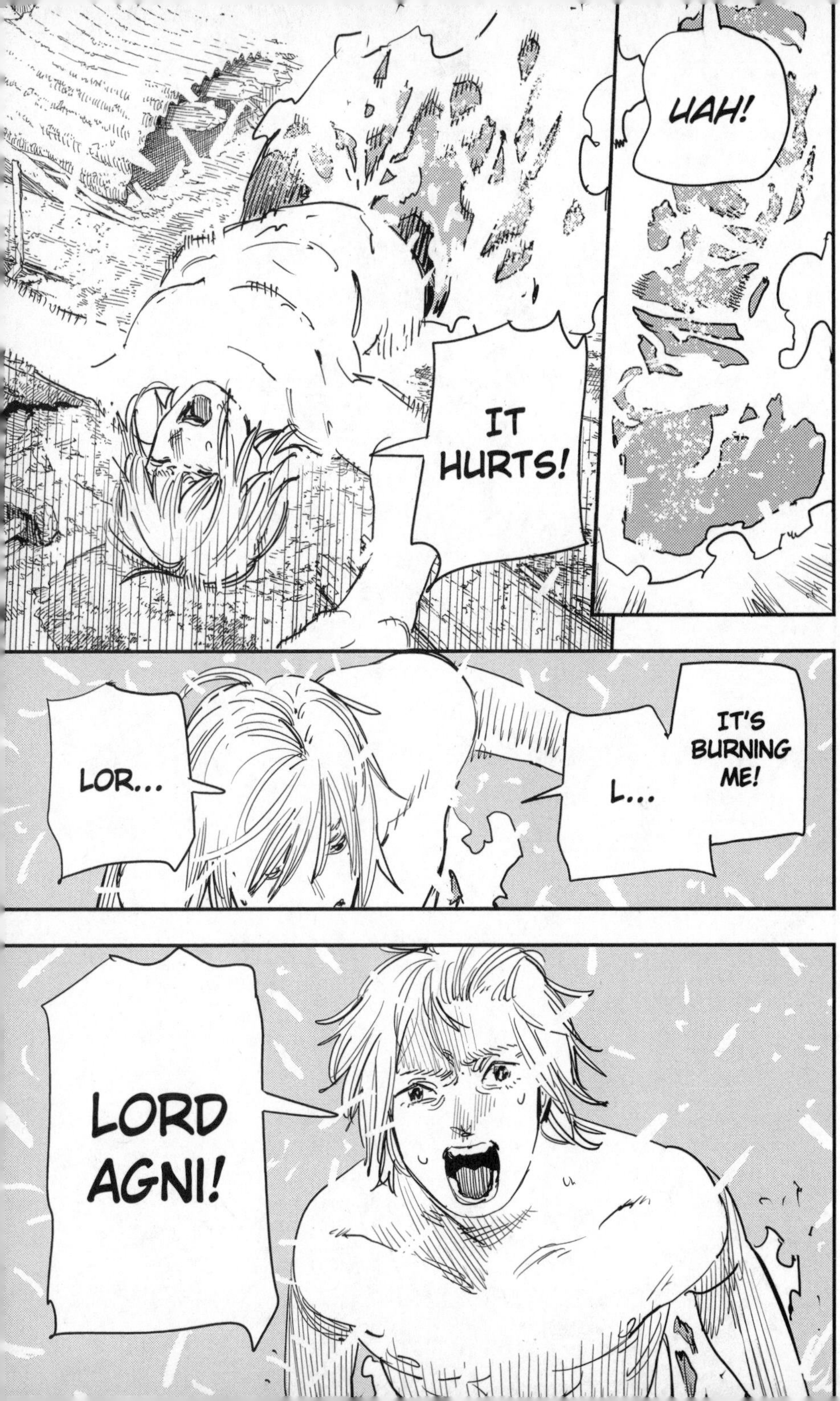
UAH!
IT HURTS!
IT'S BURNING ME!
L...
LOR...
LORD AGNI!

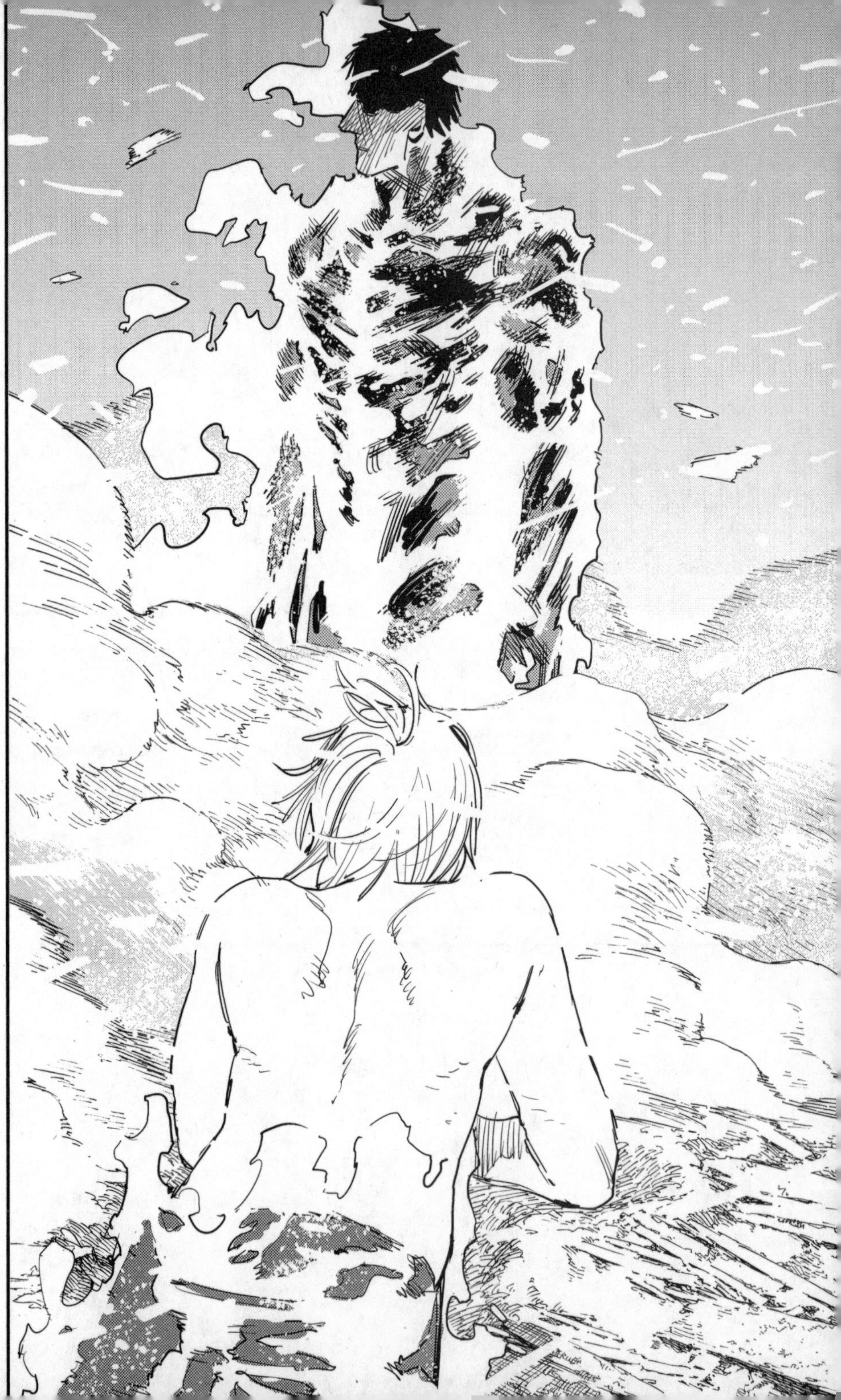

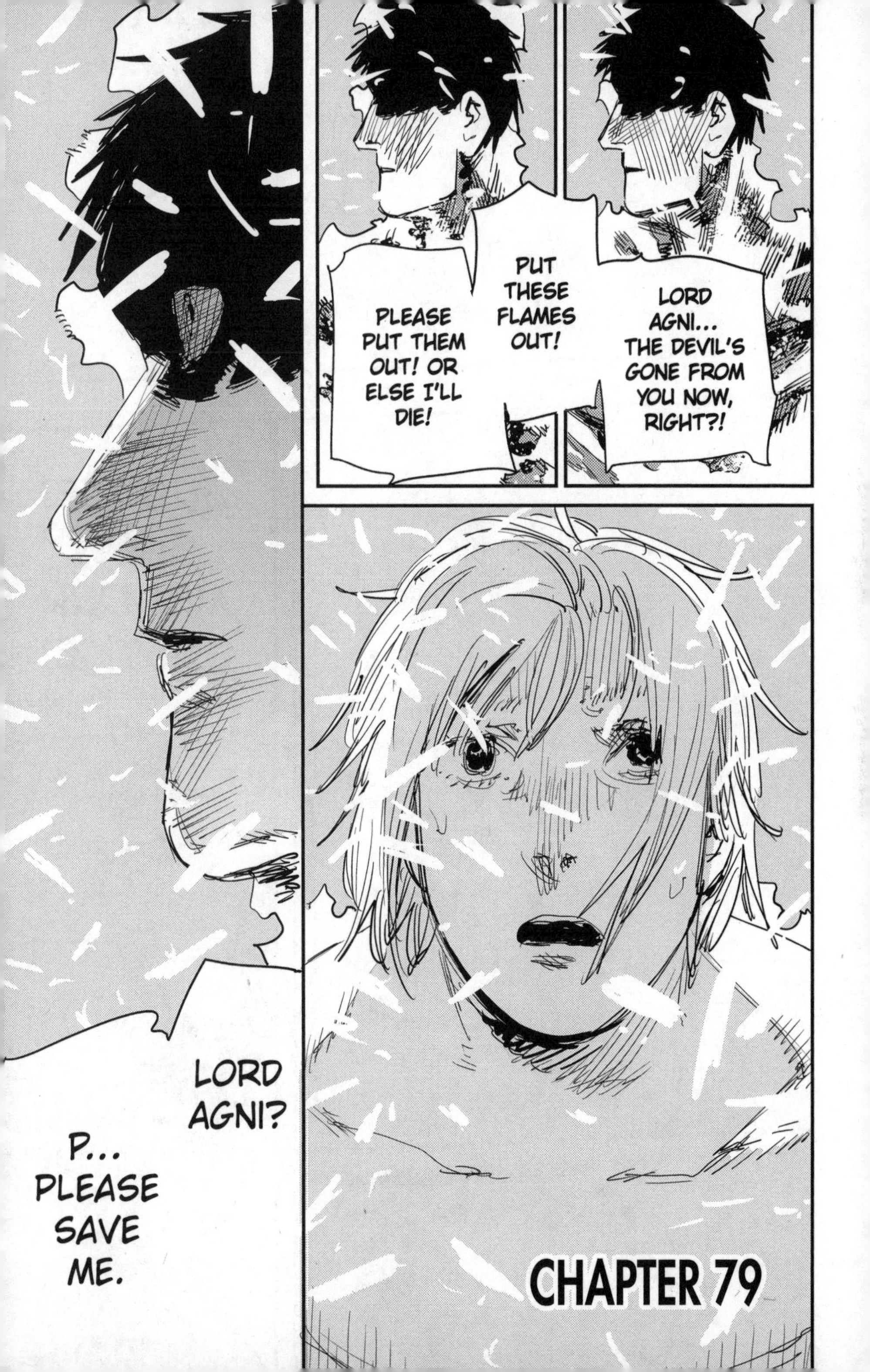
LORD AGNI... THE DEVIL'S GONE FROM YOU NOW, RIGHT?!
PUT THESE FLAMES OUT!
PLEASE PUT THEM OUT! OR ELSE I'LL DIE!
CHAPTER 79
LORD AGNI?
P... PLEASE SAVE ME.

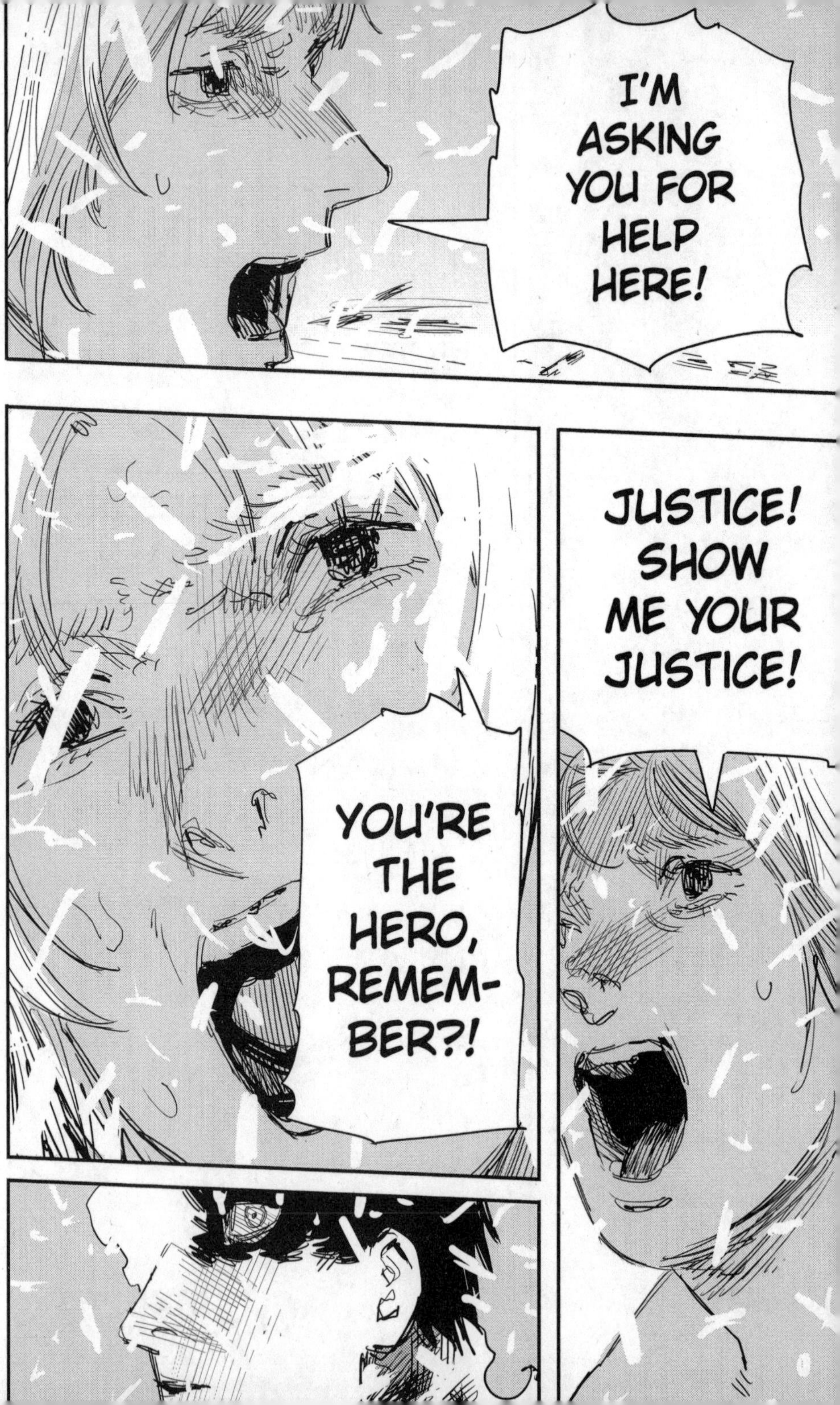
I'M ASKING YOU FOR HELP HERE!
JUSTICE! SHOW ME YOUR JUSTICE!
YOU'RE THE HERO, REMEM-BER?!

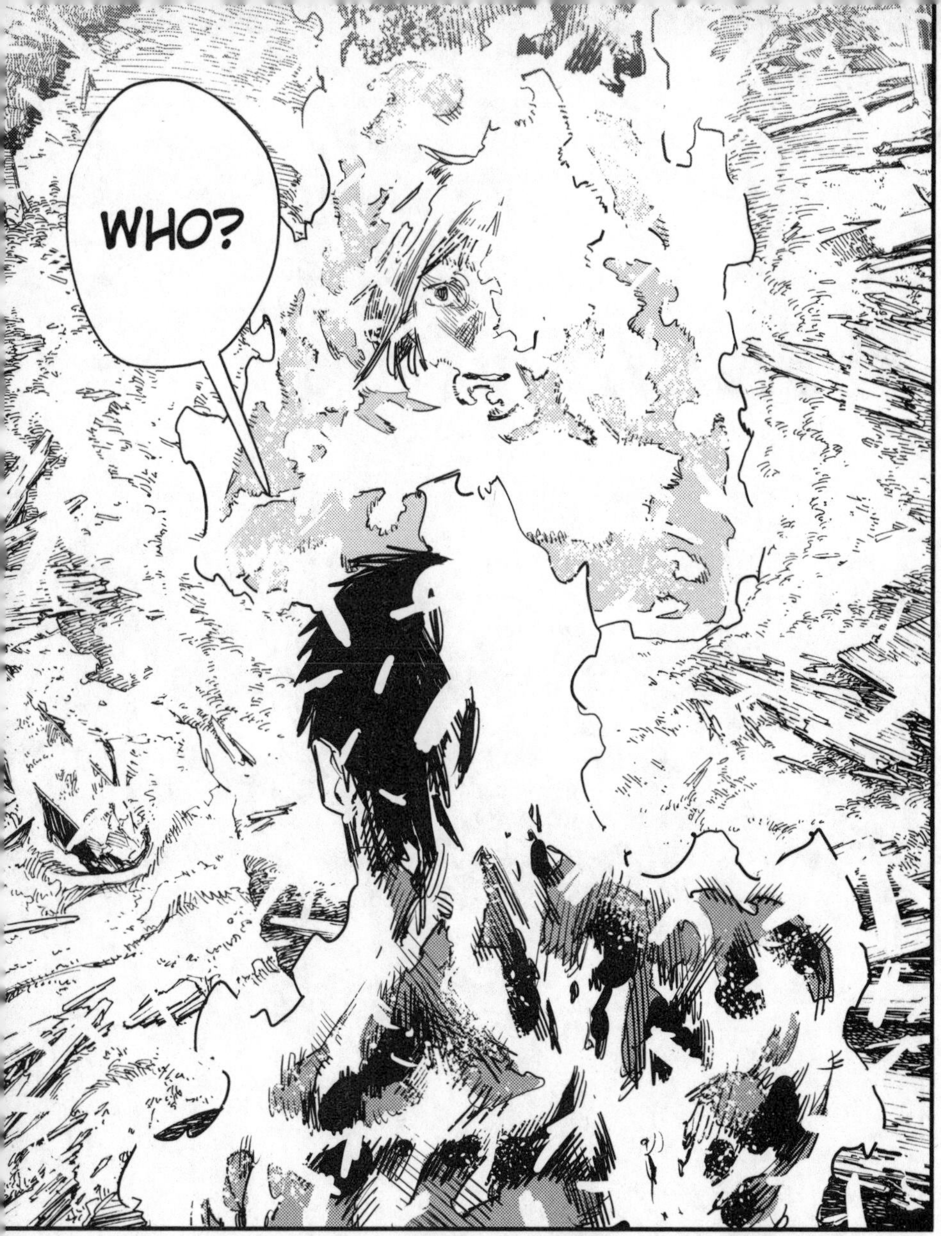
WHO?

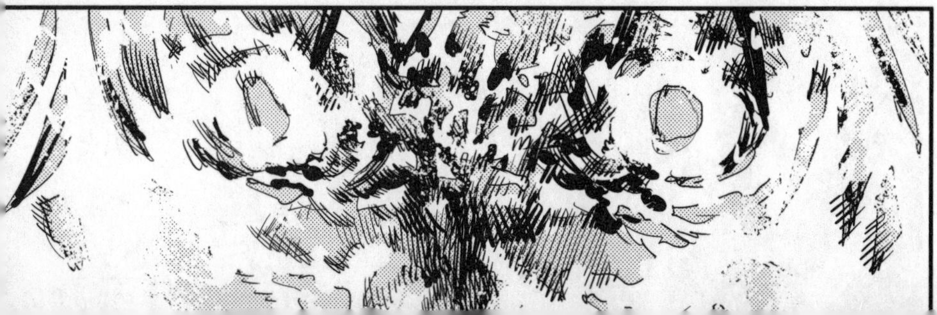

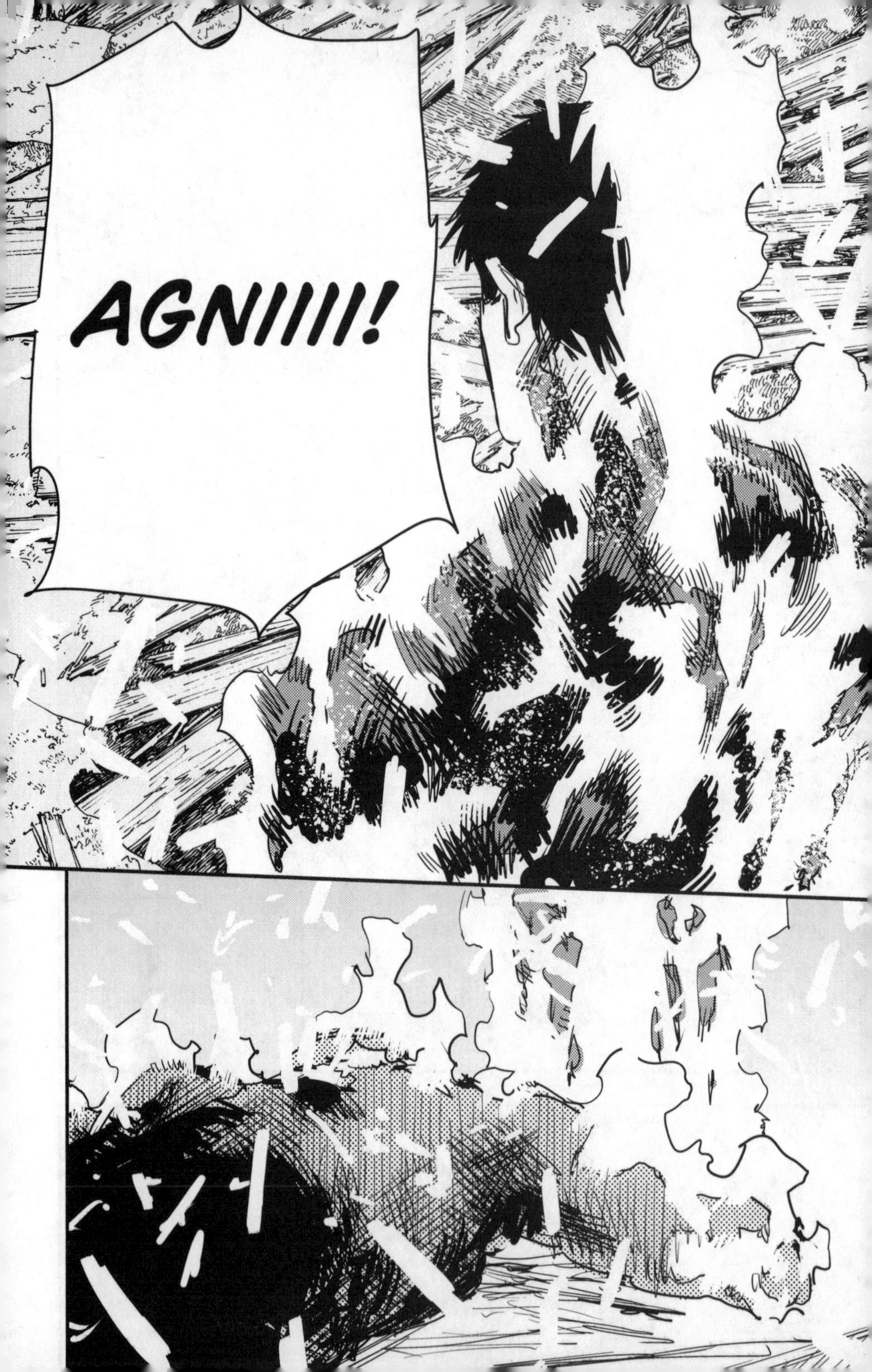
AGNIIIII!

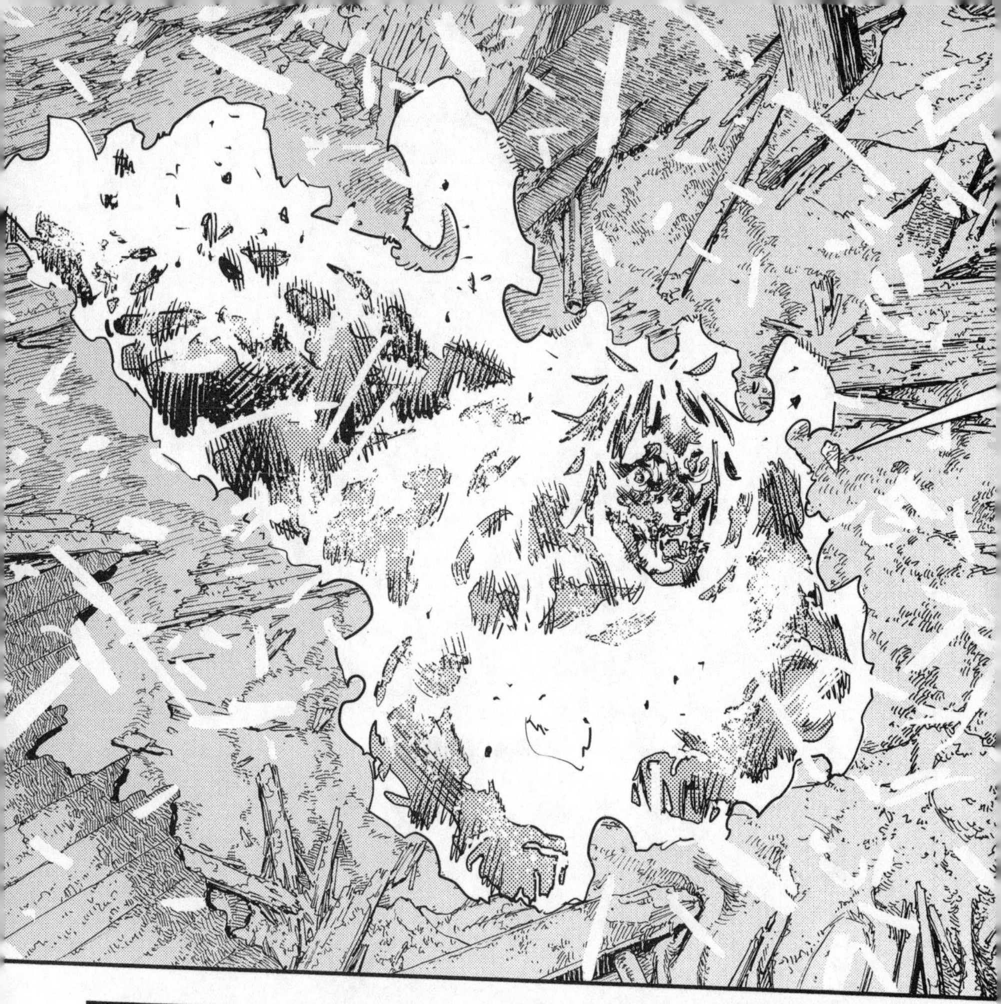
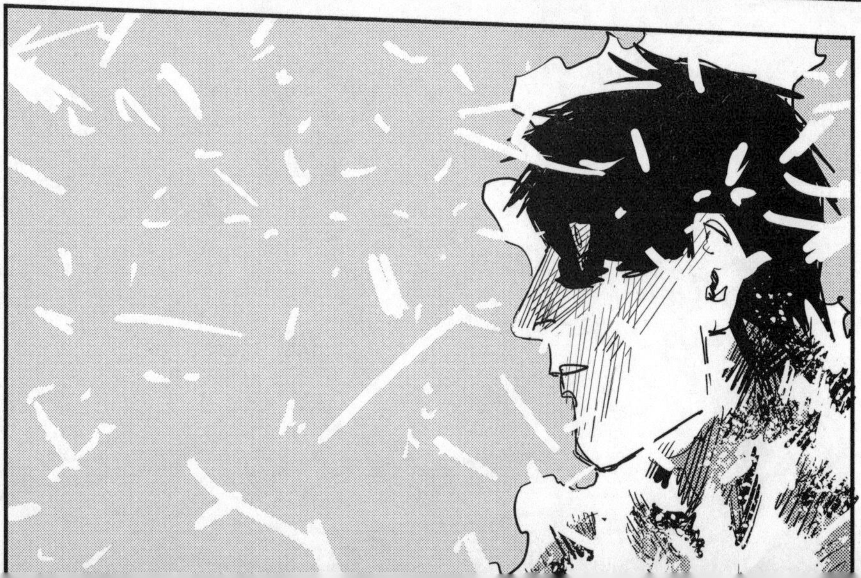

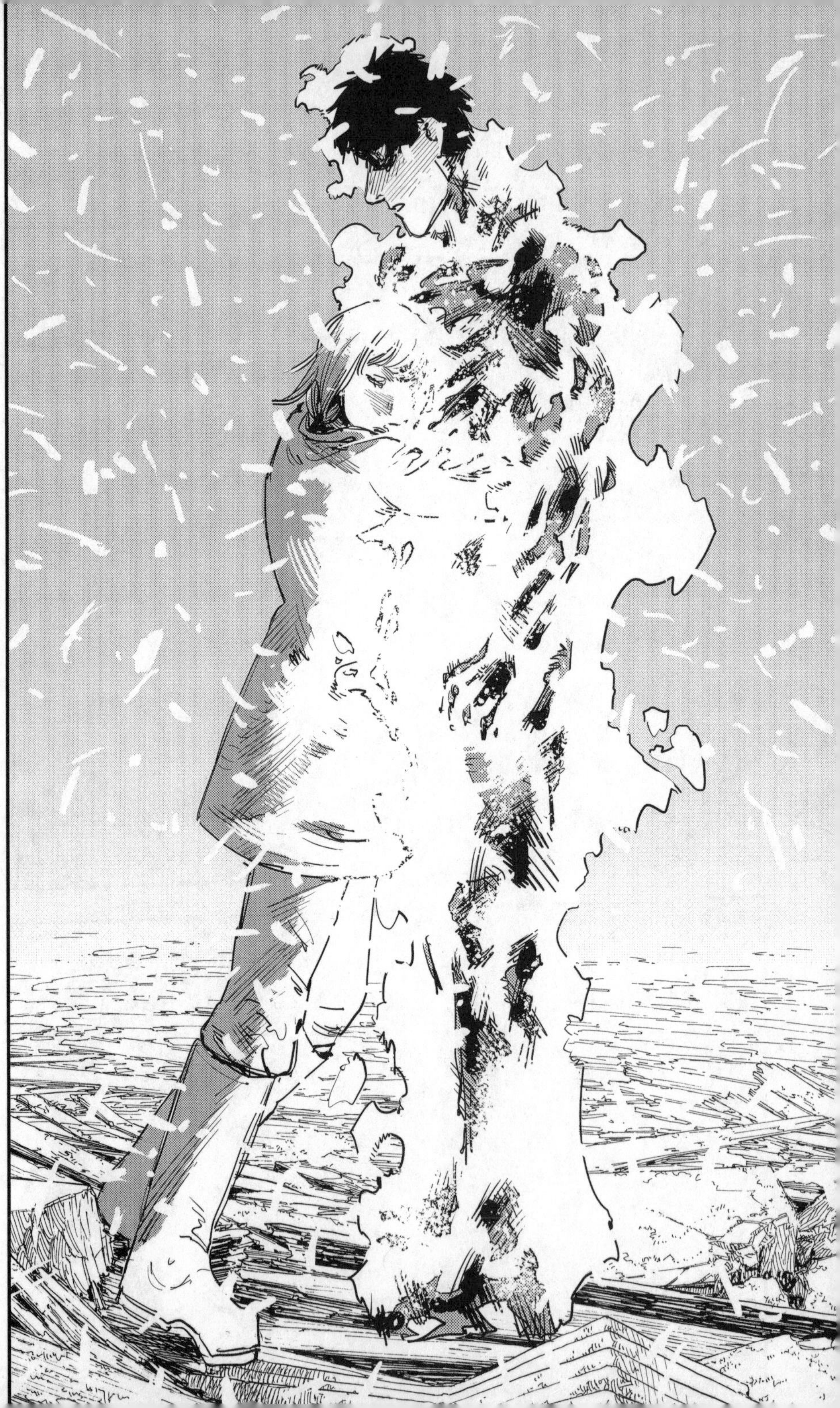

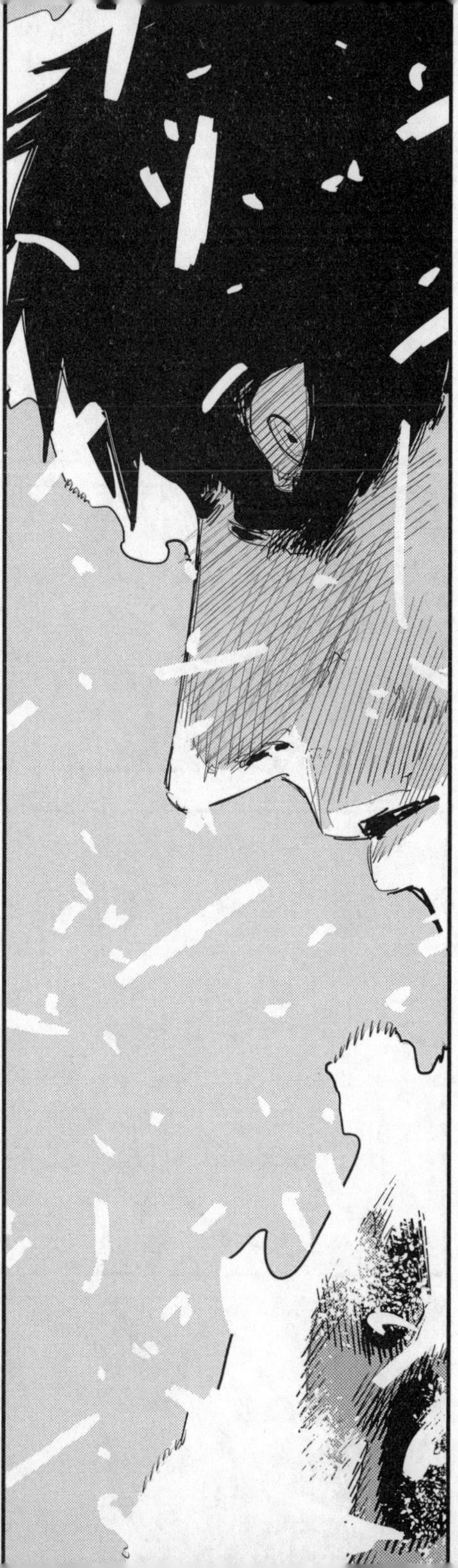
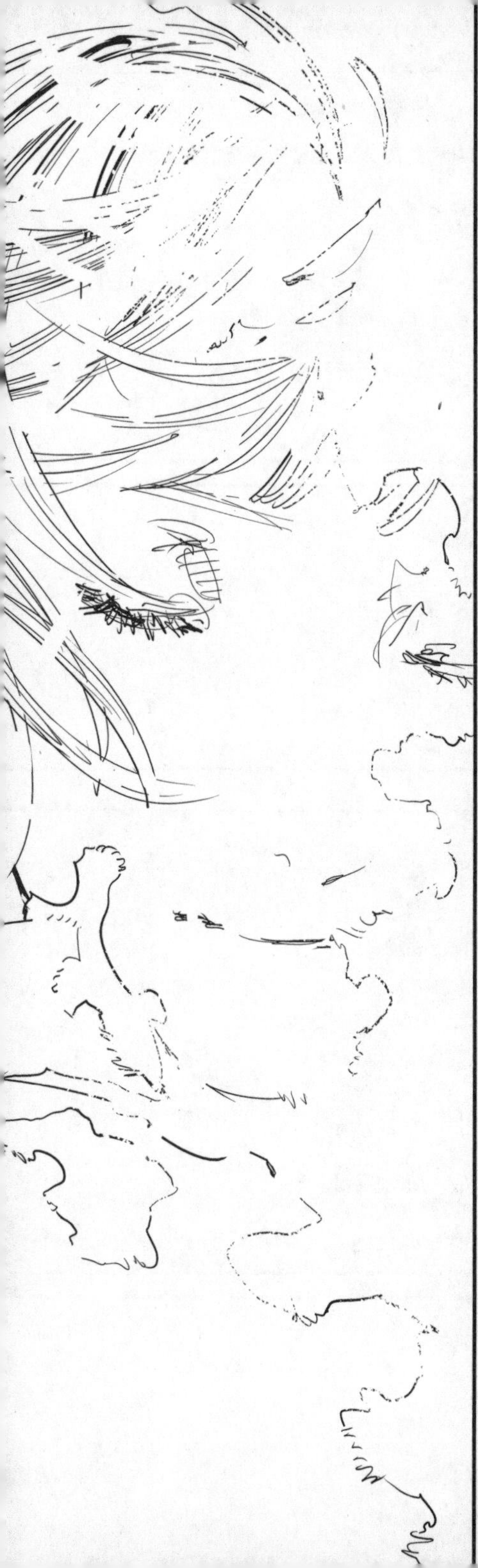

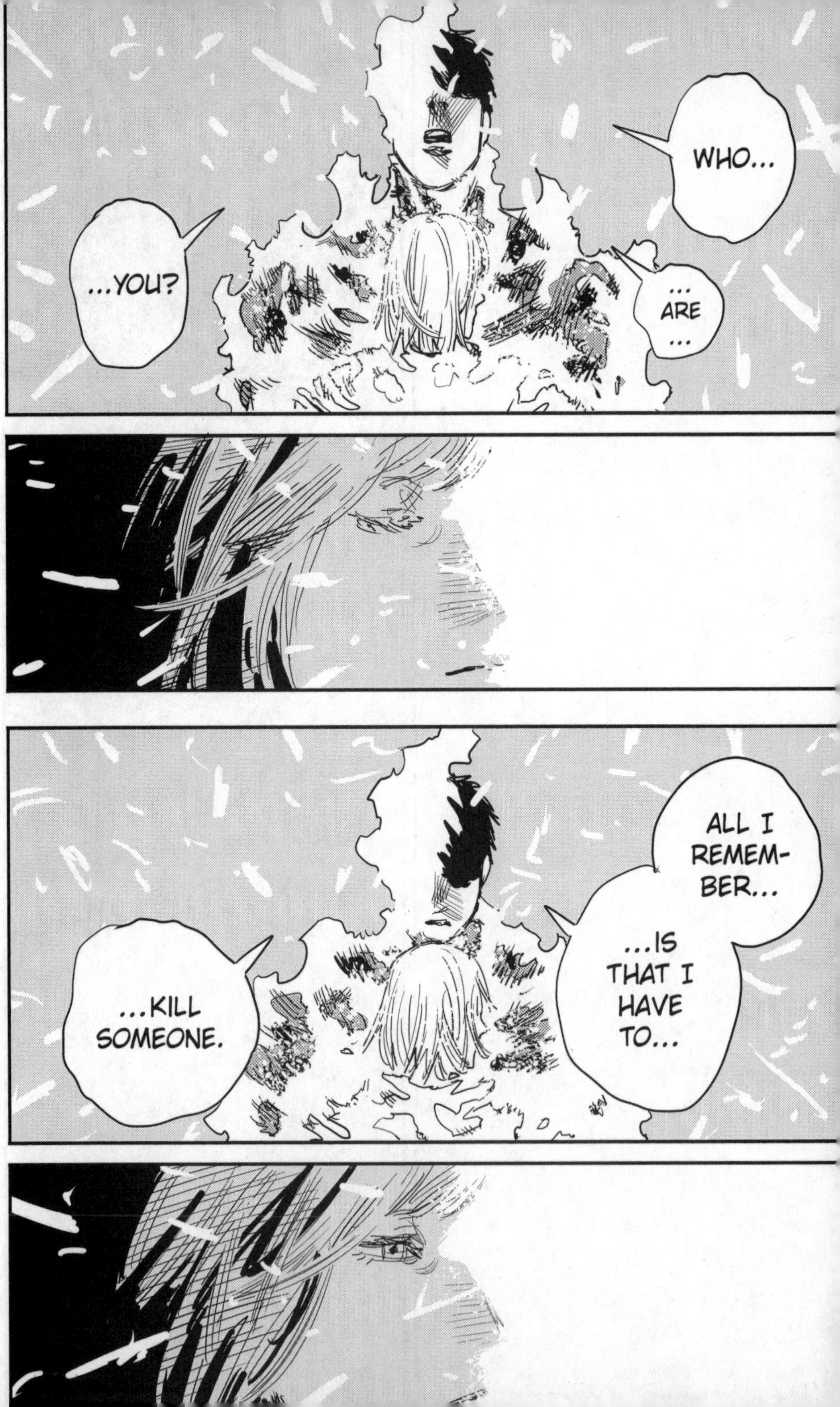
WHO...
...ARE...
...YOU?
ALL I REMEMBER...
...IS THAT I HAVE TO...
...KILL SOMEONE.

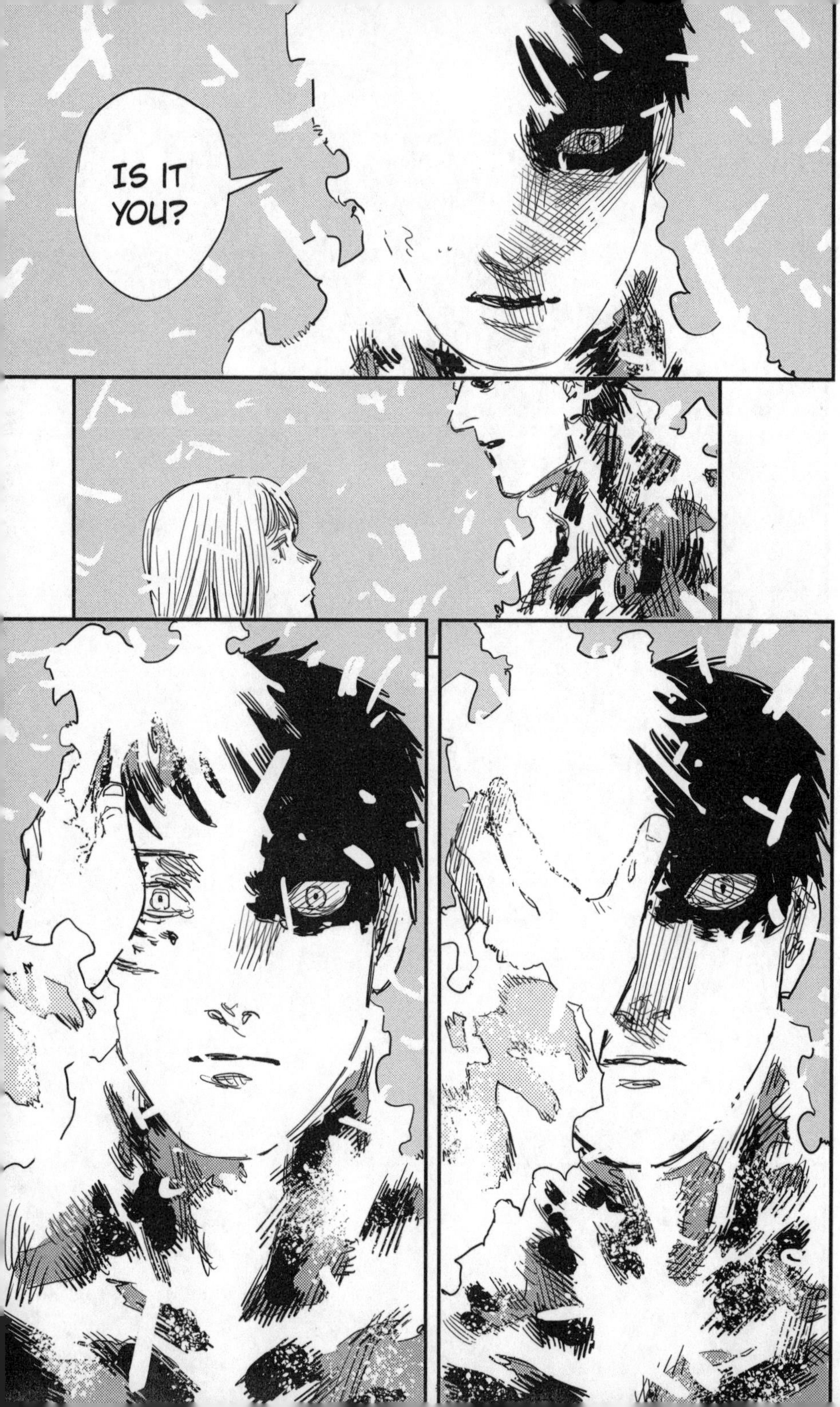
IS IT YOU?

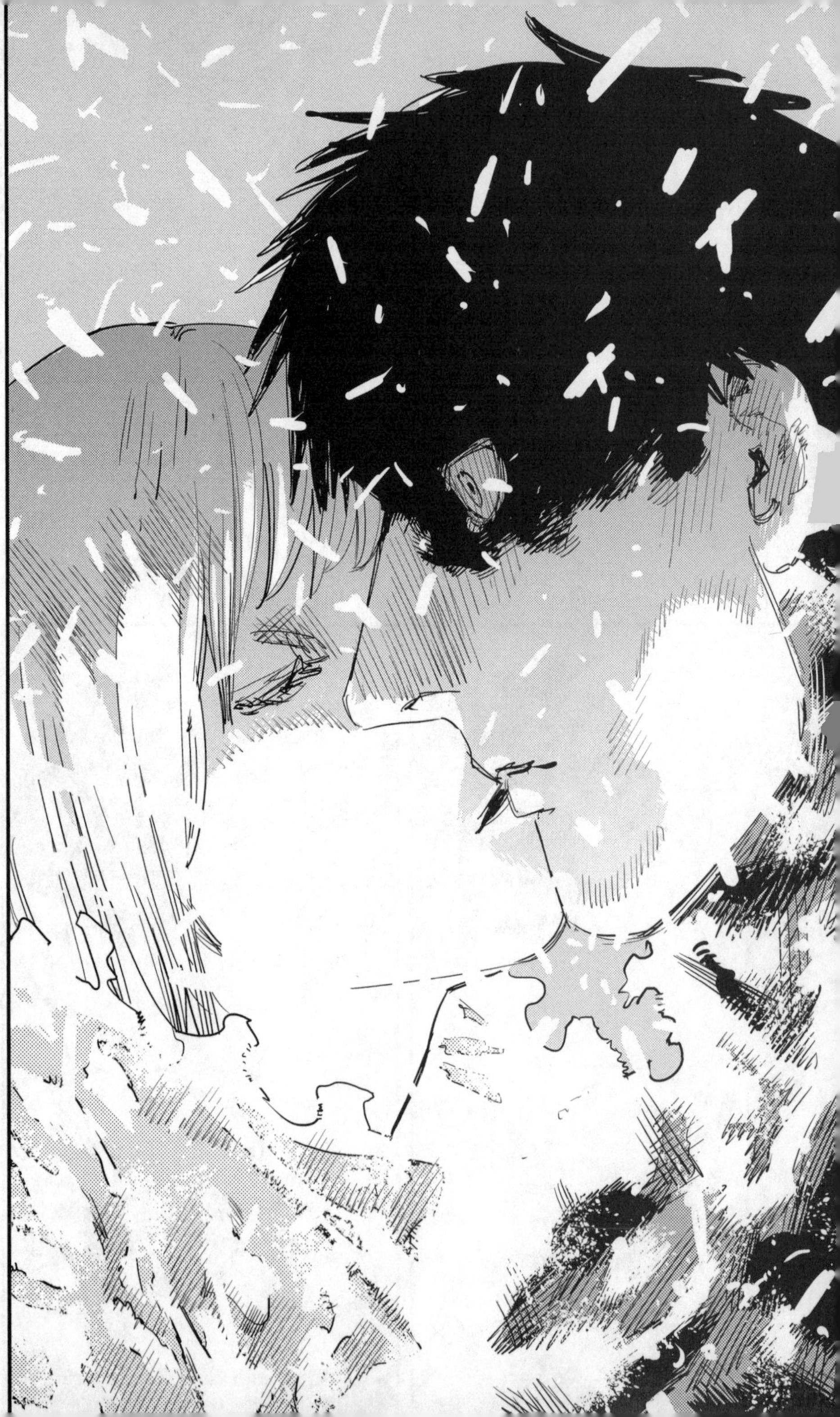

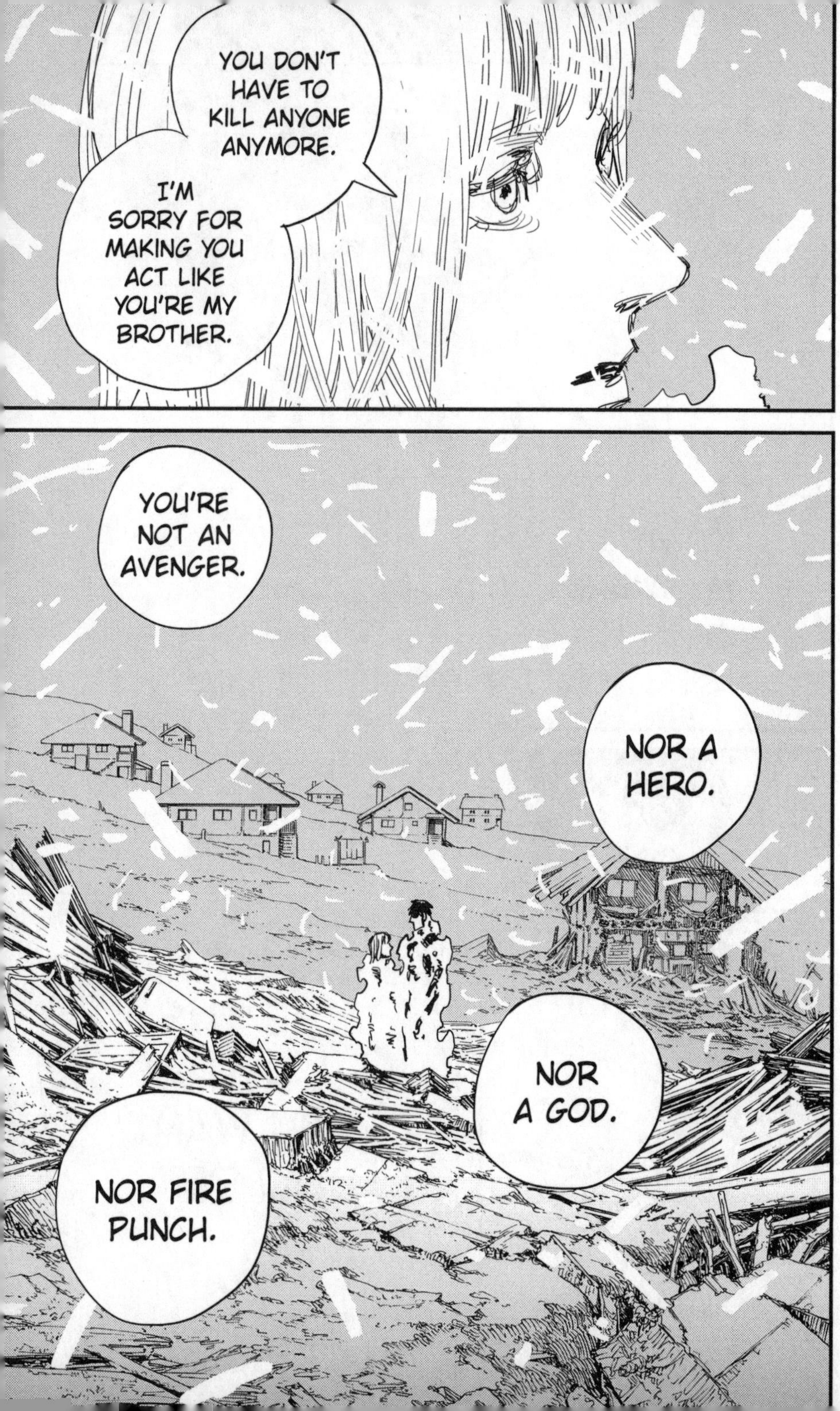
YOU DON'T HAVE TO KILL ANYONE ANYMORE.
I'M SORRY FOR MAKING YOU ACT LIKE YOU'RE MY BROTHER.
YOU'RE NOT AN AVENGER.
NOR A HERO.
NOR A GOD.
NOR FIRE PUNCH.

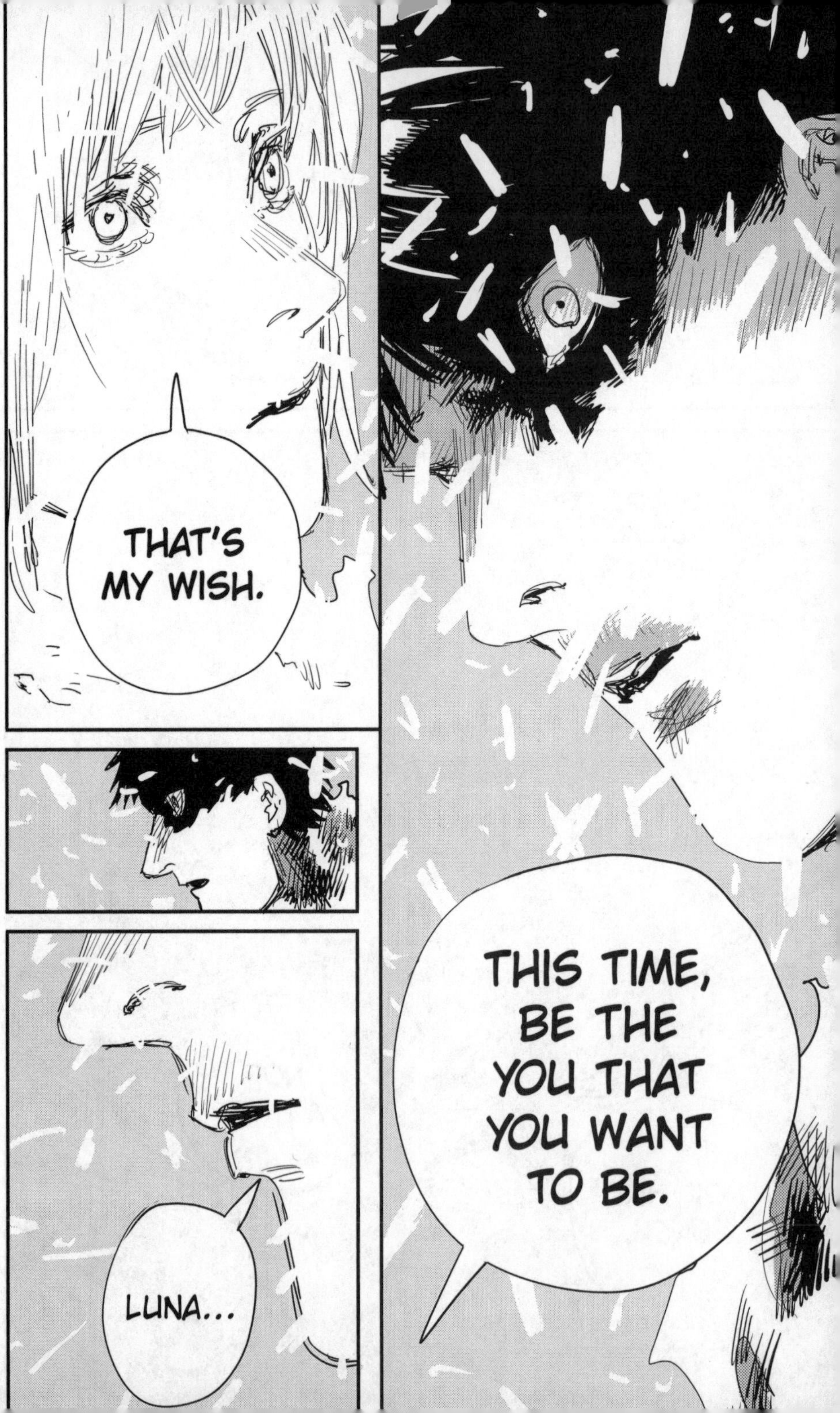
THIS TIME, BE THE YOU THAT YOU WANT TO BE.
THAT'S MY WISH.
LUNA...

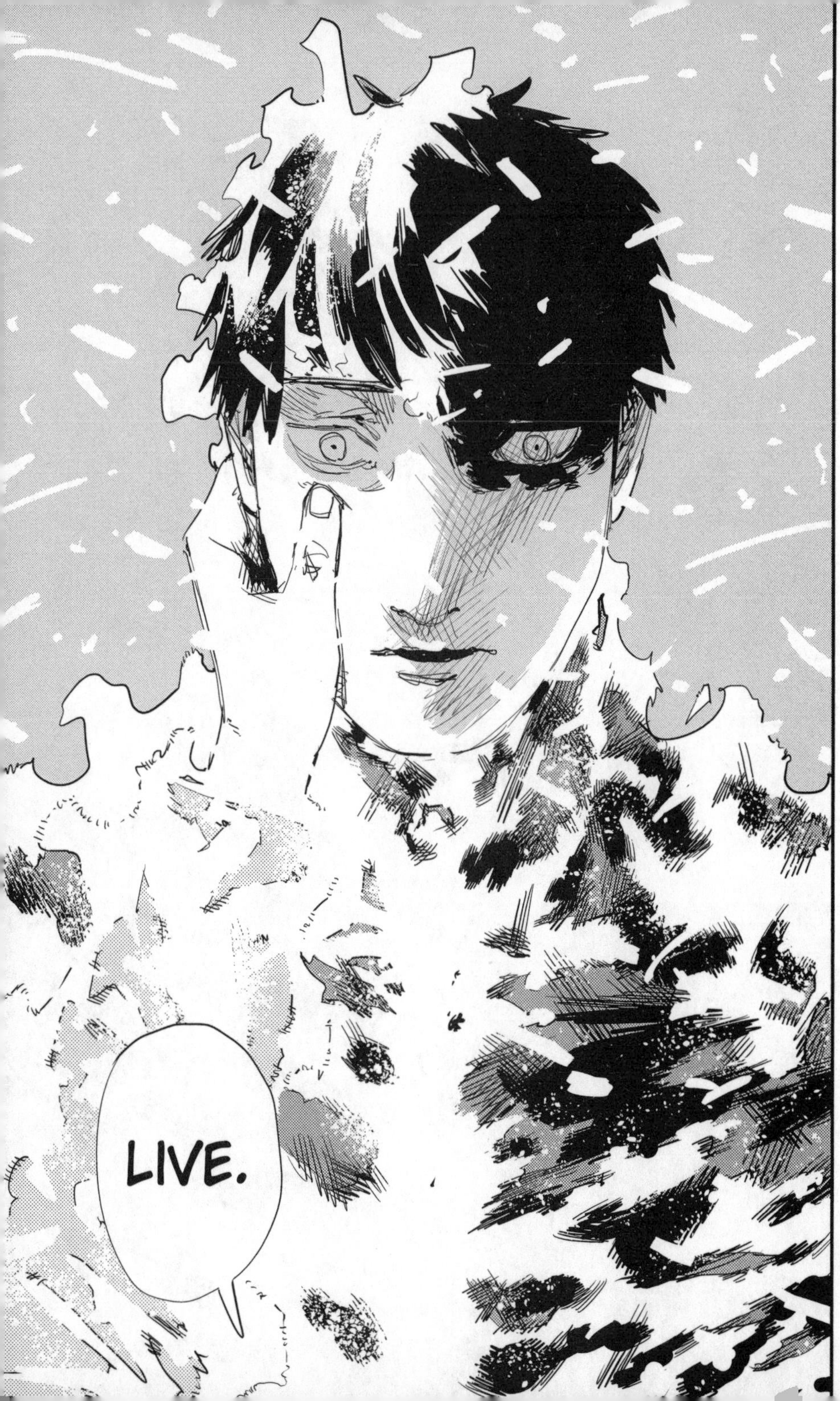
LIVE.

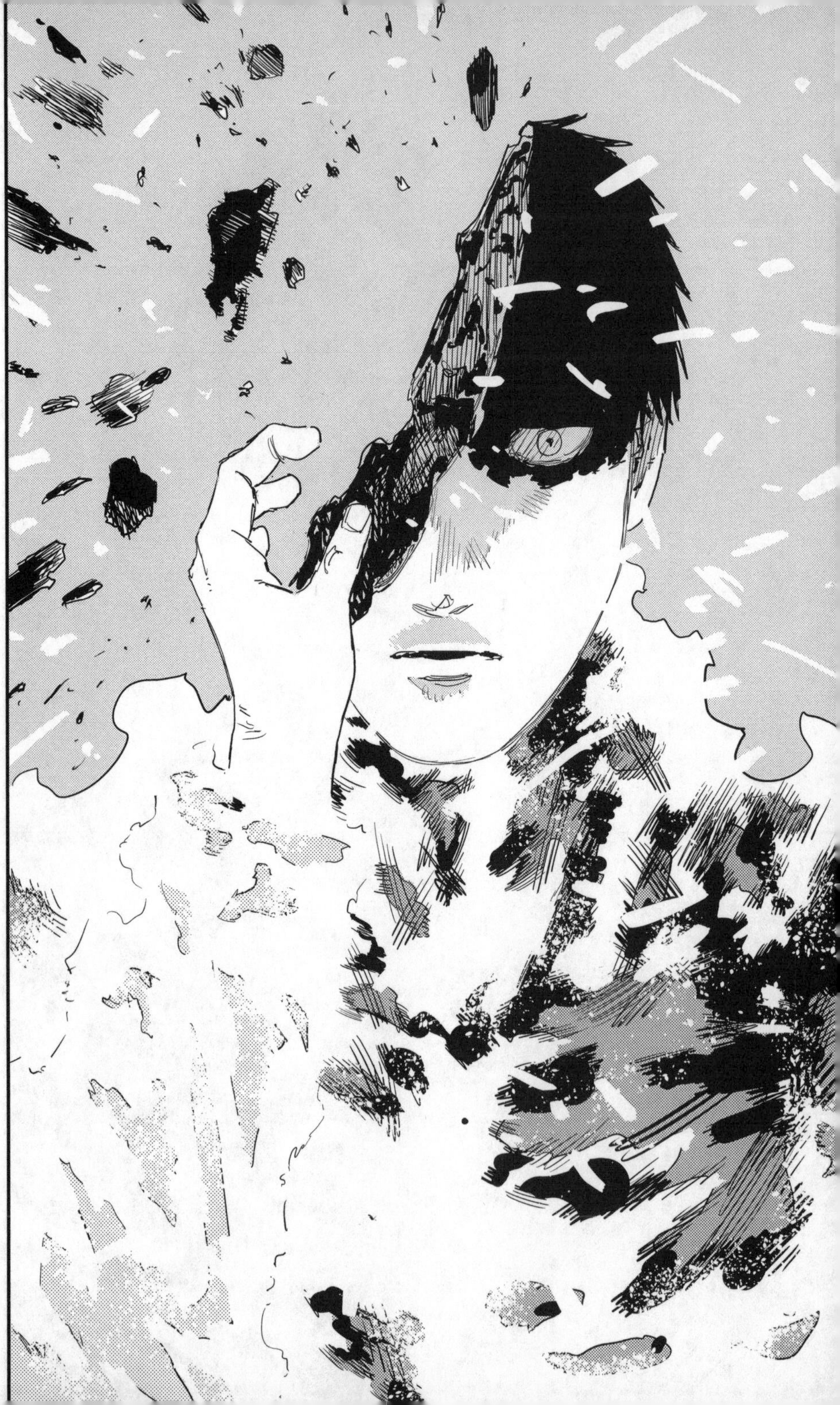

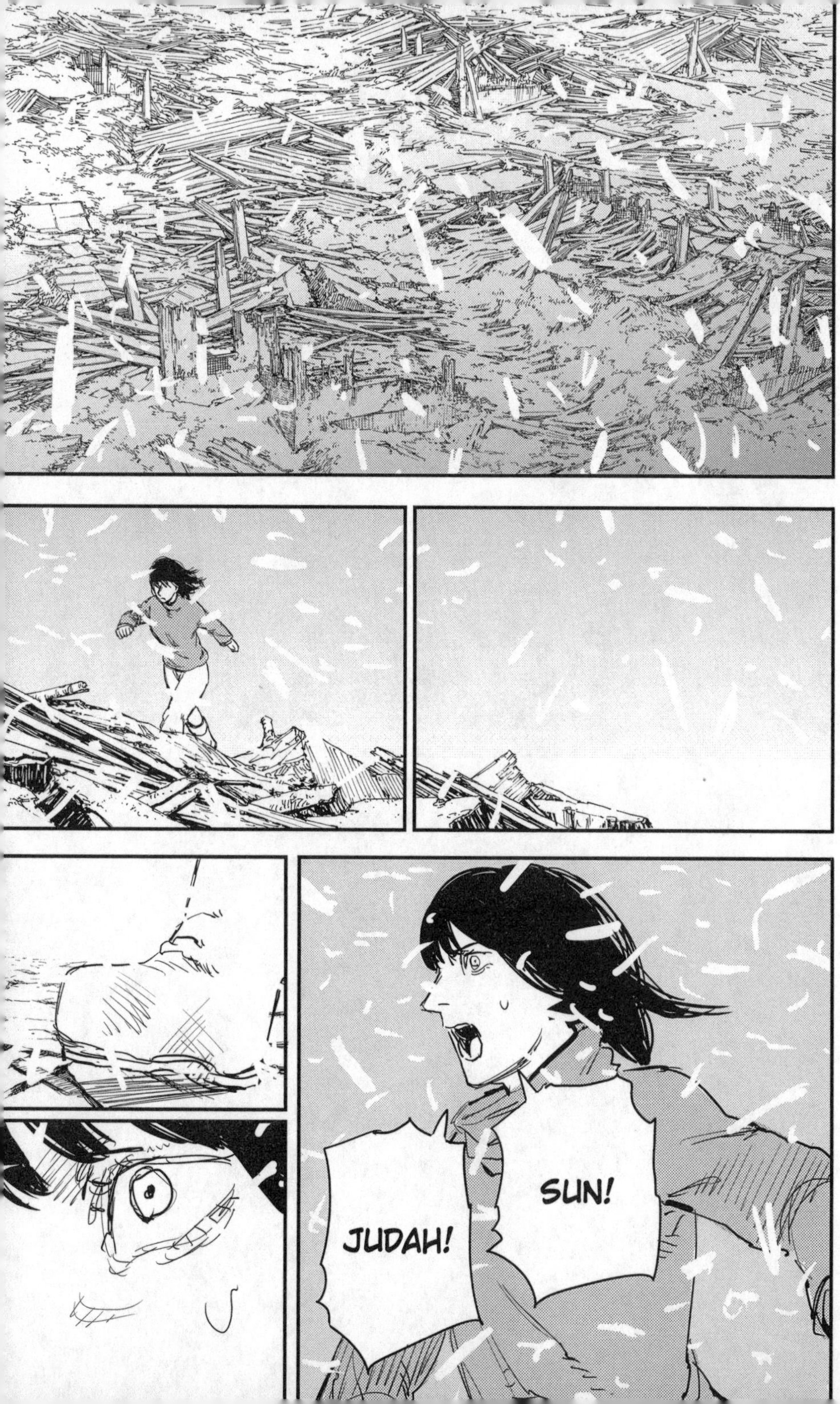
SUN!
JUDAH!

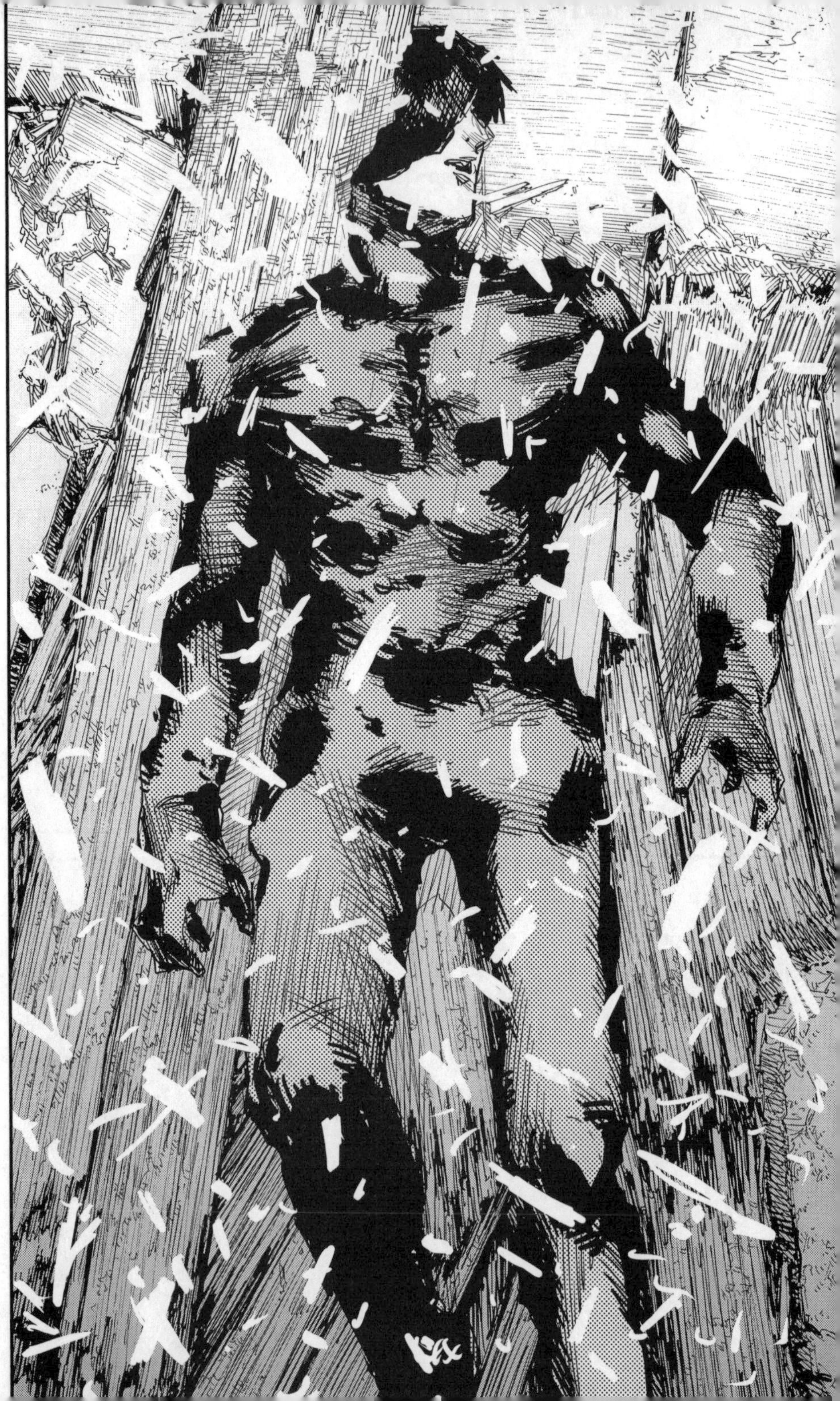

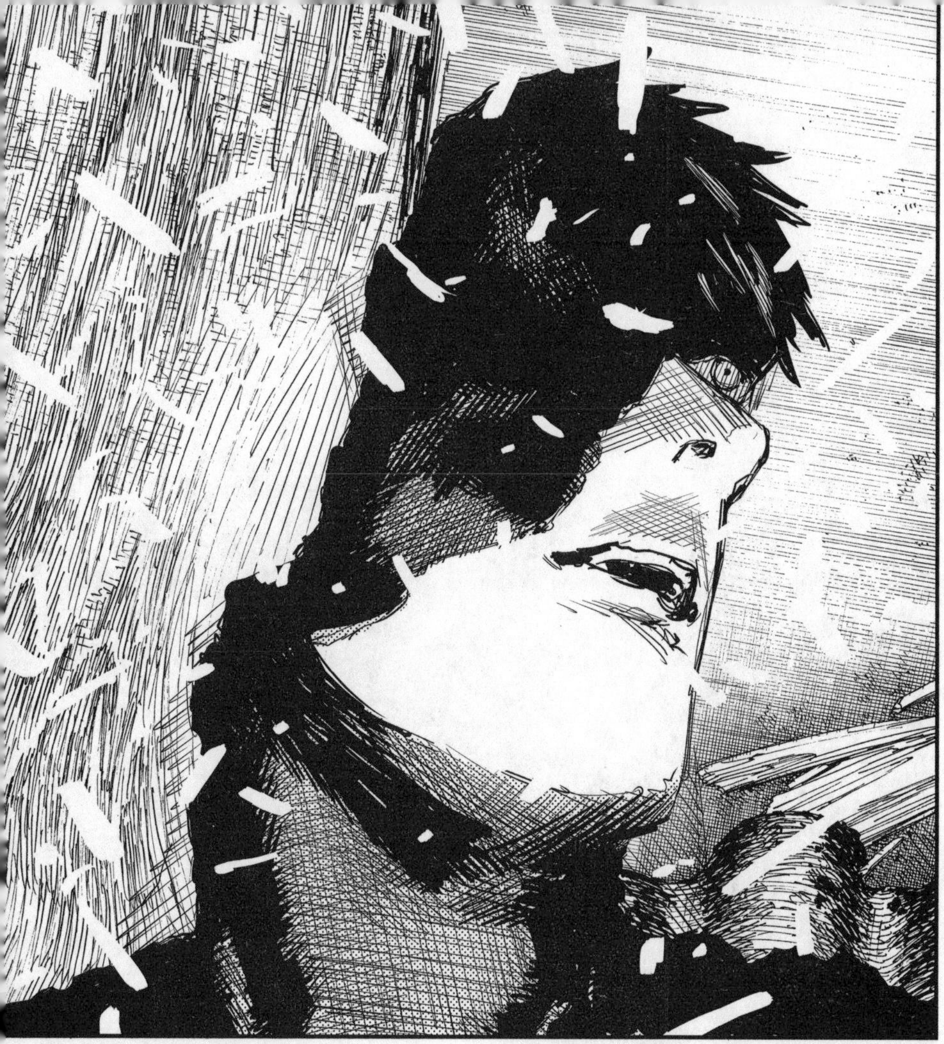
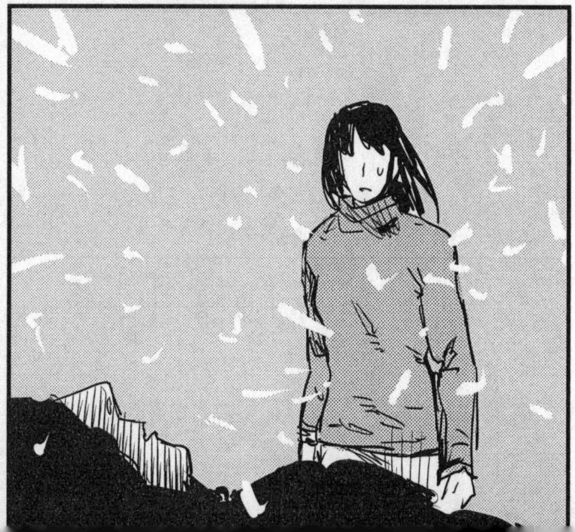
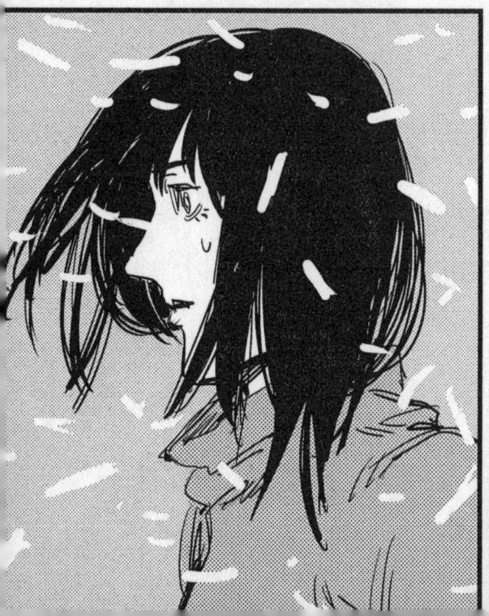

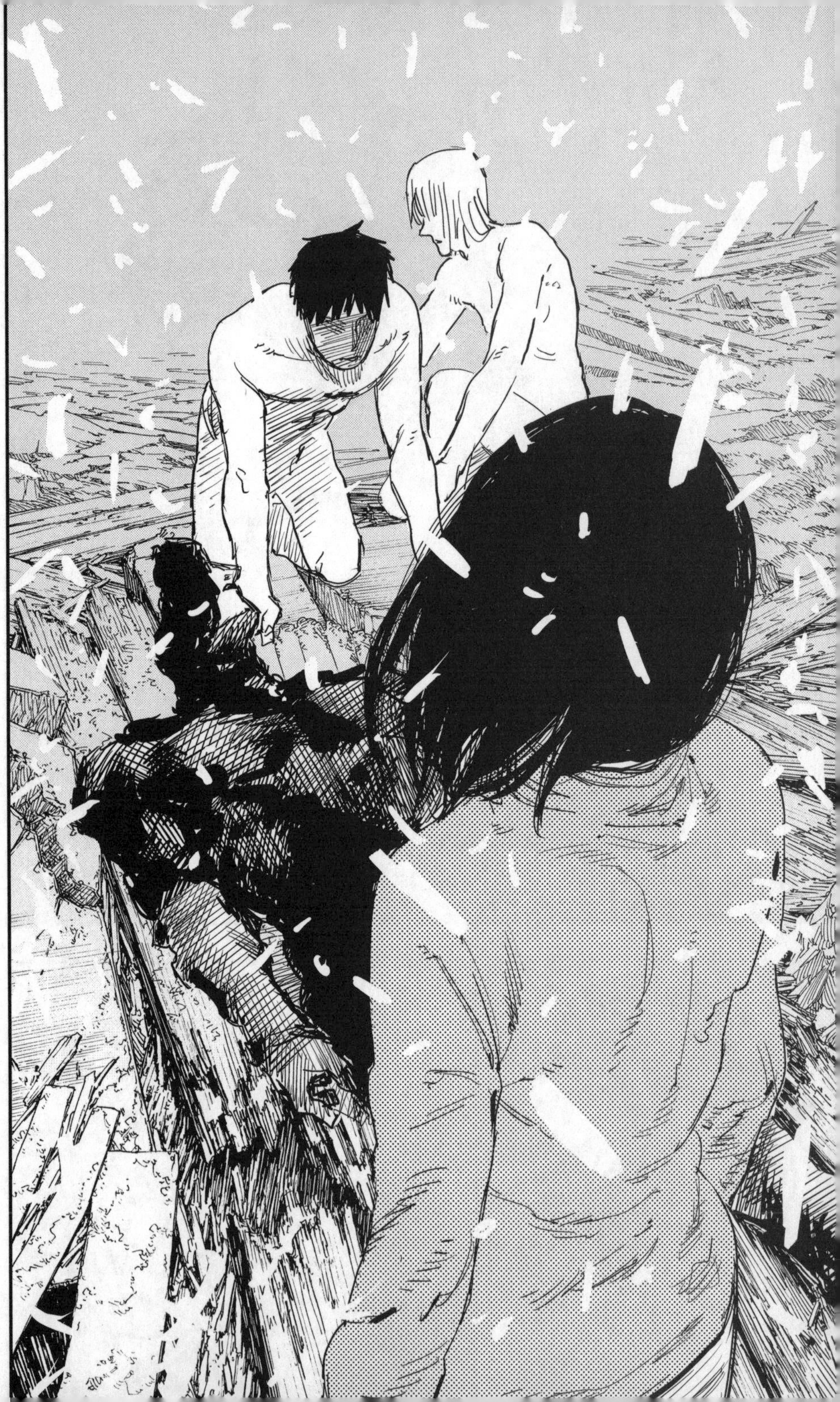

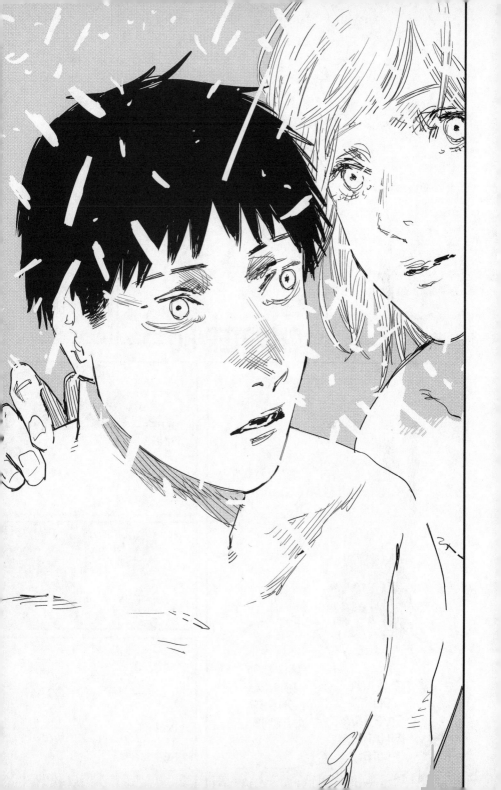

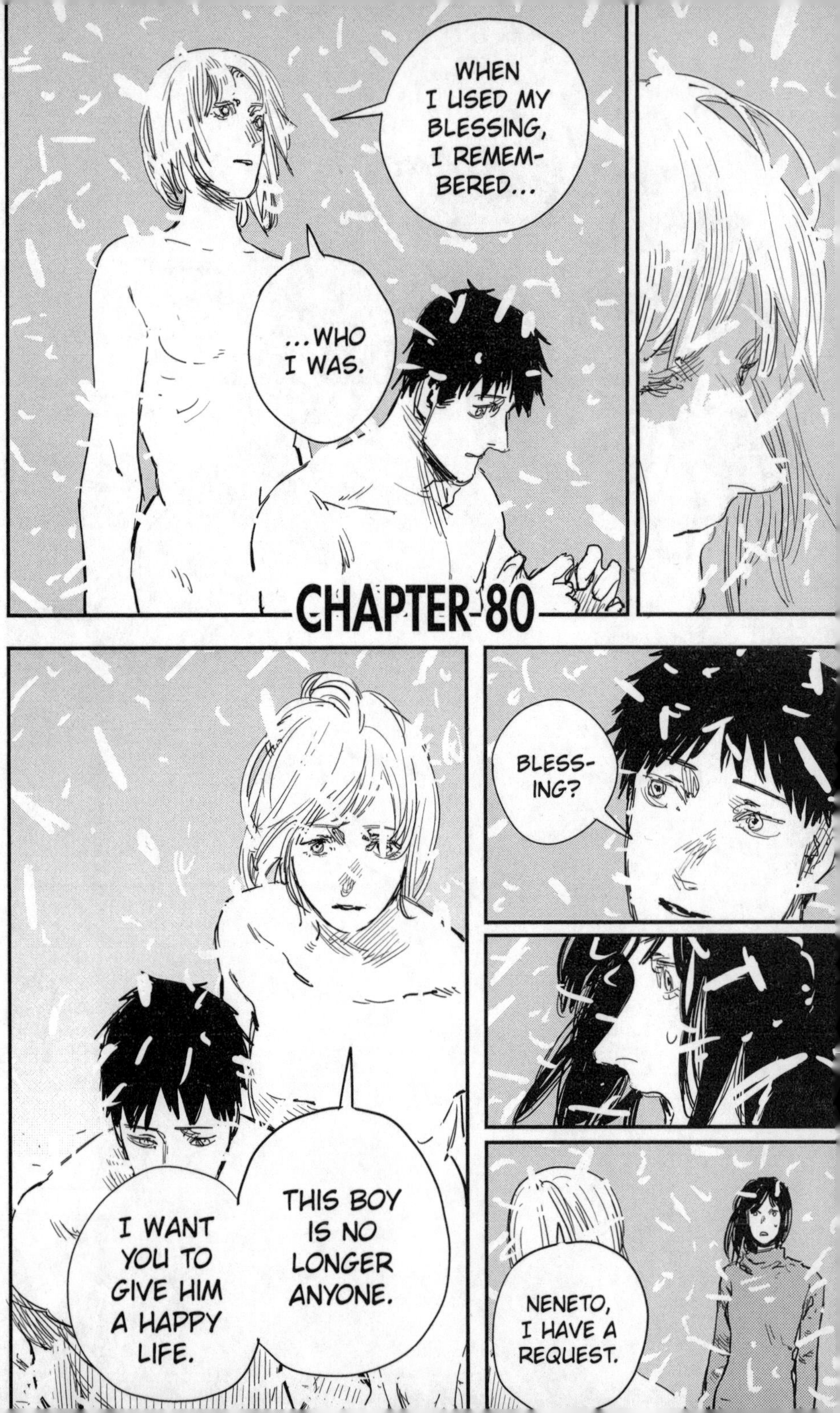
WHEN I USED MY BLESSING, I REMEMBERED...
...WHO I WAS.
CHAPTER 80
BLESSING?
NENETO, I HAVE A REQUEST.
THIS BOY IS NO LONGER ANYONE.
I WANT YOU TO GIVE HIM A HAPPY LIFE.

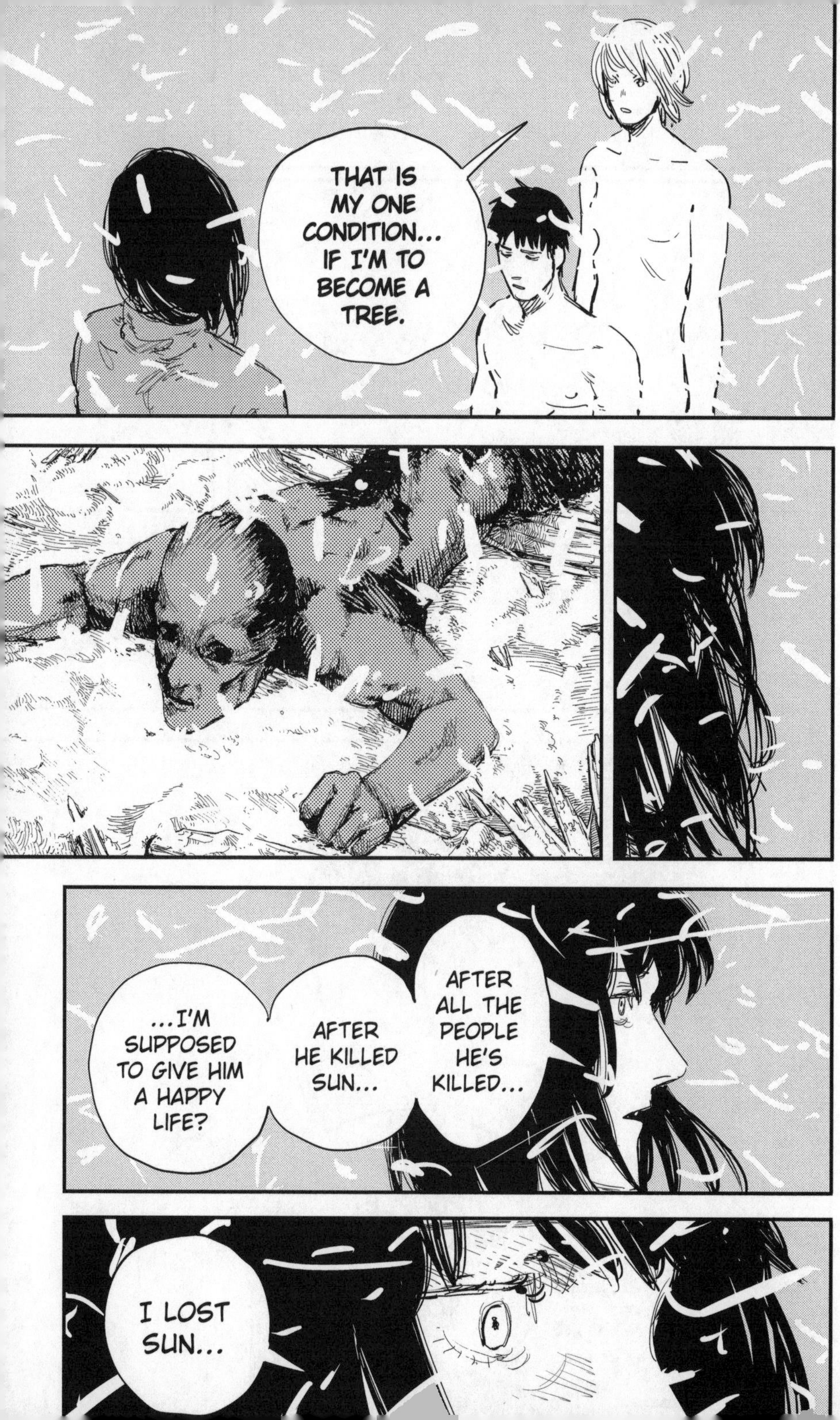
THAT IS MY ONE CONDITION... IF I'M TO BECOME A TREE.
AFTER ALL THE PEOPLE HE'S KILLED...
AFTER HE KILLED SUN...
...I'M SUPPOSED TO GIVE HIM A HAPPY LIFE?
I LOST SUN...

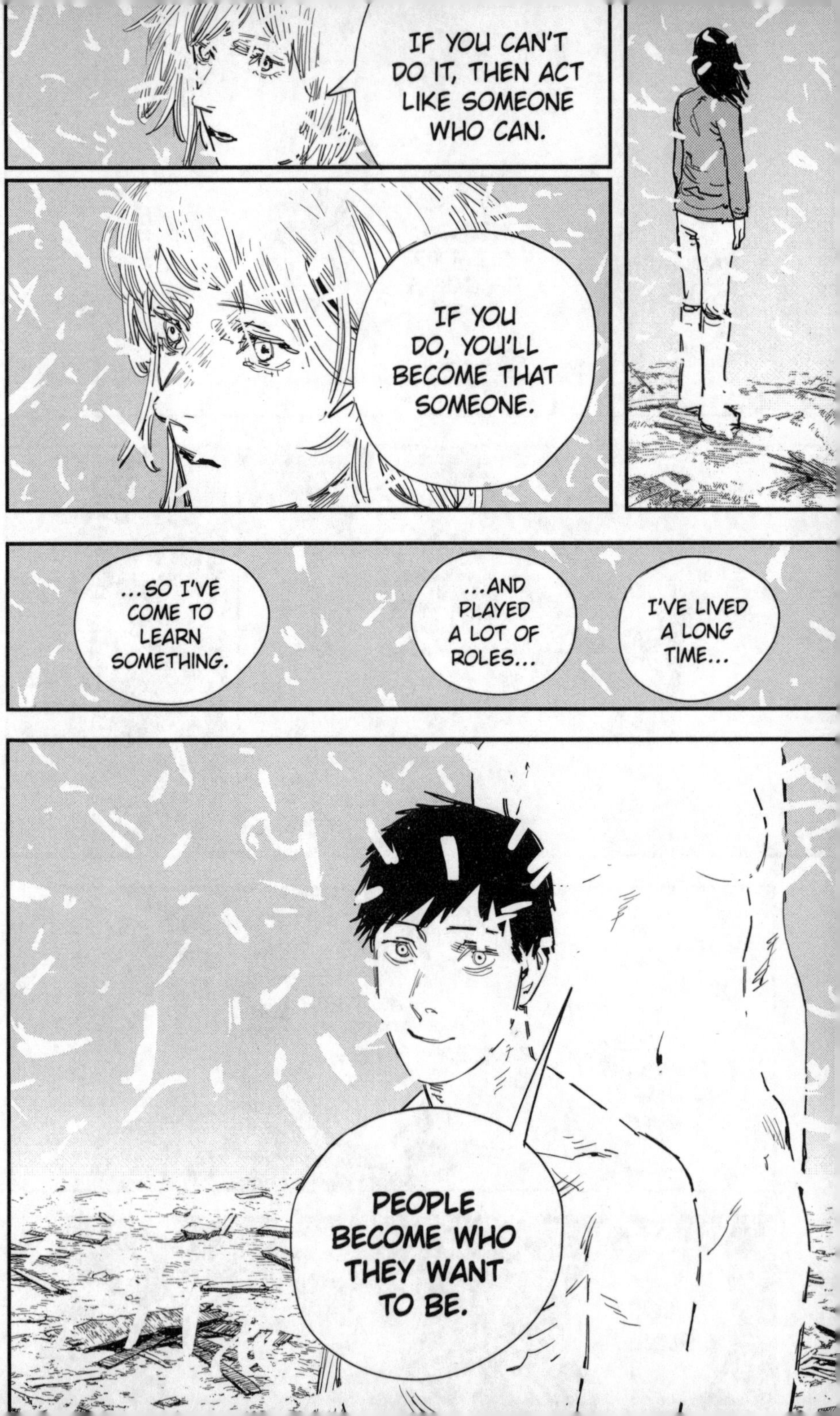
IF YOU CAN'T DO IT, THEN ACT LIKE SOMEONE WHO CAN.
IF YOU DO, YOU'LL BECOME THAT SOMEONE.
I'VE LIVED A LONG TIME...
...AND PLAYED A LOT OF ROLES...
...SO I'VE COME TO LEARN SOMETHING.
PEOPLE BECOME WHO THEY WANT TO BE.

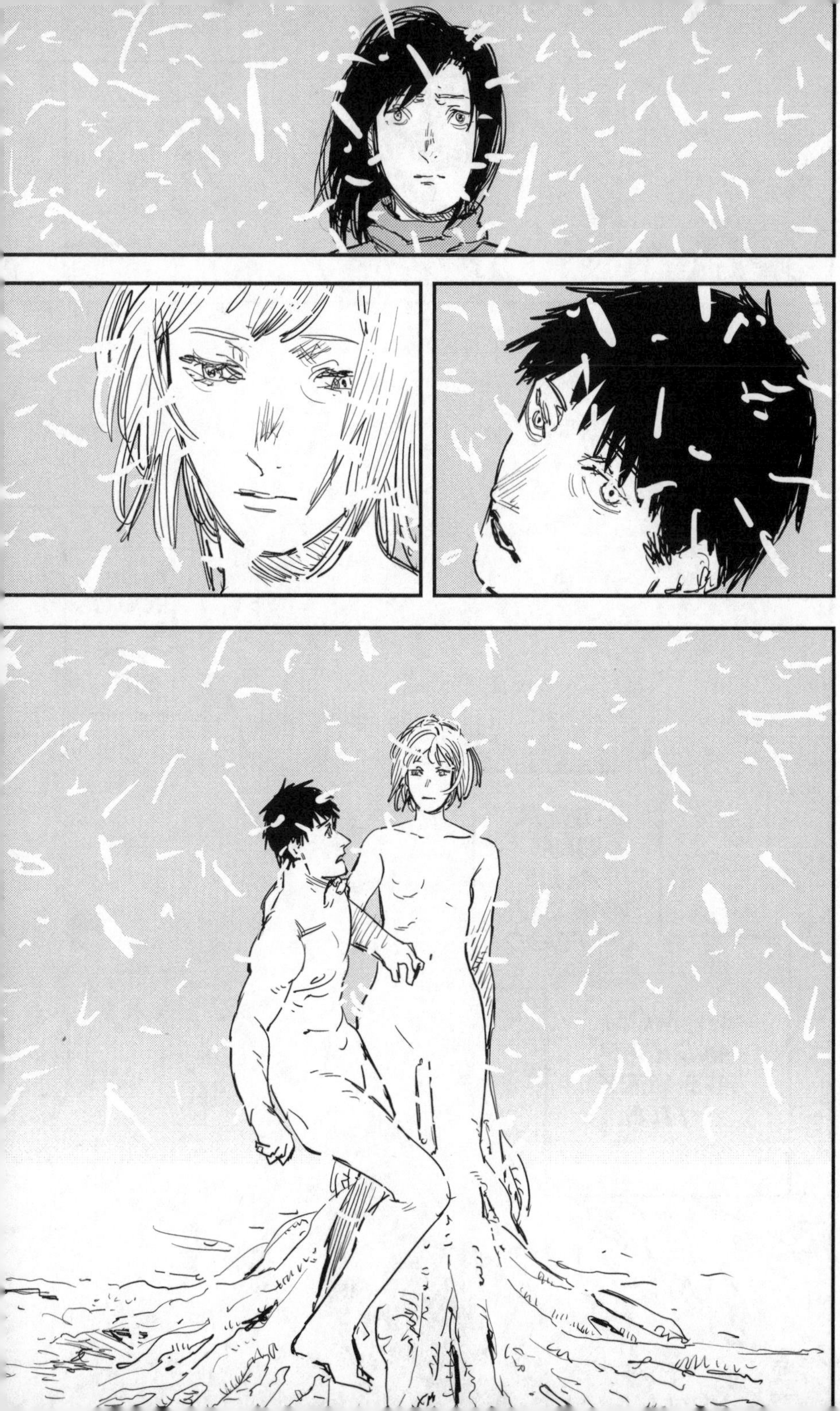

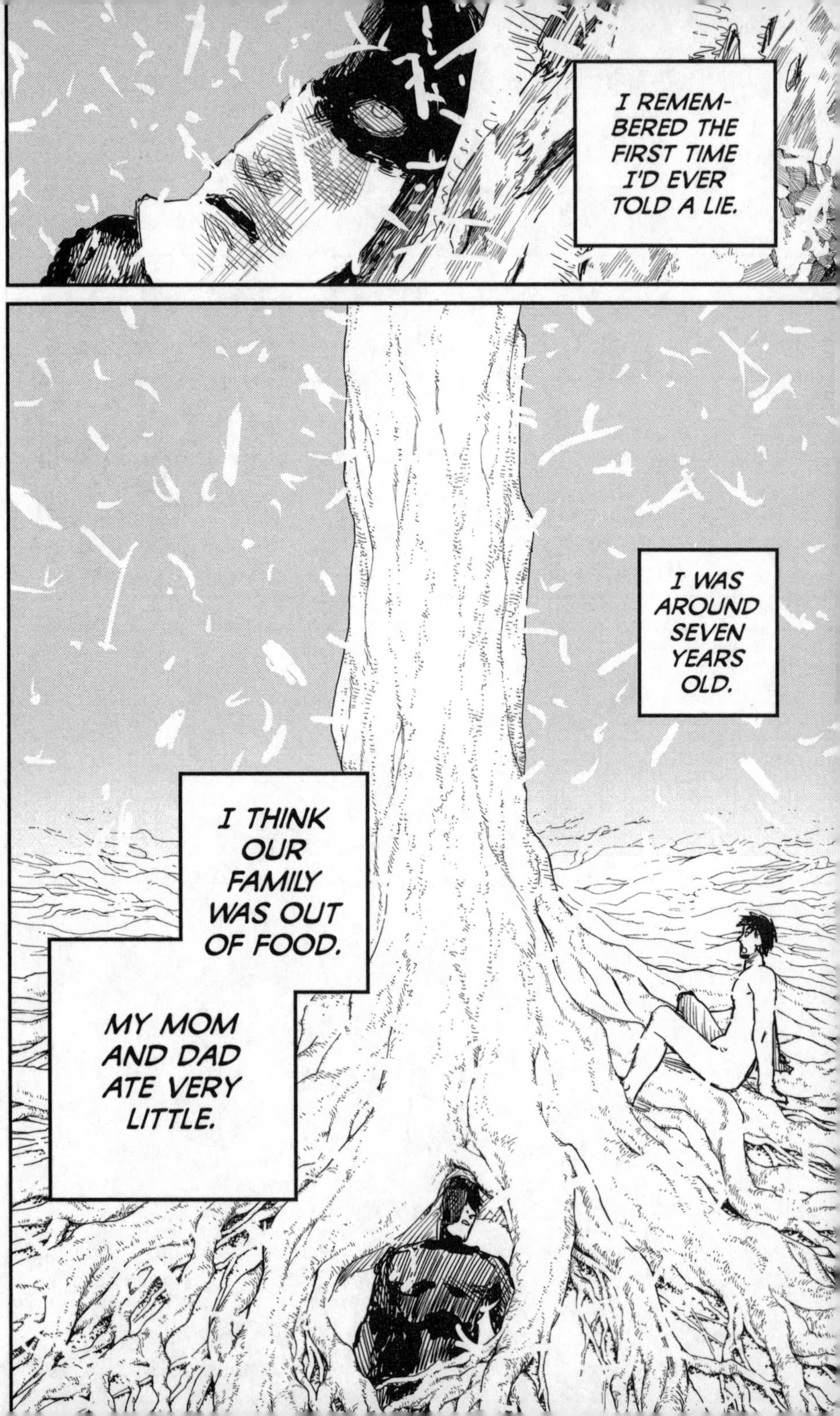
I REMEMBERED THE FIRST TIME I'D EVER TOLD A LIE.
I WAS AROUND SEVEN YEARS OLD.
I THINK OUR FAMILY WAS OUT OF FOOD.
MY MOM AND DAD ATE VERY LITTLE.

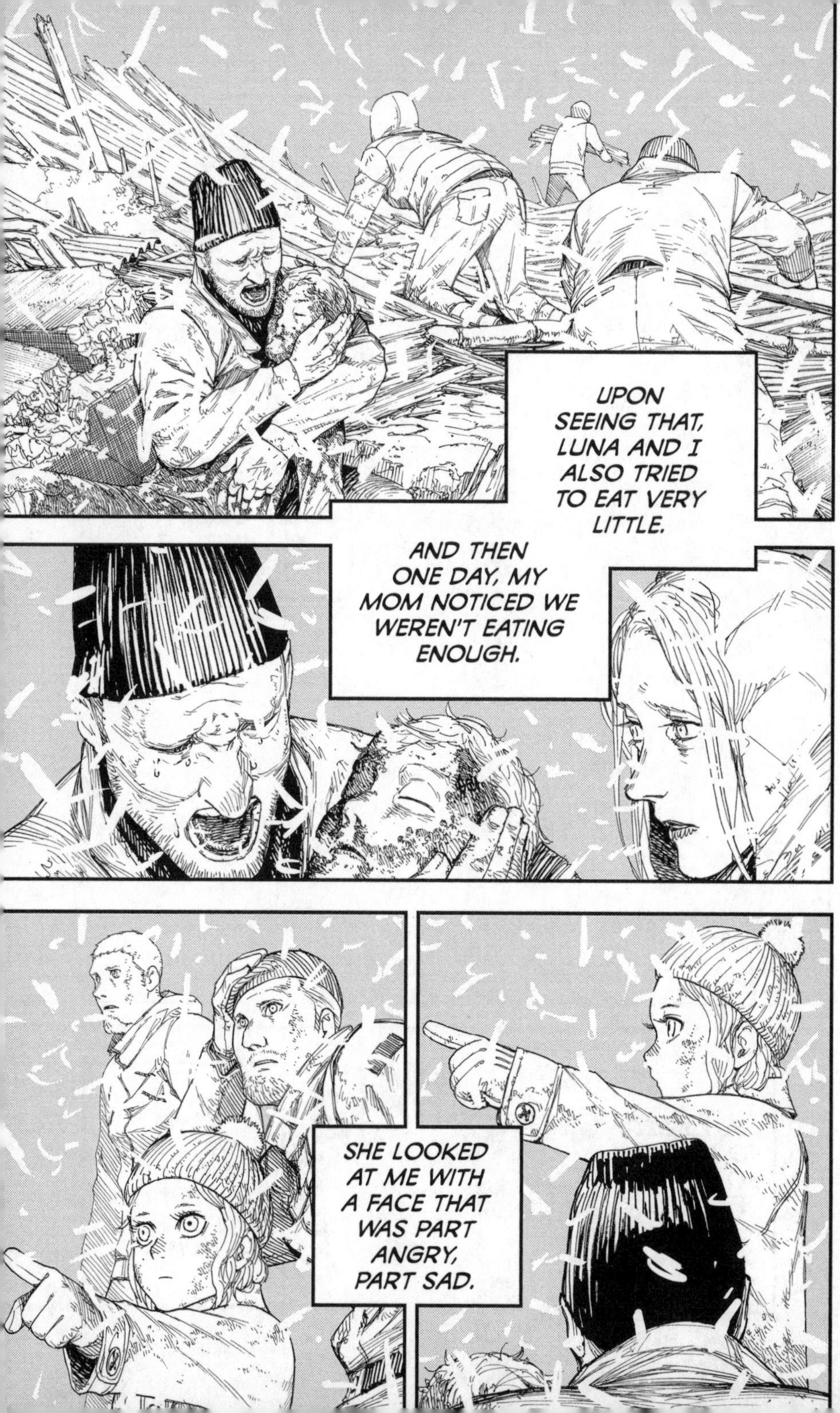
UPON SEEING THAT, LUNA AND I ALSO TRIED TO EAT VERY LITTLE.
AND THEN ONE DAY, MY MOM NOTICED WE WEREN'T EATING ENOUGH.
SHE LOOKED AT ME WITH A FACE THAT WAS PART ANGRY, PART SAD.

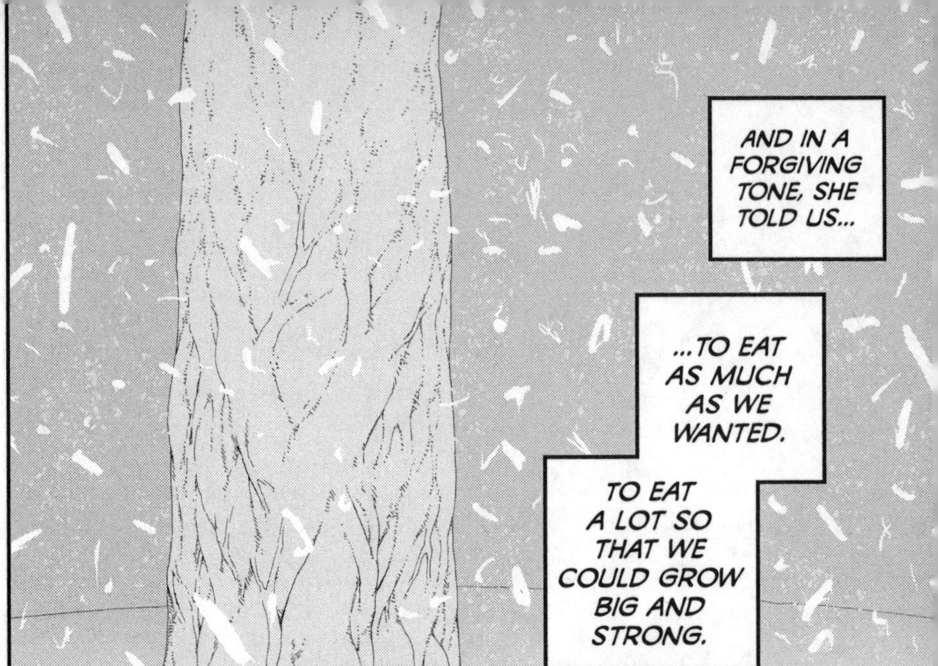
AND IN A FORGIVING TONE, SHE TOLD US...
...TO EAT AS MUCH AS WE WANTED.
TO EAT A LOT SO THAT WE COULD GROW BIG AND STRONG.
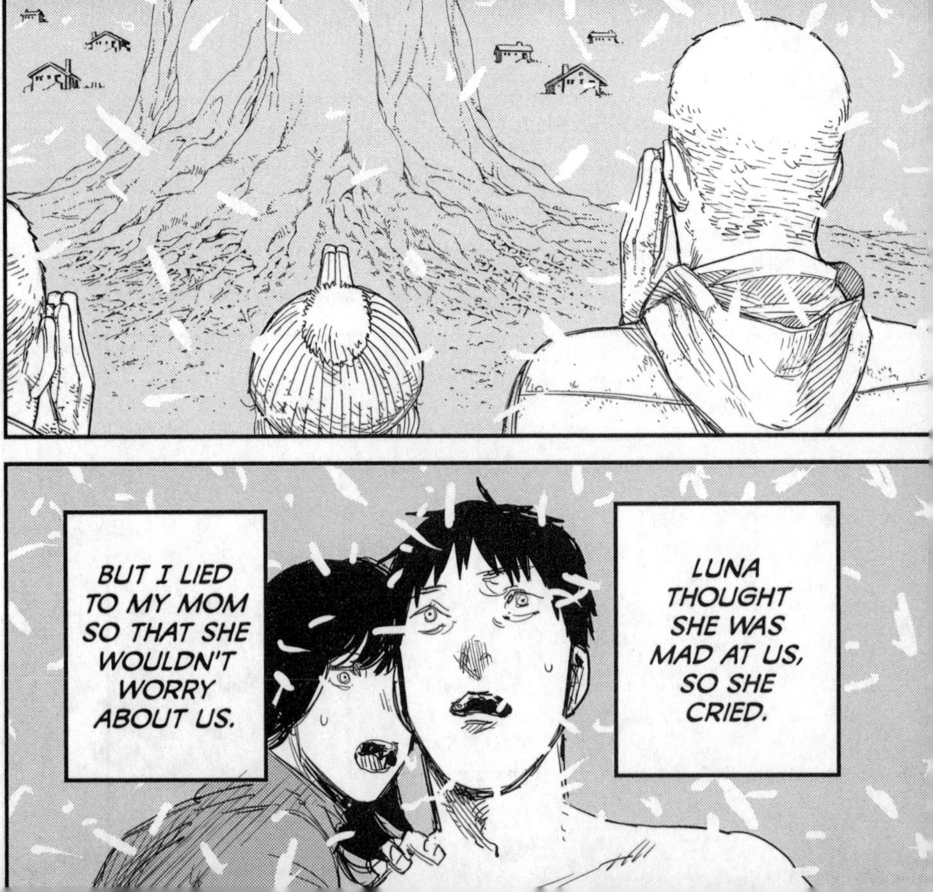
LUNA THOUGHT SHE WAS MAD AT US, SO SHE CRIED.
BUT I LIED TO MY MOM SO THAT SHE WOULDN'T WORRY ABOUT US.

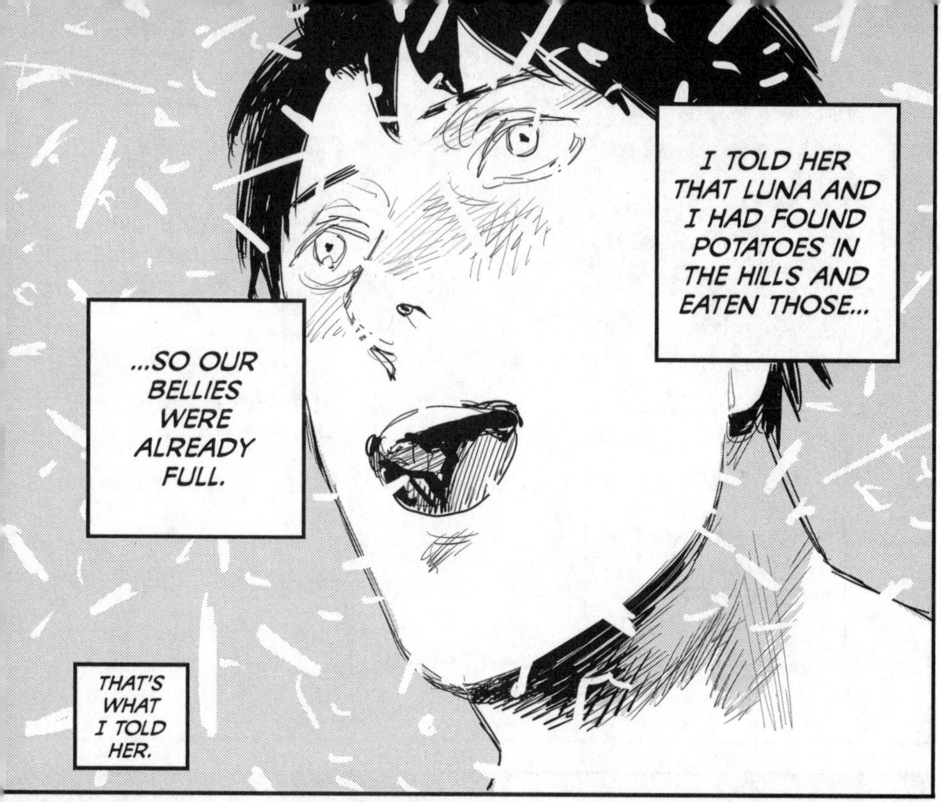
I TOLD HER THAT LUNA AND I HAD FOUND POTATOES IN THE HILLS AND EATEN THOSE...
...SO OUR BELLIES WERE ALREADY FULL.
THAT'S WHAT I TOLD HER.
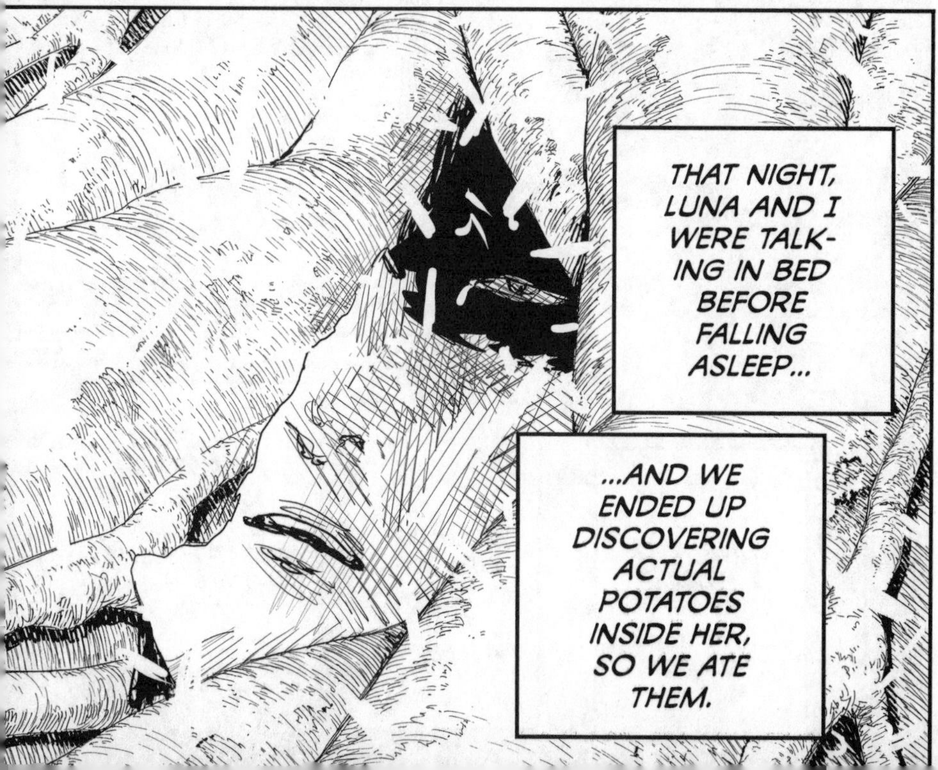
THAT NIGHT, LUNA AND I WERE TALK-ING IN BED BEFORE FALLING ASLEEP...
...AND WE ENDED UP DISCOVERING ACTUAL POTATOES INSIDE HER, SO WE ATE THEM.

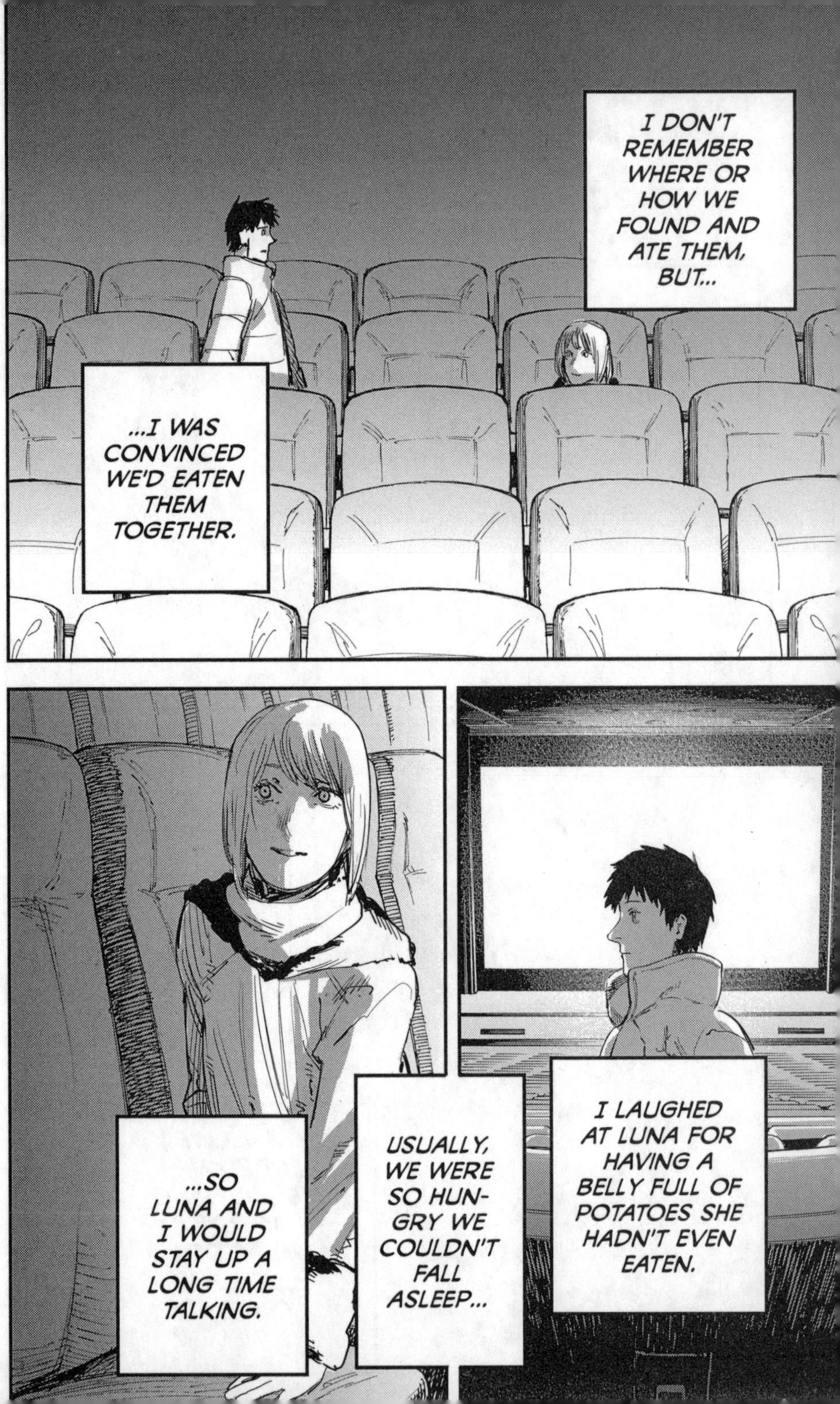
I DON'T REMEMBER WHERE OR HOW WE FOUND AND ATE THEM, BUT...
...I WAS CONVINCED WE'D EATEN THEM TOGETHER.
I LAUGHED AT LUNA FOR HAVING A BELLY FULL OF POTATOES SHE HADN'T EVEN EATEN.
USUALLY, WE WERE SO HUN-GRY WE COULDN'T FALL ASLEEP...
...SO LUNA AND I WOULD STAY UP A LONG TIME TALKING.

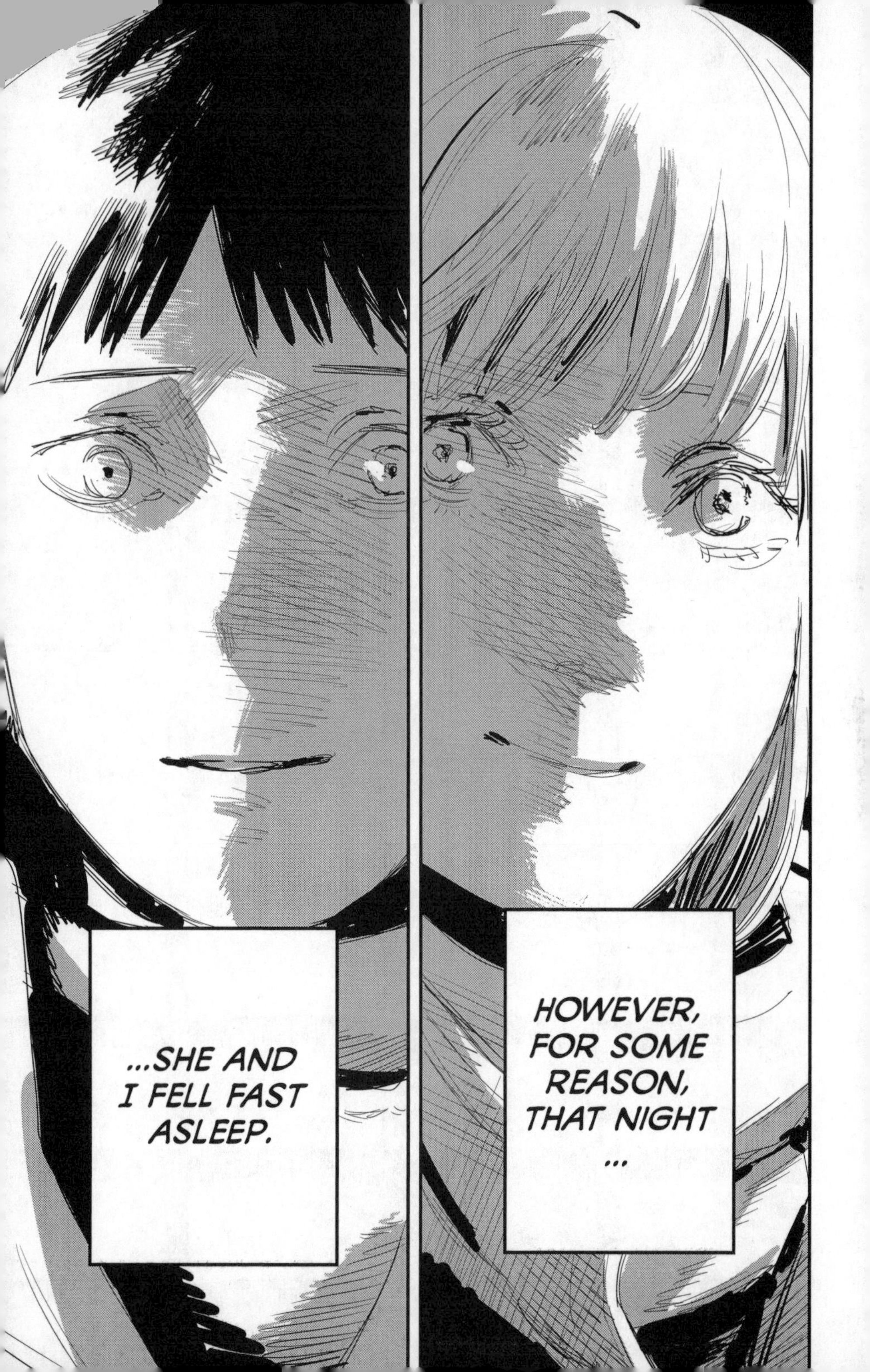
HOWEVER, FOR SOME REASON, THAT NIGHT ...
...SHE AND I FELL FAST ASLEEP.

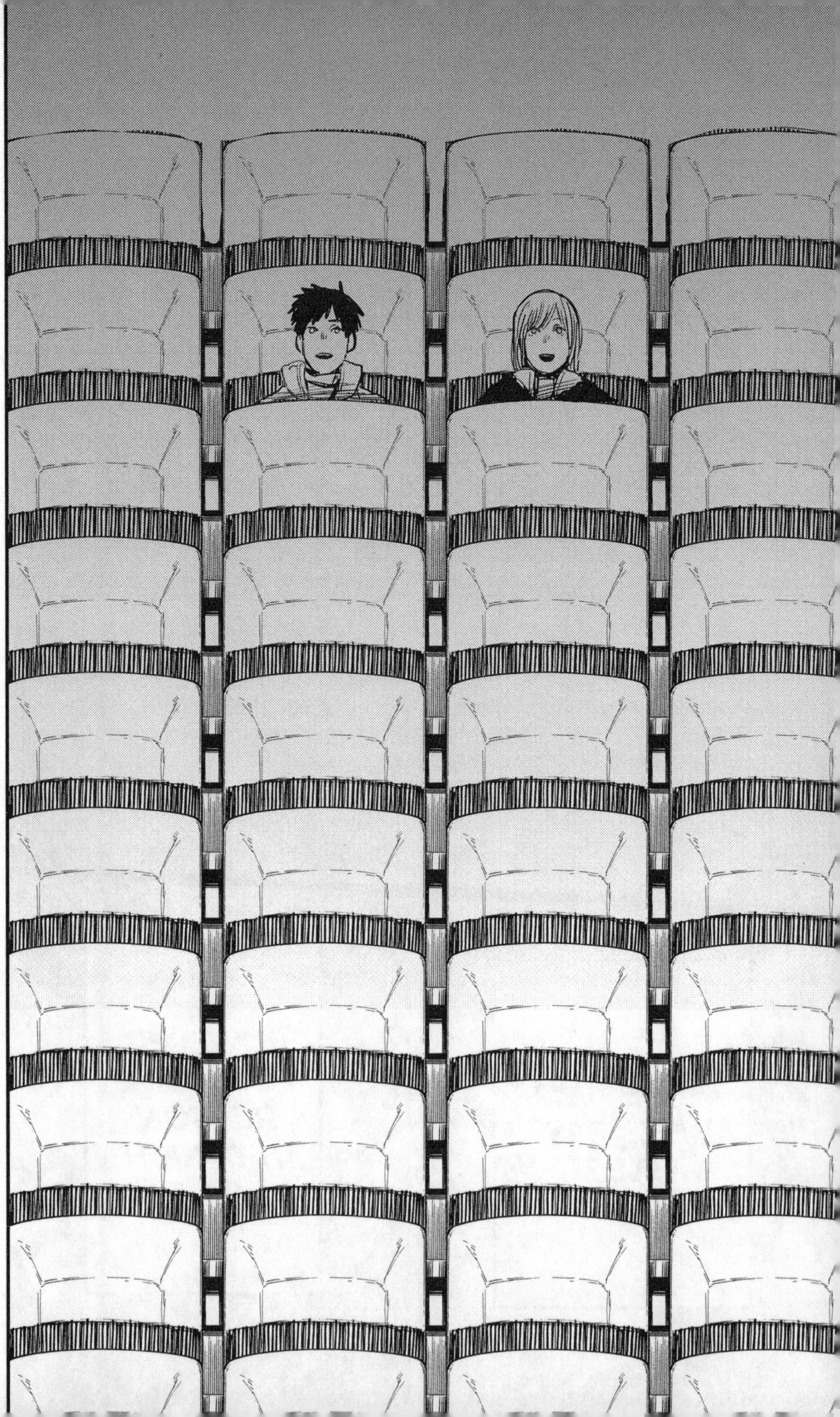

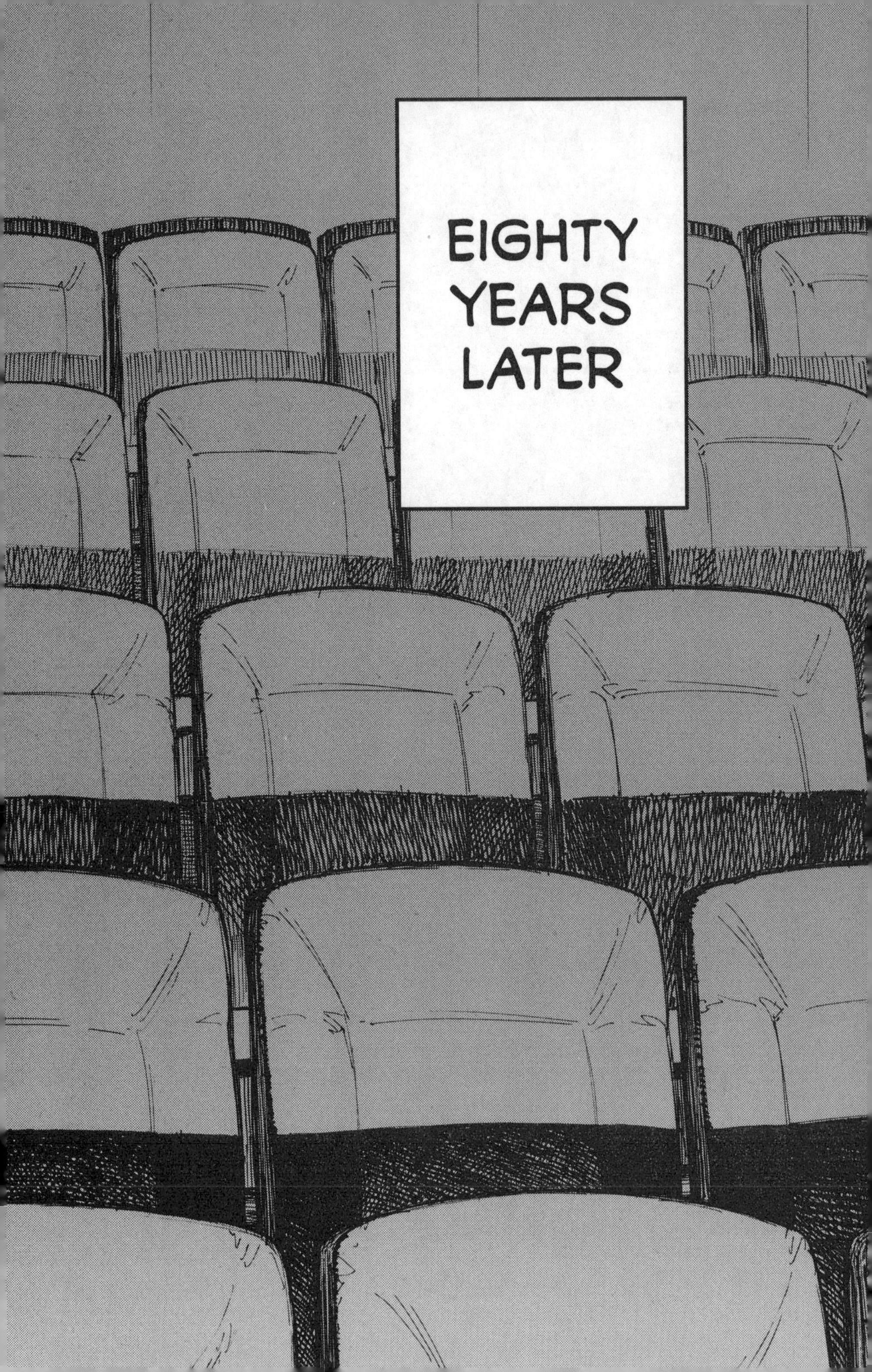
EIGHTY YEARS LATER

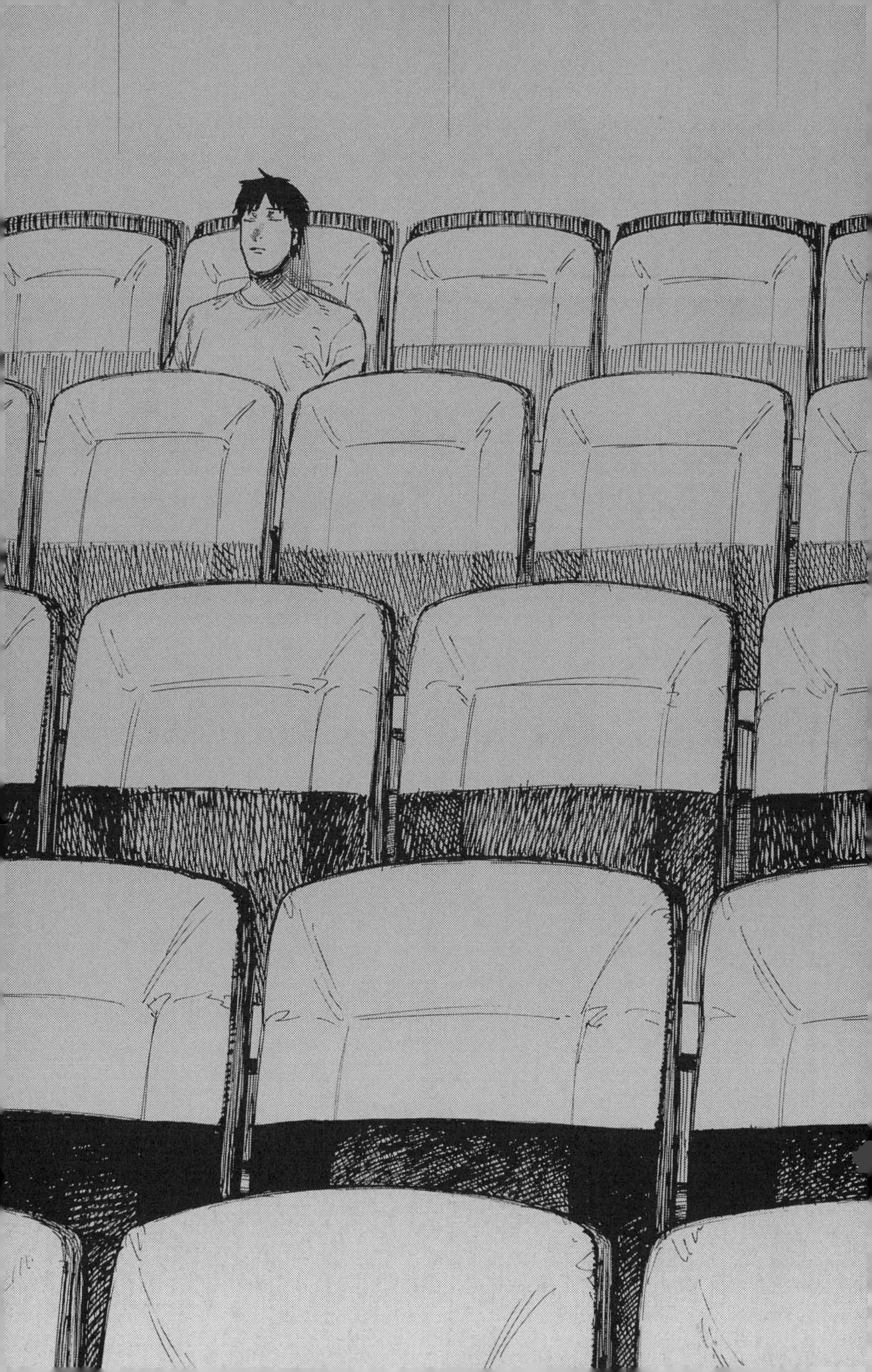

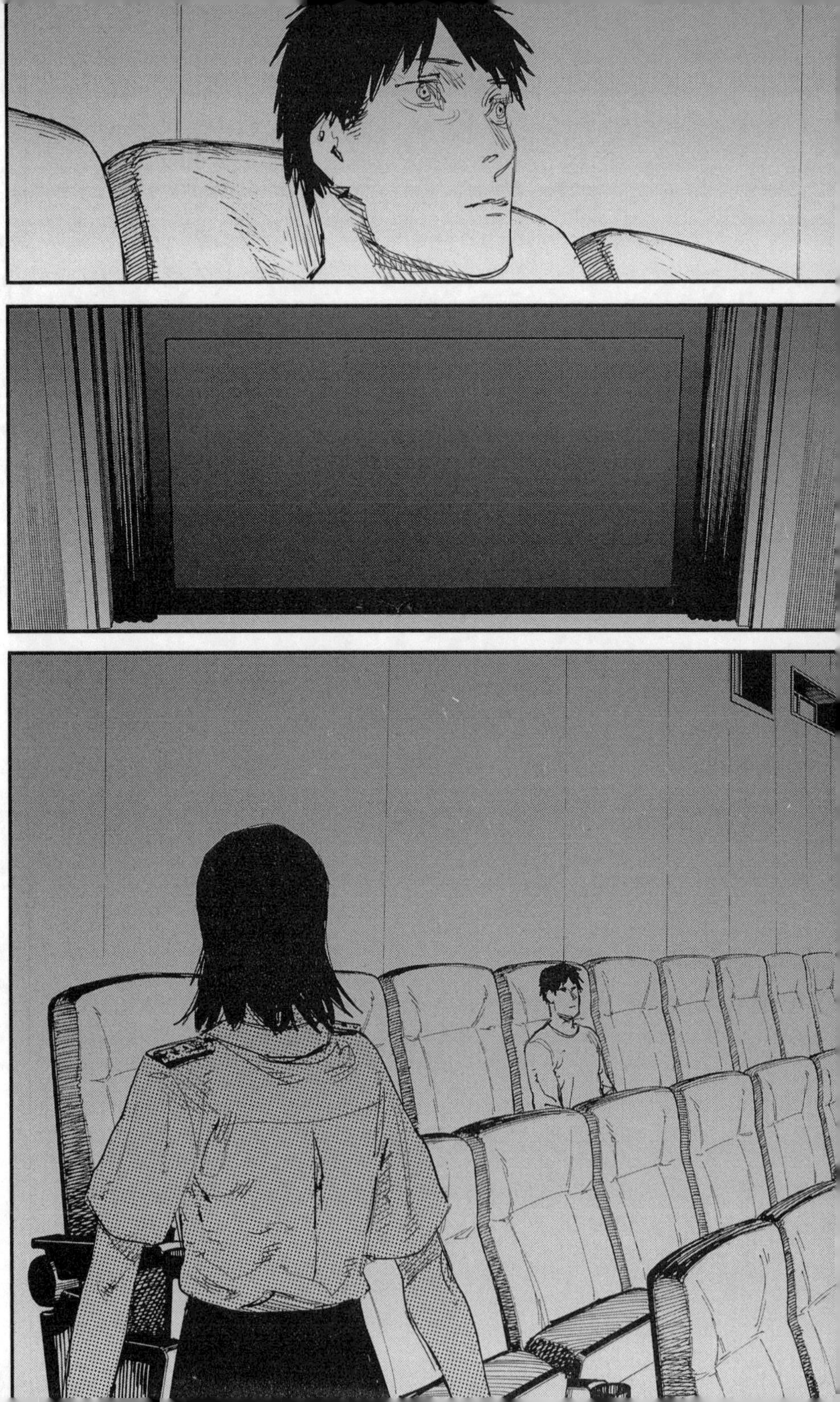

SUN, SIR.

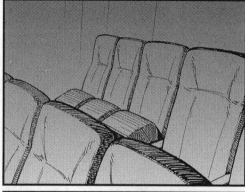

GOT IT.

MADAM NENETO WILL BE GOING TO HEAVEN SOON.

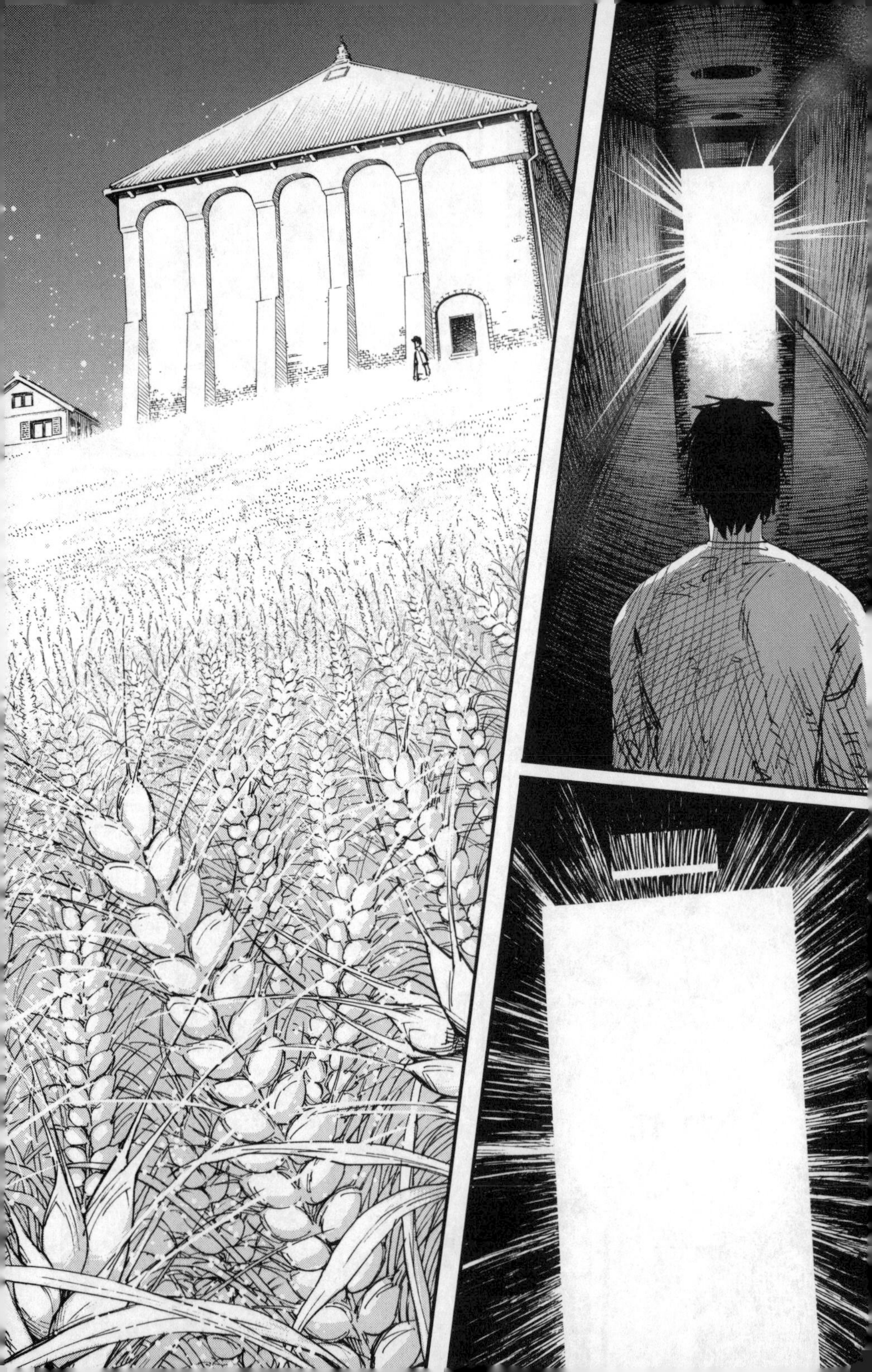

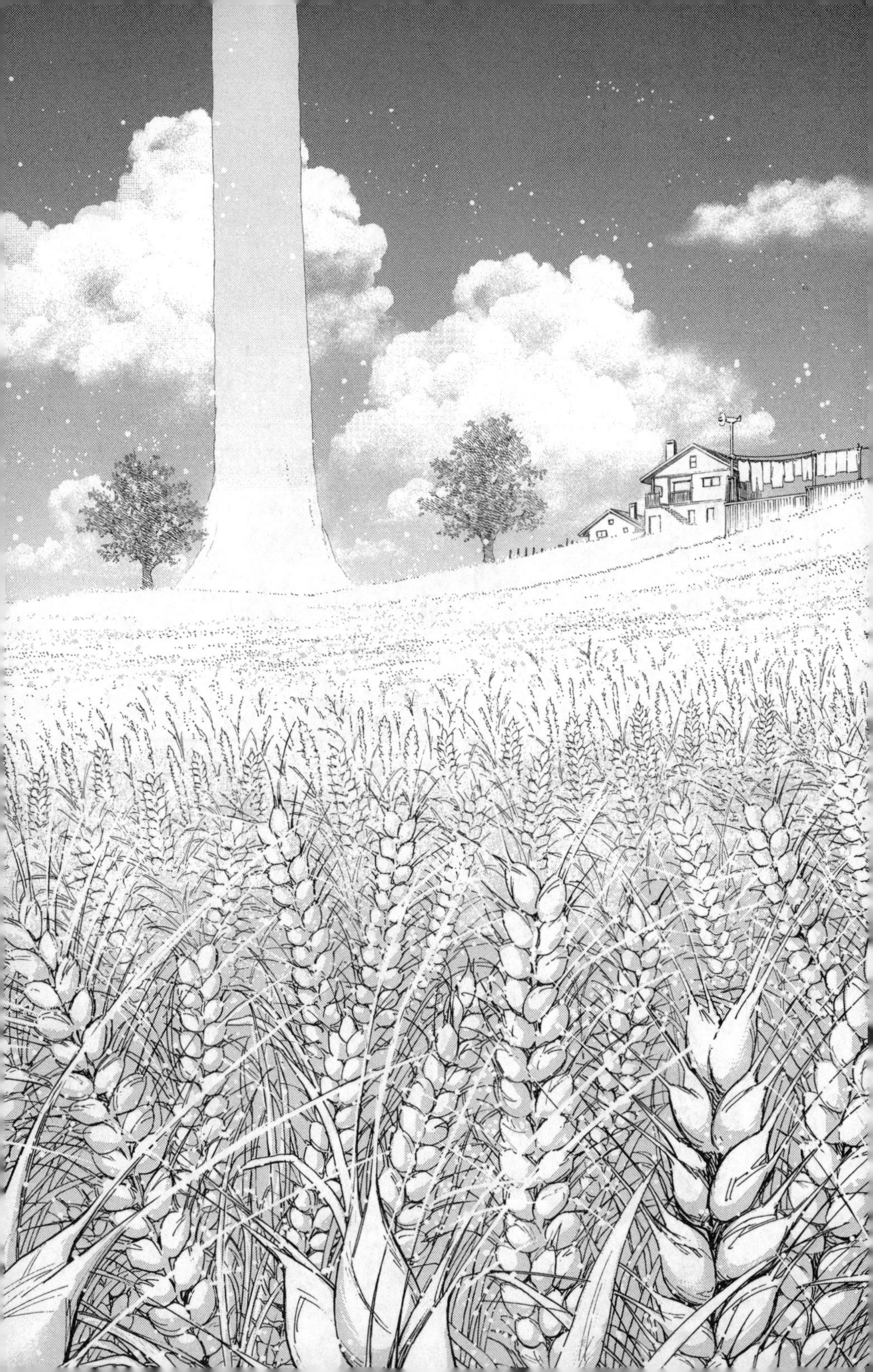

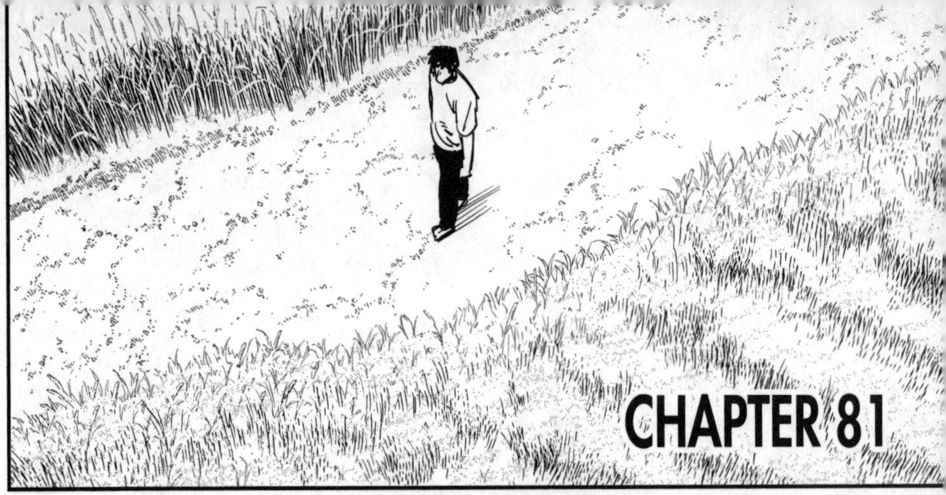
CHAPTER 81
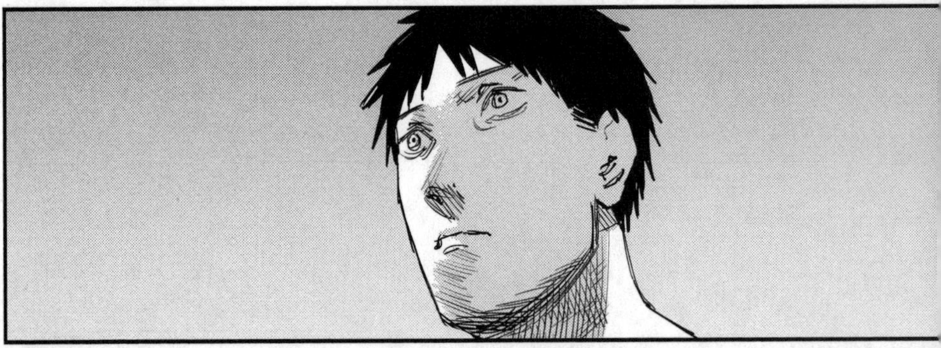
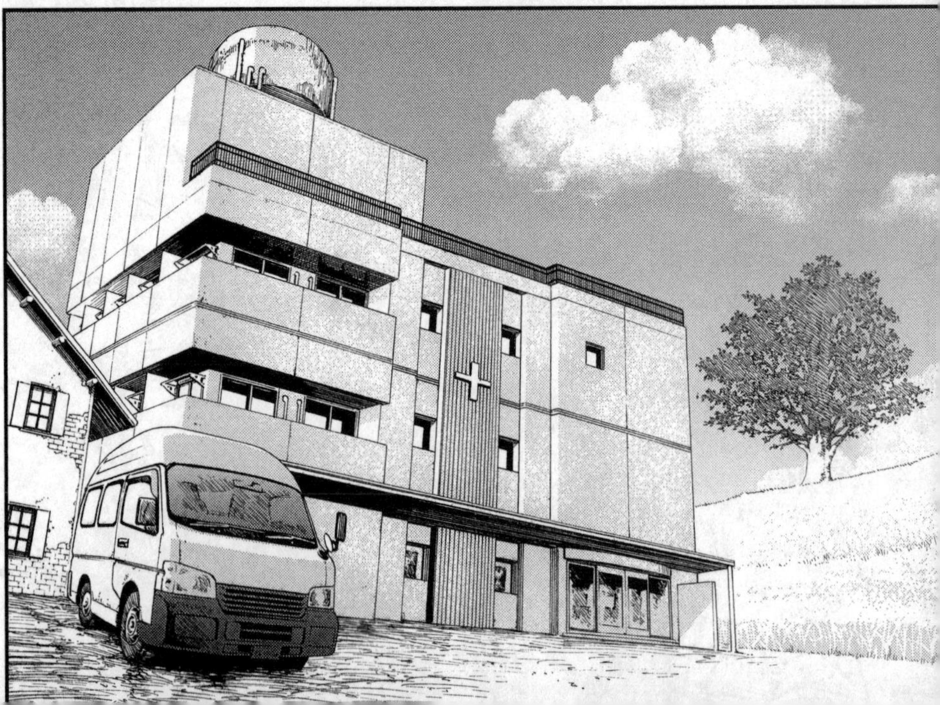

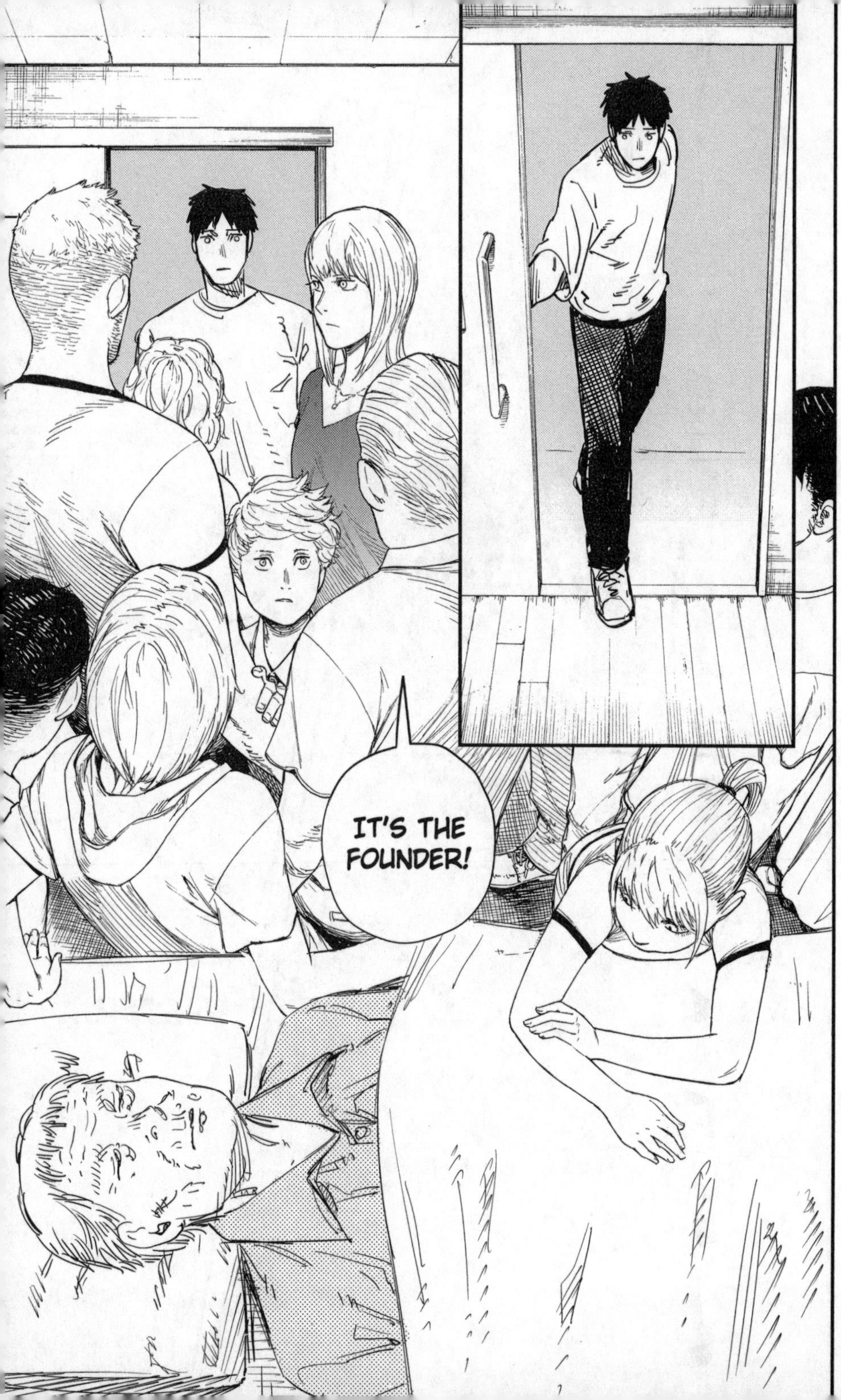
IT'S THE FOUNDER!

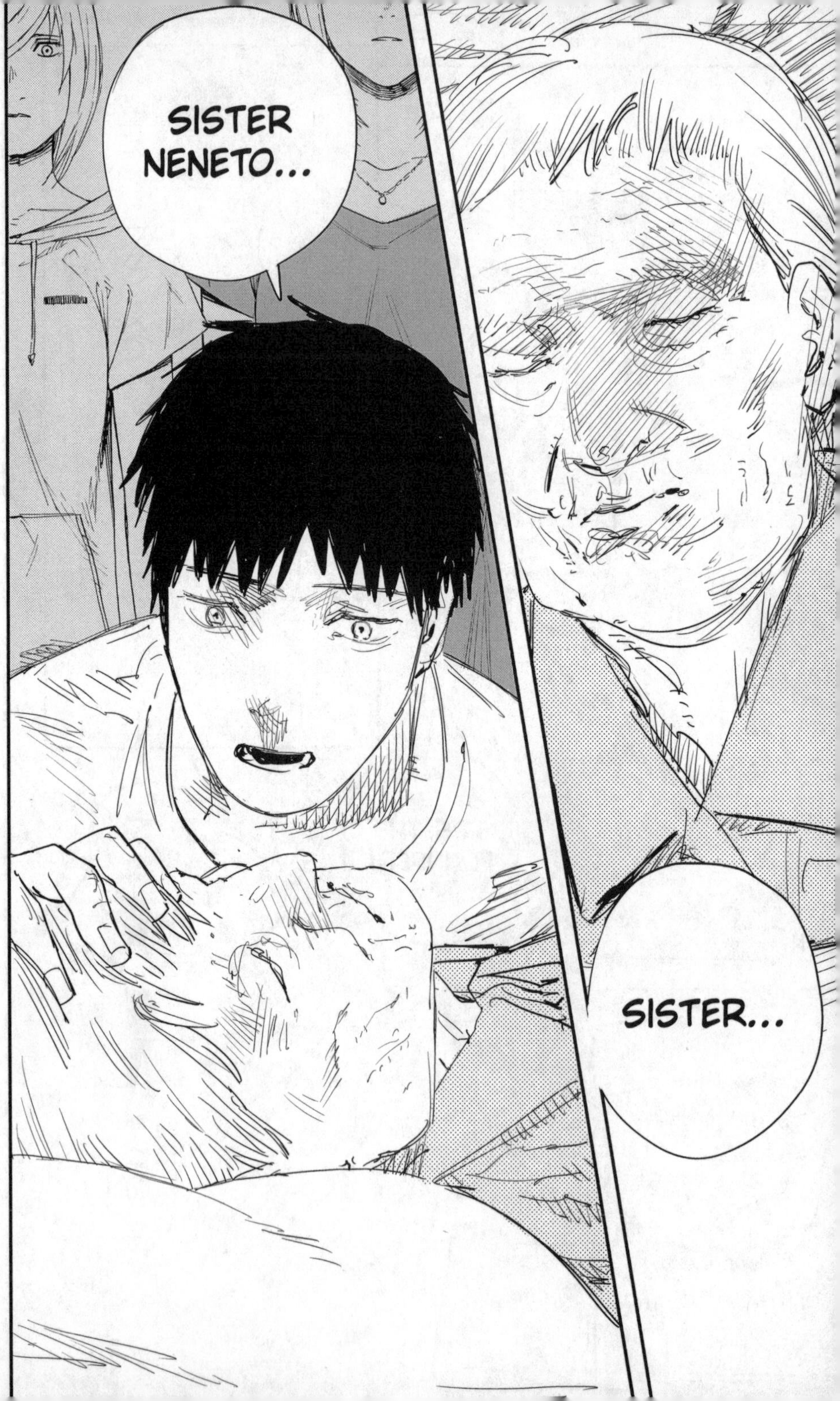
SISTER...
SISTER NENETO...

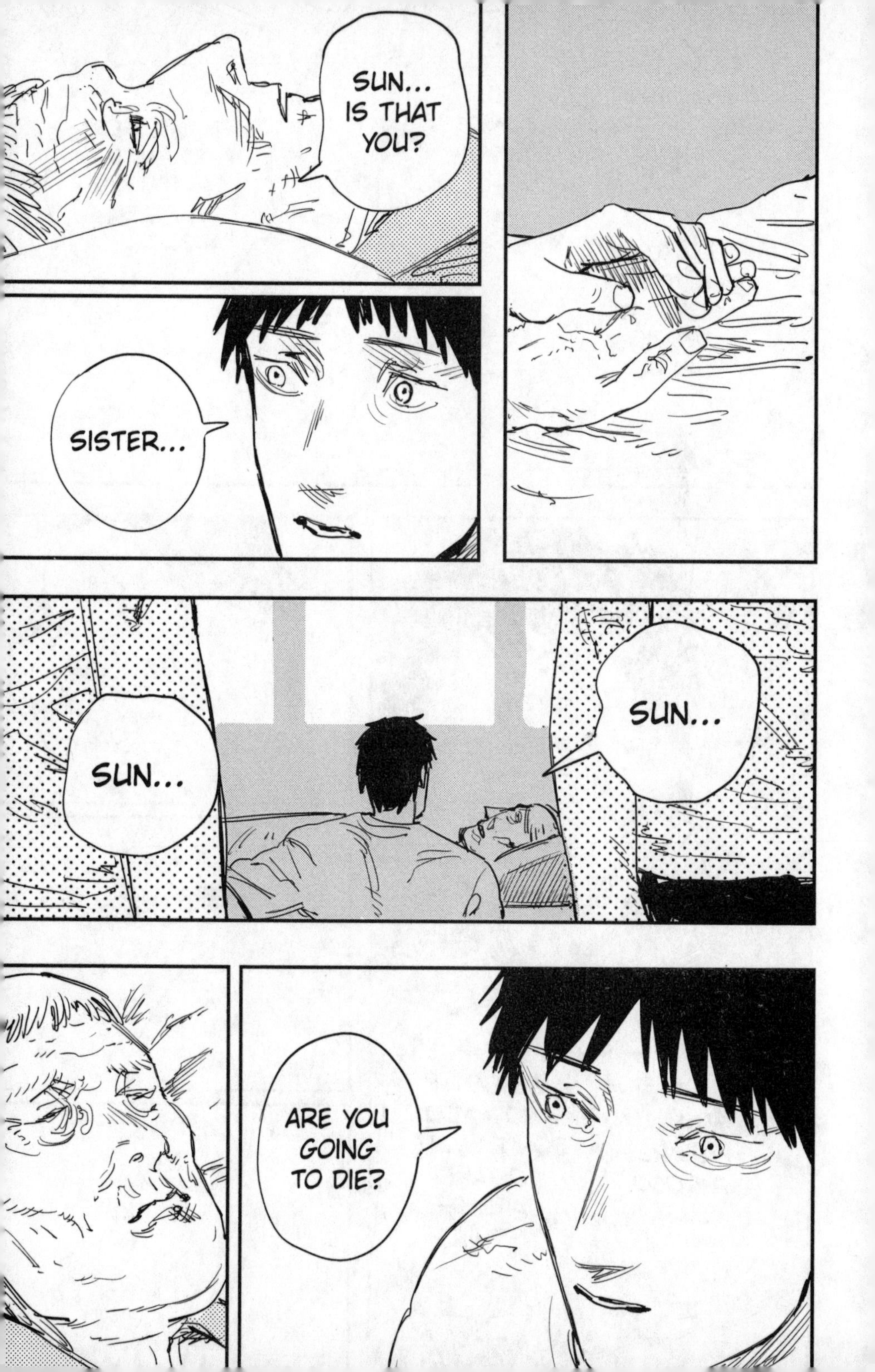
SUN... IS THAT YOU?
SISTER...
SUN...
SUN...
ARE YOU GOING TO DIE?

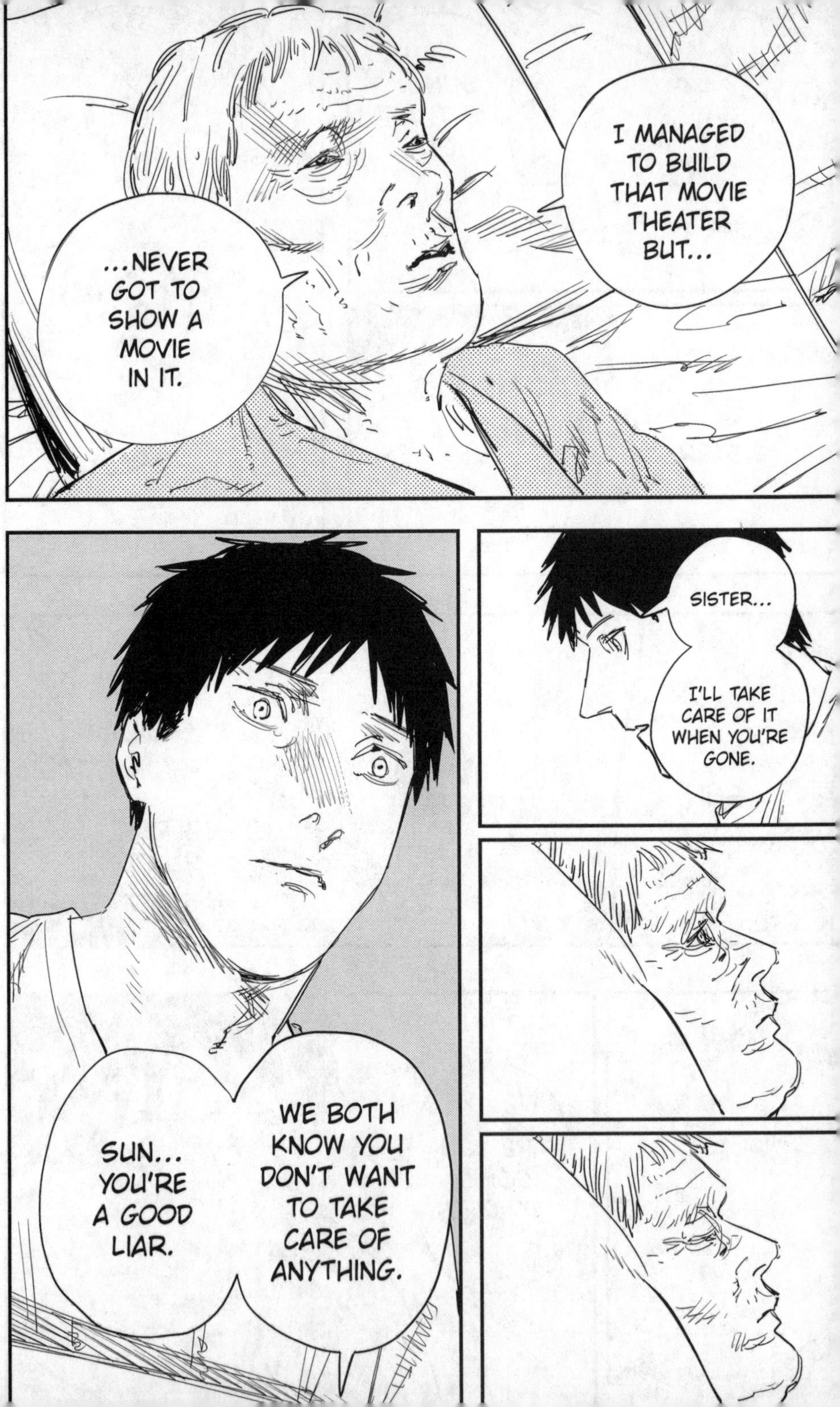
I MANAGED TO BUILD THAT MOVIE THEATER BUT...
...NEVER GOT TO SHOW A MOVIE IN IT.
SISTER...
I'LL TAKE CARE OF IT WHEN YOU'RE GONE.
WE BOTH KNOW YOU DON'T WANT TO TAKE CARE OF ANYTHING.
SUN... YOU'RE A GOOD LIAR.

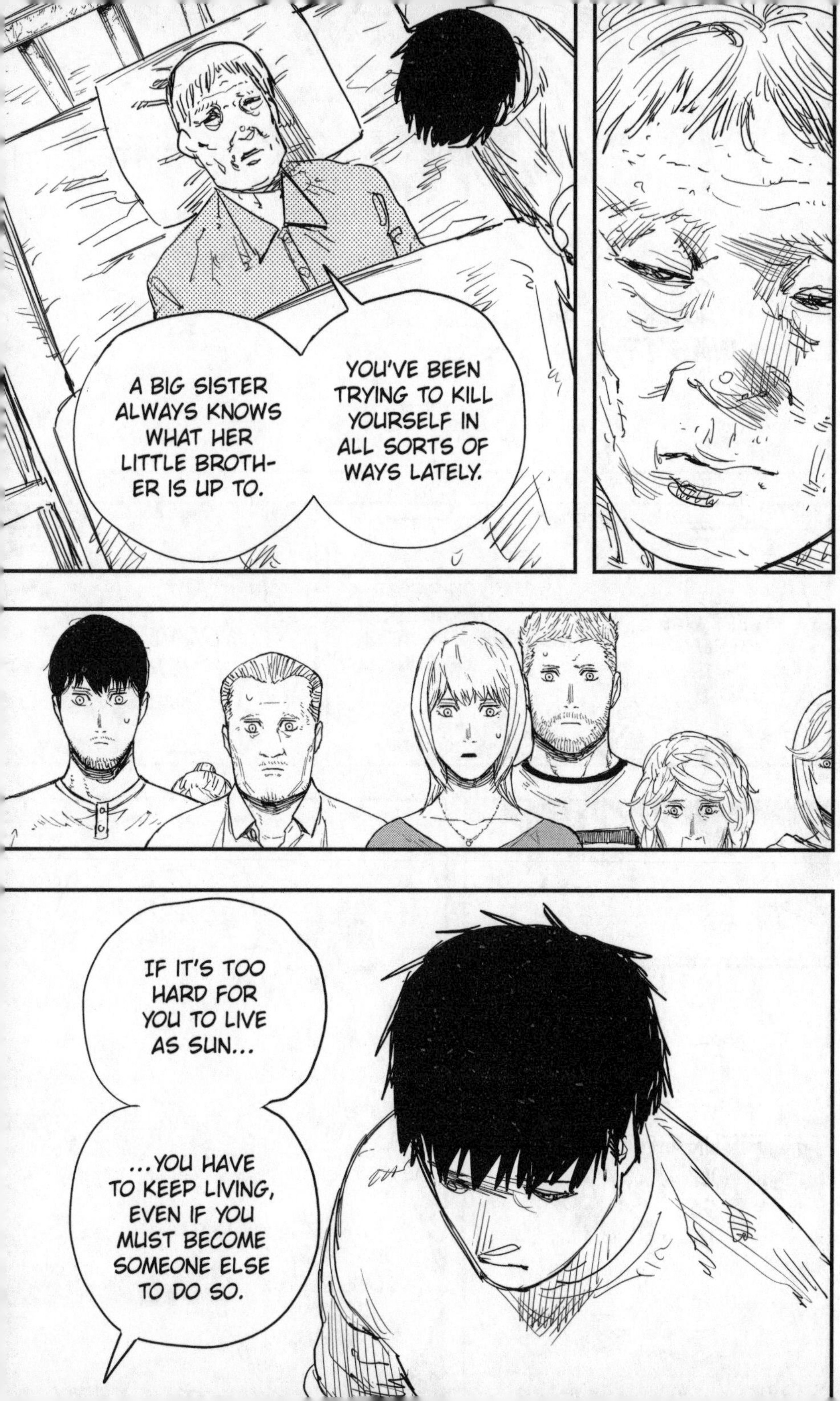
YOU'VE BEEN TRYING TO KILL YOURSELF IN ALL SORTS OF WAYS LATELY.
A BIG SISTER ALWAYS KNOWS WHAT HER LITTLE BROTH-ER IS UP TO.
IF IT'S TOO HARD FOR YOU TO LIVE AS SUN...
...YOU HAVE TO KEEP LIVING, EVEN IF YOU MUST BECOME SOMEONE ELSE TO DO SO.

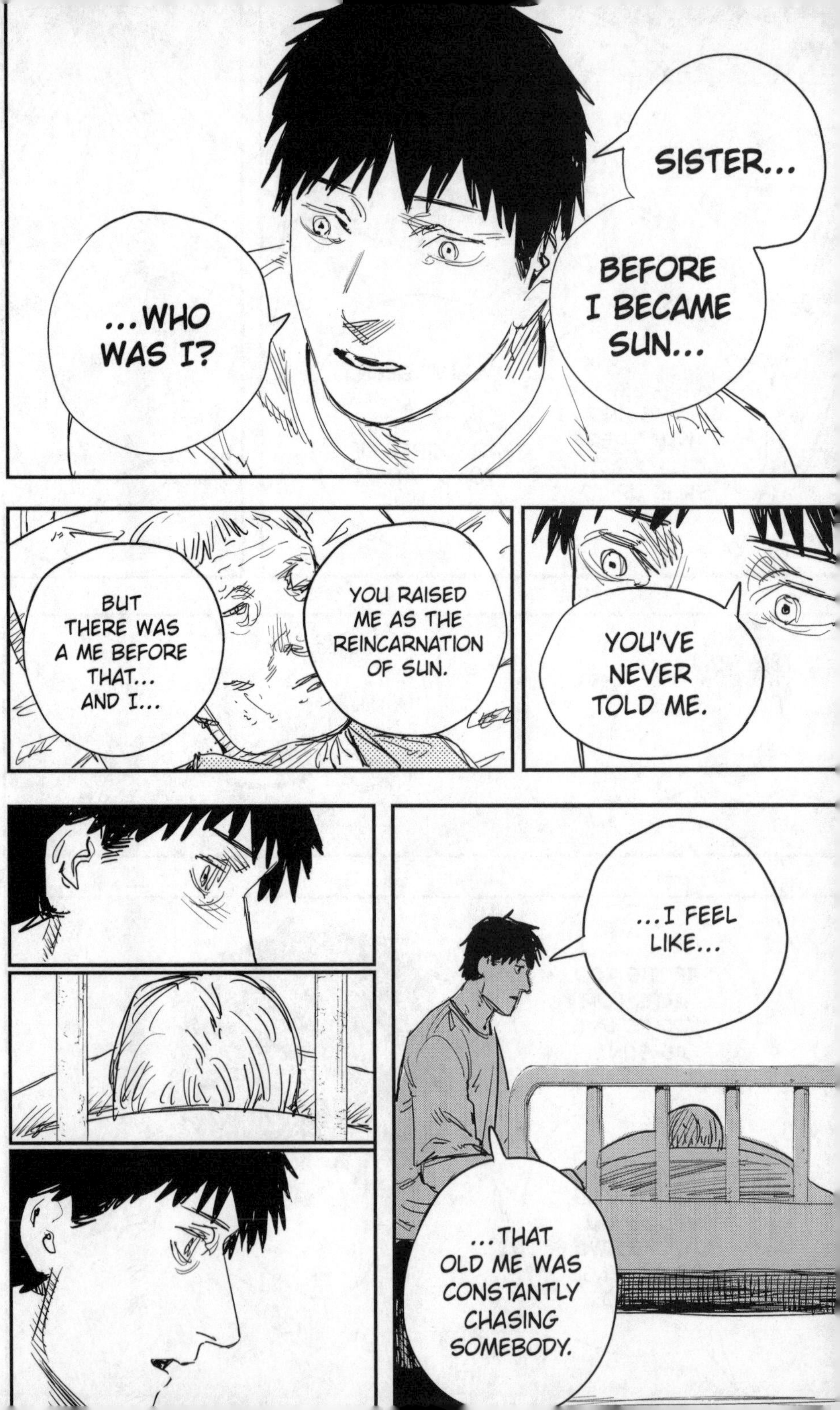
SISTER...
BEFORE I BECAME SUN...
...WHO WAS I?
YOU'VE NEVER TOLD ME.
YOU RAISED ME AS THE REINCARNATION OF SUN.
BUT THERE WAS A ME BEFORE THAT... AND I...
...I FEEL LIKE...
...THAT OLD ME WAS CONSTANTLY CHASING SOMEBODY.

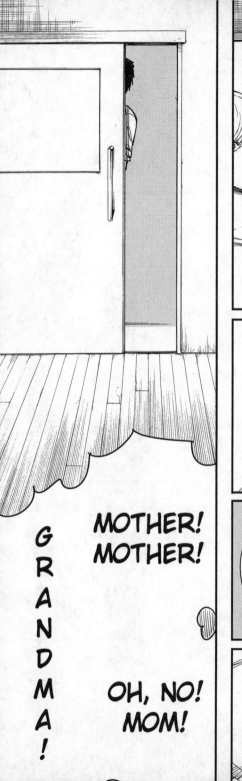

MOTHER! MOTHER!

G R A N D M A !

OH, NO! MOM!

SHE'S DEAD.

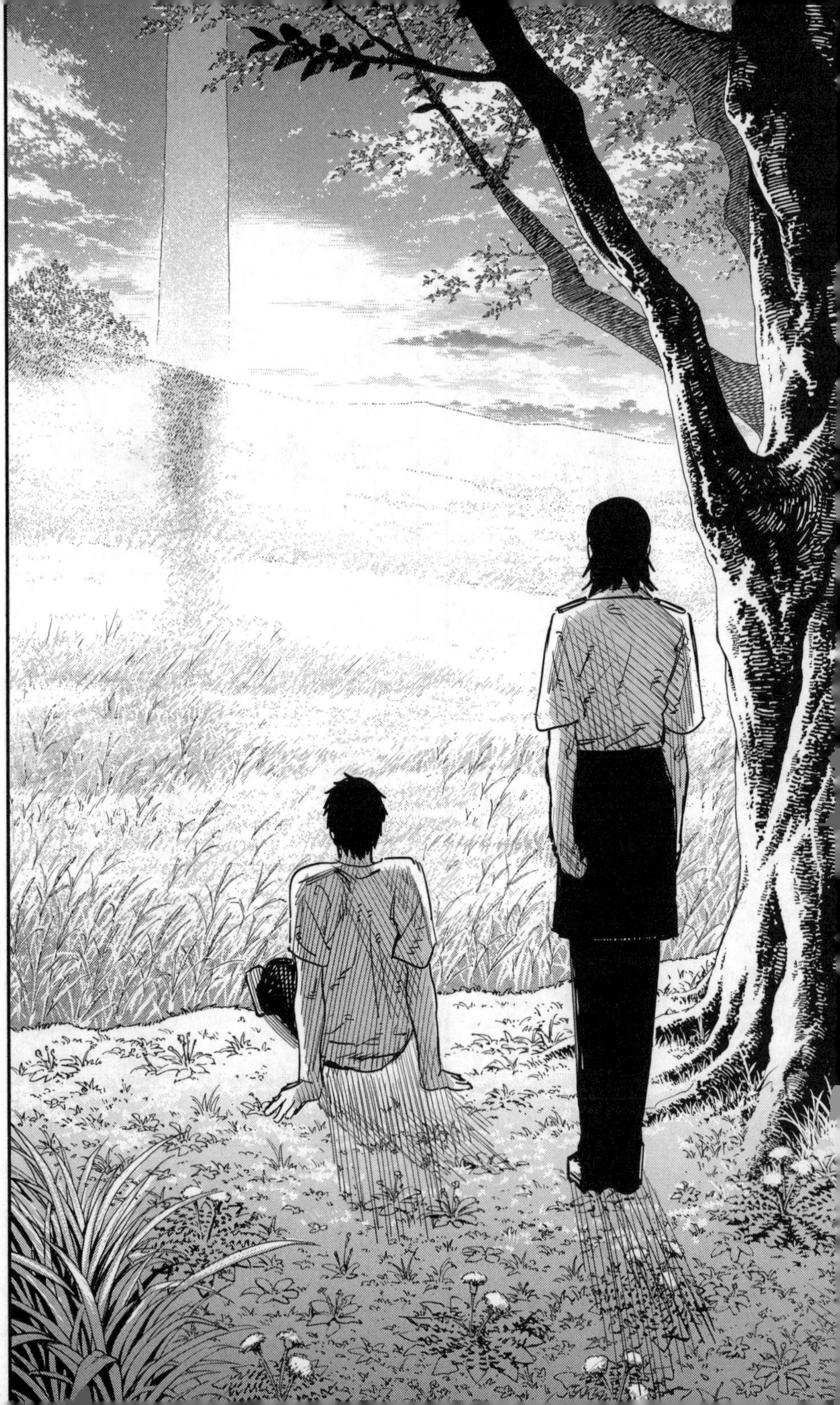

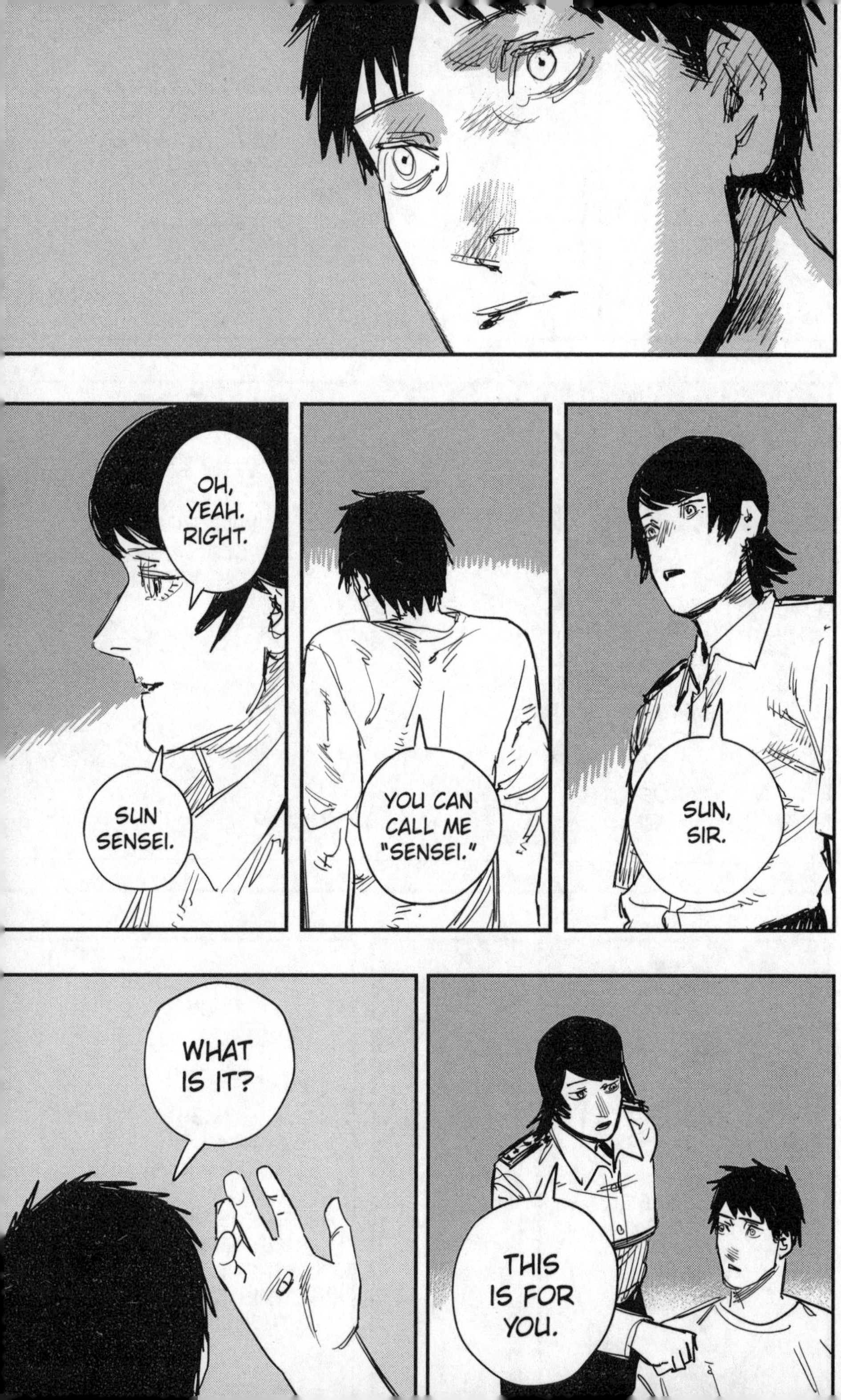
SUN, SIR.
YOU CAN CALL ME "SENSEI."
OH, YEAH. RIGHT.
SUN SENSEI.
THIS IS FOR YOU.
WHAT IS IT?

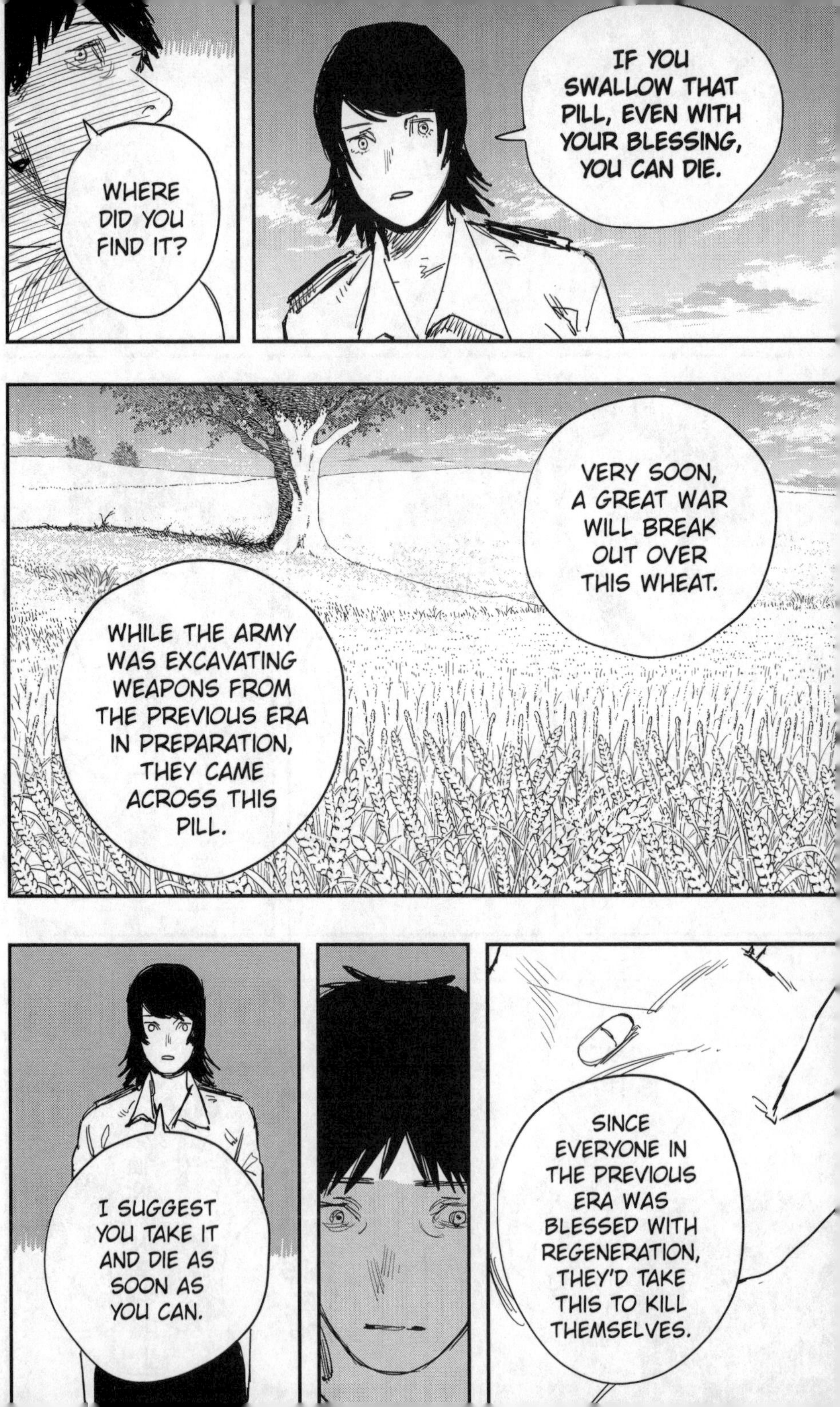
IF YOU SWALLOW THAT PILL, EVEN WITH YOUR BLESSING, YOU CAN DIE.
WHERE DID YOU FIND IT?
VERY SOON, A GREAT WAR WILL BREAK OUT OVER THIS WHEAT.
WHILE THE ARMY WAS EXCAVATING WEAPONS FROM THE PREVIOUS ERA IN PREPARATION, THEY CAME ACROSS THIS PILL.
SINCE EVERYONE IN THE PREVIOUS ERA WAS BLESSED WITH REGENERATION, THEY'D TAKE THIS TO KILL THEMSELVES.
I SUGGEST YOU TAKE IT AND DIE AS SOON AS YOU CAN.

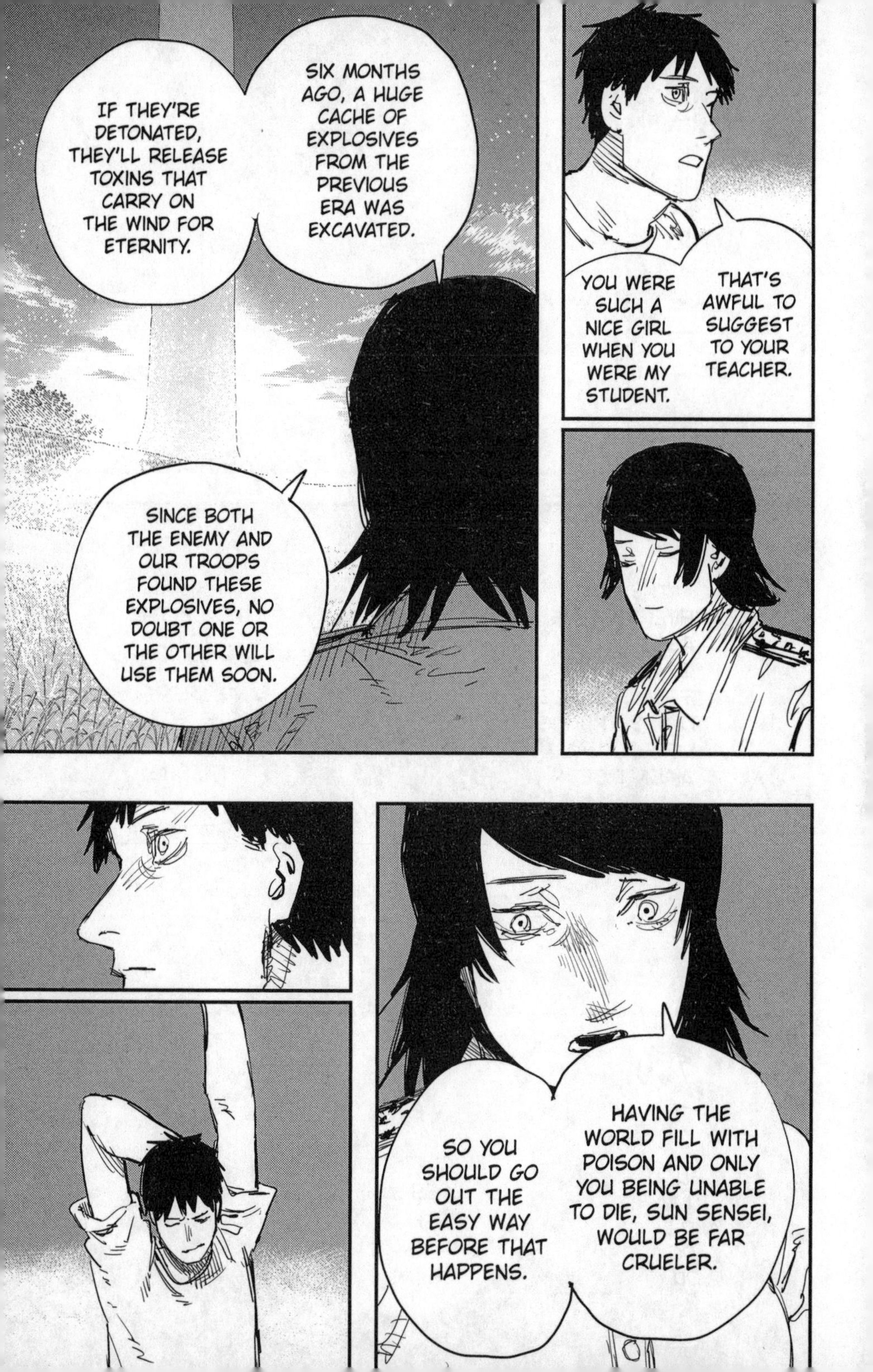
SIX MONTHS AGO, A HUGE CACHE OF EXPLOSIVES FROM THE PREVIOUS ERA WAS EXCAVATED.
IF THEY'RE DETONATED, THEY'LL RELEASE TOXINS THAT CARRY ON THE WIND FOR ETERNITY.
SINCE BOTH THE ENEMY AND OUR TROOPS FOUND THESE EXPLOSIVES, NO DOUBT ONE OR THE OTHER WILL USE THEM SOON.
THAT'S AWFUL TO SUGGEST TO YOUR TEACHER.
YOU WERE SUCH A NICE GIRL WHEN YOU WERE MY STUDENT.
HAVING THE WORLD FILL WITH POISON AND ONLY YOU BEING UNABLE TO DIE, SUN SENSEI, WOULD BE FAR CRUELER.
SO YOU SHOULD GO OUT THE EASY WAY BEFORE THAT HAPPENS.

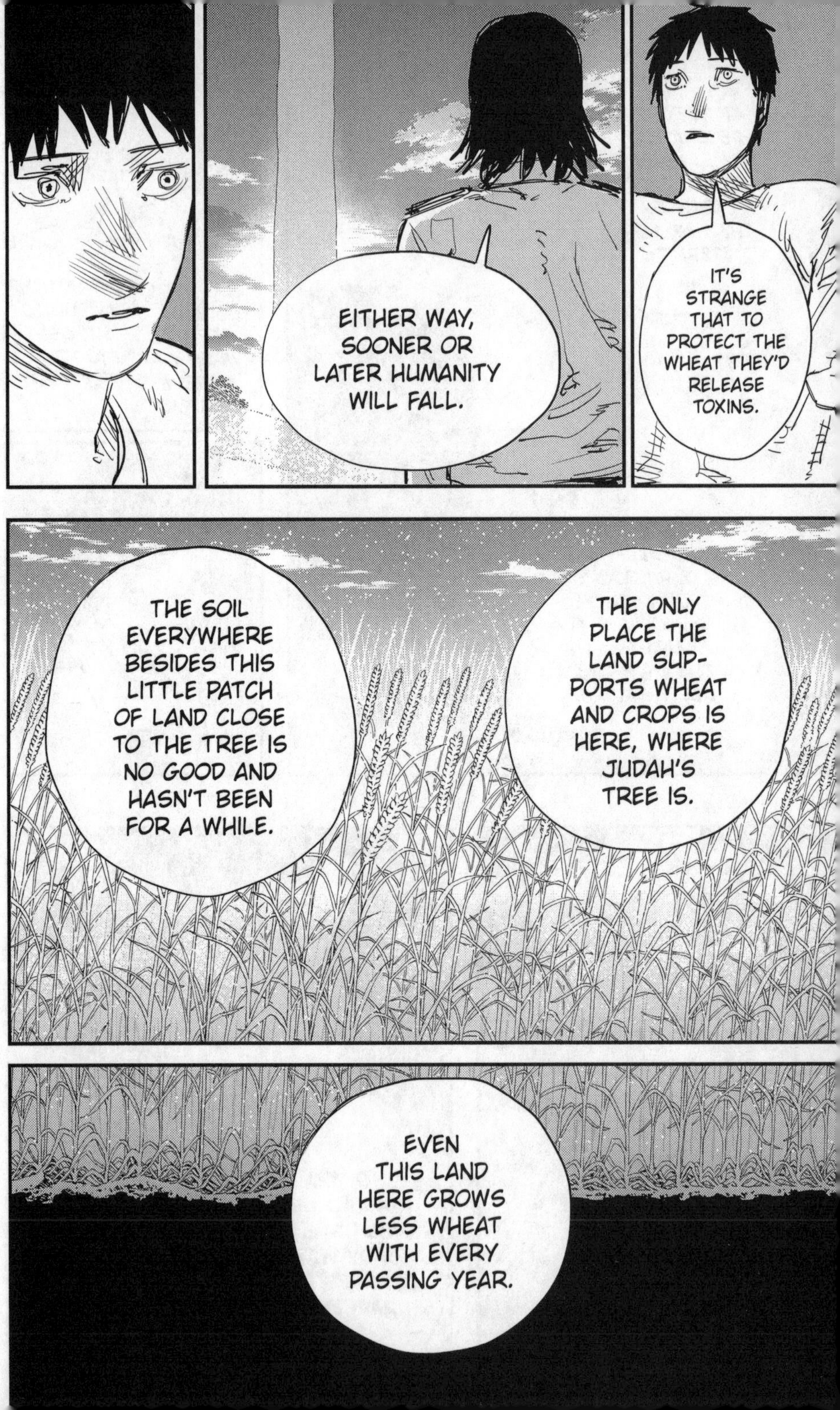
IT'S STRANGE THAT TO PROTECT THE WHEAT THEY'D RELEASE TOXINS.
EITHER WAY, SOONER OR LATER HUMANITY WILL FALL.
THE ONLY PLACE THE LAND SUP-PORTS WHEAT AND CROPS IS HERE, WHERE JUDAH'S TREE IS.
THE SOIL EVERYWHERE BESIDES THIS LITTLE PATCH OF LAND CLOSE TO THE TREE IS NO GOOD AND HASN'T BEEN FOR A WHILE.
EVEN THIS LAND HERE GROWS LESS WHEAT WITH EVERY PASSING YEAR.

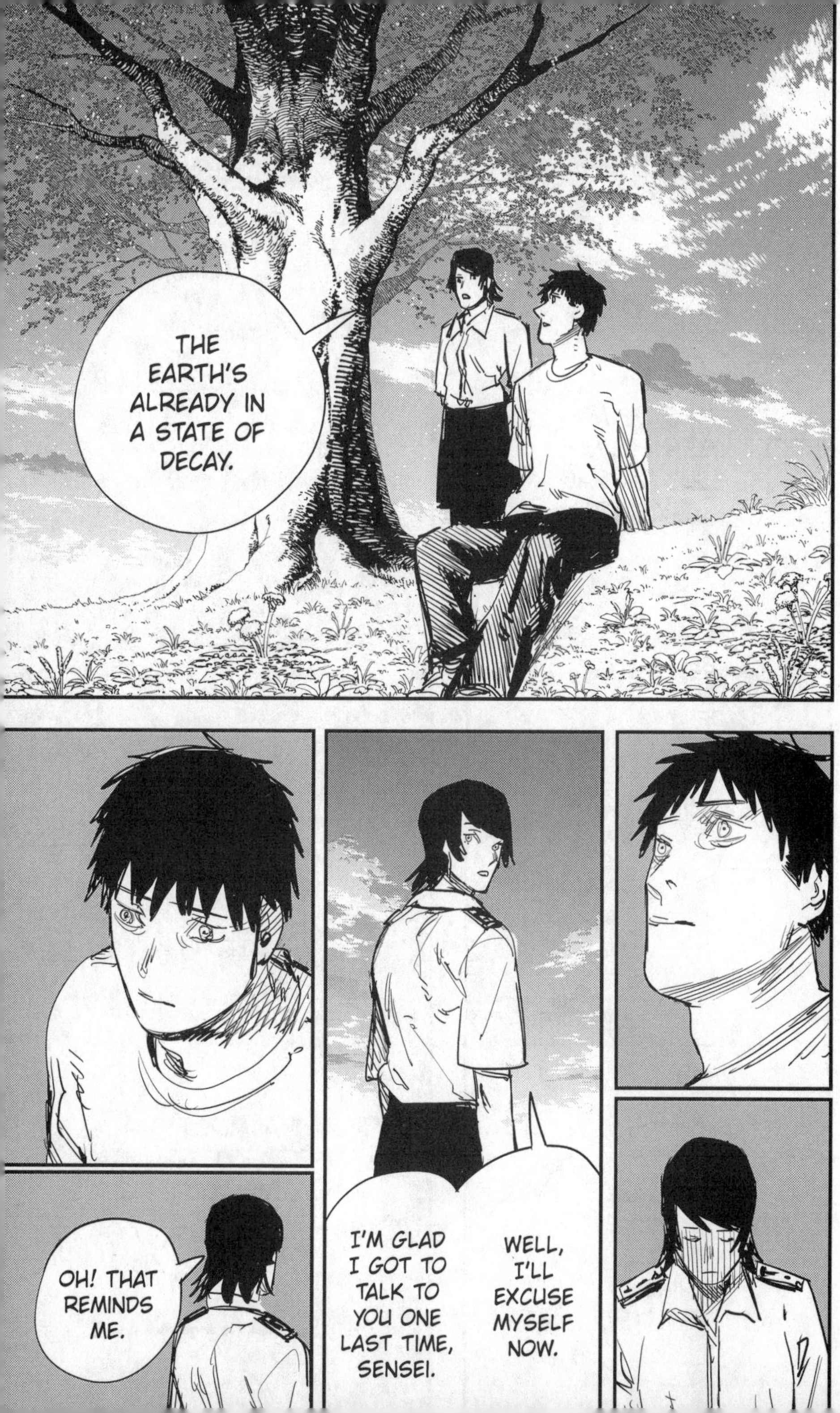
THE EARTH'S ALREADY IN A STATE OF DECAY.
WELL, I'LL EXCUSE MYSELF NOW. I'M GLAD I GOT TO TALK TO YOU ONE LAST TIME, SENSEI.
OH! THAT REMINDS ME.

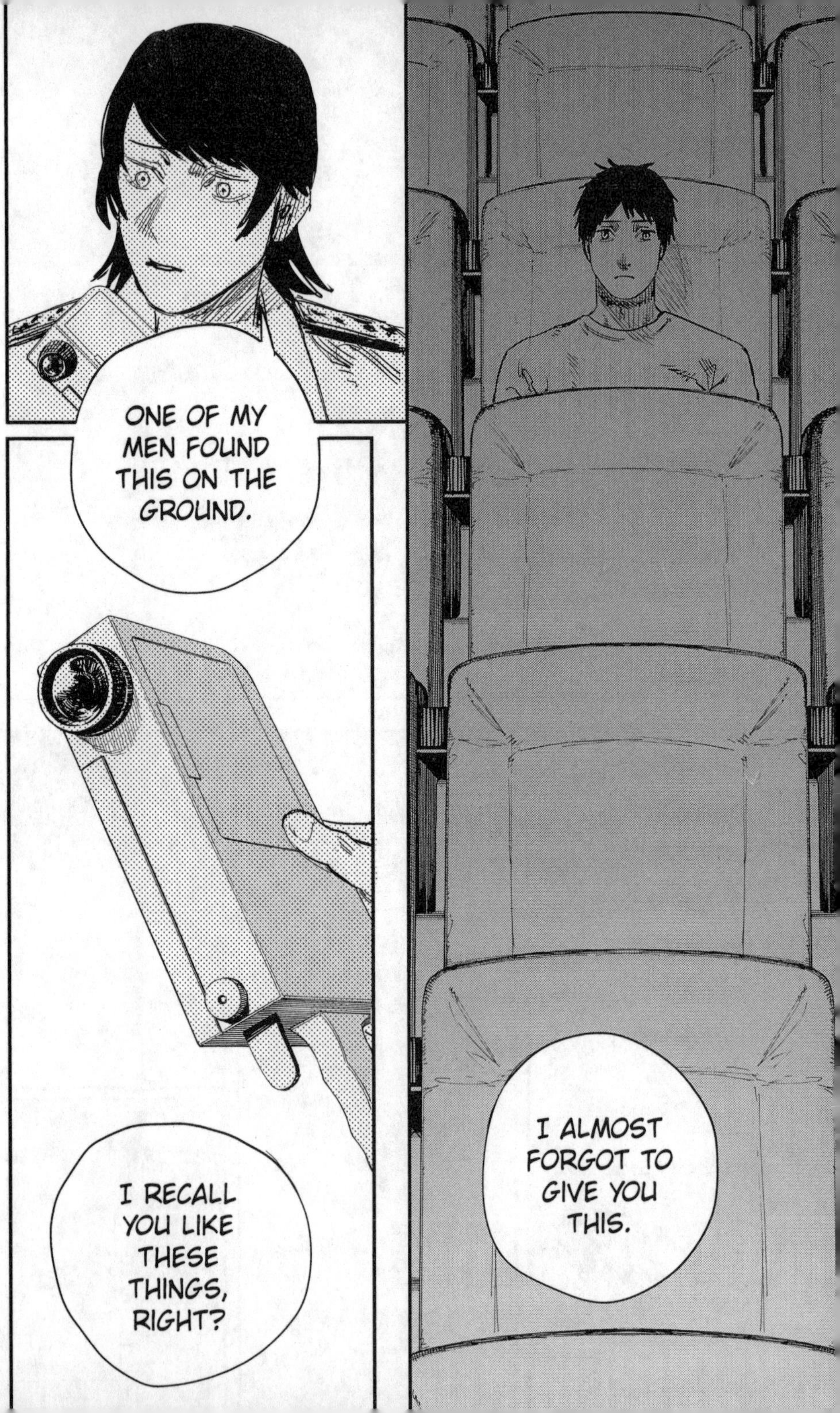
I ALMOST FORGOT TO GIVE YOU THIS.
ONE OF MY MEN FOUND THIS ON THE GROUND.
I RECALL YOU LIKE THESE THINGS, RIGHT?

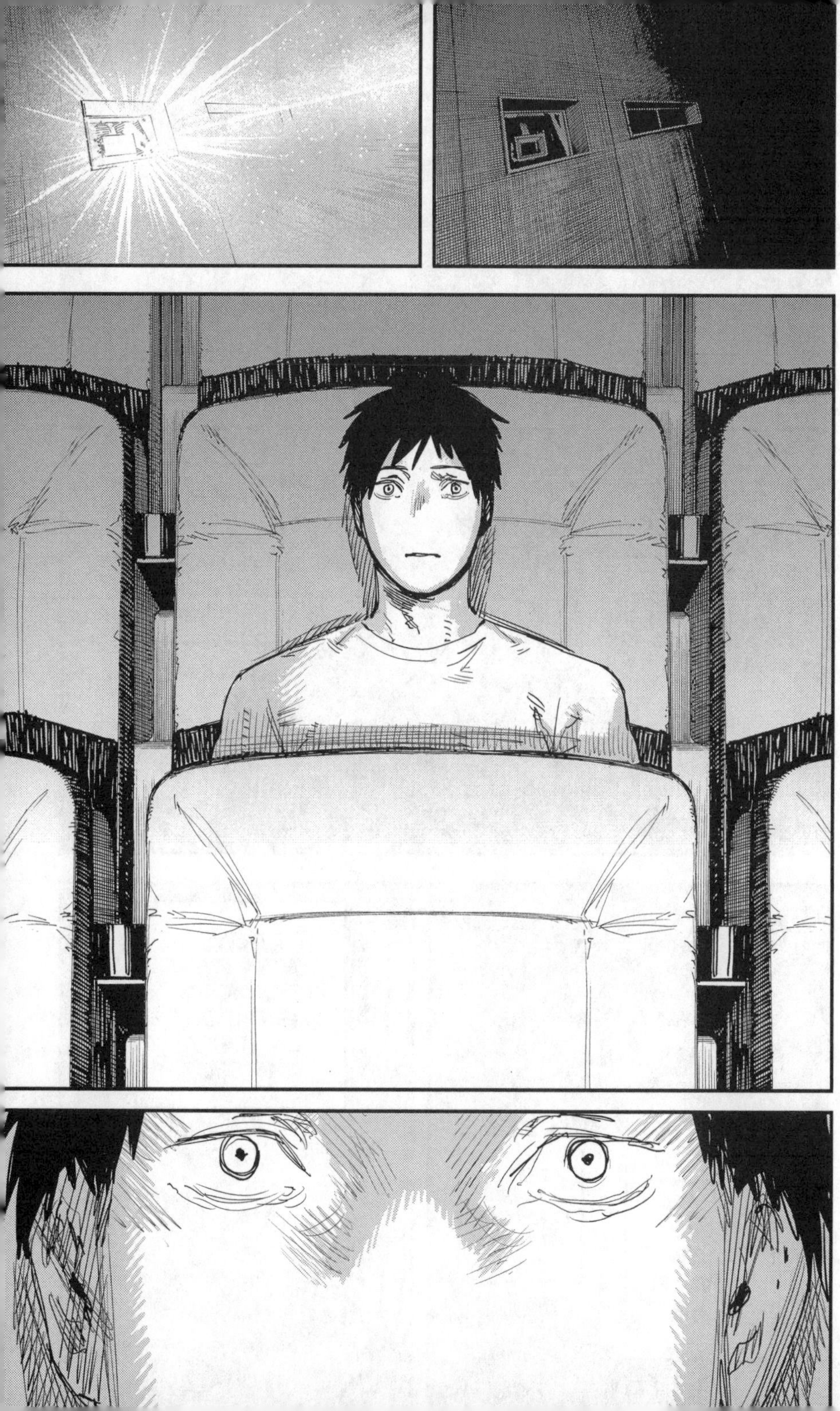

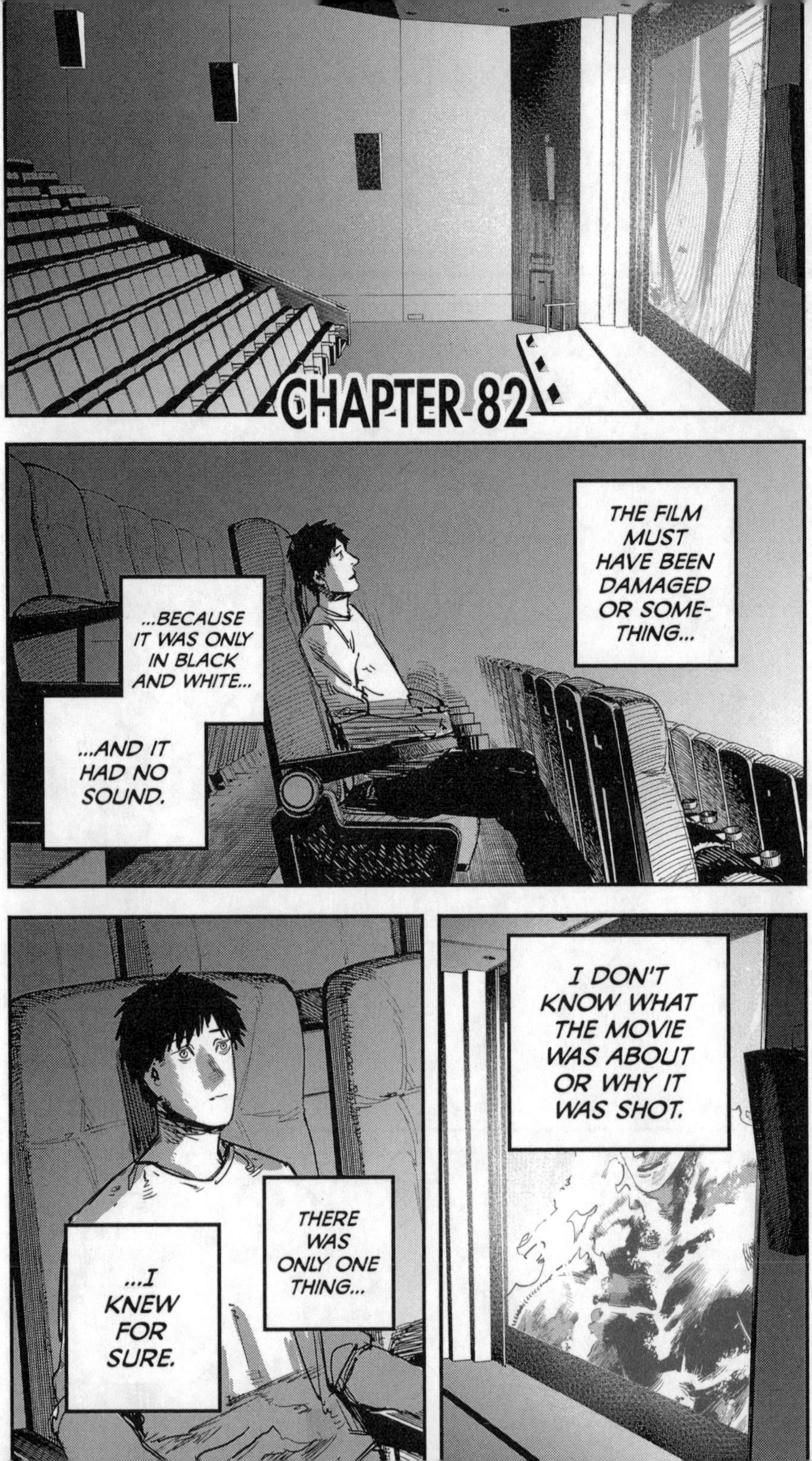
CHAPTER 82
THE FILM MUST HAVE BEEN DAMAGED OR SOME-THING...
...BECAUSE IT WAS ONLY IN BLACK AND WHITE...
...AND IT HAD NO SOUND.
I DON'T KNOW WHAT THE MOVIE WAS ABOUT OR WHY IT WAS SHOT.
THERE WAS ONLY ONE THING...
...I KNEW FOR SURE.

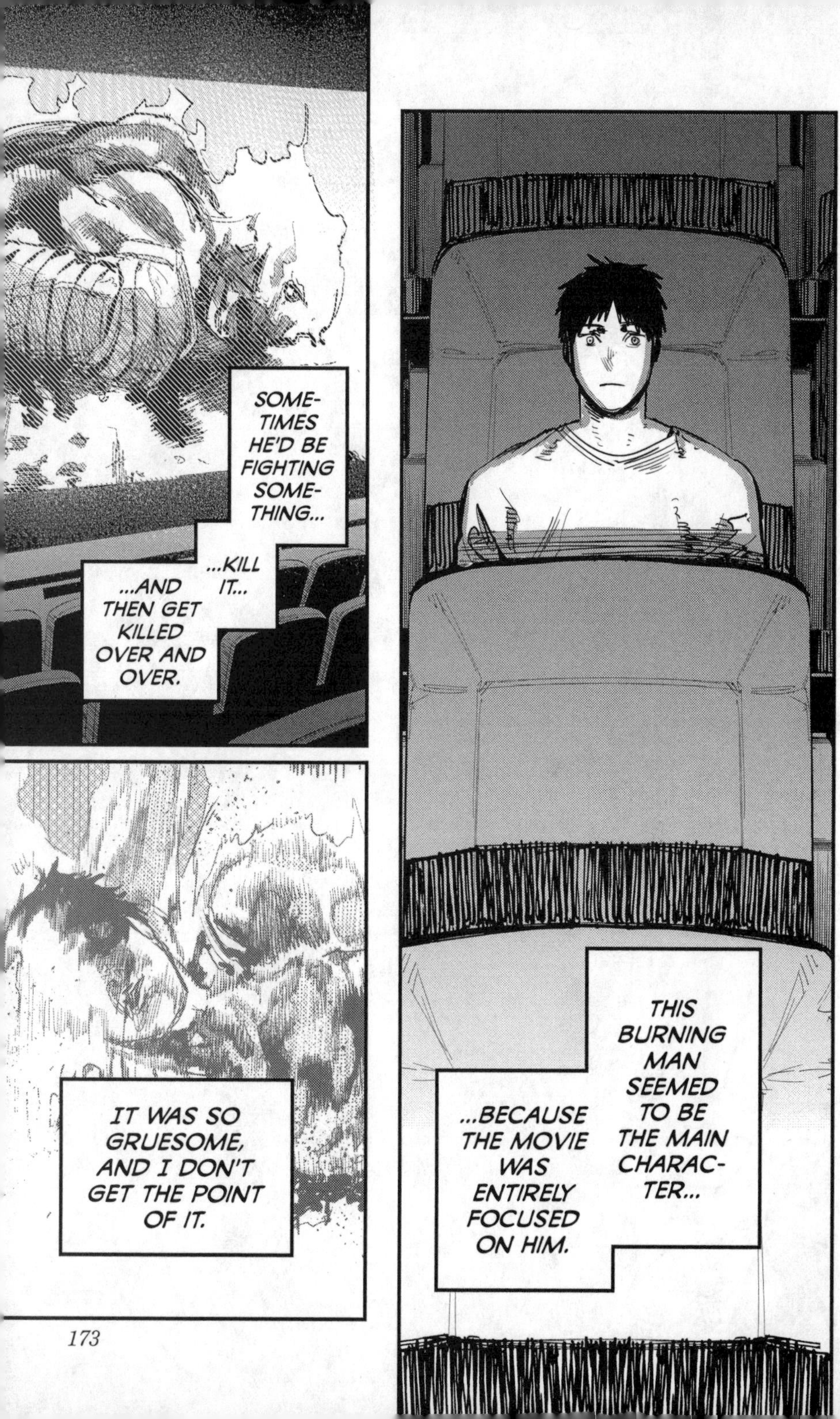
THIS BURNING MAN SEEMED TO BE THE MAIN CHARACTER...
...BECAUSE THE MOVIE WAS ENTIRELY FOCUSED ON HIM.
SOMETIMES HE'D BE FIGHTING SOMETHING...
...KILL IT...
...AND THEN GET KILLED OVER AND OVER.
IT WAS SO GRUESOME, AND I DON'T GET THE POINT OF IT.

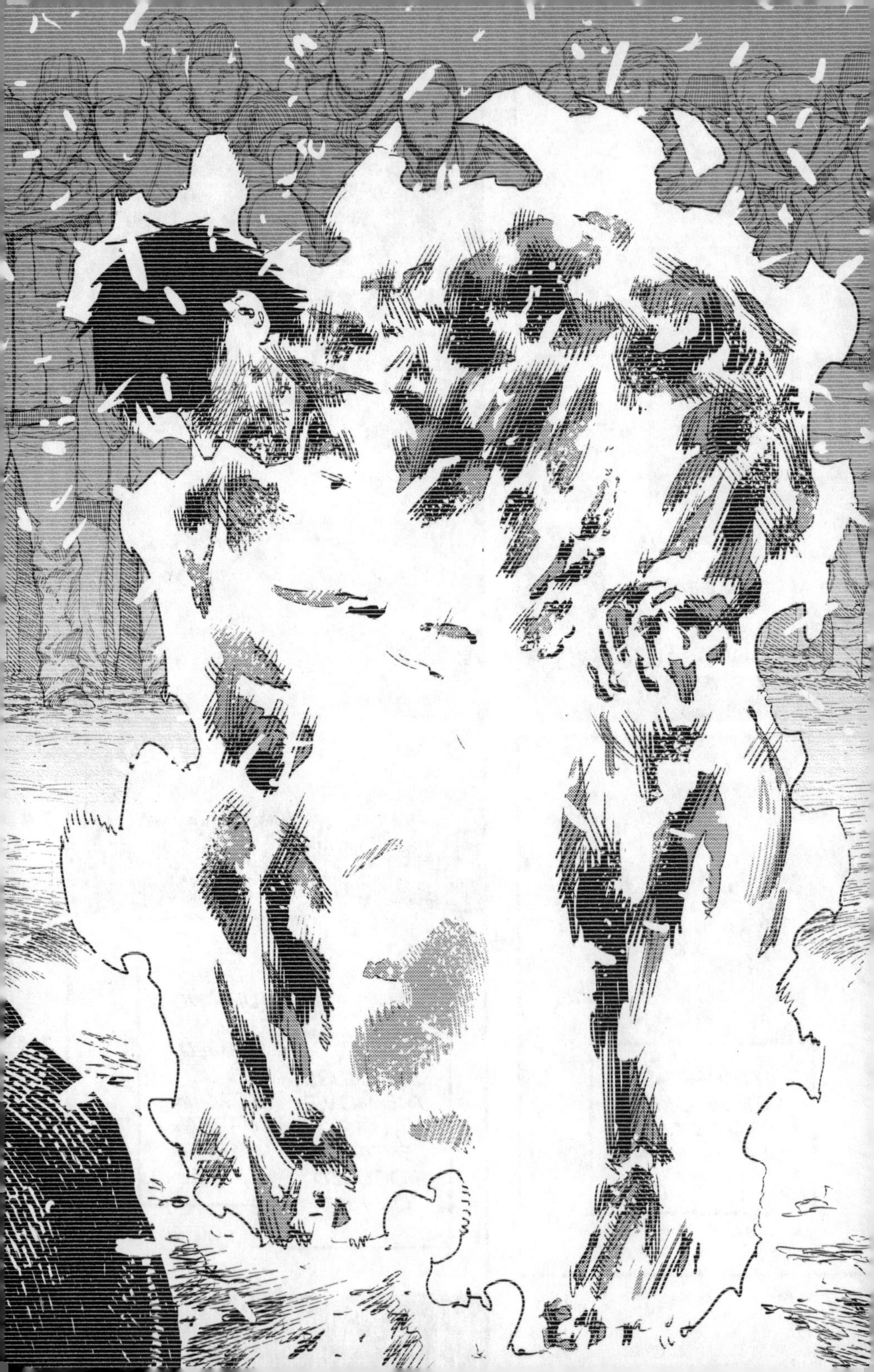

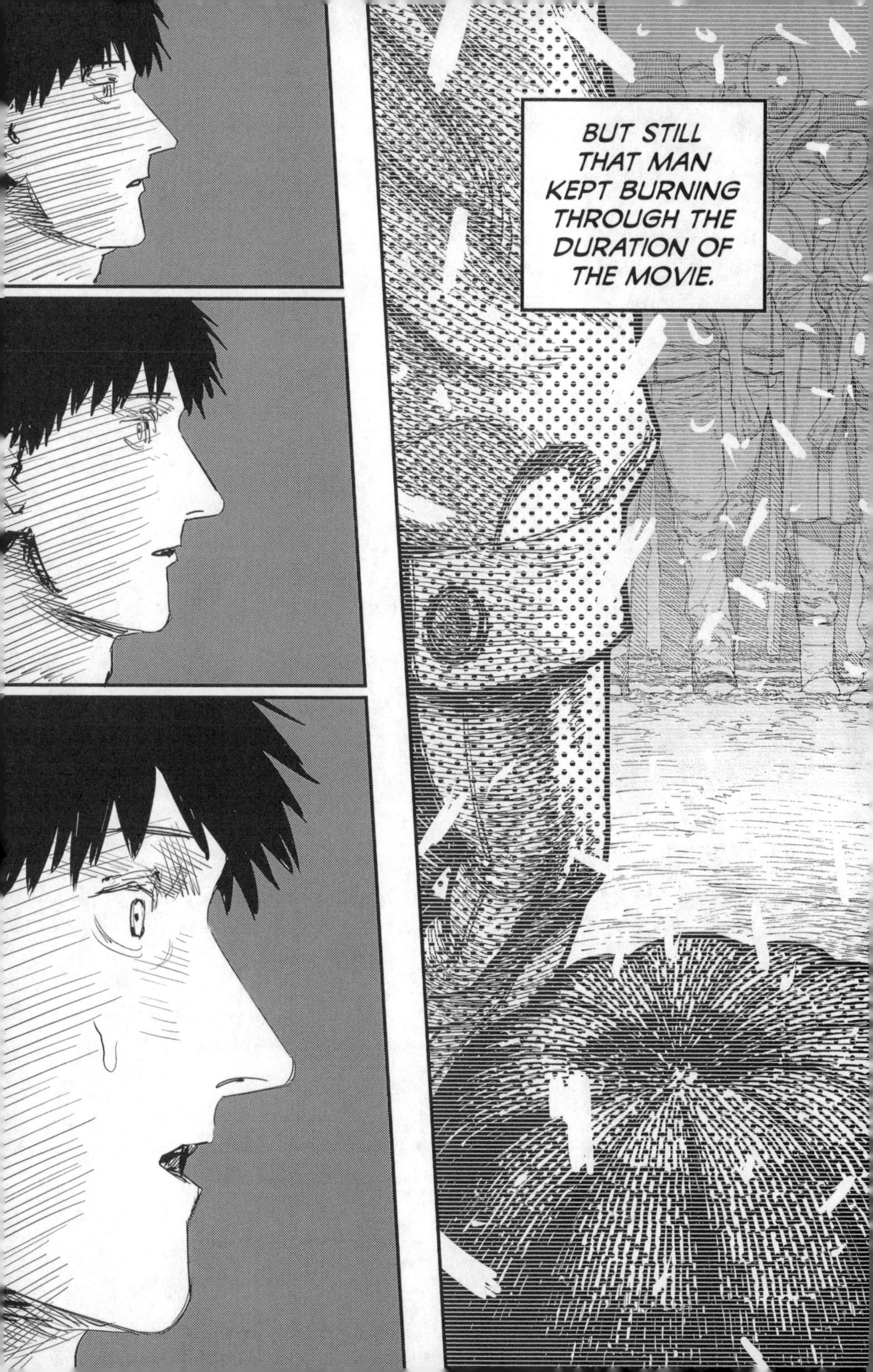
BUT STILL THAT MAN KEPT BURNING THROUGH THE DURATION OF THE MOVIE.

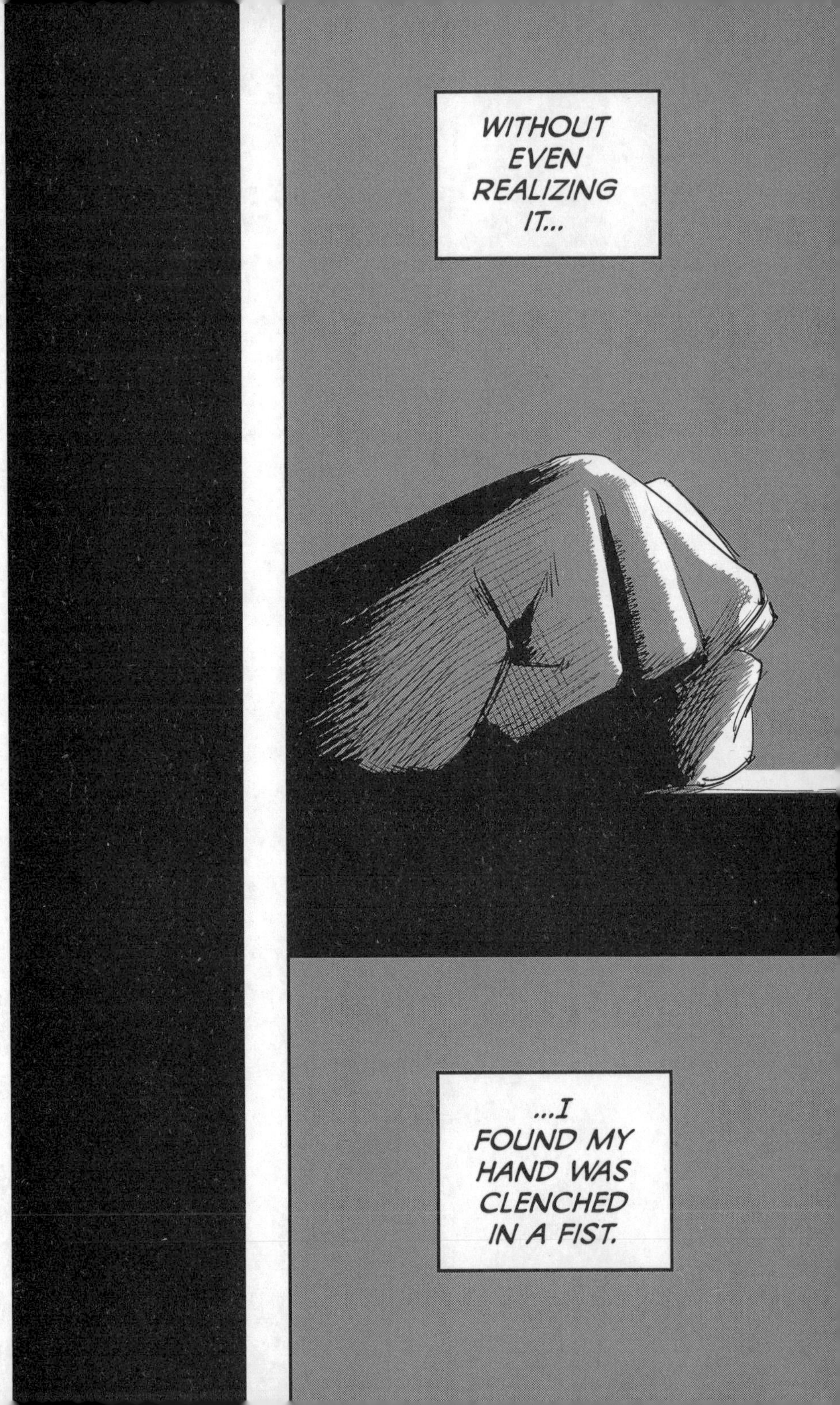
WITHOUT EVEN REALIZING IT...
...I FOUND MY HAND WAS CLENCHED IN A FIST.

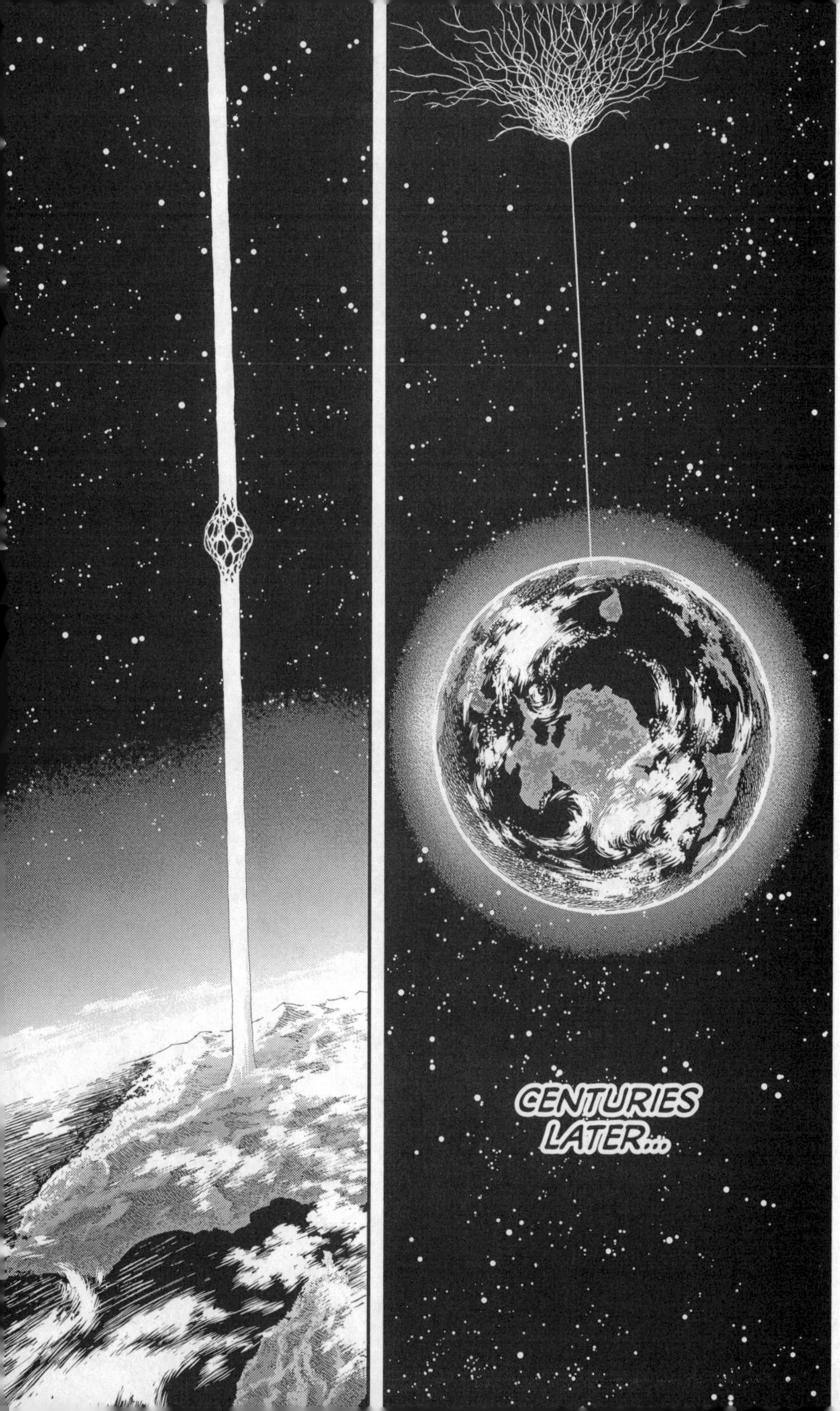
CENTURIES LATER...

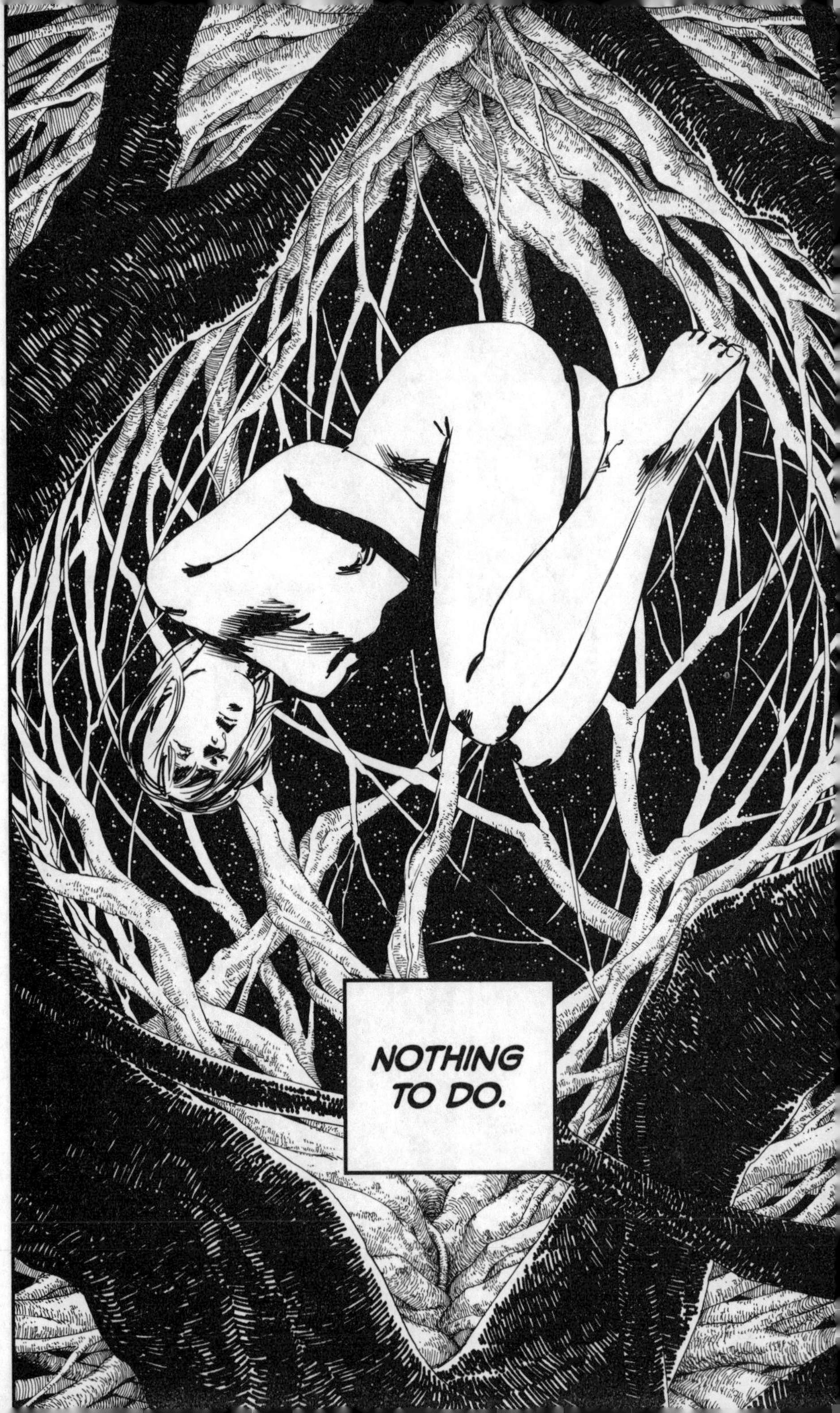
NOTHING
TO DO.

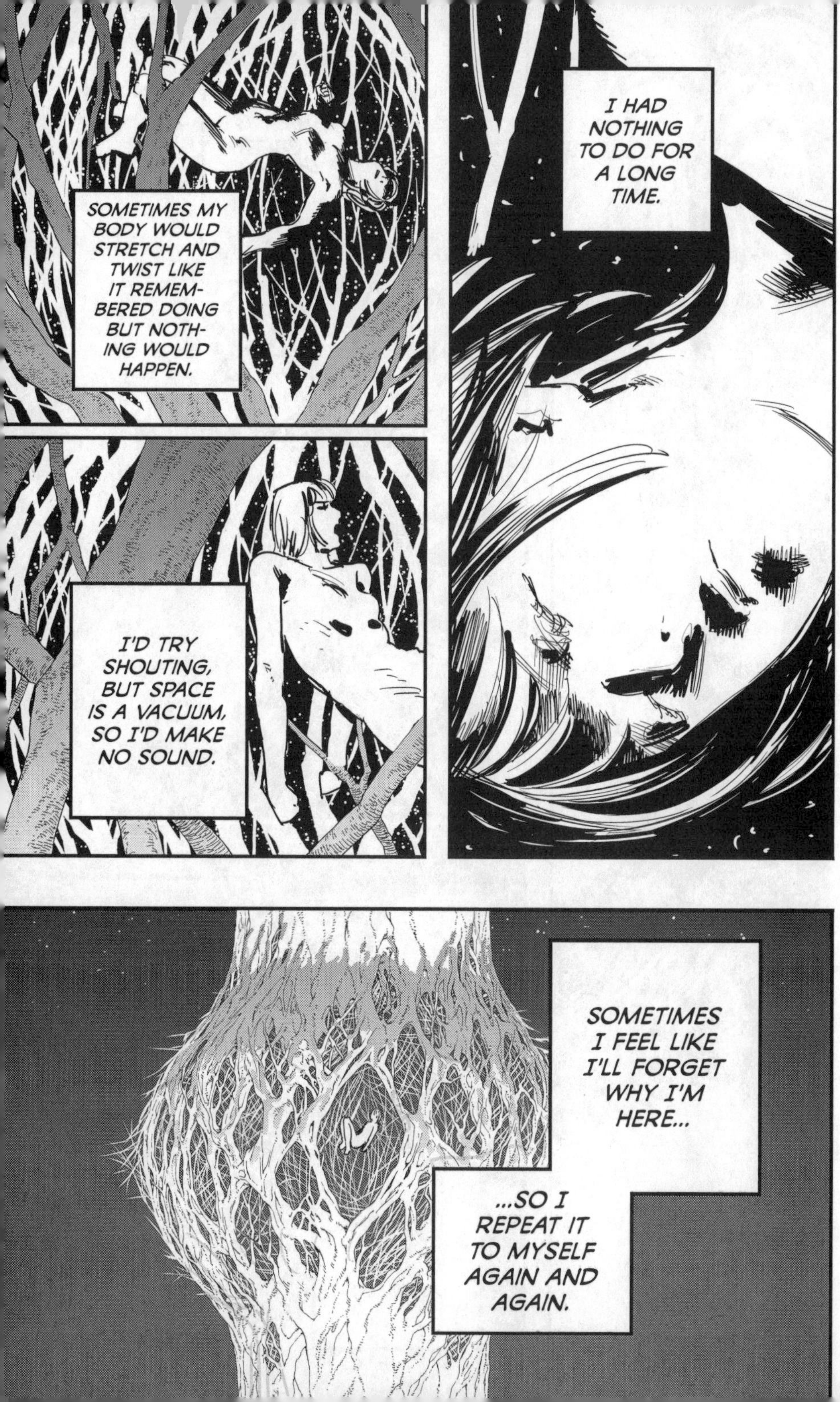
I HAD NOTHING TO DO FOR A LONG TIME.
SOMETIMES MY BODY WOULD STRETCH AND TWIST LIKE IT REMEMBERED DOING BUT NOTHING WOULD HAPPEN.
I'D TRY SHOUTING, BUT SPACE IS A VACUUM, SO I'D MAKE NO SOUND.
SOMETIMES I FEEL LIKE I'LL FORGET WHY I'M HERE...
...SO I REPEAT IT TO MYSELF AGAIN AND AGAIN.

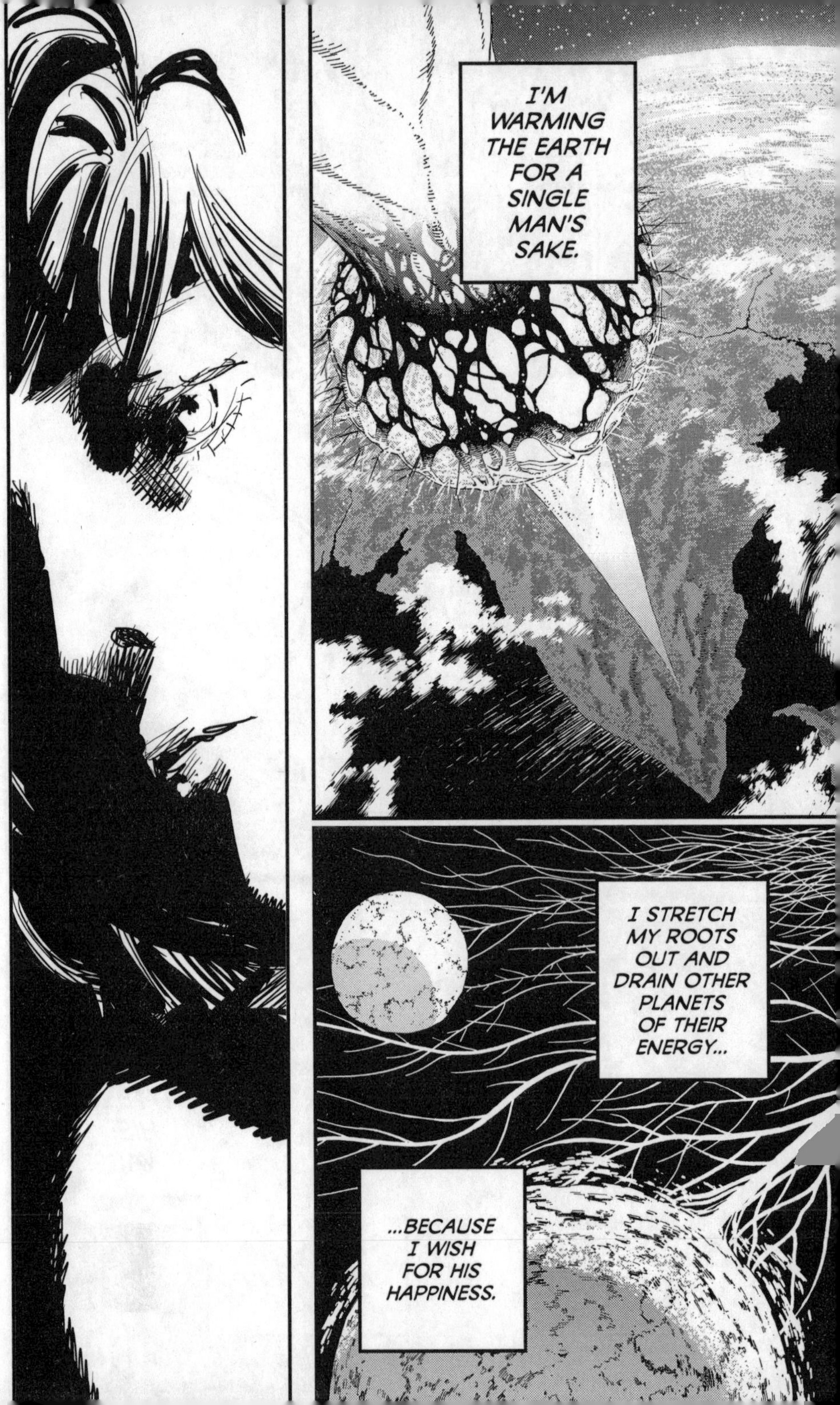
I'M WARMING THE EARTH FOR A SINGLE MAN'S SAKE.
I STRETCH MY ROOTS OUT AND DRAIN OTHER PLANETS OF THEIR ENERGY...
...BECAUSE I WISH FOR HIS HAPPINESS.

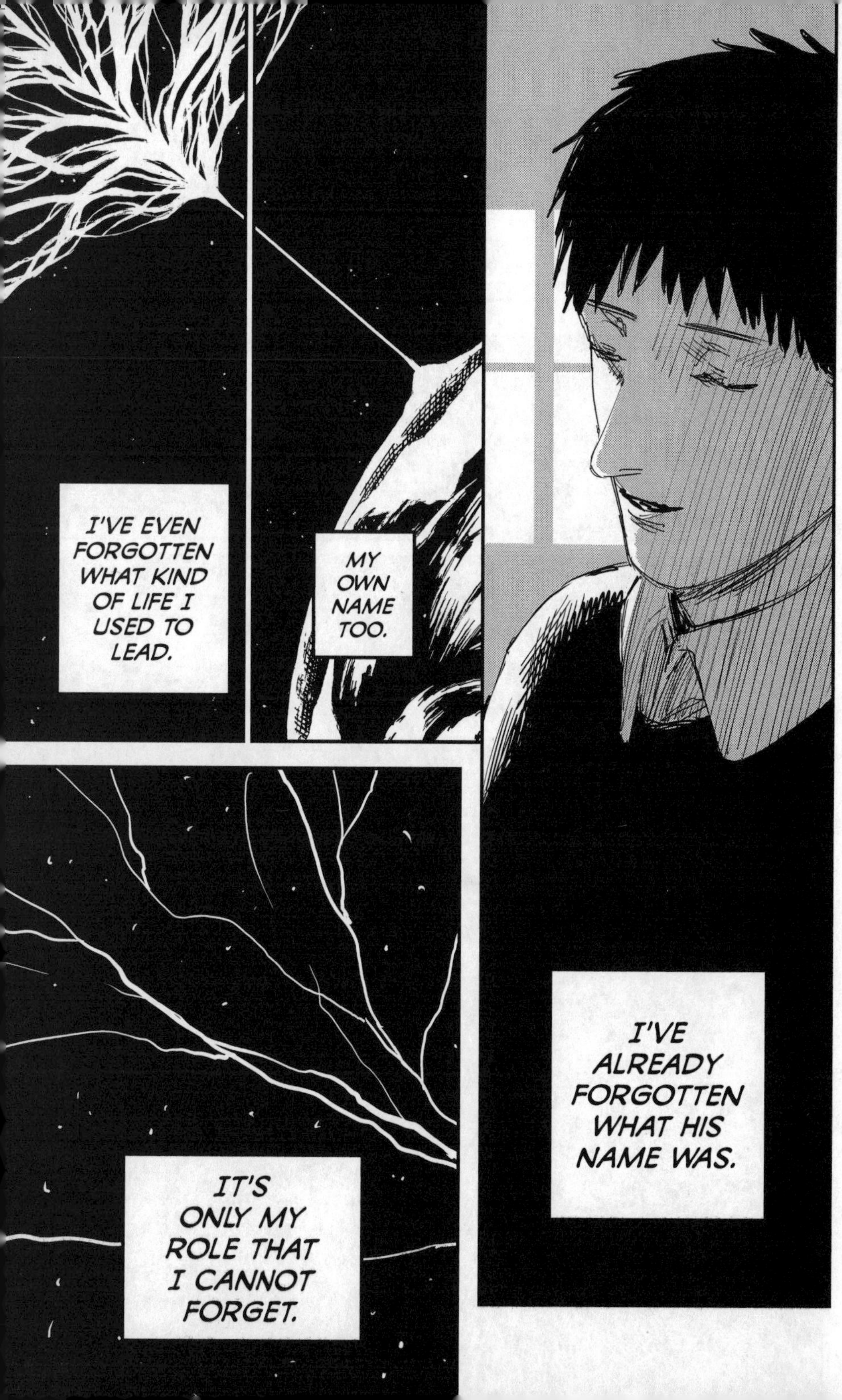
I'VE ALREADY FORGOTTEN WHAT HIS NAME WAS.
MY OWN NAME TOO.
I'VE EVEN FORGOTTEN WHAT KIND OF LIFE I USED TO LEAD.
IT'S ONLY MY ROLE THAT I CANNOT FORGET.

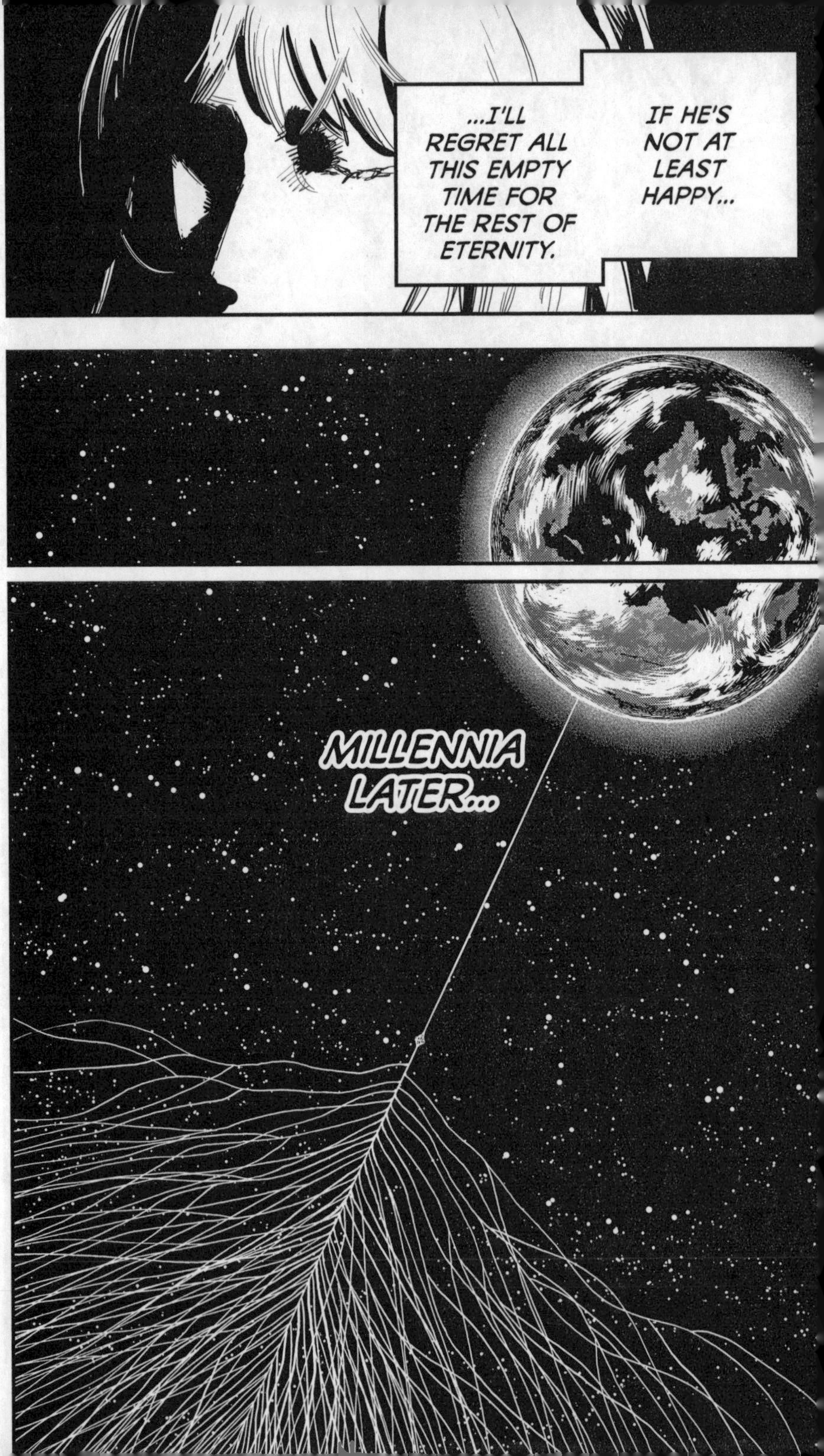
IF HE'S NOT AT LEAST HAPPY...
...I'LL REGRET ALL THIS EMPTY TIME FOR THE REST OF ETERNITY.
MILLENNIA LATER...

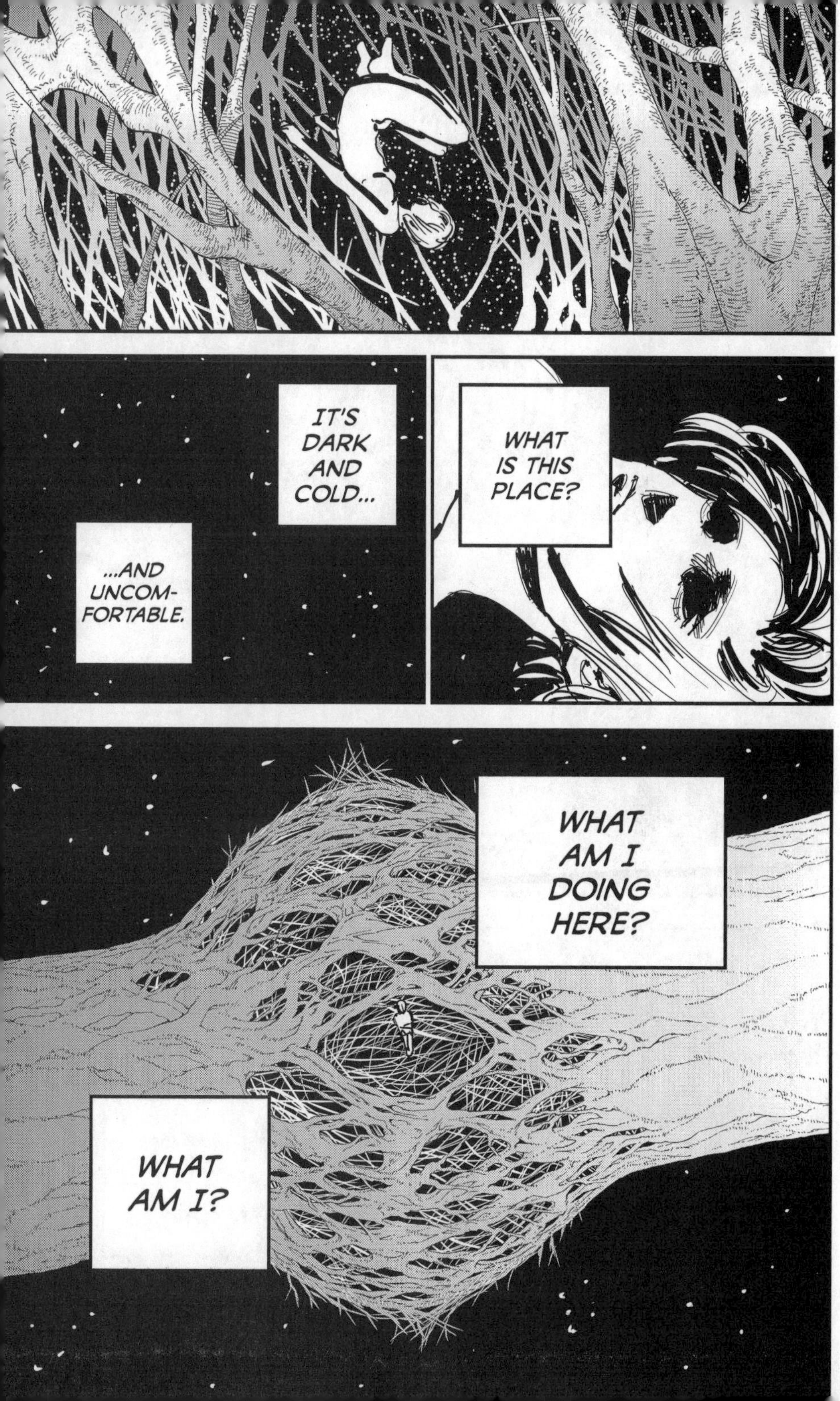
WHAT IS THIS PLACE?
IT'S DARK AND COLD...
...AND UNCOM-FORTABLE.
WHAT AM I DOING HERE?
WHAT AM I?

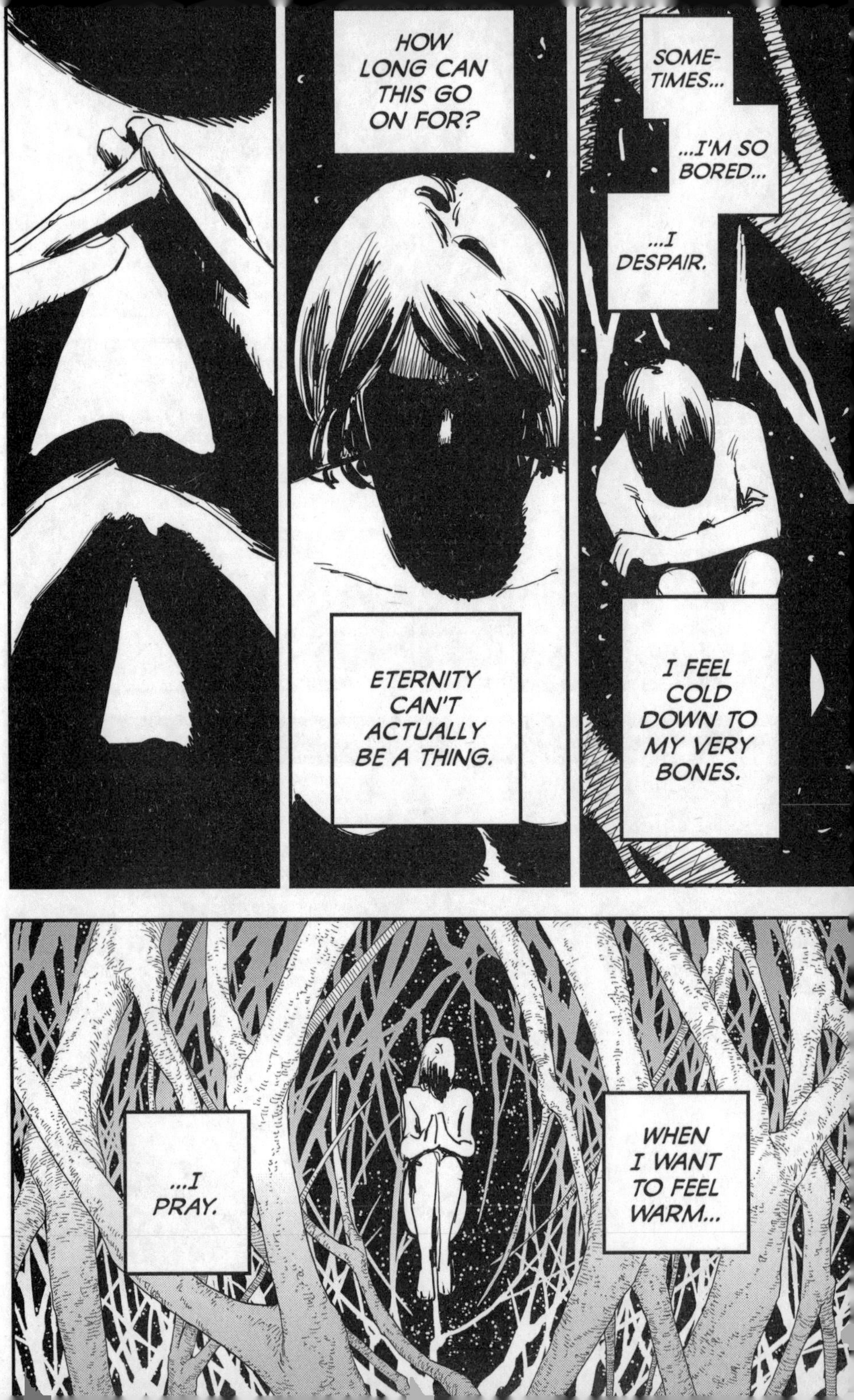
SOME-TIMES...
...I'M SO BORED...
...I DESPAIR.
I FEEL COLD DOWN TO MY VERY BONES.
HOW LONG CAN THIS GO ON FOR?
ETERNITY CAN'T ACTUALLY BE A THING.
WHEN I WANT TO FEEL WARM...
...I PRAY.

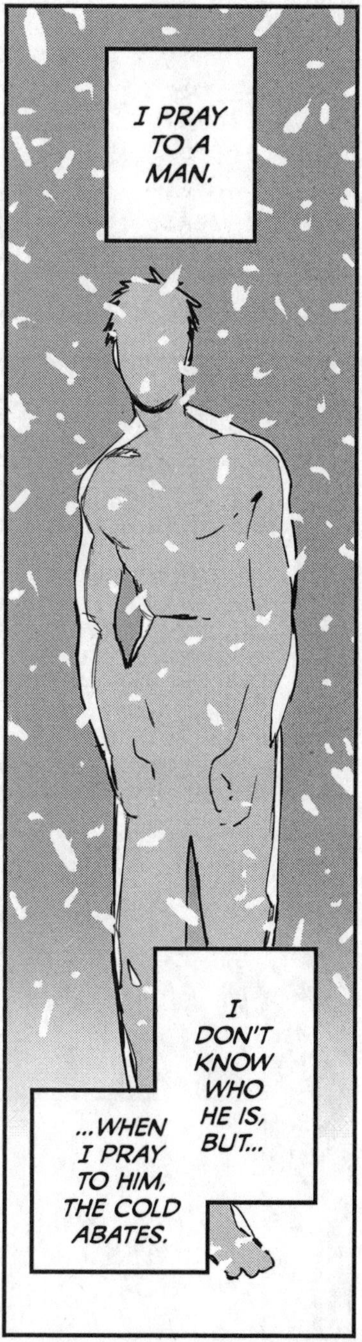
I PRAY TO A MAN.
I DON'T KNOW WHO HE IS, BUT...
...WHEN I PRAY TO HIM, THE COLD ABATES.
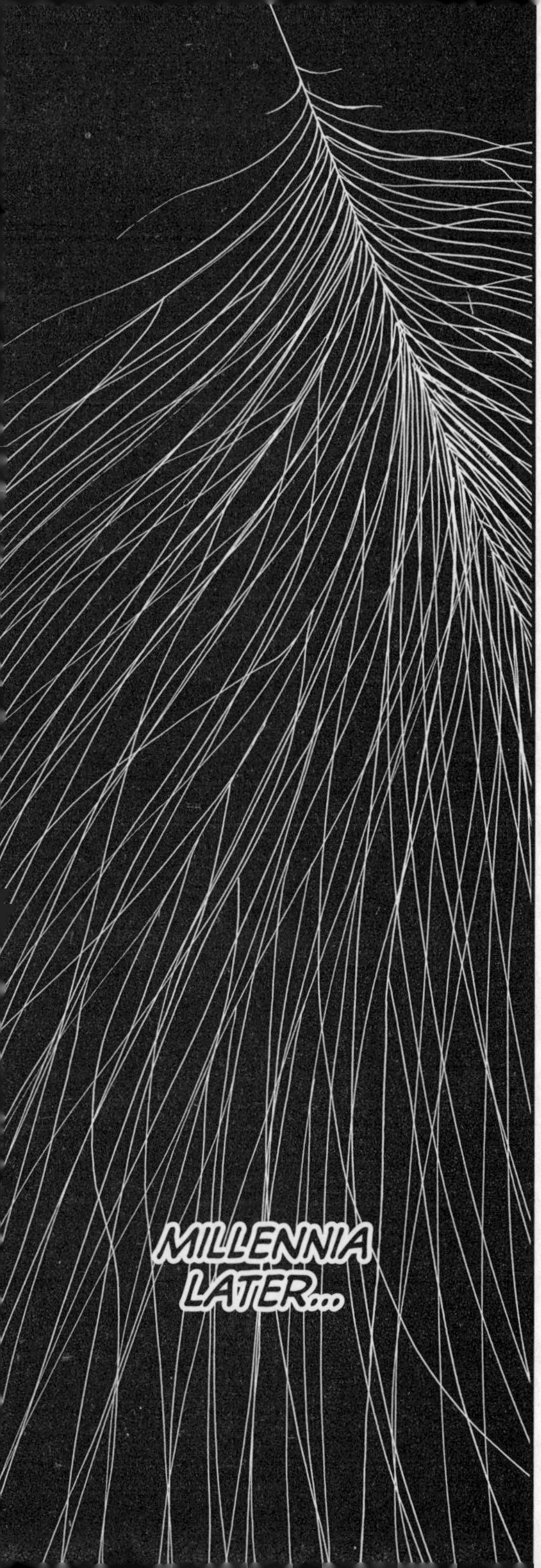
MILLENNIA LATER...

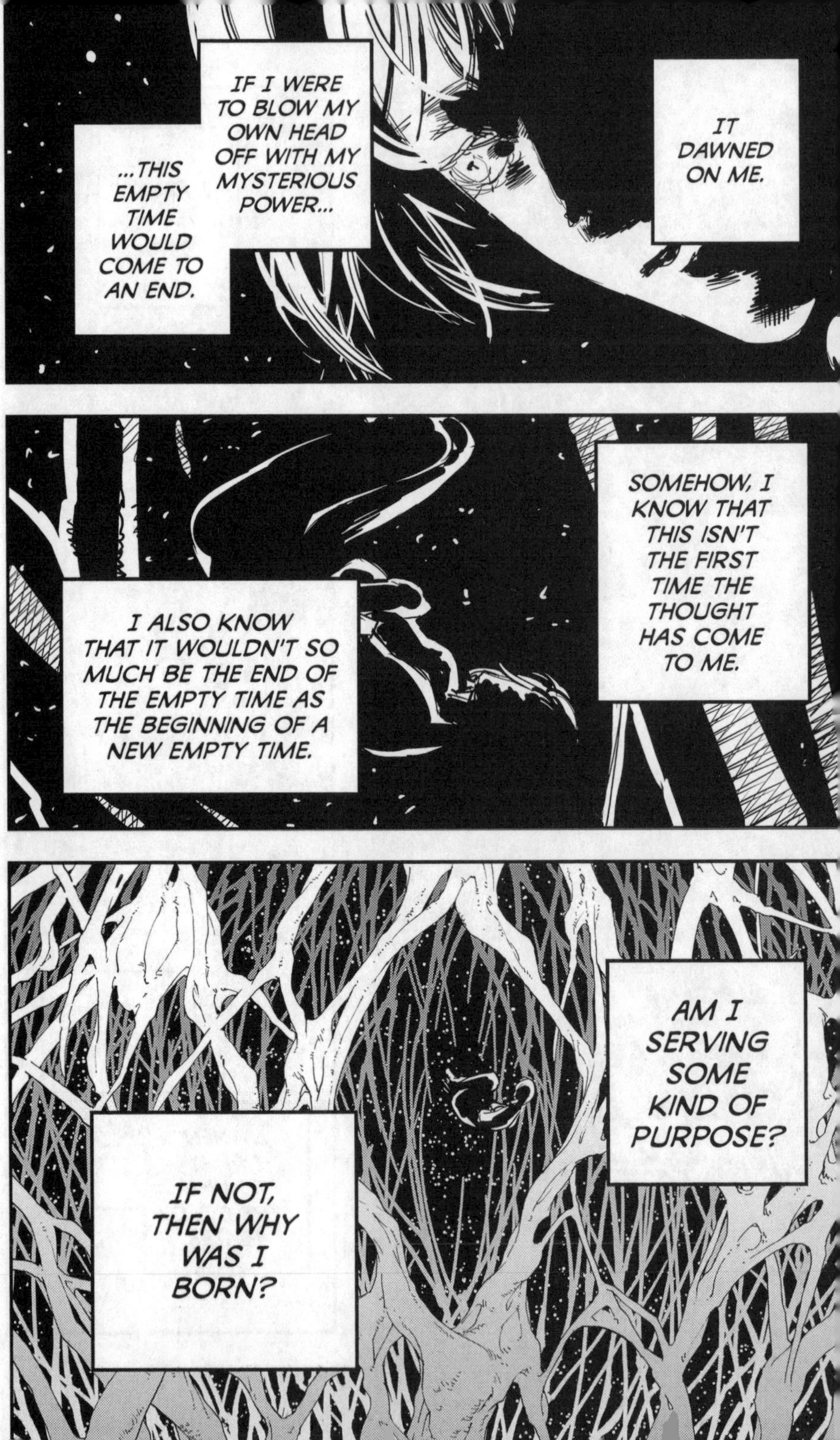
IT DAWNED ON ME.
IF I WERE TO BLOW MY OWN HEAD OFF WITH MY MYSTERIOUS POWER...
...THIS EMPTY TIME WOULD COME TO AN END.
SOMEHOW, I KNOW THAT THIS ISN'T THE FIRST TIME THE THOUGHT HAS COME TO ME.
I ALSO KNOW THAT IT WOULDN'T SO MUCH BE THE END OF THE EMPTY TIME AS THE BEGINNING OF A NEW EMPTY TIME.
AM I SERVING SOME KIND OF PURPOSE?
IF NOT, THEN WHY WAS I BORN?

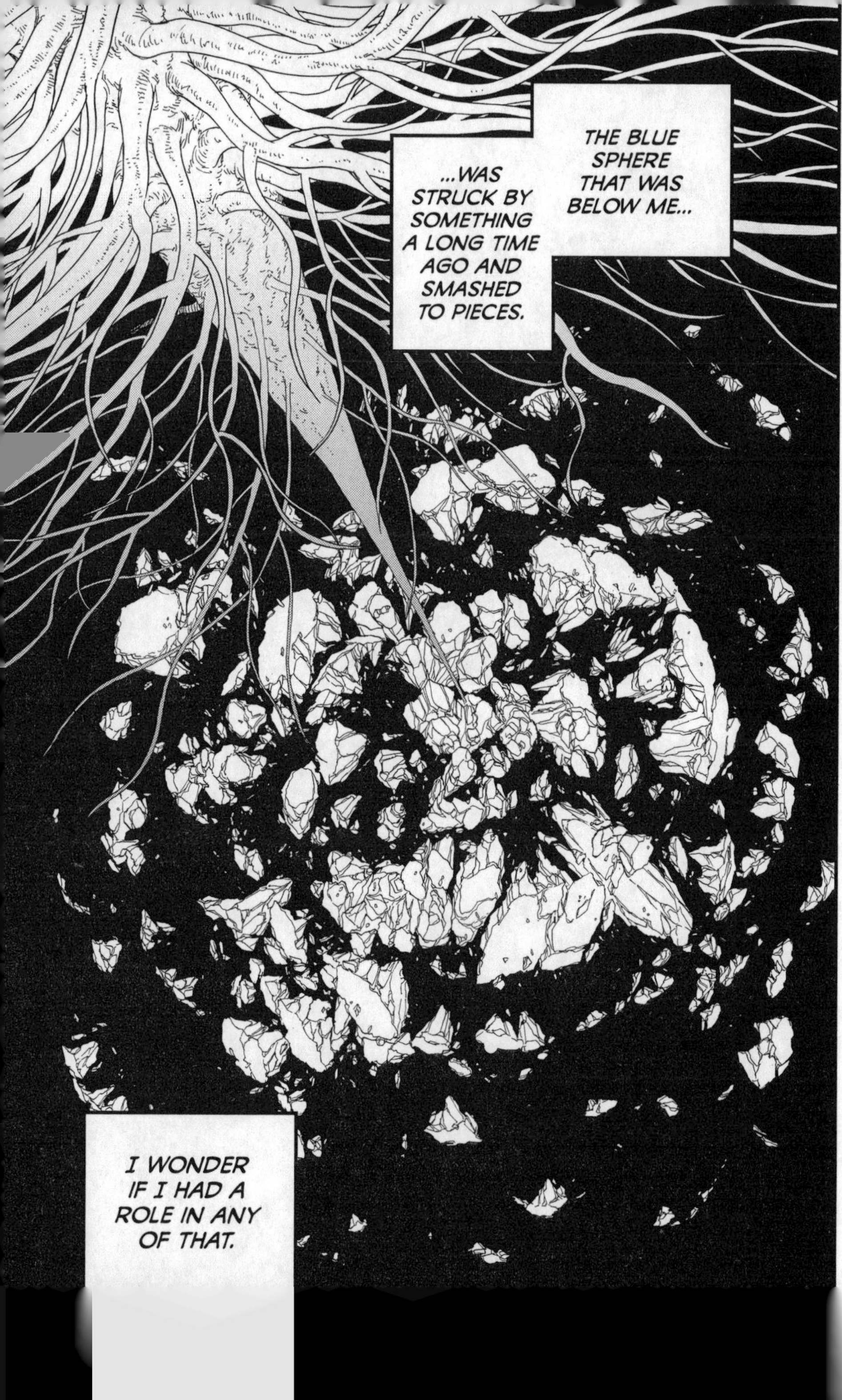
THE BLUE SPHERE THAT WAS BELOW ME...
...WAS STRUCK BY SOMETHING A LONG TIME AGO AND SMASHED TO PIECES.
I WONDER IF I HAD A ROLE IN ANY OF THAT.

MORE
MILLENNIA
LATER...

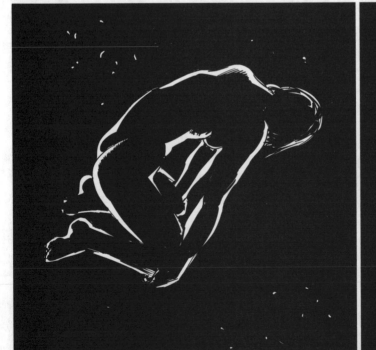

EVEN
MORE
MILLENNIA
LATER...

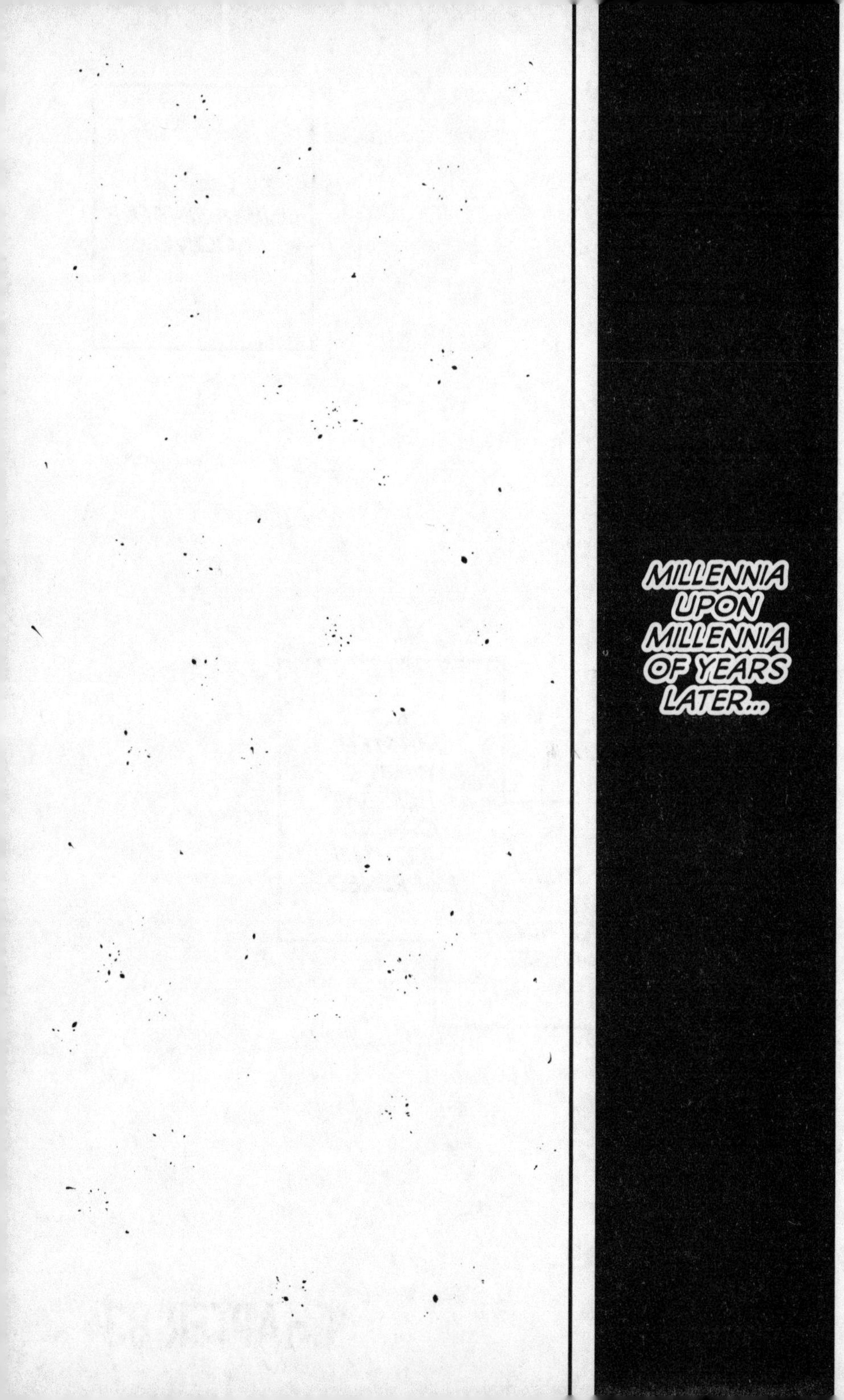
MILLENNIA UPON MILLENNIA OF YEARS LATER...

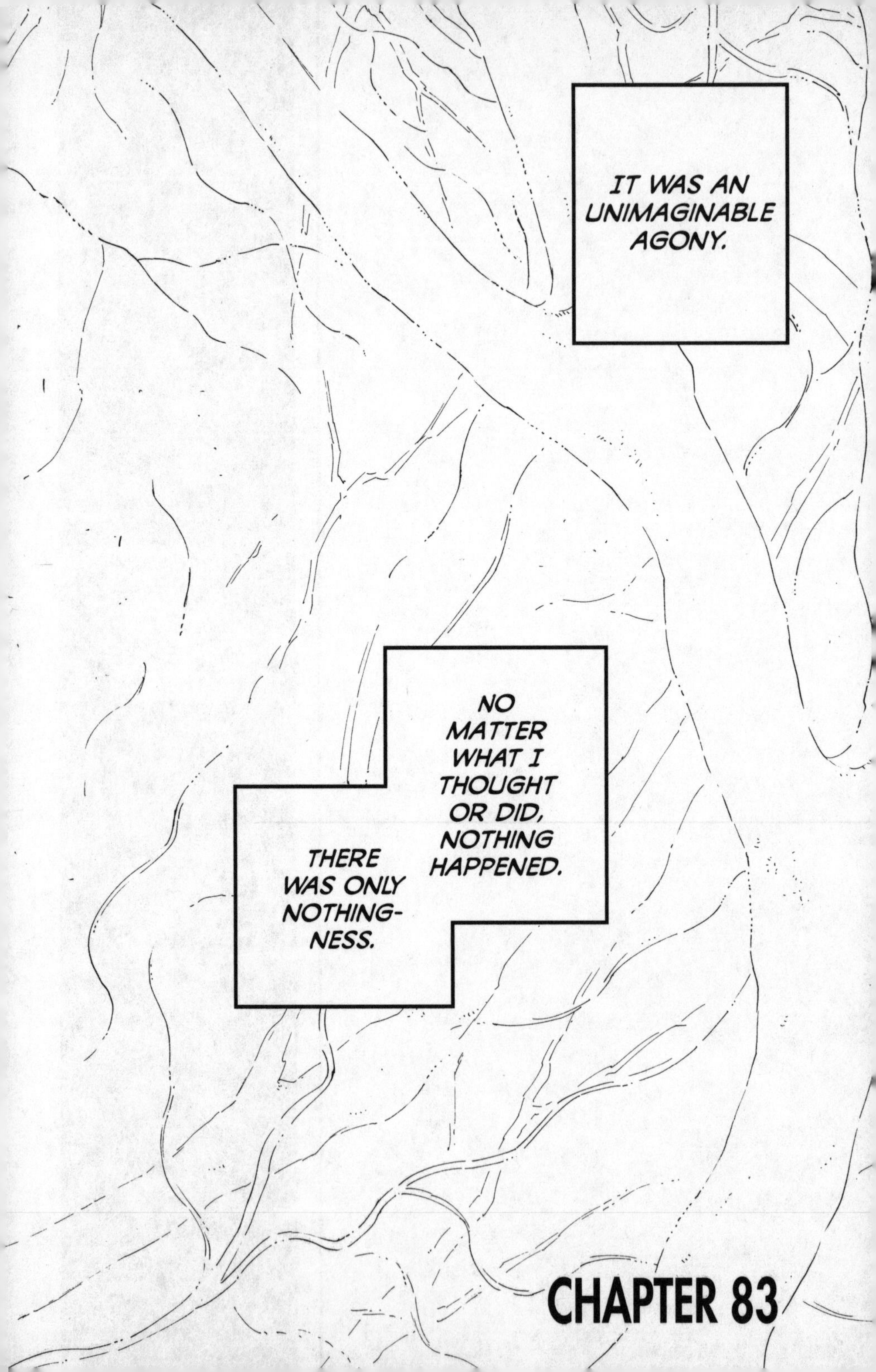
IT WAS AN UNIMAGINABLE AGONY.
NO MATTER WHAT I THOUGHT OR DID, NOTHING HAPPENED.
THERE WAS ONLY NOTHING-NESS.
CHAPTER 83

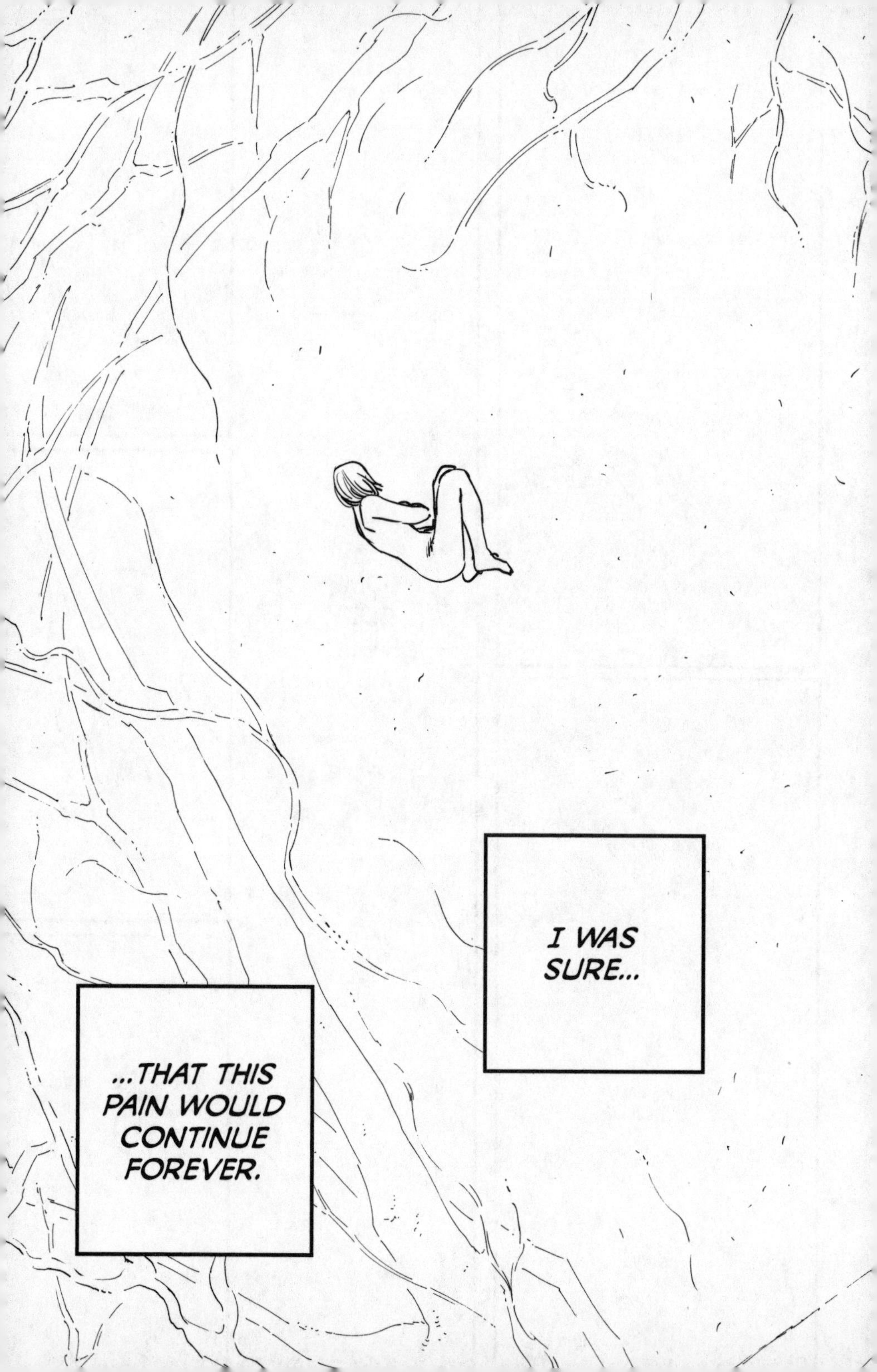
I WAS SURE...
...THAT THIS PAIN WOULD CONTINUE FOREVER.

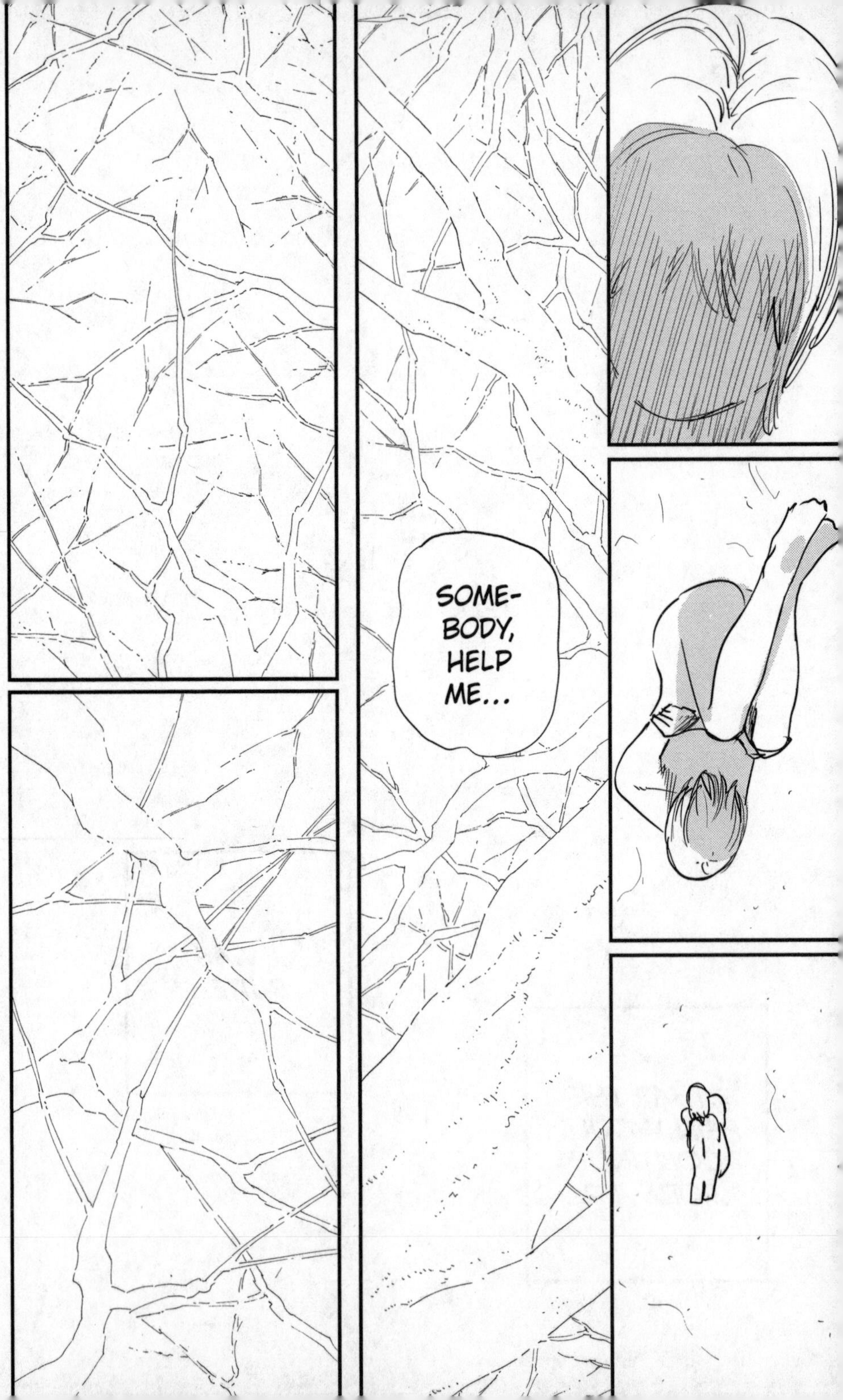
SOME-BODY, HELP ME...

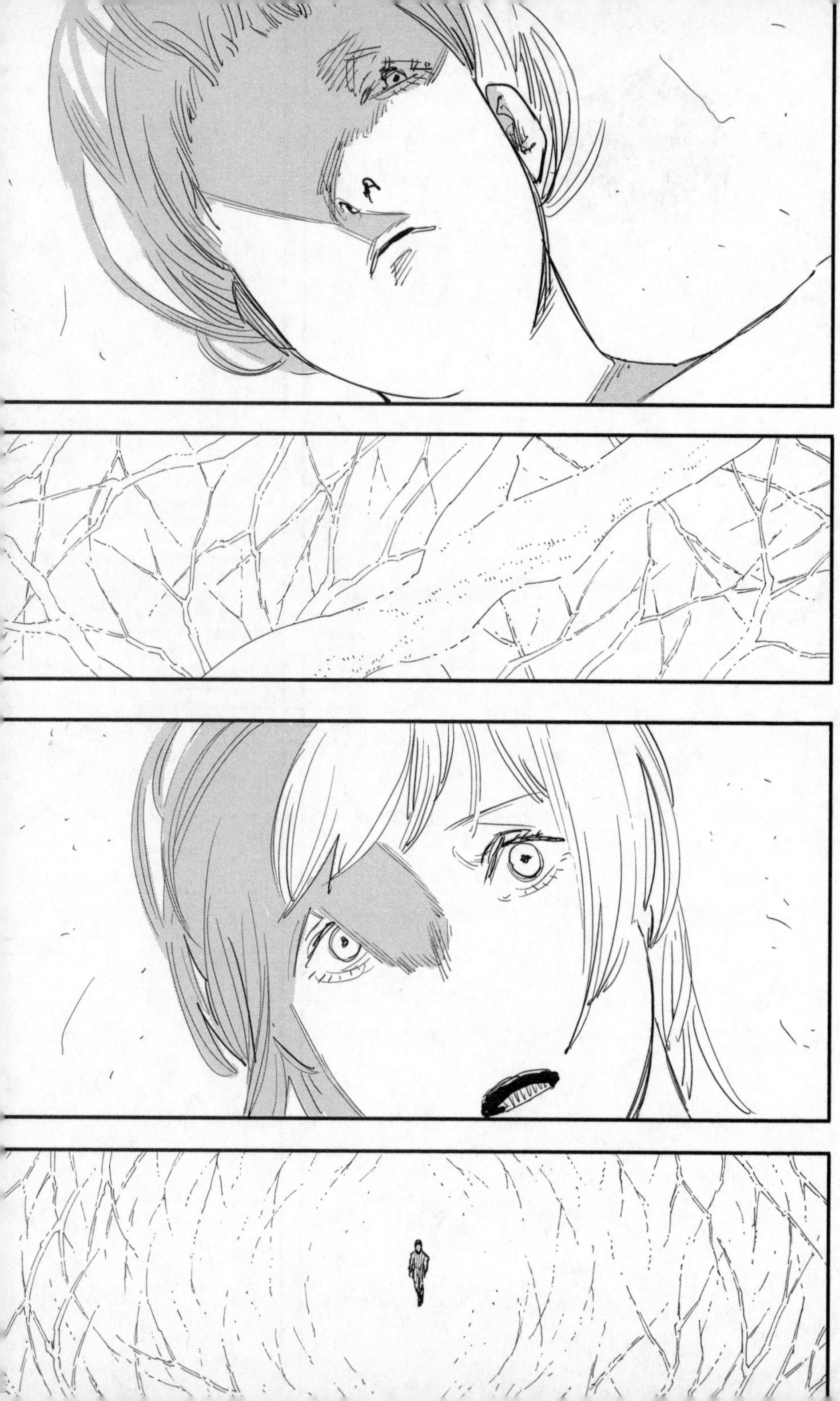

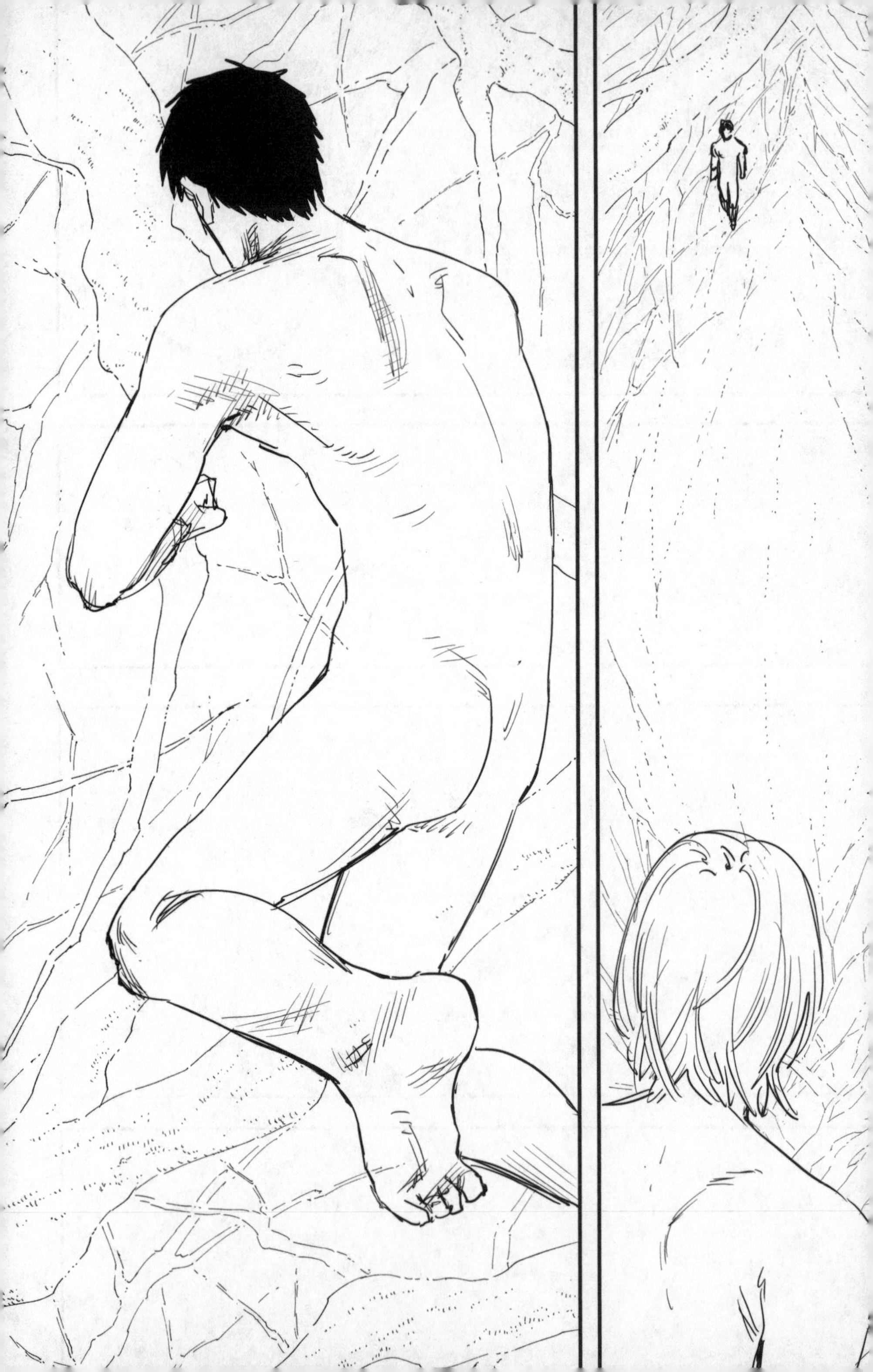

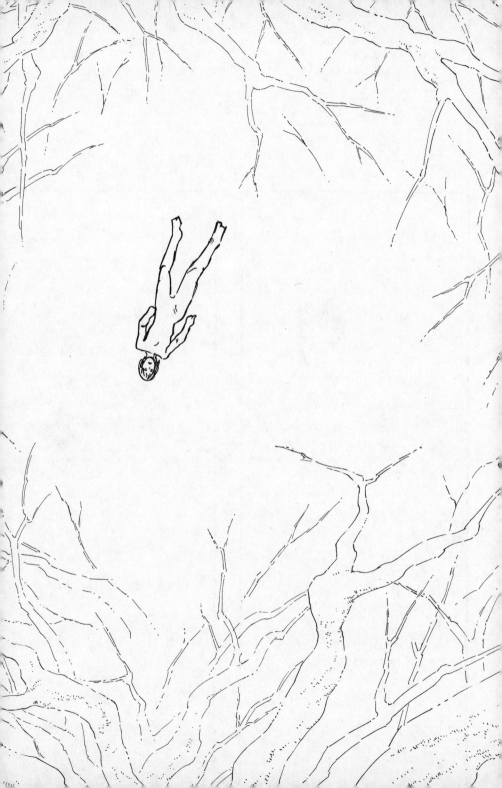

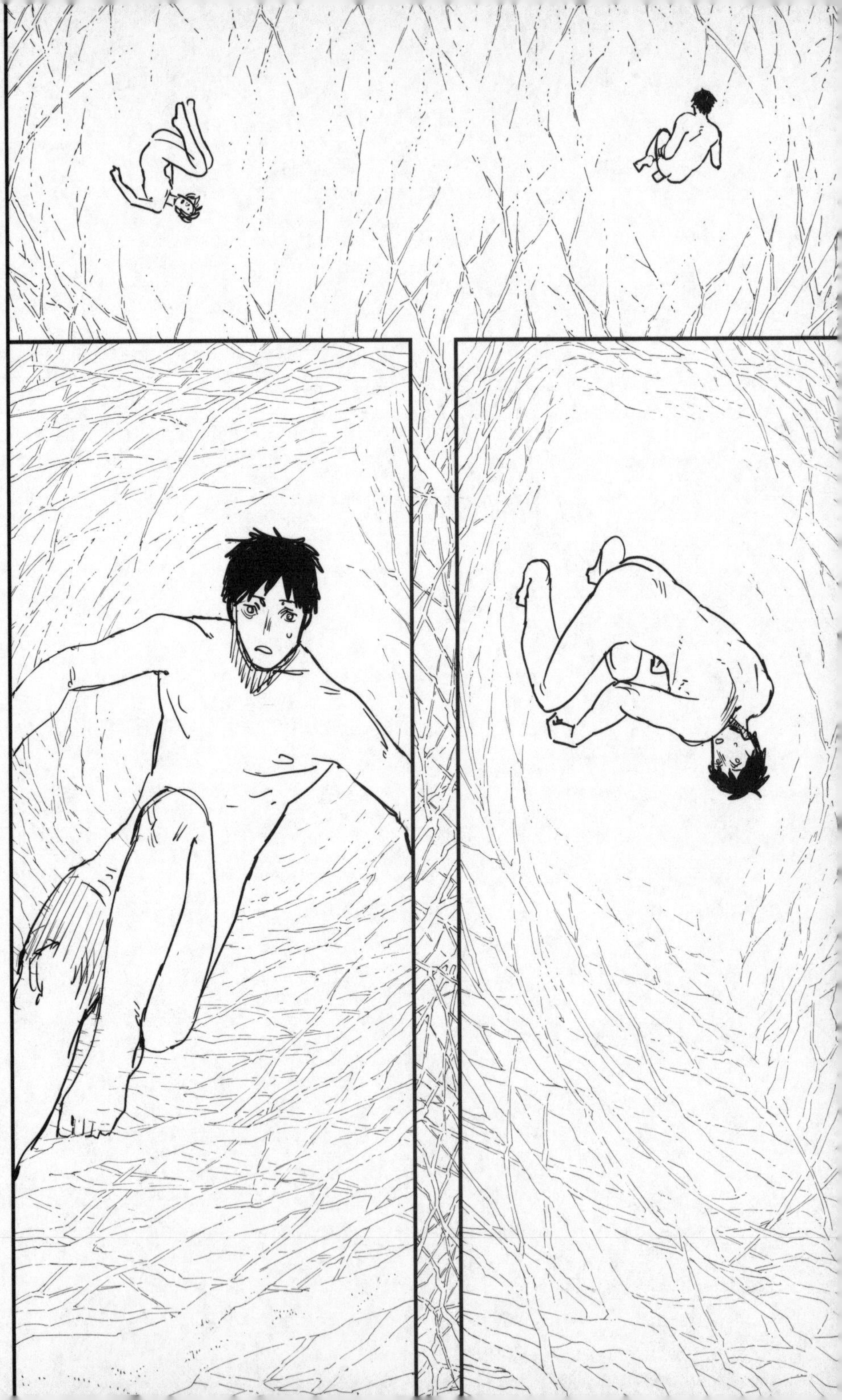

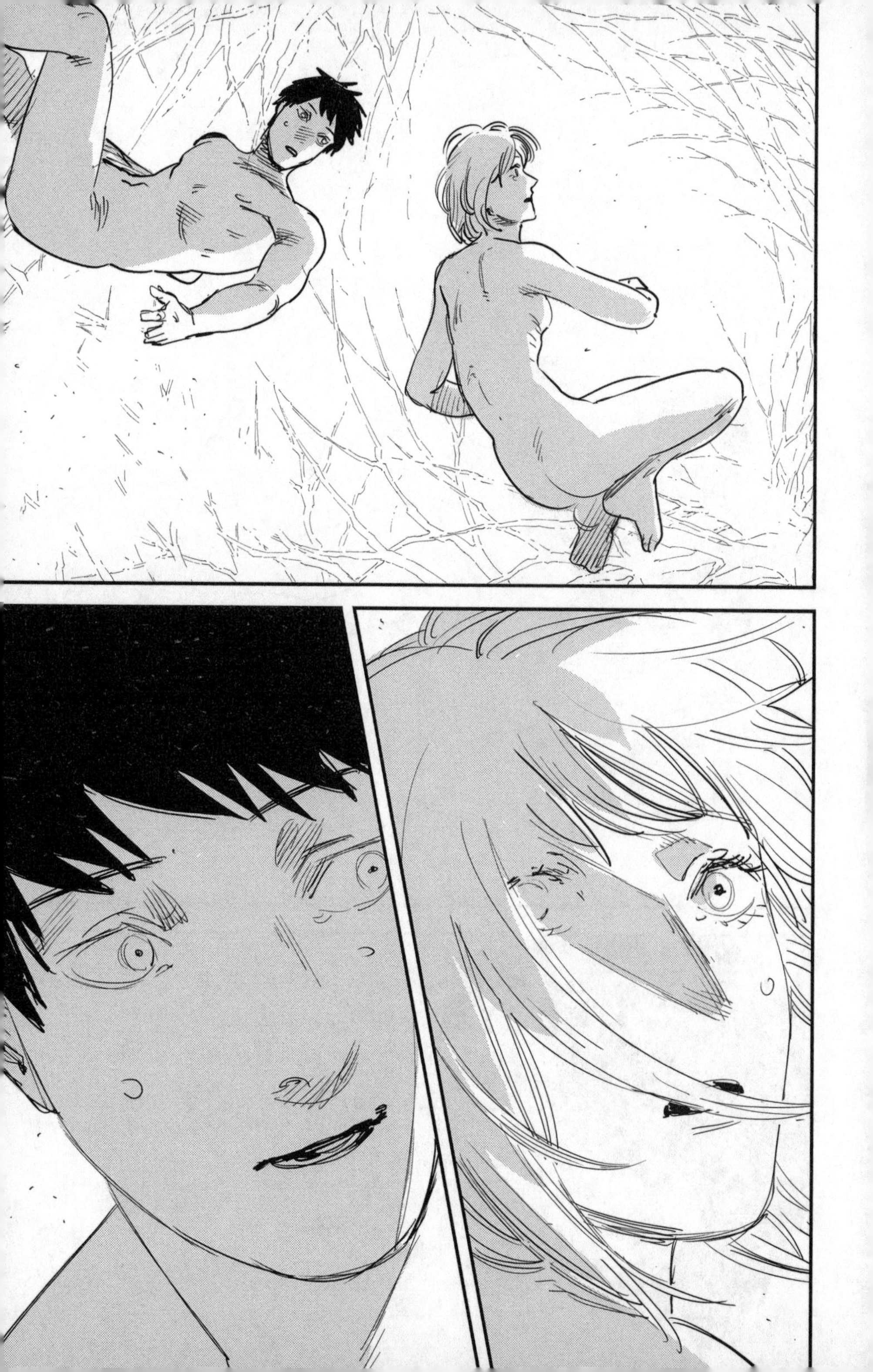

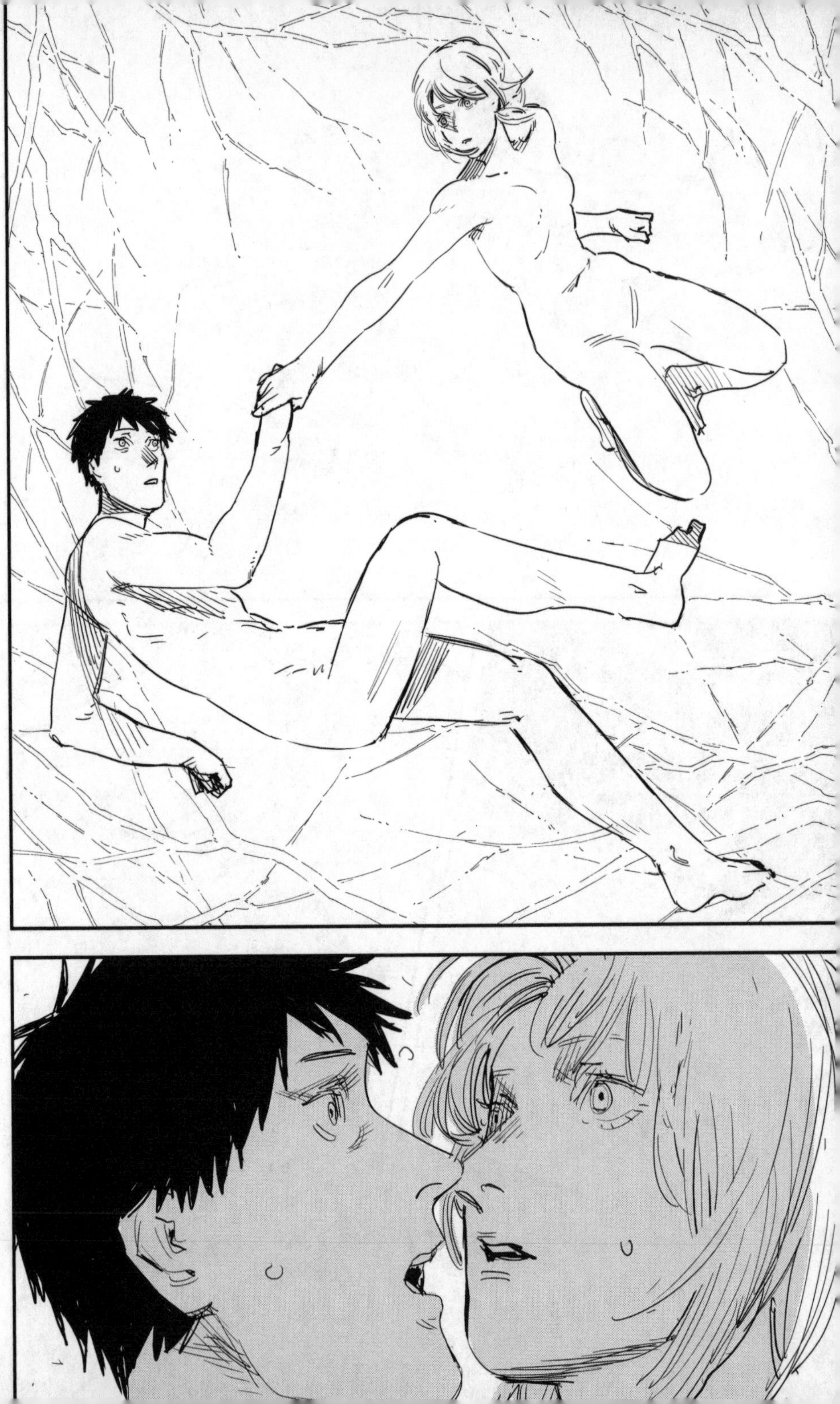

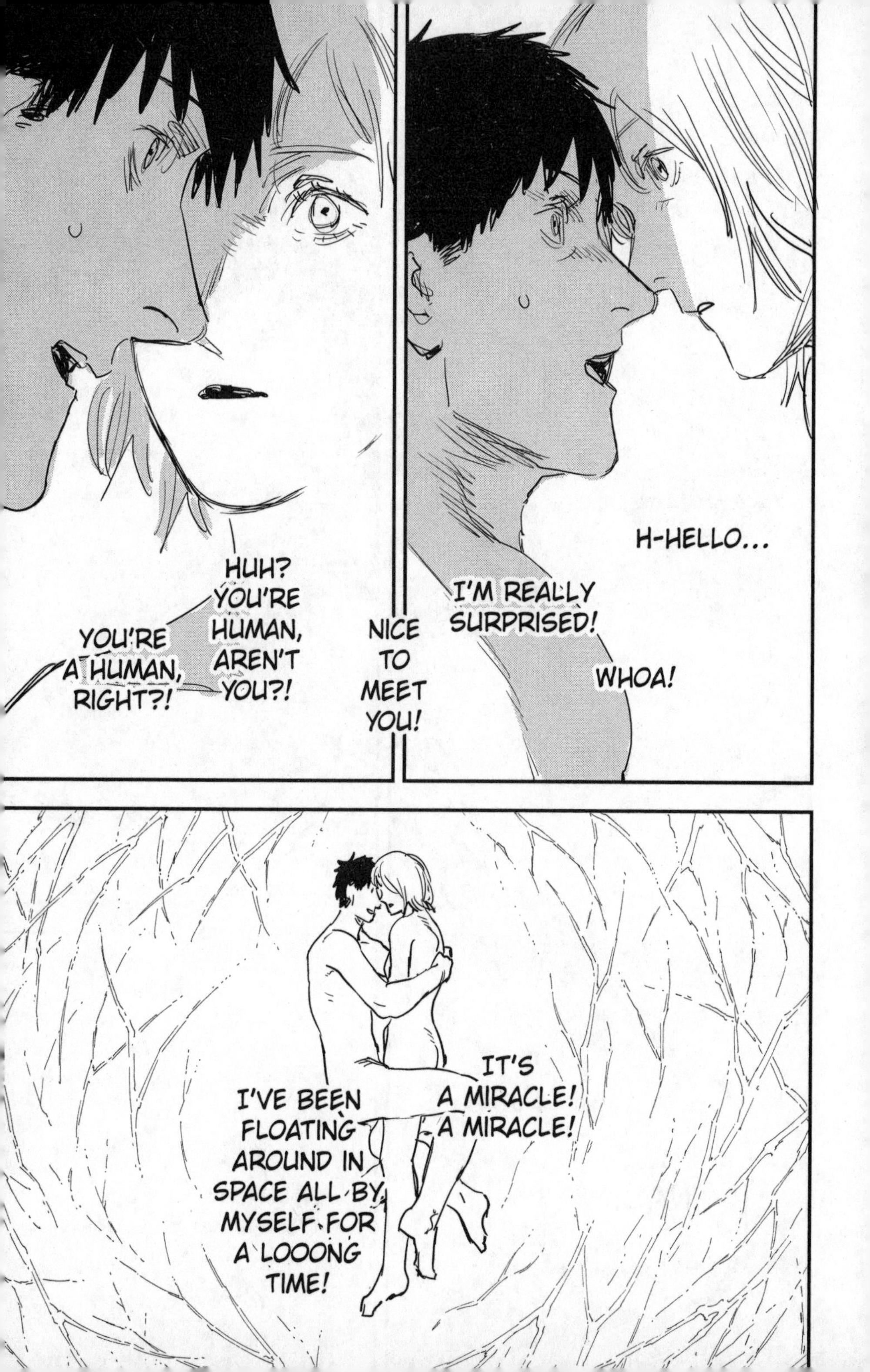
H-HELLO...
WHOA!
I'M REALLY SURPRISED!
NICE TO MEET YOU!
HUH? YOU'RE HUMAN, AREN'T YOU?!
YOU'RE A HUMAN, RIGHT?!
IT'S A MIRACLE! A MIRACLE!
I'VE BEEN FLOATING AROUND IN SPACE ALL BY MYSELF FOR A LOOONG TIME!

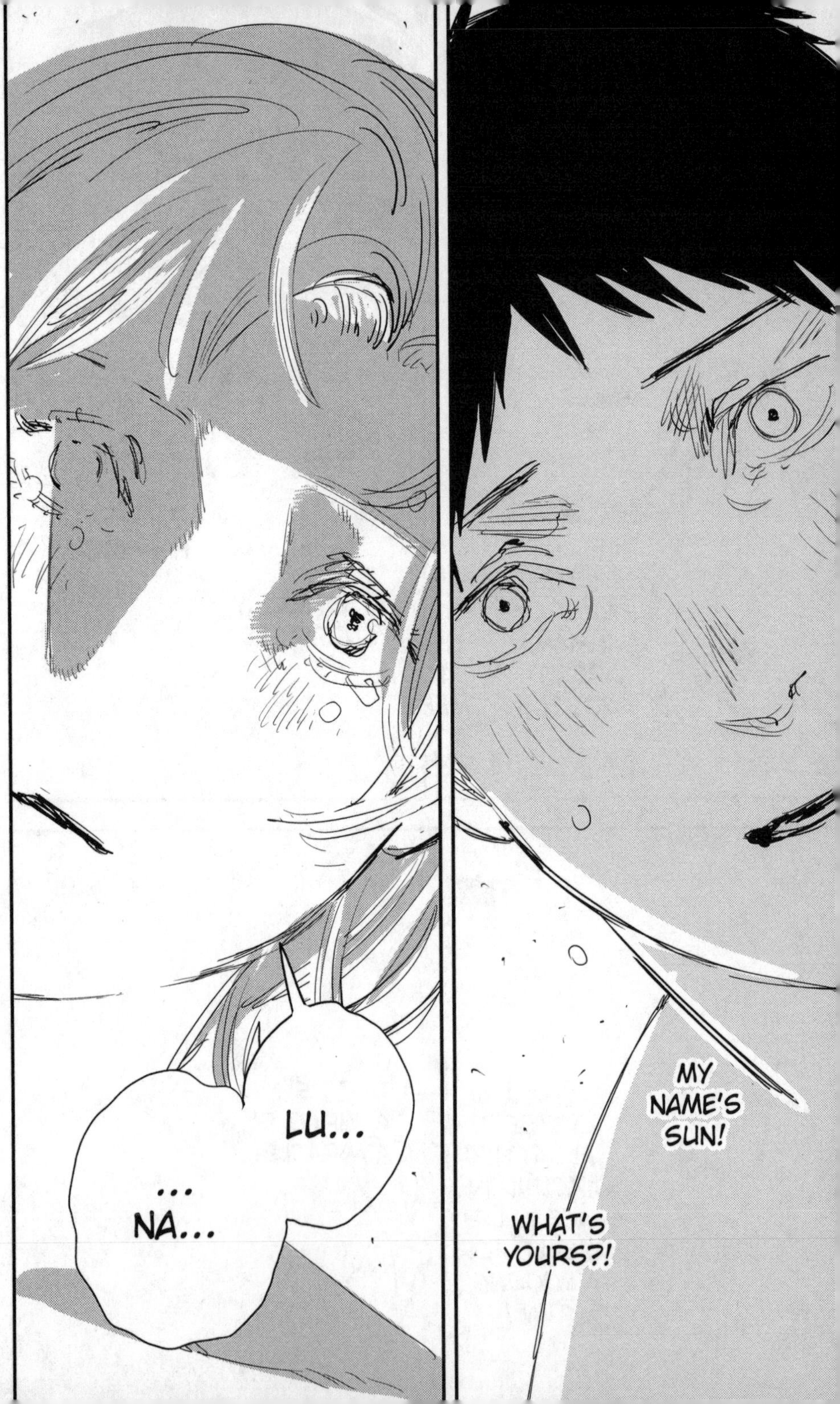
MY NAME'S SUN!
WHAT'S YOURS?!
LU...
... NA...

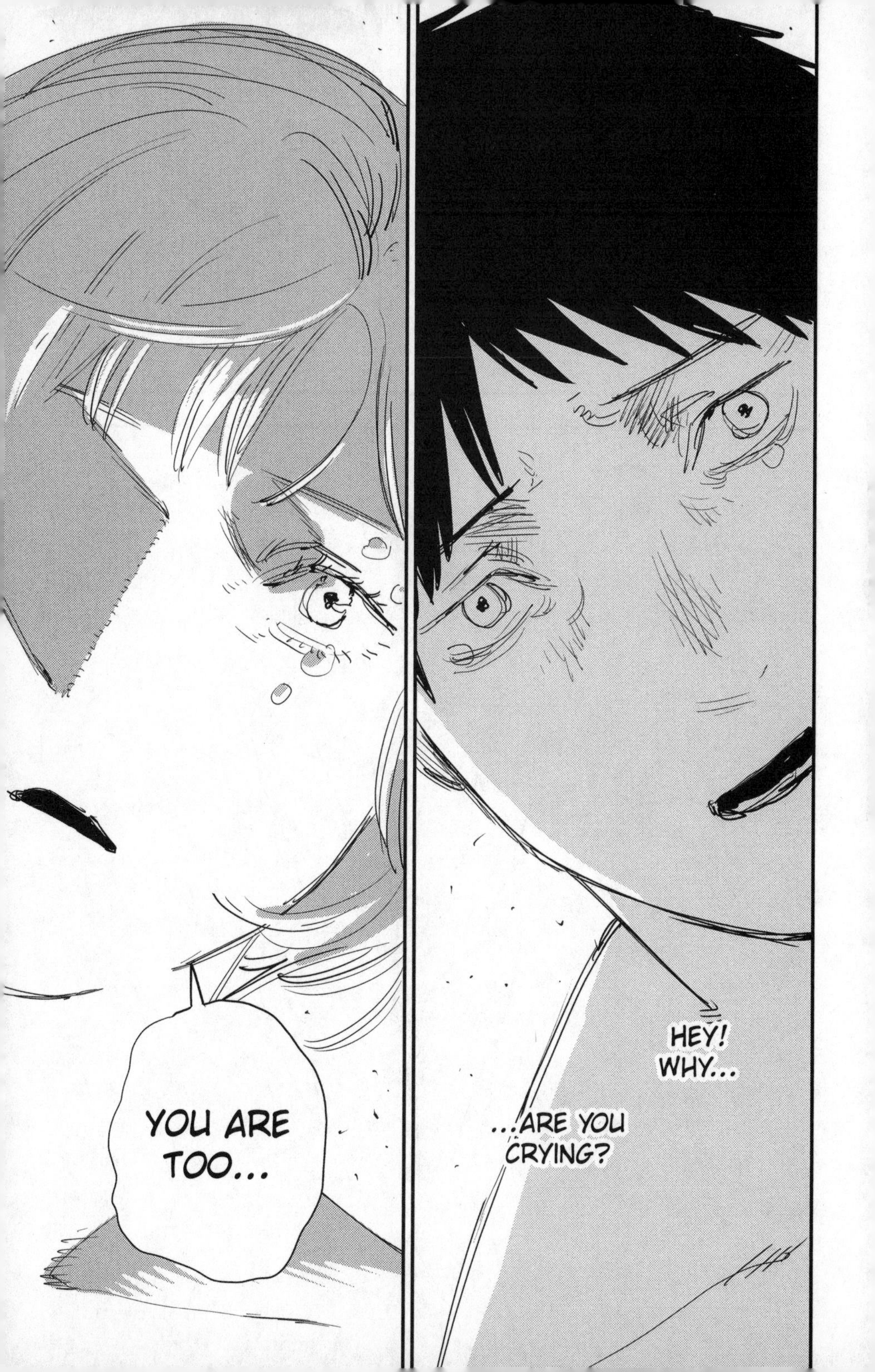
HEY! WHY...
...ARE YOU CRYING?
YOU ARE TOO...

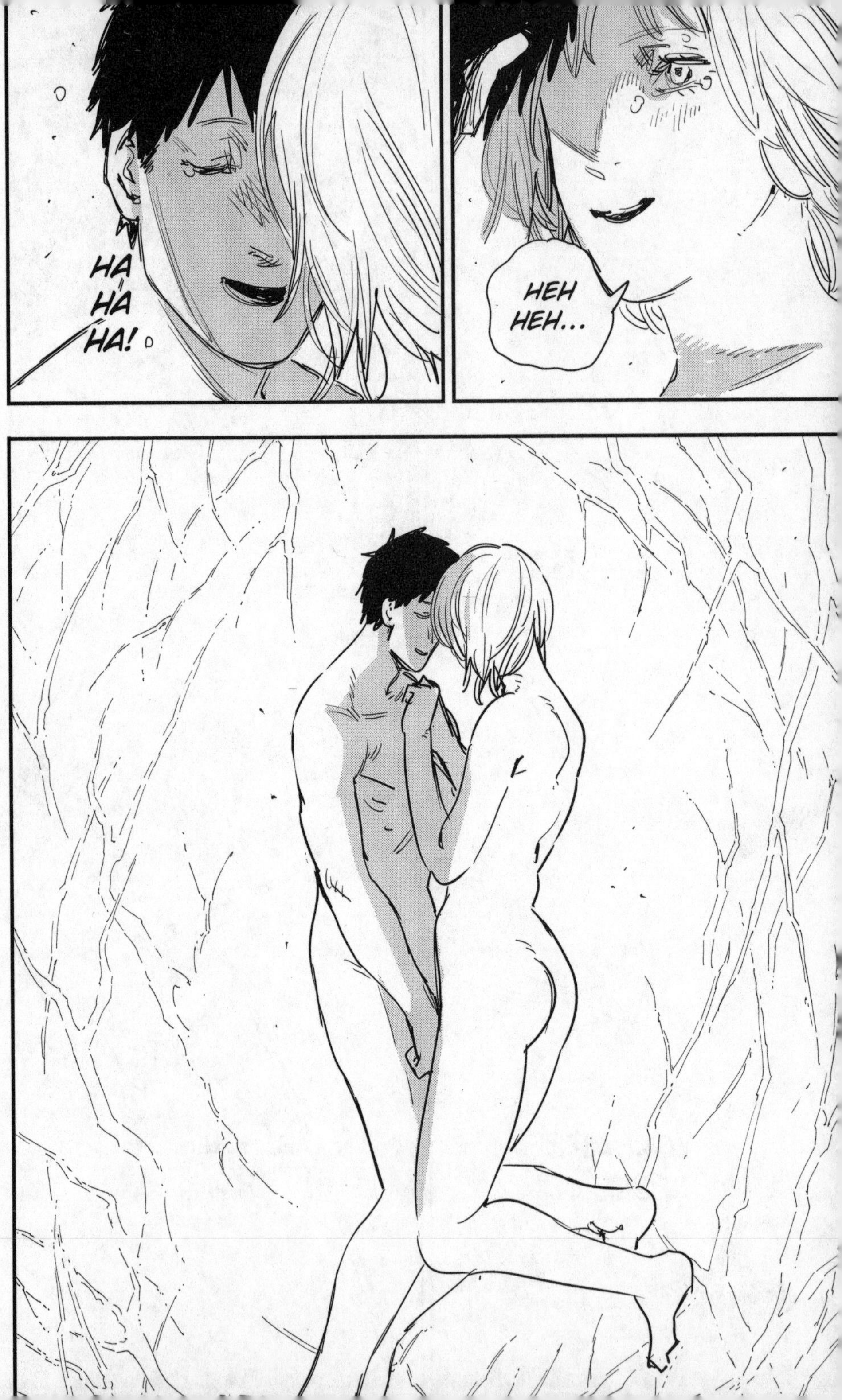
HEH HEH...
HA HA HA!

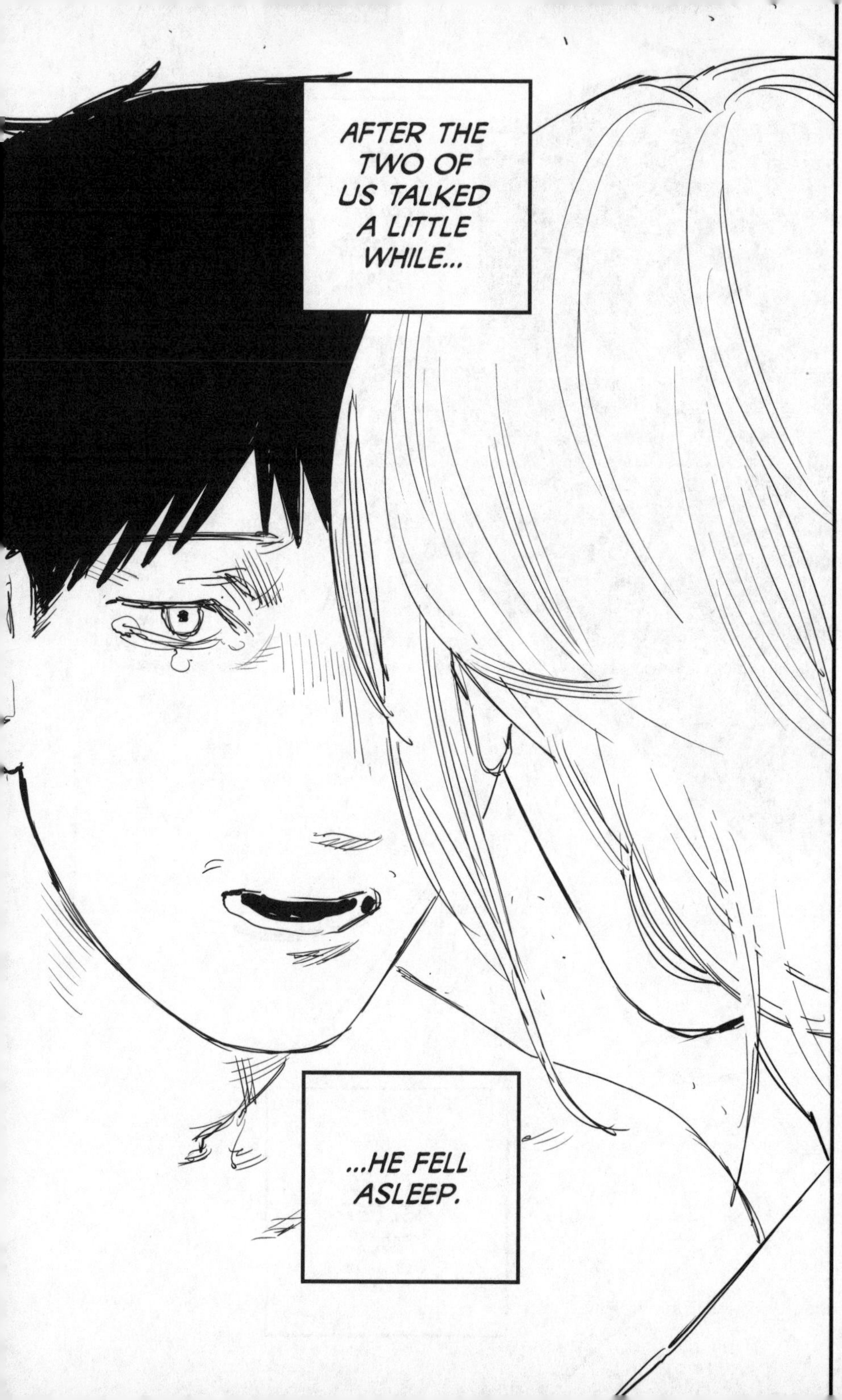
AFTER THE TWO OF US TALKED A LITTLE WHILE...
...HE FELL ASLEEP.

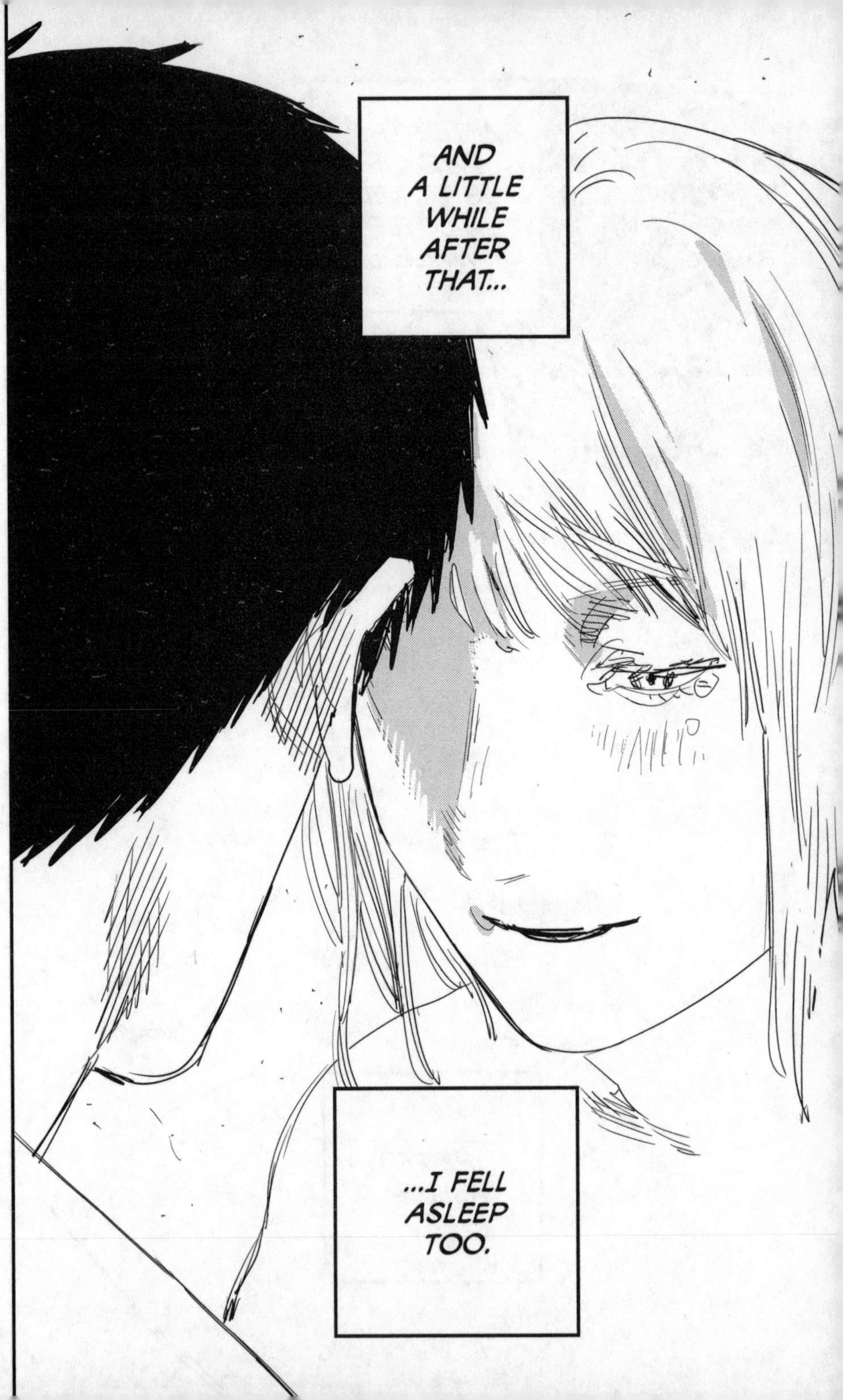
AND A LITTLE WHILE AFTER THAT...
...I FELL ASLEEP TOO.

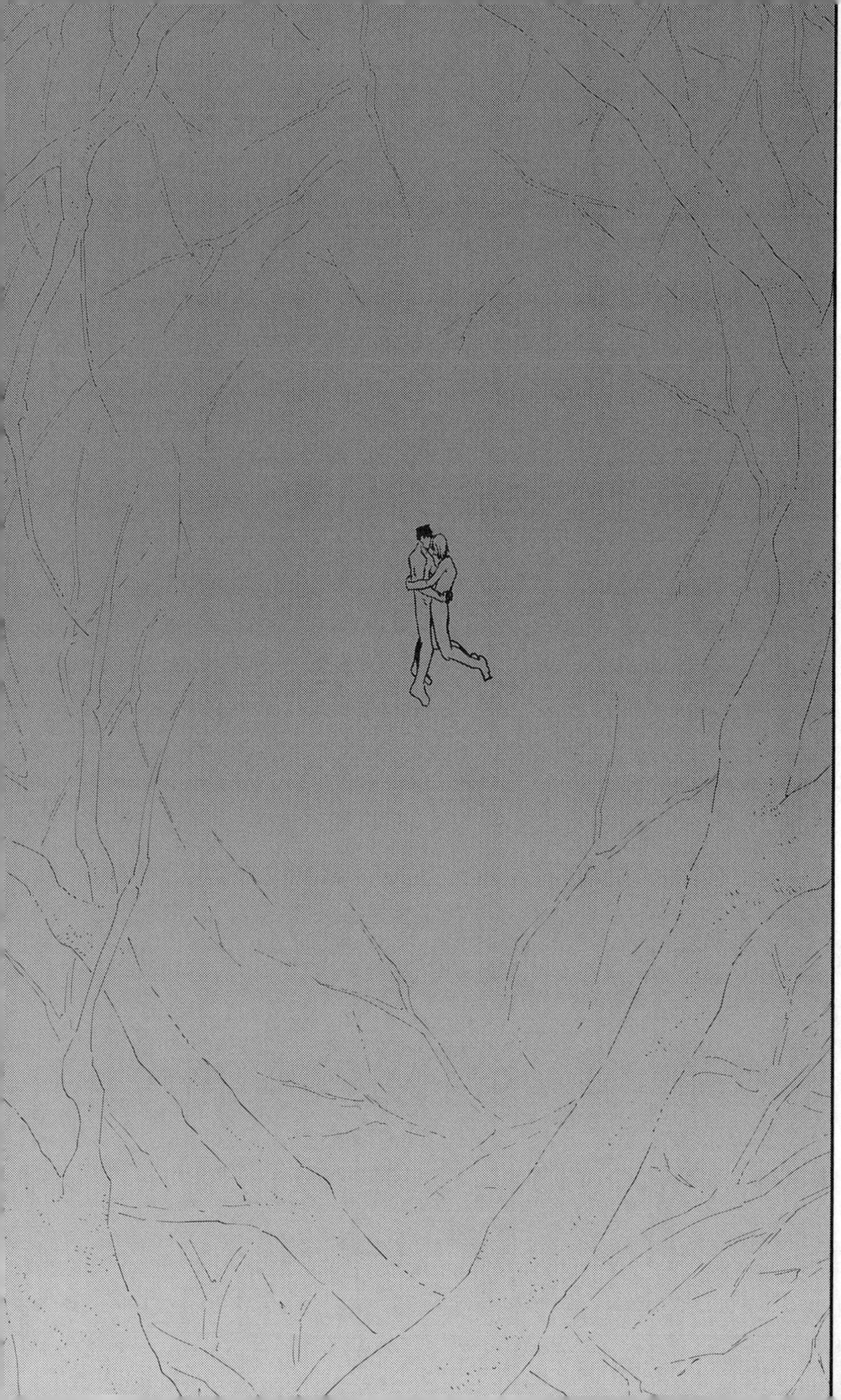

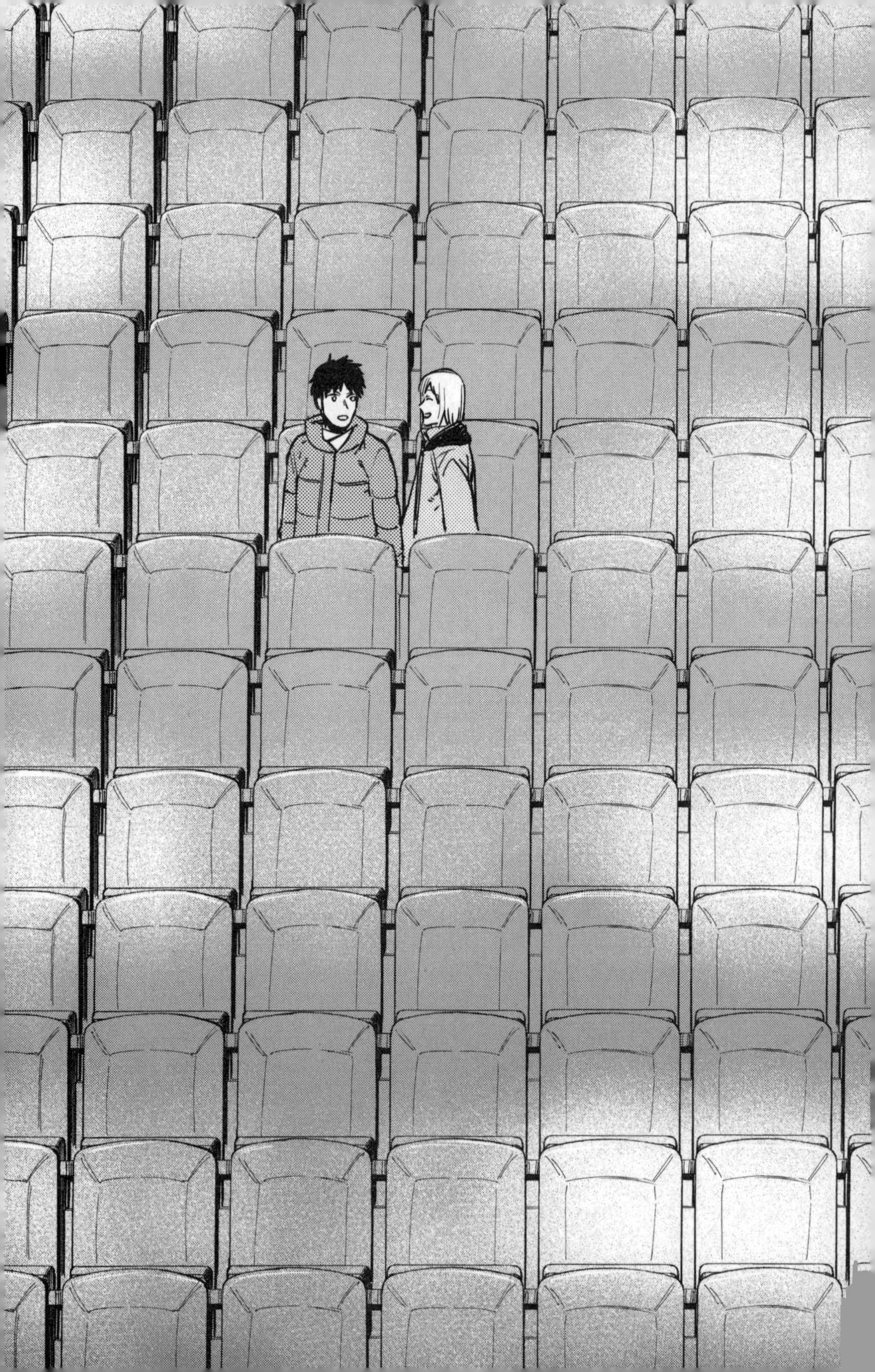

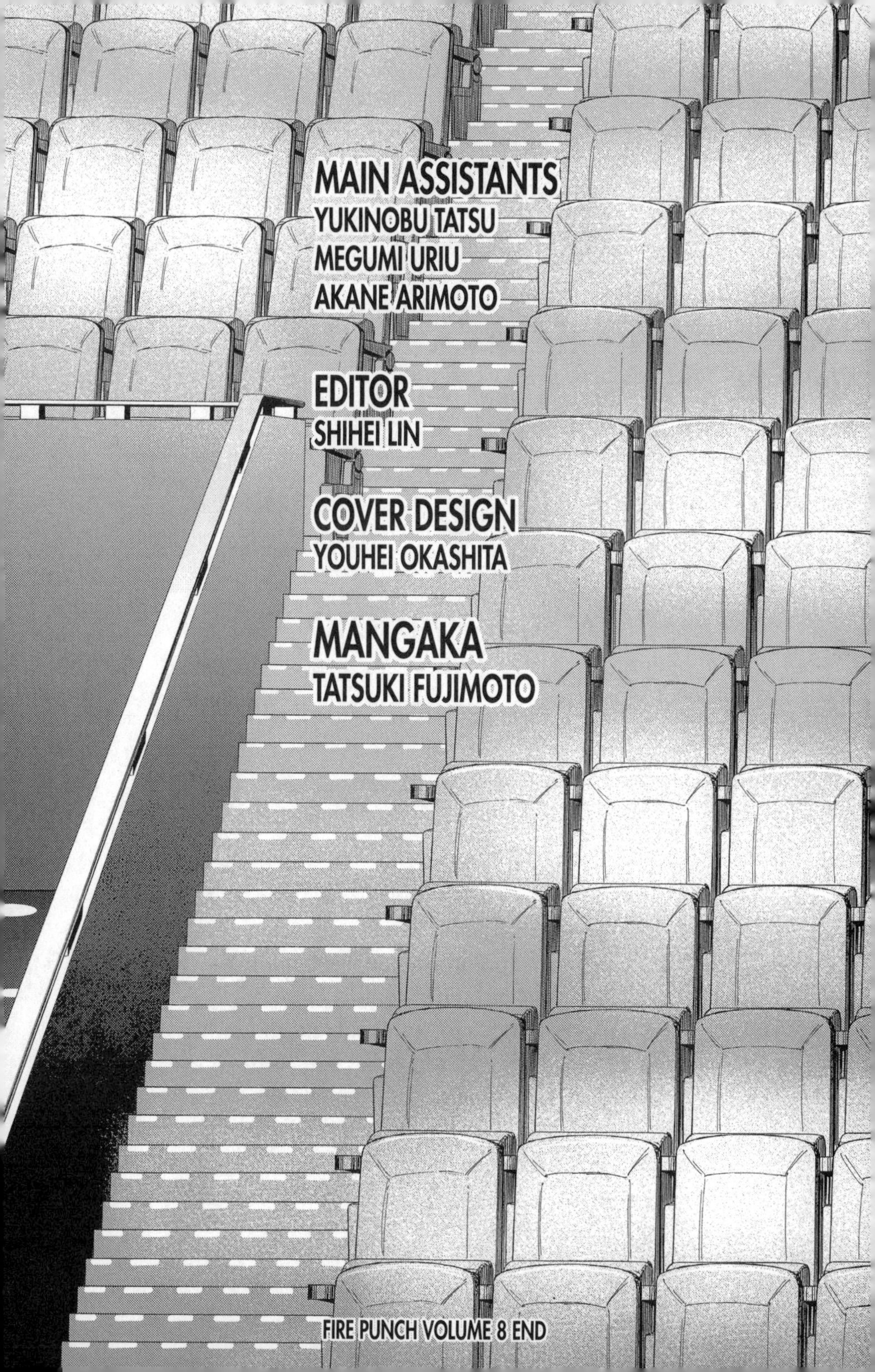
MAIN ASSISTANTS
YUKINOBU TATSU
MEGUMI URIU
AKANE ARIMOTO
EDITOR
SHIHEI LIN
COVER DESIGN
YOUHEI OKASHITA
MANGAKA
TATSUKI FUJIMOTO
FIRE PUNCH VOLUME 8 END

TATSUKI FUJIMOTO

This work is fiction.

Tatsuki Fujimoto won Honorable Mention in the November 2013 Shueisha Crown Newcomers' Awards for his debut one-shot story "Love Is Blind," which was published in volume 13 of *Jump SQ.19*. Fujimoto's follow-up series, *Fire Punch*, is the creator's first English-language release.

FIRE PUNCH

Volume 8
VIZ Signature Edition

Story and Art by Tatsuki Fujimoto

Translation: Christine Dashiell
Touch-Up Art & Lettering: Snir Aharon
Design: Julian [JR] Robinson
Editor: Jennifer LeBlanc

FIRE PUNCH © 2016 by Tatsuki Fujimoto
All rights reserved.
First published in Japan in 2016 by SHUEISHA Inc., Tokyo.
English translation rights arranged by SHUEISHA Inc.

The stories, characters and incidents mentioned in
this publication are entirely fictional.

Printed in the U.S.A.

Published by VIZ Media, LLC
P.O. Box 77010
San Francisco, CA 94107

10 9 8 7 6 5 4 3
First printing, October 2019
Third printing, September 2022

viz.com

vizsignature.com

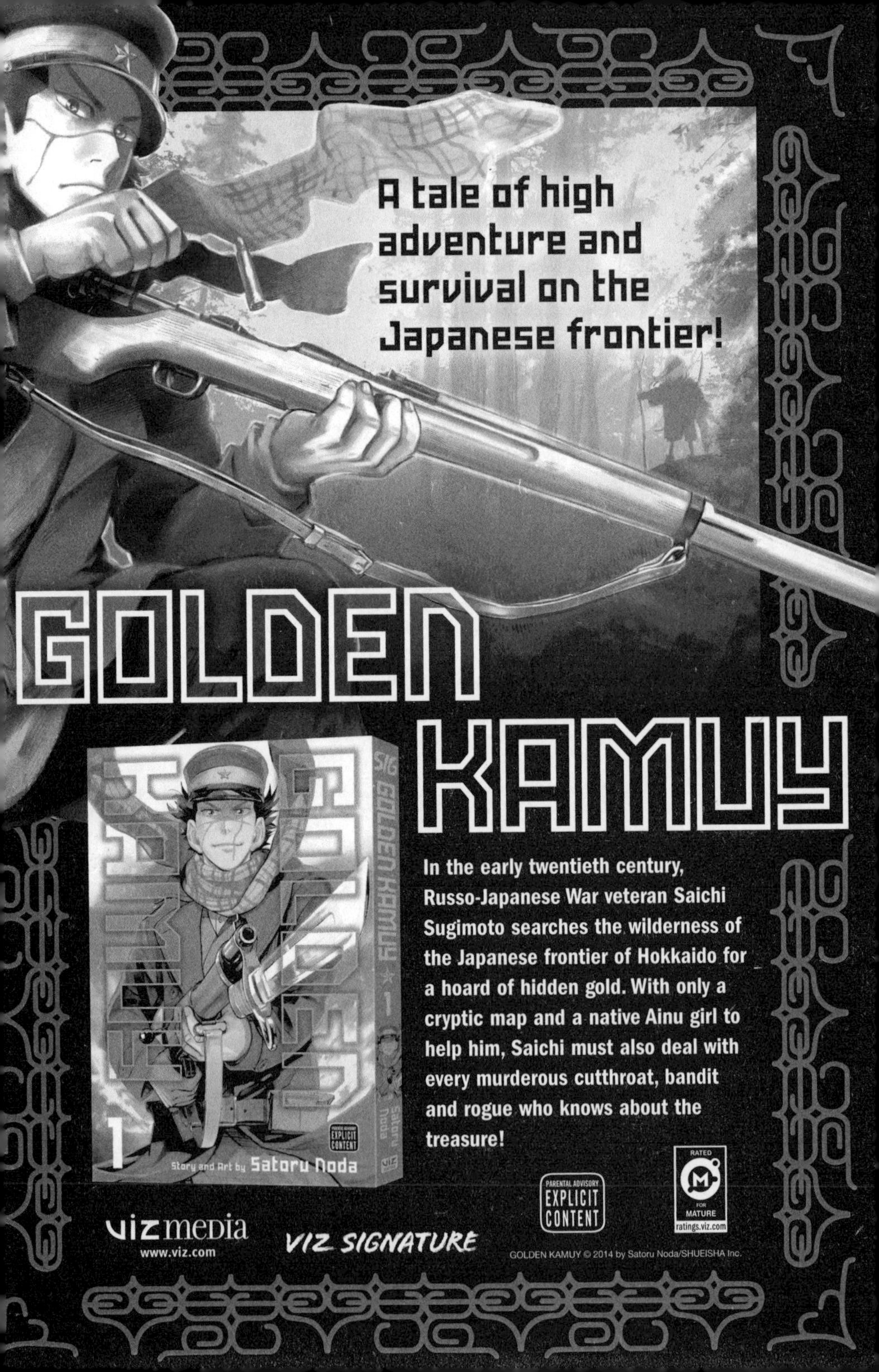

A tale of high adventure and survival on the Japanese frontier!
GOLDEN KAMUY
SIG GOLDEN KAMUY 1
1
Story and Art by Satoru Noda
Satoru Noda
In the early twentieth century, Russo-Japanese War veteran Saichi Sugimoto searches the wilderness of the Japanese frontier of Hokkaido for a hoard of hidden gold. With only a cryptic map and a native Ainu girl to help him, Saichi must also deal with every murderous cutthroat, bandit and rogue who knows about the treasure!
PARENTAL ADVISORY EXPLICIT CONTENT
RATED M FOR MATURE ratings.viz.com
viz media
www.viz.com
VIZ SIGNATURE
GOLDEN KAMUY © 2014 by Satoru Noda/SHUEISHA Inc.

A RACE TO SAVE A WORLD BEYOND HOPE

BIOMEGA

STORY & ART BY
TSUTOMU NIHEI

WELCOME TO EARTH'S FUTURE: A NIGHTMARISH
WORLD INFECTED BY A VIRUS THAT TURNS MOST
OF THE POPULATION INTO ZOMBIE-LIKE DRONES.
WILL THE SYNTHETIC HUMAN ZOICHI KANOE BE
MANKIND'S SALVATION?

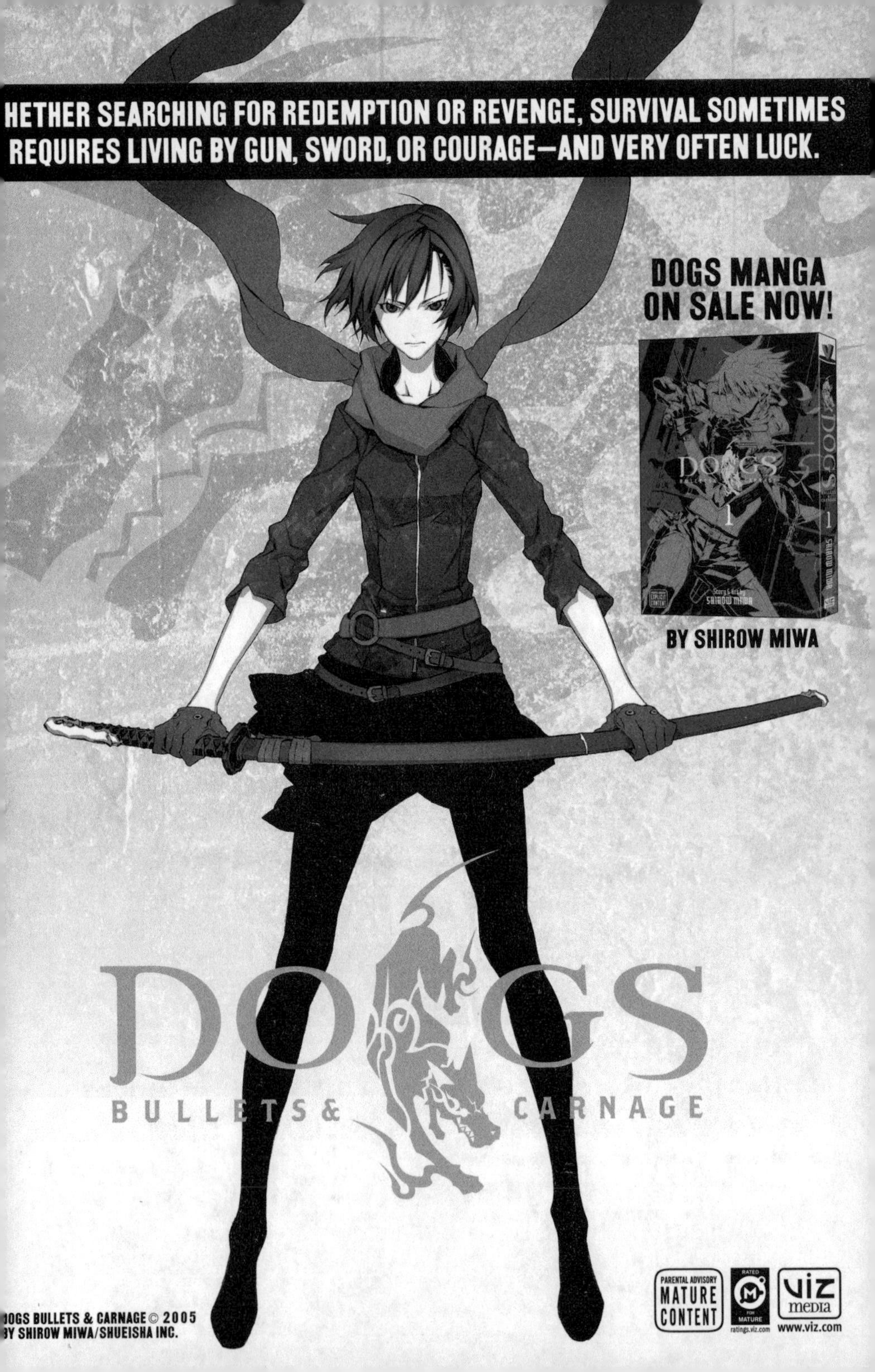
HETHER SEARCHING FOR REDEMPTION OR REVENGE, SURVIVAL SOMETIMES REQUIRES LIVING BY GUN, SWORD, OR COURAGE—AND VERY OFTEN LUCK.
DOGS MANGA ON SALE NOW!
DOGS
BY SHIROW MIWA
DOGS
BULLETS & CARNAGE
PARENTAL ADVISORY MATURE CONTENT
RATED M FOR MATURE
ratings.viz.com
VIZ media
www.viz.com
DOGS BULLETS & CARNAGE © 2005 BY SHIROW MIWA/SHUEISHA INC.

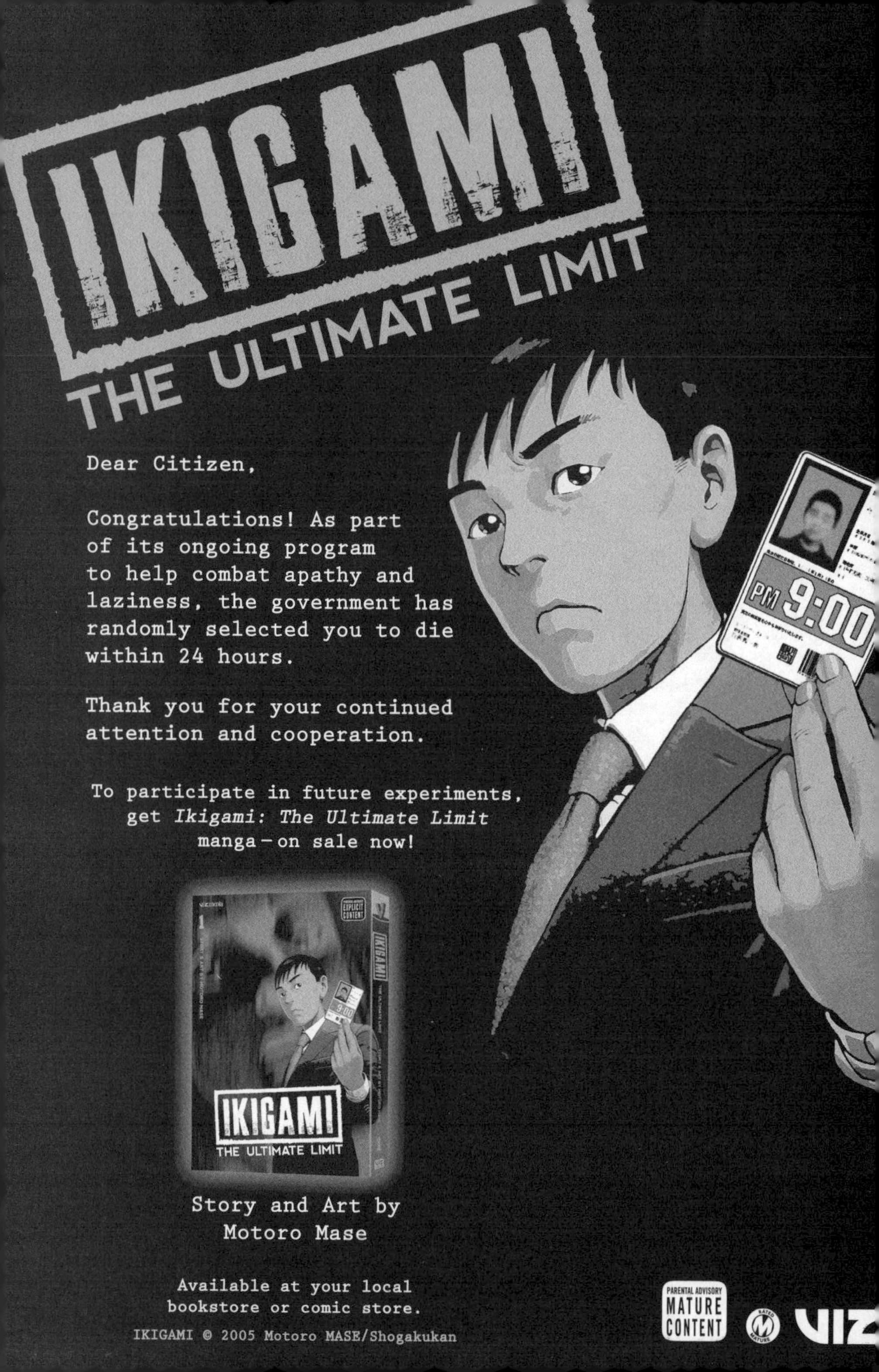
IKIGAMI
THE ULTIMATE LIMIT
Dear Citizen,
Congratulations! As part of its ongoing program to help combat apathy and laziness, the government has randomly selected you to die within 24 hours.
Thank you for your continued attention and cooperation.
To participate in future experiments, get Ikigami: The Ultimate Limit manga – on sale now!
PM 9:00
IKIGAMI
THE ULTIMATE LIMIT
Story and Art by Motoro Mase
Available at your local bookstore or comic store.
IKIGAMI © 2005 Motoro MASE/Shogakukan
PARENTAL ADVISORY
MATURE CONTENT
VIZ

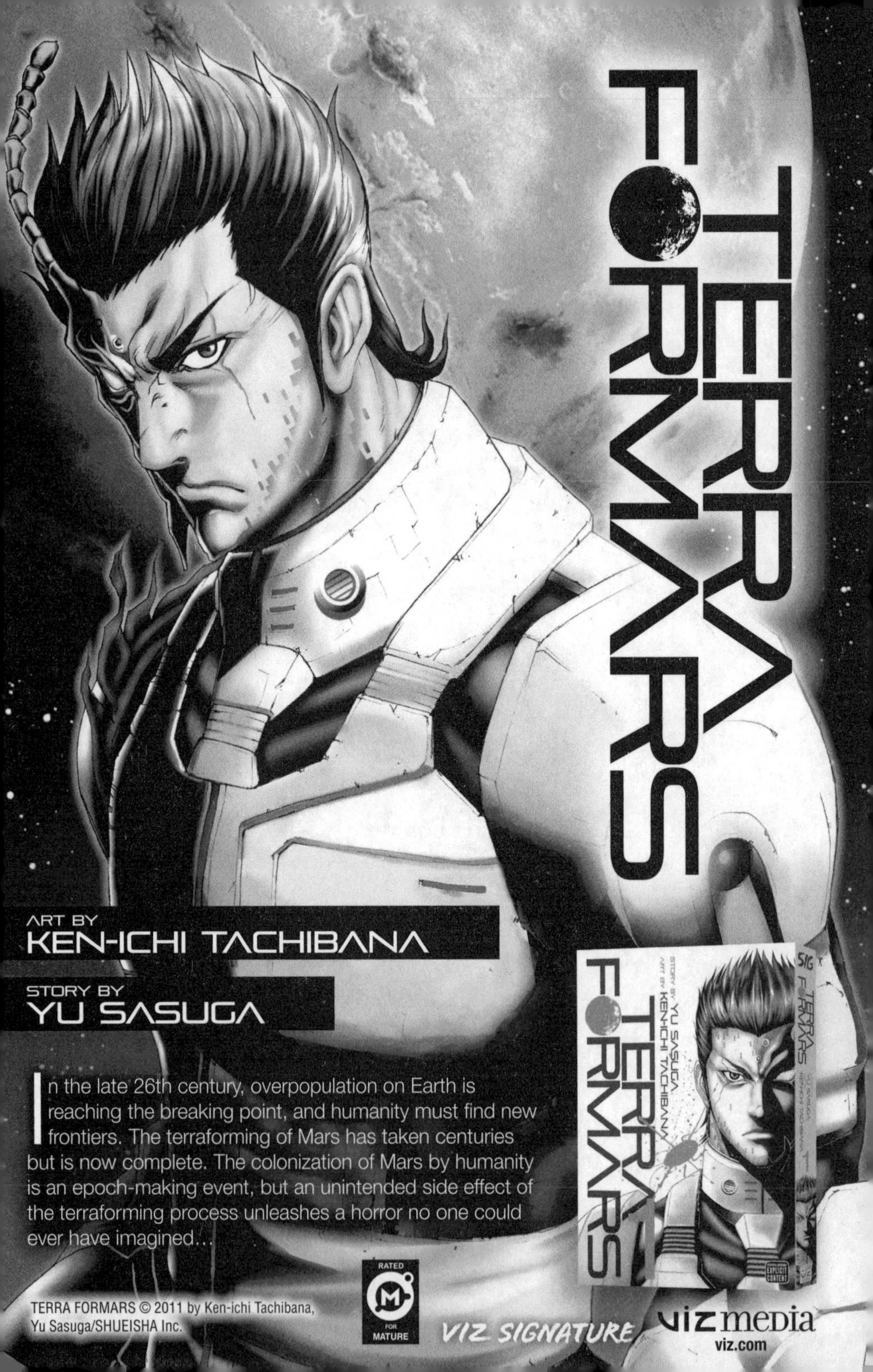
TERRA FORMARS
ART BY
KEN-ICHI TACHIBANA
STORY BY
YU SASUGA
In the late 26th century, overpopulation on Earth is reaching the breaking point, and humanity must find new frontiers. The terraforming of Mars has taken centuries but is now complete. The colonization of Mars by humanity is an epoch-making event, but an unintended side effect of the terraforming process unleashes a horror no one could ever have imagined...
STORY BY YU SASUGA
ART BY KEN-ICHI TACHIBANA
TERRA FORMARS
RATED M FOR MATURE
TERRA FORMARS © 2011 by Ken-ichi Tachibana, Yu Sasuga/SHUEISHA Inc.
VIZ SIGNATURE
viz media
viz.com

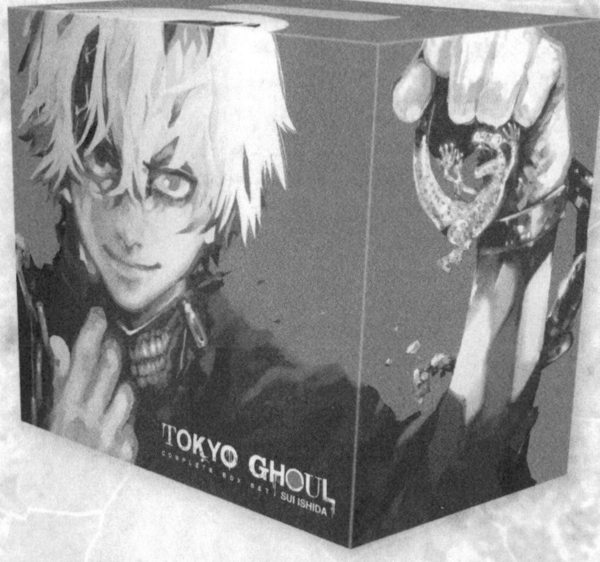
TOKYO GHOUL
COMPLETE BOX SET
SUI ISHIDA

TOKYO GHOUL

COMPLETE BOX SET

STORY AND ART BY **SUI ISHIDA**

KEN KANEKI is an ordinary college student until a violent encounter turns him into the first half-human, half-Ghoul hybrid. Trapped between two worlds, he must survive Ghoul turf wars, learn more about Ghoul society and master his new powers.

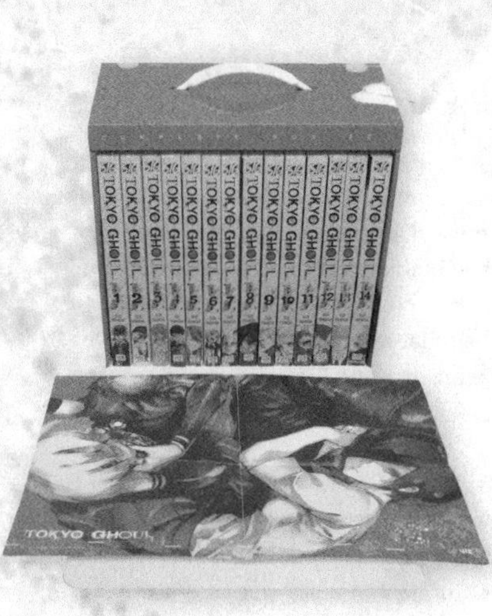
TOKYO GHOUL

Box set collects all fourteen volumes
of the original *Tokyo Ghoul* series.
Includes an exclusive double-sided poster.

COLLECT THE COMPLETE SERIES

RATED T+ OLDER TEEN

VIZ

ABARA
COMPLETE DELUXE EDITION
TSUTOMU NIHEI

A visually stunning work of sci-fi horror from the creator of **BIOMEGA** and **BLAME**!

A vast city lies under the shadow of colossal, ancient tombs, the identity of their builders lost to time. In the streets of the city something is preying on the inhabitants, something that moves faster than the human eye can see and leaves unimaginable horror in its wake.

Tsutomu Nihei's dazzling, harrowing dystopian thriller is presented here in a single-volume hardcover edition featuring full-color pages and foldout illustrations. This volume also includes the early short story "Digimortal."

RATED T+ OLDER TEEN

VIZ